D1560221

The Choice to Be

JEREMY KAGAN

The Choice to Be

A Jewish Path to
Self and Spirituality

The author may be contacted at:
17/10 Brand St.
Har Nof, Jerusalem 93878
Email: rjkagan@yahoo.com

ISBN 978-1-59826-821-8

Distributed by:
FELDHEIM PUBLISHERS
POB 43163 / Jerusalem, Israel
208 Airport Executive Park
Nanuet, NY 10954

www.feldheim.com

Printed in Israel

הרב אהרן פעלדמאן

RABBI AHARON FELDMAN

409 YESHIVA LANE, BALTIMORE, MD 21208
TEL.: 410-6539433 FAX: 410-6534694
STUDY: 410-4847200 EXT. 114

ROSH HAYESHIVA
NER ISRAEL RABBINICAL COLLEGE

ראש הישיבה
ישיבת נר ישראל

B.H. 19 Elul 5771/ September 18, 2011

TO WHOM IT MAY CONCERN:

Rabbi Jeremy Kagan, Principal of Midreshet Tehillah in Jerusalem, has written an outstanding book. Based on RAMCHAL and classical sources, the book presents the basic concepts of G-d, Man and the Jewish People in a clear, modern idiom and convincingly demonstrates how exercising free-will to subordinate oneself to G-d's will is the path to creating a true sense of Self, and how Torah satisfies man's deepest longings for meaning and purpose.

At a time when most books are intended for superficial, cursory reading, this book is directed to the thinking reader and is unusual in its ability to present some of the deepest and most basic ideas of Judaism in a manner that every serious reader will be able to understand and apply to his personal life.

I highly recommend this book to all those who seek to discover the reason for their existence. It will immeasurably enrich the life of anyone who reads it.

With deep respects,

Rabbi Aharon Feldman

Contents

THE PURPOSE:
Actualizing Self to Connect to God

THE MEANS:
Free Will

Acknowledgments

I MUST BEGIN WITH EXPRESSING my gratitude to the Creator for all that He has given me. At this moment I am specifically aware of the Divine blessing that was required to complete this project: the teachers, the ability, the opportunity, the assistance… whatever was needed was always there when it was needed. I am thankful not only for the *zechut* of being the vehicle for this book, but also for all that I have gained personally from working on the project. No one could possibly derive as much benefit from reading this as I have derived from writing it.

I will discuss in the introduction my debt to my principal teachers, Rabbi Moshe Shapiro and Rabbi Aharon Feldman. For now, it will be enough to say that the vision each presents has provided me with the inspiration to understand my world on a deeper level than I could have imagined possible. Whatever grasp I have of the philosophical side of Torah is a consequence of the foundations laid by these rebbeim. Had I not had the opportunity to learn from them, this book would not exist.

By this I do not mean to discount the debt I hold to the many other rebbeim I have learned from; Rabbi Shapiro and Rabbi Feldman are, however, the ones under whom I studied the material presented here. Special mention must also be made of Rabbi Uziel Milevsky *ztz"l*, my first rebbi, who guided the original development of my Torah learning and established the foundations of my outlook to a degree that I will probably never fully appreciate. It was an incomparable blessing to have begun my journey through Torah under the tutelage of so great a man, so clear a thinker, and so remarkable an educator. I am indebted to Ohr Somayach and all those responsible for that institution for being the agents of that blessing and, more generally, for creating a place that allowed me to enter the world of Torah.

Once this project reached an advanced stage, there was need of a great deal of input. Many of the ideas presented here are subtle and sensitive and I needed advice on both their accuracy and the appropriateness of their presentation. A number of individuals were extraordinarily kind in taking time from their pressured schedules to assist me.

I first wish to thank Rabbi Moshe Shapiro who, beyond the role he played in so much of what is written here, generously granted me a lengthy meeting to discuss the book — his insights and suggestions were invaluable as was his request that Rabbi Akiva Tatz and Rabbi Marcel Bordon look at the manuscript. Rabbi Tatz, an old *chavruta* and continuing inspiration, actually belongs at the beginning of any thanks, for he provided the initial impetus to actually write this. In a "chance" meeting with him in Yerushalayim he galvanized me to stop procrastinating and get started on a project I had been thinking about for a long time. But Rabbi Tatz also returned later to do me the tremendous honor of editing a late version of the text. This required an enormous dedication of time by an individual with a very busy life. I lack adequate words to express my gratitude for this kindness. The book is both clearer and more accurate as a result of his valuable input. Rabbi Bordon read an early version of important parts of the text. On a trip to Israel and through many emails, he generously dedicated a great deal of time to both reading and discussing a number of important issues in the book. I am deeply indebted for that caring and time; his stamp is evident on the final product.

Rabbi Moshe Meiselman was also generous with his time, reading the chapters relating to science and discussing related points. Rabbi Dovid Kamenetsky has the misfortune of *davening* in the same *Shacharit minyan* as I do and so was delayed on his way to many morning appointments as he lent his valuable advice and insight to several important topics in the book. He also arranged for his brother to read two chapters, leaving me also indebted to Rabbi Shalom Kamenetsky. Rabbi Dovid Miller generously read the manuscript, making valuable comments. Rabbi Menachem Gross was also kind enough to read several chapters and alerted me to some important errors. Rabbi David Sedley also read through the manuscript and provided valuable feedback. Rabbi Zachariah Greenwald showed genuine friendship by reading a number of chapters; his support for the project was much needed and appreciated.

Finally, I must mention Rabbi Zevulun Shwartzman, whose generosity of spirit I am incapable of describing. Though he was not able to read the manuscript to the point of commenting on the actual writing, he dedicated many hours that he did not have to discussing various points in or relevant to the book. The opportunity to partake of the vastness and depth of his Torah and experience his *middot* was a benefit beyond measure.

I will mention in the introduction that "both my training and interest are directed toward the cultural and experiential context within which people view their world and how that affects the way they see it." That "training and interest" has much to do with the approach of this book. The credit for that goes to Prof. Karsten Harries, one of my professors at Yale University. It was through trying to understand some of the ideas he spoke about that I was sensitized to hear aspects of what my rebbeim in Yerushalayim were teaching. It is hard for me to imagine I could have written this particular book without his influence.

I would like to thank Rabbi Dovid Refson. I have been teaching for more than fifteen years in institutions that exist through his tireless dedication. This has given me an opportunity to clarify many of the thoughts expressed in this book.

I would also like to thank my parents. Though first thanks for any abilities I have go to the Creator, the agents through which they came must also be recognized. My sensitivities and respect for truth are something I learned growing up in my home and are my most precious inheritance. When I mention my parents I include in my thoughts the many generations of ancestors who came before them and whose sacrifices I hope are evident in this book. I am also deeply gratified that my family has made it possible to partially dedicate this book to my father, Dr. Abraham Kagan *z"l*.

This book would not have been published without the financial support of several very special individuals. Suffice it to say that I feel truly fortunate to have their genuine friendship.

Apart from the content of the book, a large support staff is required to bring a book out once the manuscript is written. I wish to express my thanks to Feldheim Publishers for agreeing to distribute this book even though the possibility exists that it will not make the *New York Times* best seller list. Mrs. Ita Olesker put time into editing the book at an early stage. Mrs. Aliza Magram did the copyediting and proofing with Mrs. Tziporah Frankel doing the final proofread. Mrs. Eden Chachamtzedek showed patience as well as skill in setting the type more than once. Ben Gasner and his very capable assistant, Mindel Kassorla, contributed their genius by designing the cover.

Sof ma'aseh b'machshavah techilah — last but not least, I wish to thank my family. They have not seen that much of me the last few years — except my back as I sat in front of my computer typing. But no one has given more to completing this project than my beloved wife. I cannot say more than that her name belongs under the title of this book as much as mine.

Introduction

THIS BOOK IS VERY much a reflection of its author. I came to Torah in the middle of my pursuit of an undergraduate degree. I was not consciously looking for God and I don't think I would have been voted the person most likely to become religious in my predominantly Japanese prep school in Honolulu. But on a trip to Israel to explore my roots I felt it important to at least spend a day in a yeshivah finding out what it used to be like to be a Jew. Helped by some gentle prodding by the then ubiquitous Rabbi Meir Schuster, I ended up in Ohr Somayach, a yeshivah designed for people like me, and I was quite surprised by what I found there. My education at Yale had not prepared me for the existence of people who were extremely bright, very knowledgeable and thought through, and still deeply religious. After getting over the initial shock, I was intrigued by the things I heard there. I was also taken by the genuine dedication to learning and understanding displayed by the students — here was an example of a true intellectual community the likes of which I had not seen before. I stayed for only a short while, but left with much to think about. Back at Yale I changed my major from physics to philosophy, and returned to Yerushalayim a year later for what became an extended stay.

Needless to say, I eventually made some adjustments to my direction in life, moving from a secular life to one based in Torah. This represented a fundamental shift in worldview. It is not easy to understand how a person can make changes on this level. A worldview is an integrated whole; how can any well-adjusted person (I considered myself reasonably well-adjusted at the time) move beyond the one he is in? This book is in part a product of my fascination with this question.

I looked to my own process to understand how such a transition can happen. I had always found the western intellectual tradition a coherent system that faithfully reflected the world as I experienced it. But there was a part of me that was not satisfied. The way that I expressed it then was: "Being nice is more than just a nice thing to do — it's not *just nice* to be nice," but I could not find a way to integrate that into my understanding of the world on a level that I found satisfying. Today, the language I would use to describe my disquiet is that the western picture is intellectually satisfying — consistent, sophisticated, and deep — but that there are other aspects to a human being more fundamental than his intellect. A vision of the world built wholly from the perspective of the intellect will leave deeper spiritual aspects troubled and the person himself, if he is sufficiently connected to those parts of himself, will feel the unease. Sometimes this will be strong enough to lead him to test the limits of his world and even to push beyond it.

The transition from one worldview to another, then, is not catalyzed by the intellect. But it certainly can be blocked by the intellect. When a thinking person feels some form of awakening to press beyond the world he is in, the world he is reaching toward must be intelligible. Otherwise, he will feel that the move compromises an essential and familiar aspect of himself for the sake of another that is less familiar and stop the process. At the highest stages of religious commitment faithfulness to intellect is not an inviolable principle — Avraham's binding of Yitzchak illustrates this. Our spiritual root is the foundation of our humanity, intellect a mere tool of that spiritual connection. The intellect must give way when a conflict arises with the spirit. But when someone is standing outside the walls looking in, this is not relevant. Understanding is needed.

This book, then, is my search for coherence in the world of Torah. But is this need limited to those standing outside the walls? Even when we recognize that at the heights of spiritual attainment we may need to sacrifice our understanding before our commitment, the two conflict only under the most extreme of circumstances. And even if we recognize that there are things we cannot understand, there is much that *is* within reach. When Ramchal investigated the principles of Divine oversight he taught us that accepting the existence of things we cannot understand does not undermine the validity of striving to understand what we can.[1] We were given the Torah at Har Sinai only after agreeing to "do and understand."[2] Though the Sages emphasize that our commitment to obey preceded our commitment to understand, this was primarily to ensure our actions were motivated by our dedication to God rather than by our ego-based rationality;[3] it does not imply a contradiction between the two. After all, regardless of which was first we also had to obligate ourselves to strive to understand in order to get the Torah. Rabbeinu Bechaya in *Duties of the Heart* requires that our faith and understanding of God's connection to reality not consist solely of acceptance of pronouncements by the wise simply because the wise say them. Rather, we should utilize our intellect to investigate their ideas until we attain personal conviction that they are true.[4] Maharal explains that at the Passover Seder the son who does not know how to ask is given the same answer as the evil son because the indifference of not caring enough to notice irregularities and ask questions is as destructive of true faith as outright hostility.[5]

And even if it were that only those standing outside the walls need this understanding, how many of us are not, at least to some degree, standing on the outside? There are some who live wholly within the walls of the Torah, but most of us do not even know what a wall is anymore. We are very familiar with the secular world and if we understood deeply what the secular world is about we would realize just how much we are a part of it. The Torah is far from us and therefore needs to make sense.

---

1. Ramchal, *Daʾat Tevunot* 7–11.
2. *Shemot* 24:7.
3. *Shabbat* 88a.
4. Rabbeinu Bechaya, *Chovot HaLevavot, Hakdamah.*
5. Maharal, *Gevurot HaShem*, ch. 53.

If we seek an intelligible Torah, what are we to do with the fact that Torah describes a world that does not conform to the reality of our experience? The Torah is a prophetic document. Prophecy is no longer part of our world. In fact, anyone claiming prophecy finds his home in a locked ward. The Torah describes numerous miraculous events, yet God does not split seas before us any more. On the contrary, as we saw in the previous century, when we get chased into the water most of us drown. And what of the question of evil in a world theoretically created to give good? Why is a world created by the all-powerful God not perfect from its inception?

Despite all these difficulties, what makes the Torah seem really foreign is not our lack of singular events like miracles and prophecy or answers to specific questions. Rather, we are primarily separated from the Torah by our overall sense of the world as empty of God. In the Torah, God's presence is pervasive. He is the foundation of our awareness of reality, gives context to our social relations, and invests even the most mundane of our activities with spiritual meaning and significance. Today, while we may soar in the books and touch majesty when we pray, as soon as our focus returns to the world we experience it as hollow. Outside the study hall or synagogue any mention of spirituality has a certain flatness to it, sounding as relevant as a quote from Kant on a playground at recess.

God does not just lack presence in our world. Rather, we don't even notice His absence — because He doesn't seem to have a place. Our world is filled with physical things. Our pursuits are disconnected from any spiritual concerns. Even when we detach ourselves from our purely physical focus, parting for a moment the veil that separates us from God, only darkness is revealed and we must take the initiative to construct any connection to what lies beyond. Efforts at spirituality seem strangely artificial; a relationship with God has become unnatural. The force of our tradition pushes us to soldier on, but how many of us succeed in making God a genuine reality in our lives, let alone its central reality? Do most of us not suffer some level of compromise in our faith occasioned by the distance between the Torah and our world? What do we have to say about this matter to the inquisitive nonreligious person or to those of our youth who are restive and aching for relevance and authenticity?

Why is it like this? To brush off the barrenness of our reality with the observation that we are in exile is insufficient — at least without further explanation. We all intuitively understand that life is supposed to be challenging, but are our circumstances really what we would expect in a world created for the sole purpose of man's relationship with God? We are willing to climb mountains, but shouldn't we at least see the goal, or at least that there is a goal? We are willing to sacrifice for the relationship, but shouldn't the relationship be there for us?

*   *   *

The awareness that we are in a relationship is crucial to understanding our situation. What is the process of forming a relationship? What kind of relationship is it that we are forming? We do not have direct access to spiritual matters so we rely on metaphors from our experience in this world to understand them. In *Shir HaShirim* (The Song of Songs), Shlomo HaMelech (King Solomon) depicts the evolving historical relationship of the Jewish people with God using the metaphor of a bride and groom. What can we learn from this choice of metaphor?

When two people meet and their love blossoms, they pledge eternal dedication to one another in their marriage vows. They recognize that they will have to work for each other. But in their immaturity, they imagine that the love they feel will always be there and that the effort they are accepting is external to the actual relationship. They soon discover the primary struggle is for the relationship itself.

The initial attraction that a bride and groom experience derives from each being incomplete alone and feeling that the other fills the lack. Love is always becoming one, but in its raw form it is actually a selfish emotion; for each, the unity comes in the other becoming his or her extension — they are not so much a couple as they are a couple of individuals. Only once the relationship becomes a reality and they find that they must sacrifice some of their individuality for it to develop can a real process of unification begin. Each must transform himself from who he was as a single person to who he must be in a relationship with the other. Instead of a *he* and a *she*, they become a *we*. But there is a pe-riod after they discover that their original love was not grounded when their connection is only potential but not actual. They must accept that finding one another was not finding love but, rather, finding one with whom they could dedicate themselves to the goal of creating love. Real relationships are built, not found.

There are many levels on which this metaphor can apply to the evolv-ing relationship between God and the Jewish people. The point that is relevant to us now is that while striving to achieve a relationship with God, though we may move through a period when the bond is easy and intuitive, this is only an initial, immature stage in a developing relation-ship. For the connection to be real, we must enter a time when we take responsibility for the connection — which means taking responsibility for ourselves as a partner in the relationship — and transform ourselves into a party capable of being truly connected to God. Once the inspiration has dissipated, however, until the transformation of self is completed the actual bond, though it exists, will not be apparent: "As I lay in my bed in the nights I sought my beloved but I could not find Him."[6]

This necessity of a period of separation is confirmed by the other relationship that serves as a metaphor for our developing connection with God — that of a child to his or her parent. A mother begins her relationship with her daughter when the daughter is a suckling infant. The closeness in those moments is immeasurable. Yet we instinctively recognize that, for all its intimacy and importance to the future health of the child, it would be unnatural for the connection to continue in this manner. The duty of every mother is to train her daughter to be an individual in her own right. The child herself intuitively feels this. This shows itself at an early age in the child's need to stand alone from the parent, albeit checking regularly to make sure Mom is close at hand. When the child reaches adolescence she wants real independence and breaks away. She will return later — on the deepest level everything

---

6. *Shir HaShirim* 3:1.

craves return to its source.[7] But the daughter needs to establish her own individuality first. Once this is accomplished, that very individuality becomes the basis of a new kind of closeness — one built on emulation. The mother and daughter will be most profoundly connected when the daughter herself becomes a mother with her own suckling infant, resonating with the shared experiences she will then have with her mom.

Just as a daughter must separate to develop the independence by which she eventually emulates and connects to her mother so, too, we in our relationship with God. The parallel to the metaphorical independence of adolescence in our bond with God is a period when we turn away from Him. We then experience God's hiddenness and must take responsibility for finding Him. Through meaningful choices, we build ourselves as partners in the relationship — by recreating ourselves we achieve connection through emulating God the Creator.

*   *   *

Our painfully brief overview creates more questions than it answers. But it sets the stage for this book, in which we strive to understand our distance from God by examining, in much more detail, this process of building relationship with Him and, hopefully, answer more questions than we create. The book is divided into four sections. In the first section we recognize that our purpose is to develop ourselves as creations of God, recovering the connection to Him that was broken by our entry into individual existence. We work on this in all arenas of human experience using the commandments of the Torah as our guide. Based on this understanding of our purpose, we begin the second section by asking questions about how and why the world is set up the way that it is. Those readers solely interested in the more analytical aspects of this book may want to move quickly to this second section but, otherwise, the first section provides a strong foundation for what follows.

We start the second section with the basic question of why, in a

---

7. Ramchal, *Daat Tevunot* 24; Maharal, *Gevurot HaShem*, ch. 47.

world created for relationship with God, is He so hard to find? This leads to an investigation of free will and its necessity to accomplish the purpose of creation, both in terms of our attaining individuality and our ability to recognize God. In the third section we examine the development that we undergo both individually and nationally as we face the difficulties of creating relationship with God. We trace the actual history of the Jewish people as we move through this process — our evolving separation from God, how it impacts our perception of Him, and how we grow from it. In the final section we take a hard look at modern experience to understand the nature of our distance from God today, why it is so challenging, and how we are to use it as an opportunity to achieve full relationship with the Creator.

*   *   *

In a work like this it can be easy for readers to become so involved in understanding a particular idea in the discussion that they lose sight of how that idea advances the larger themes that are the backbone of the project. I have therefore provided a synopsis at the end of the book. Readers who are already familiar with the concepts of free will, exile, and modern consciousness might try looking at the synopsis first to provide a framework to guide them in their reading. They can refer back to it occasionally while making their way through the material to keep clarity on where they are in the argument and where it is going. Readers for whom these ideas are new may find the synopsis difficult before going through the book. For them, the synopsis provides a review after finishing the book that can tie it all together and recover a focus on the forest, having examined all the trees. Obviously, reading the synopsis is no substitute for reading the book. That would be like visiting a museum gift shop and skipping the museum — many of the most important items are not represented and even those that are lack their true power because they are viewed outside of their full context. The purpose of the synopsis is only to give a sense for the flow and structure of the ideas. Readers may also find that they gain a deeper appreciation for the ideas and their integration by reading the book more than once.

Certain basic Hebrew terms are used in transliteration where I felt the English was especially laden with associations best kept out of the discussion. The first time each appears, and whenever there has been a lengthy break since its previous usage, the English translation is given. A glossary is provided at the back for quick reference.

I also need to warn the reader that you may find certain parts of the book noticeably more challenging than others — for example, the sixth chapter. These are sections where ideas are taken to a greater level of depth, and understanding them, necessarily, requires more effort. I would urge you if you reach a section that gives you difficulty not to give up on the whole venture, but to go over the troublesome part again, or even skip it and return to reread it after you have finished the book. Many ideas are revisited several times throughout the work and become clearer as the context of the overall discussion develops. The main thing is not to assume when things get particularly hard that they will continue that way and, as a result, abandon the project.

Reading this book requires commitment. The reader needs to be engaged and thinking while working through it. But I believe you will find your investment compensated. A few very basic questions are explored deeply. The answers presented are not mine. They are those of our Sages as refracted through certain commentaries, primarily Maharal, Ramchal, and Rabbi Tzaddok HaKohen, as well as my principal teachers, Rabbi Moshe Shapiro *shlita* and Rabbi Aharon Feldman *shlita*. The foundations upon which the edifice is built are therefore strong and deep. That being said, I have certainly developed what I heard from the perspective of my particular interests and transposed it into a language that speaks to and for me. Therefore, the possibility exists that errors have crept into my understanding or presentation and I am solely responsible for them.

I walk a bit of a tightrope here. On one hand, I must give credit where it is very much due for the ideas presented here and the methodology by which they were developed. On the other, I must not burden those sources with any distortions that may result from the particular development and slant I have applied to them.

I have not had the merit of hearing classes from Rabbi Feldman for over twenty years. But once upon a time he took pains to bang into my unresponsive mind certain ideas about the nature of the *yetzer ha-ra* (the evil inclination), which remain with me to this day and lie at the core of parts of this book. Those ideas can be found in his own words in his masterpiece, *The Juggler and the King*. Perhaps the most important concept I took from my time with him, beyond the example he set and continues to set for me, is the fact that no idea, regardless of how abstract, is understood sufficiently until it is made personal.

I have had the fortune to hear classes from Rabbi Moshe Shapiro almost continually for over 25 years. What I have taken from those lectures is so intimately woven into my thinking at this point, even more so in approach than in content, that it would be difficult to identify any area of my understanding that he has not affected. I say "what I have taken from his lectures" as opposed to "what he said in them" because there are few who can rightfully claim to fully understand what he presents and I do not count myself in their company. Here, especially, I am in a quandary over giving credit where it is due without burdening Rabbi Shapiro with any distortions I may have introduced. There is no simple solution to this problem; suffice it to say that the few footnotes that directly reference Rabbi Shapiro in regard to specific points cannot do justice to his influence both on me and on the contents of this book.

*   *   *

I find the questions asked in this book urgent and the answers provided by our Sages deeply satisfying. I think I can say with confidence that if you are the type of person who would attempt this book, you also will find the questions important. But I cannot guarantee that the manner in which I have framed the answers will speak to you as much as it does to me. My hope is that it will. The goal, however, is not merely to resolve the difficulty that generated the question. Rather, it is that as a result of examining the Sages' approach to the issues the reader gains a deeper and more satisfying understanding of his world that resonates powerfully within him — I find that the most compelling indication of truth.

I also hope that readers will appreciate through studying the book that there is nothing to fear from delving into Torah. Pure intentions are required, for the intellectual process can be easily commandeered by external agendas. And in the body of the book I explain why critiquing the Torah from outside itself is illegitimate. But Torah is only strengthened by sincere scrutiny; when examined from within its own confines and with a genuine spirit of inquiry — the more we ask, the more clearly we appreciate just how deep our Torah is. Not that we ever achieve full understanding. There is always that bit left to comprehend, which when we take the time and effort to probe it, opens a little door behind which is a cavernous chamber at the end of which is another little door.

I learned more from working on this project than I could have imagined. On numerous occasions, points that seemed peripheral to the central discussion revealed themselves upon examination to be fundamental to understanding the topic and shifted the focus of the book subtly but significantly. I hope the reader will be able to taste some of the excitement that comes from unfolding ideas that I experienced while writing it.

Any work dealing with modern understanding and experience must grapple with the place of science in consciousness. The relationship between Torah and science is a controversial topic at present, and the intensity with which people often hold opinions on it can lead to misreading. I would like to caution readers against hastily categorizing positions developed in the book. With regard to this issue, as is often the case with me, I am more interested in *why* people think the way they do and *how* their thinking is connected to the rest of their awareness than *what* they actually think. Both my training and interest are directed toward the cultural and experiential context within which people view their world and how that affects the way they see it. It is in the framework of investigating these larger issues of modern consciousness and spirituality that the relationship between Torah and science is explored. The specifics of the controversy are not examined for they are not relevant to the topic of this book. I do believe, however, that placing the controversy within this larger context gives it much needed perspective.

As theoretical as this book is, it remains eminently practical. By identifying the challenges that characterize modern experience, it indicates where the real work of faith lies, thus giving focus to our efforts. And while the intellectual understanding of Torah is no substitute for a personal relationship with God, which is Torah's heart and purpose, it provides a strong context in which that relationship can flourish.

THE PURPOSE:

Actualizing Self to Connect to God

CHAPTER 1

A Guide to Action

[When a positive commandment and a prohibition conflict]
the positive commandment nullifies the prohibition,[1] because
positive commandments connect to a higher spiritual source
than prohibitions.[2]

M OST OF US DO not walk around consciously feeling lonely. But the
rush of pleasure we experience when we meet someone with whom
we genuinely connect makes us realize how incomplete we really are.

Once in a while, when quietly gazing at a sunset, that inexplicable
switch takes place, and instead of looking at our surroundings we become part of them. We then become aware that much of our lives are
spent sharply cut off from our world.

We are so distracted by life we hardly ever notice our existence.
When we do we are often disturbed by our emptiness. Yet, we can have
moments of contemplation and deep understanding that bring a sense
of wholeness and satisfaction.

In every dimension of our experience — in our relationships with
others, in our connection to reality, in our awareness of self — the situation

---

1. *Shabbat* 132b.
2. Maharal, *Tiferet Yisrael*, ch. 37 and *Chiddushei Aggadot* IV, p. 7.

is the same.[3] We pass almost all of our time isolated in ourselves. Though we are usually asleep to the inadequacy of this detachment, in those moments when we break through the walls, our satisfaction is startling in its depth — and reveals just how much we have a need to connect beyond ourselves. What is this need? Why does it run so deep? How do we explain our general oblivion to this lack that is clearly so significant to us?

This need is an expression of our intrinsic desire to return to our Source.[4] Before we entered individual existence, we were one with the immensity of unitary Being. We were broken off into a distinct life and the boundedness of physical reality which is its necessary context. From our core we crave to escape from the limitations our individual existence imposes upon us and return to our boundless origin. Our life is powered by this need and shaped by our response to it. That it can be masked from our consciousness poses a question that is the concern of much of this book. But we cannot begin answering that question until we understand the framework within which we strive to recover connection to our infinite Source. What is the nature of the connection we are trying to achieve and how do we achieve it?

A RELATIONSHIP FORMED OF ACTIONS

The way people connect is through relationships; that is as true of our connection to our Source, the Creator, as any other connection we make. A full relationship has as many facets as we have parts to our personality. We experience our self in our conscious awareness — obviously that must be involved in any significant relationship we have. If

---

3. These three dimensions of experience correspond to the three categories of mitzvot: *bein adam l'chaveiro* (between man and his fellow man), *bein adam l'Makom* (between man and God), and *bein adam l'atzmo* (between man and himself). See *Pirkei Avot* 1:2 with Maharal, *Derech Chayim*, on that *mishnah*.

4. See *Kohelet Rabbah* 6:6 and *Da'at Tevunot* 24. The greatness we find within ourselves and the dignity we sense in others are both consequences of man being created in *tzelem Elokim* (the image of God). Our communion with existence is an effort to break the limits of our individuality and reunite with the all-encompassing Source of reality.

awareness constituted the whole person perhaps we would be satisfied with relationships restricted to sharing thoughts and emotions. But our awareness arises from a complex melding together of spiritual and physical roots and is profoundly impacted by the subconscious of both of them. Involving these deeper aspects is at least as important as our conscious self since, whether we are aware of it or not, they largely govern our personality.[5]

Pen pals are nice but don't last because the connection never goes beyond ideas. A husband can tell his wife he loves her, but if he does not do something that conveys that love, the relationship will inevitably flounder. This is not only because there is something missing in what the other receives. It is also because without actual deeds the self we commit to the relationship is critically deficient. Full relationships need actions to incorporate our physical energies.[6] And those actions must also give expression to our spiritual root so that it, too, is joined to the other. But how can we know what actions will accomplish this when our spiritual self lies beyond our conscious reach?

We turn to the Torah for guidance. In fact, the word "Torah" comes from the root *hora'ah* which means to teach in a practical way — to guide.[7] Though Torah conveys an understanding of reality that is deep beyond measure, it is essentially a book of commands to action — mitzvot.[8] Obviously, those mitzvot assume and manifest all the spiritual depth that is in the Torah. When we are required, for example, to give

---

5. Torah sources have recognized these influences for a very long time. For a recent source that lays it out clearly, see *Peirush HaGra al Megillat Esther* 7:6. There the Gra attributes the idea of subconscious influence to the Sages. More recently the depth psychologists have investigated the impact of the subconscious. For the physical subconscious we can look to Freud and Adler; for the influence of the spiritual, Jung and Frankel among many others.
6. *Sefer HaChinuch* 16. Our will arises from the synthesis of our spiritual and physical aspects and much more closely approximates our essential humanity than our thoughts (we will discuss free will later). Thoughts constitute an aspect of us, not our total being. Only through the combination of intention with action do we reach, affect, and give expression to our essential will. Therefore, to bring our self to relationship we must act.
7. Maharal, *Gur Aryeh, Bereishit* 1:1.
8. *Rashi, Bereishit* 1:1.

charity, it is not as a utilitarian Band-Aid to inequity — God can take care of His poor. Rather, it is because giving charity profoundly impacts the nature of our humanity.

In general, when fulfilling a command out of obedience we are nullified to its commander; our action becomes a vehicle of his will, endowing it with his intention. In the case of the Torah's mitzvot, obedience invests our action with the Creator's purpose, a spiritual content which transcends human understanding. The mitzvot of the Torah thus bind our spiritual root to our awareness and physical being, fostering a relationship of the whole self with our Source, the Creator.

But, just as an assembly of disjointed acts cannot form the basis for a relationship between two people, so a bunch of random commandments cannot form the basis for a relationship between man and God. Torah is not a mere jumble of mitzvot. Rather, the mitzvot are a system through which a relationship with the Creator develops and takes on physical expression. Understanding the relationship we are striving to form with the Creator and our overall responsibilities in achieving it requires that we grasp all the mitzvot together as a structured whole — i.e., what they are about as a system.

But discerning the essential principle that unifies the disparate mitzvot and makes of them a coherent whole is daunting. There are 613 distinct obligations,[9] and there is no obvious commonality between them. What ties together refraining from work on Shabbat, giving charity, wearing phylacteries, not eating cheese with meat, and observing the laws of family purity? It is very difficult to deduce from the mitzvot themselves what their overall purpose is. Yet, not identifying this purpose would leave any intent we bring to our observance without context or foundation.

If our difficulty deriving the underlying principle of the Torah's system of mitzvot is due to its complexity, we could solve our problem by locating a simpler set of the Creator's commandments to man. Since

---

9. *Makkot* 23b.

the relationship we are striving to achieve with the Creator is man's purpose, and purpose in creation does not change, we can be confident that any set of commandments from God to man will aim at the same goal, merely achieving it through different means.[10]

Adam and Chavah in Gan Eden had only a few commandments; since they were on a higher spiritual plane than us they needed less structure to achieve the same end. Gan Eden is, then, a natural laboratory to analyze the command relationship with the Creator. By identifying the essential character of Adam and Chavah's system we can discover what defines ours.

THE SEED FROM WHICH ALL COMMANDS SPRING

Our method of distinguishing the essence of Adam's relationship with the Creator will be to determine the first command God gave him.[11] Beginning and essence are equivalent in creation, for the Creator does not recreate from scratch every individual element of existence. Rather, first creations are the equivalent of templates that take on expression

---

10. God's purpose does not change but, rather, is inevitably accomplished. "Like the snow and rain that descend from the heavens never to return there, but rather water the ground and bring budding and growth and seed to the sower and bread to eat. So will be My word that goes forth from My mouth; it will not return to me empty until it has done that which I have desired and succeeded in that for which I have sent it" *Yeshayah* 55:10–11. See also Rabbi Yosef Albo, *Sefer HaIkarim* 1:4 where, when discussing the three fundamentals of *emunah* (faith), he states that they are the foundations of any *Torat Elokim*, whether it be that of Adam, Noach, Avraham, or Moshe.

11. If this is our approach, why not search for the first of the 613 mitzvot? There are several levels of answer to this question. (1) The first of the 613 is not the first mitzvah ever, so it does not represent the truest beginning. (2) In a moment we will learn that creations of the first six days have a special, more fundamental character. (3) The first of the 613 comes after the Jews have fallen away from the Creator and are recovering themselves and their relationship, which introduces a prior, preparatory stage to the actual pursuit of the goal. The first of the 613 mitzvot commanded to the Jews was the sanctification of the new month. We will learn in Chapter 7 that the new month is deeply connected to *teshuvah* (repentance) — recovery from the fall.

in various forms over the course of time.[12] The Torah effectively states this when it says that on the first Shabbat of creation, God rested "from all that He had created *to do*." The meaning of "to do" at the end of the verse is difficult to understand. The commentaries explain that the first six days expressed the essence of all that would follow in history; it was created then "to do" later, to come out transposed and stretched over longer periods of time.[13]

Finding the first appearance of any creation, then, locates the essential expression of that creation, containing all its potential. If we can identify the first commandment given to Adam, we will have found the essence of his commandments and, therefore, of all commandments.

What was the first commandment that was given to mankind?[14] The Torah does not provide an obvious answer to this question. Two separate passages record God commanding Adam. In one, God requires Adam to reproduce; in the other, God prohibits Adam from eating from the Tree of Knowledge:

> So God created man in His image, in the image of God He created him; male and female He created them. And God blessed them and God said to them, "Be fruitful and multiply, fill the earth and subdue it..."[15]
>
> *Bereishit* (Genesis) 1:27–28

> HaShem God took the man and placed him in Gan Eden to work it and to guard it. And HaShem God commanded the man, saying, "Of every tree of the garden you may freely eat; but of the Tree of the

---

12. See Chapter 16, note 9 for another treatment of this idea.

13. See *Ramban, Bereishit* 2:2.

14. The approach that follows is based on material from Rabbi Beryl Gershenfeld.

15. This translation is from the Stone *Chumash*. The original Hebrew text is:

בראשית א (כז) וַיִּבְרָא אֱלֹקִים אֶת הָאָדָם בְּצַלְמוֹ בְּצֶלֶם אֱלֹקִים בָּרָא אֹתוֹ זָכָר וּנְקֵבָה בָּרָא אֹתָם: (כח) וַיְבָרֶךְ אֹתָם אֱלֹקִים וַיֹּאמֶר לָהֶם אֱלֹקִים פְּרוּ וּרְבוּ וּמִלְאוּ אֶת הָאָרֶץ וְכִבְשֻׁהָ וּרְדוּ בִּדְגַת הַיָּם וּבְעוֹף הַשָּׁמַיִם וּבְכָל חַיָּה הָרֹמֶשֶׂת עַל הָאָרֶץ:

Knowledge of Good and Evil you must not eat; for on the day you eat from it you will die." And HaShem God said, "It is not good for man to be alone; I will make him a helper."[16]

Bereishit 2:15–18

In the text of the Torah, the passage that directs man to "be fruitful" precedes the one that prohibits eating from the Tree of the Knowledge of Good and Evil. At first glance, then, it would appear that the obligation to procreate is the first commandment. However, things are not so simple. *Bereishit* narrates the creation story twice, telling it each time from a different perspective.[17] Each version mentions only one of the mitzvot. Since both passages are describing the same event, their order of appearance provides no information from which to determine the relative chronology of details recorded in each one.

It is like interviewing two people who witnessed the aftermath of the same accident. When we ask a child what he saw, he tells us with great excitement that there was a bright red fire truck spraying water everywhere. When we ask an adult what she remembers, she tells us that she saw an ambulance and was very concerned. Both are describing the same event but focusing on the details of particular interest to them. Just because we interview the child before the adult we cannot conclude that the fire truck arrived before the ambulance. So, also, in the two creation stories in *Bereishit*. The order of appearance of the mitzvot in the text gives us no clue as to their relative chronology, for they come in different accounts of the same event. How are we to determine which commandment was given first in the Garden, in order to identify the essential root of our relationship with the Creator?

---

16. Translation from the Stone *Chumash*. The original Hebrew text is:

בראשית ב (טו) וַיִּקַּח ה' אֱלֹקִים אֶת הָאָדָם וַיַּנִּחֵהוּ בְגַן עֵדֶן לְעָבְדָהּ וּלְשָׁמְרָהּ: (טז) וַיְצַו ה' אֱלֹקִים עַל הָאָדָם לֵאמֹר מִכֹּל עֵץ הַגָּן אָכֹל תֹּאכֵל: (יז) וּמֵעֵץ הַדַּעַת טוֹב וָרָע לֹא תֹאכַל מִמֶּנּוּ כִּי בְּיוֹם אֲכָלְךָ מִמֶּנּוּ מוֹת תָּמוּת: (יח) וַיֹּאמֶר ה' אֱלֹקִים לֹא טוֹב הֱיוֹת הָאָדָם לְבַדּוֹ אֶעֱשֶׂה לּוֹ עֵזֶר כְּנֶגְדּוֹ:

17. The first version goes from 1:1 until 2:3. This encompasses the description of the first seven days of Creation. The second version, which revisits the sixth day when man was created, begins in verse 2:4.

If we return to the command regarding the tree in the second version, we find that it is immediately followed by God stating, "It is not good for man to be alone; I will make him a helper." This refers to the fact that Adam was originally created androgynous and was subsequently split into two parts, male and female.[18] This split only comes after the command was given regarding the Tree. It would seem logical that a prerequisite for being obligated in procreation is that man exist in distinct male and female forms. Though on a mystical level this is not necessarily so (especially when we remember that Adam was androgynous),[19] the text of the first chapter in *Bereishit* makes it clear that man was separated into two before the command to multiply was announced: "God created the man in His image, in the image of God He created *him*; male and female He created *them*. And God blessed *them* and said to *them*, 'Be fruitful and multiply...'" The shift from the singular pronoun "him" to the plural "them" marks the split of man into two separate individuals.[20] The subsequent command to multiply is addressed to the plural "them."

Since the splitting of man into male and female precedes the command to reproduce and follows the command regarding the Tree, it is clear that the command about the Tree inaugurates the command relationship between man and God. It would seem we must conclude that the prohibition against eating from the Tree of the Knowledge of Good and Evil defines the essence of all commandments, with all that this implies.

LOST IN TRANSLATION

But we have been working under false pretenses. Following the translation in all common English versions of the *Chumash* (the Five Books

---

18. *Berachot* 61a.
19. See *Ramban, Bereishit* 2:18.
20. See *Rashi* and *Chizkuni, Bereishit* 1:27.

of Moses), we have rendered the text regarding the command of the Tree as, "Of every tree of the garden you *may* freely eat; but of the Tree of the Knowledge of Good and Evil you *must not* eat..." According to this translation, there was only one command regarding the tree — a prohibition against eating from the Tree of Knowledge; regarding all the other trees of the Garden man was told he "may" eat from them, meaning he had permission to eat from them if he chose, but he was never commanded to do so.

Relationship with God is the purpose of creation and therefore incumbent upon us.[21] The contents of that relationship are, therefore, commanded — they are not optional. We are only interested in what man must do — there lies meaning — not in how he fills his idle time. According to the translation of the text we are now using, man's essential relationship with God — the relationship mediated through commands — begins with the prohibition against eating from the Tree of Knowledge.

If we look directly at the original Hebrew, however, a different story emerges. A more accurate translation would read, "From all the trees of the garden you *must* eat. And from the Tree of the Knowledge of Good and Evil you must not eat..."[22] According to this more precise translation, there were actually two mitzvot regarding the trees: a positive obligation to eat from all the trees of the garden as well as a prohibition against eating from the Tree of Knowledge, with the positive requirement to eat coming first.

Remember, our search for the first commandment to Adam was motivated by a desire to identify the root from which all the commands arise. Once we recognize that eating the fruit of the Garden was the first

---

21. See Chapter 4, pp. 45–47.
22. See Rabbeinu Bechaya, *Aderet Eliyahu*, and *Meshech Chochmah* on *Bereishit* 2:16. Also Rabbi Tzaddok HaKohen, *Pri Tzaddik*, *Shevuot* 12. That God is commanding man is stated in the verse before the invitation to eat from the trees of the Garden, and that invitation to eat comes in a double verb "*achol tocheil*," which is a command form. See for example *Vayikra* 19:17 and *Devarim* 24:13. (See Rabbi Cooperman's commentary to *Meshech Chochmah*, *Bereishit* 2:16.)

command, it must define all commands, with the prohibition against eating from the Tree of Knowledge a mere limitation of this positive obligation.

A POSITIVE GUIDE

The implications of this reversal are resounding. What is the Torah principally about? Is it a guide to action and how to be in the world? Or is it restrictive, primarily concerned with distancing us from certain experiences — a guide to how not to be in the world? With the positive obligation to eat from the fruit of the Garden defining the command system, we must conclude that the Torah is a guide to action.

Recognizing the primacy of the positive mitzvot gives a distinct tone to our experience of Torah. This can be illustrated by contrasting two different focuses on Shabbat. There are two kinds of mitzvot involved in Shabbat observance: There is the positive obligation to rest — which really means to turn inward, striving for a different level of self and, with it, a different level of connection to others and to God. And there are the negative commands to refrain from all manner of creatively changing our physical environment. The feel of Shabbat is dependent upon which of these two commands defines the day.

Imagine entering a Shabbat-observant home for the first time. What is our first impression? Are we soothingly ushered to a chair where we are struck with the sublime serenity of a mother seated on the couch playing with her children, Shabbat candles flickering their magic from the mantel at her side? Or, as we open the door, are we immediately whisked to our seat at the table, being told by our hostess to please not touch the light switch, be careful to take the fish from the bones and not the bones from the fish, and to be especially vigilant to use the cold water faucet on the right side of the sink when going to wash?

Prohibitions are an essential and significant part of Shabbat, but they do not define the day. Refraining from writing reports, speaking on the phone, or jumping in a car creates a protective bubble that allows us to achieve the serenity, elevation, and dignity that are the essence of the Shabbat experience.[23] Abstaining from our involvement in the outer world is not meant to leave us desolate. Rather, it allows the full inward turn. The prohibitions of Shabbat exist to serve the positive obligation to rest, enabling and protecting its accomplishment. The priority in the Garden given to the positive obligation to eat from all the fruits reveals this as the general relationship of the negative mitzvot to the positive ones throughout the Torah.

The opposite view of the Torah as primarily restrictive, as well as being unsupported by the text, is, on a practical level, unsustainable. The snake coaxed Chavah to eat the forbidden fruit precisely by framing the Torah in this negative manner:

Now the snake was more clever than any animal of the field which HaShem God had made. And he said to the woman, "Has God really said you cannot eat from any tree of the garden?" And the woman said to the snake, "We may eat from the fruit of the trees of the garden. But from the fruit of the tree that is in the center of the garden God said, 'You cannot eat of it and you cannot touch it, lest you die.'" And the snake said to the woman, "You will not die; God knows that on the day you eat from it your eyes will be opened, and you will be like gods knowing good and evil."[24]

Bereishit 3:1–5

---

23. On the more profound subconscious level, any act we do that alters the physical sphere asserts our control over creation. Although we have been given responsibility for creation, this is only within a specific, limited dimension of reality. On the deepest level, God controls everything. Shabbat is a time to touch that level and testify to the omnipotence of the Creator. Any act of control, even something so slight as the flip of a light switch, contradicts that testimony.

24. Unless explicitly stated otherwise, translations of verses, Talmud, and *Midrash Rabbah* in this book are based on the Soncino editions of the Jewish Press. I have freely amended those translations where I felt it was helpful in terms of style or specific points of content. The Hebrew text of this particular translation is:

בראשית ג (א) וְהַנָּחָשׁ הָיָה עָרוּם מִכֹּל חַיַּת הַשָּׂדֶה אֲשֶׁר עָשָׂה ה' אֱלֹקִים וַיֹּאמֶר אֶל הָאִשָּׁה אַף כִּי אָמַר אֱלֹקִים לֹא תֹאכְלוּ מִכֹּל עֵץ הַגָּן: (ב) וַתֹּאמֶר הָאִשָּׁה אֶל הַנָּחָשׁ מִפְּרִי עֵץ הַגָּן נֹאכֵל: (ג) וּמִפְּרִי הָעֵץ אֲשֶׁר בְּתוֹךְ הַגָּן אָמַר אֱלֹקִים לֹא תֹאכְלוּ מִמֶּנּוּ וְלֹא תִגְּעוּ בּוֹ פֶּן תְּמֻתוּן: (ד) וַיֹּאמֶר הַנָּחָשׁ אֶל הָאִשָּׁה לֹא מוֹת תְּמֻתוּן: (ה) כִּי יֹדֵעַ אֱלֹקִים כִּי בְּיוֹם אֲכָלְכֶם מִמֶּנּוּ וְנִפְקְחוּ עֵינֵיכֶם וִהְיִיתֶם כֵּאלֹקִים יֹדְעֵי טוֹב וָרָע:

It is a common debate technique to vastly overstate an opponent's position; even if your opponent succeeds in pulling the audience back from the extreme distortion you have made of his views it is difficult for him to return them to an accurate, balanced understanding. The snake utilized this manipulation, presenting God's relationship with man as insufferably limiting — "You cannot eat from any tree in the garden?" Chavah defended God's position, catching the snake on his false detail — "We may eat from the fruit of the trees." But the poison had entered, for she said we "may" eat where she should have corrected him by saying we "must" eat; she lost the positive mitzvah.[25] All focus of the command aspect of the relationship, the part that really counted, was on what was forbidden. The snake had influenced Chavah to recast Torah as a system of restrictions and from that point on it was only a matter of time before she broke with the system through sin.

When the center is positive and the negative protects its periphery, the constructive purpose accomplished by prohibition is clear, and restriction sits comfortably within its positive context. But when a system is exclusively prohibitive, we only see negative. We begin to wonder why things exist if they are only to be avoided. Is someone else gaining from them? If so, why are we being denied? If the system is not to our benefit, why should we submit to it? The Midrash tells us that the snake played on exactly these doubts in Chavah. He told her, "God ate from this tree to create the world. He does not want you to be a creator also. He denies it to you out of jealousy."[26] Chavah began to think about the tempting qualities of the forbidden fruit — that it was good, pleasing to the eye, and satisfying to behold[27] — and she succumbed.

Imagine walking into a candy store and being asked, "Have you tried the chocolate-covered bonbons? You must try them! They are

---

25. Here the translation of the verb as the optional form "may eat" is correct because the Hebrew does not have a double verb, whereas in the earlier passage the double verb was used. See note 22 in this chapter.
26. *Bereishit Rabbah* 19:4.
27. *Bereishit* 3:6.

divine! And what about the cherry marzipan? And I almost forgot the new vanilla truffles. Don't eat the licorice — it came out quite bitter. But look at these splendid candied apples and fruit chews. And the cream-filled éclairs — you simply haven't lived till you eat one!" Under such an onslaught, who would think about the licorice? Everything is there for you, and the warning against the licorice is just for your protection while you work your way through the rest of the store. The prohibition has significance, but it does not define the project.

Compare this to a situation where the salesperson opens with, "See the licorice? You can't eat the licorice. We don't let *you* have that licorice. Perhaps a bit of chocolate or vanilla truffle for you today?" Your whole attention will be focused on the licorice and you begin to wonder whom the licorice is for? With the licorice's denial elevated to the center, the permitted truffle appears as a trifling consolation. You will be obsessed with the licorice!

In like manner, the snake created an obsession in Chavah by focusing her attention on the prohibition of the tree. His success in perverting Chavah's perspective was evident in her response. When Chavah corrected the snake, saying that it was only the Tree of the Knowledge of Good and Evil that was forbidden, she accentuated its significance by calling it, "the tree that is in the *center* of the garden."

It is not just that a restrictive Torah is unsustainable; it is also untenable. Torah determines our place in existence. If Torah defines meaningful human activity as self-restriction, we would be at odds with the rest of creation. Life is something that grows and unfolds.[28] The universe expands. To be part of creation, we too must grow. We instinctively rebel against the idea that our goal is merely to contain ourselves. That may need to be an aspect of what we do; it can serve our essential task. But it cannot serve *as* our essential task.

✳   ✳   ✳

---

28. *Tehillim* 89:3.

The first command of the Torah, the root from which all commandments arise, is a positive command. From that alone we see that Torah is essentially a guide to action — we must develop. But what must we develop? When we turn to the actual content of the first mitzvah — to eat from all the fruits of the Garden — we are bewildered. How could the foundational command of the Torah be an obligation to eat? Our grandmothers might nod their heads knowingly, but we are startled. How do we see the essence of our spiritual quest in the command to eat?

CHAPTER 2

Developing Self,
Developing Faith

Ben Azi stated: "This is the book of the generations of man."
This verse contains the essence of the Torah.[1]

W E CONCLUDED THAT GOD'S first commandment to man was to eat
from all the trees of the Garden. This requires a positive act. Since
we understand that the first commandment is the essence of all the mitzvot, identifying this as the original command defines the Torah as a guide
to action rather than a system of restrictions. But we do not merely derive
from here *that* Torah wants us to act, we also understand *what* Torah
wants us to do — and that is eat! Why is the root command to eat?

Not only in Gan Eden, but also today, eating plays a central role in
our relationship with God. If we would ask what is the holiest day of
the year, most Jews would answer Yom Kippur — we naturally associate
fasting with holiness. In fact, Shabbat is the holiest day; its violation
brings the strongest punishment.[2] Yet, on that day, rather than fasting
we eat more on Shabbat than on any other day, as we are required to
have an additional meal.[3] Why do we spend so much time eating on

---

1. *Bereishit Rabbah* 24:7 from the verse *Bereishit* 5:1.
2. *Shulchan Aruch, Orach Chayim* 611:2. Also, the largest number of people are called to
read from the Torah on Shabbat. See *Mishnah Megillah* 4:2 with Bartenura.
3. *Shabbat* 117b. *Shulchan Aruch, Orach Chayim* 291:1.

the holiest day? What is the significance of eating?

In general, the need to eat is puzzling. Eating comes in response to hunger. Hunger is lack, and lack is painful. Why would God design creation in a manner that makes pain an intrinsic part of human experience, let alone place it at the core of human responsibility? The need to eat and its centrality is even more difficult to understand because God created the world so that man could form a relationship with Him. Every detail of reality is tailored to foster, either directly or indirectly, that relationship. Eating leads to increased involvement in our physical aspect — generally at the expense of our spiritual focus, which is the basis of our relationship with God![4] How can we form a relationship through something that is seemingly at odds with that relationship?

EATING, *EMUNAH,* AND COMPLETION

The Creator is the Source from which all reality emanates. Some dimensions of reality are close to the Creator and their dependence upon Him is clear. These are the infinite, spiritual realms, which are as hidden from our view as they are revealing of the Creator. In the dimension that is familiar to us as finite physical beings, the connection to the Creator is masked.[5] Both physical reality and spiritual reality, however, emanate from and give expression to the same Source. Thus, structurally, the physical world parallels, albeit in shadow form, its spiritual root.[6] The physical world provides a kind of map or metaphor to the metaphysical.[7]

---

4. That our internal focus is the basis of our relationship with God is seen in Maharal, *Gur Aryeh, Shemot* 2:14. At the highest levels of *kedushah* (sanctity), eating can actually lead to spiritual attainment, as evidenced by the requirement that priests eat sacrifices (*Mesillat Yesharim,* ch. 26). But this only comes after tremendous personal development — what is gained by requiring everyone to face this particular challenge?

5. Ramchal, *Daat Tevunot* 50, 84.

6. Ibid., 48.

7. A more thorough discussion of the metaphorical relationship between physical reality and spiritual reality is found in Chapter 16, pp. 299–300.

Man's need to eat — his dependence upon a source outside of himself for sustenance — is a physical manifestation of the deeper reality of man's metaphysical dependence upon the Creator for existence. The intensity of our hunger serves to reinforce that sense of dependence. Eating, when we take the time to connect our food back to its original provider, affords a profound opportunity for *emunah* (faith).

On this level, Adam's obligation to eat from the trees of the Garden was a command to become aware of his connection to, and dependence upon, God. This is in keeping with the prophet Chavakuk's understanding of the general intent behind all our mitzvot. Each one has its specific purpose, and, ideally, we should have that purpose in mind when we perform each of them. The Talmud explains, however, that when the spiritual level of the generations declined, it became difficult to keep clear the intricate web of thoughts that inform each of the mitzvot. David HaMelech (King David) simplified the task by identifying eleven broad conceptual categories of intention behind the mitzvot. This allowed us when performing each mitzvah to have in mind the appropriate one of the eleven rather than the more confusing intention unique to each mitzvah.[8] This was not a reduction in what mitzvot we do; rather, it was a generalization of our inner focus when doing them. Eventually, even these eleven broad categories became too much for us. So Chavakuk, coming at the end of the prophetic period, narrowed our focus to one fundamental recognition: "The righteous person will live through his *emunah*."[9] In other words, Chavakuk identified *emunah* as the root intention and purpose of all mitzvot.[10]

If, however, general *emunah* was all that was demanded of Adam, according to what we are saying it would have been enough to command him to eat from any tree that would sustain him. Why was he commanded to eat from all the trees of the Garden? To answer this question we must look more deeply at the concept of eating.

---

8. *Makkot* 24a. See HaGra, *Peirush L'Shir HaShirim* 1:2.

9. *Chavakuk* 2:4.

10. See also *Ramban, Shemot* 13:16.

Adam was commanded to eat from the trees of the Garden. We associate eating specifically with the consumption of food. But the Torah uses language very differently from the way we are accustomed to use it. We understand words to have specific meanings. However, in the language of the Torah, *lashon ha-kodesh*, words are expressions of conceptual categories. They take on a definite meaning, a specific expression of their concept, in each particular usage; but they never lose their connection to their broader categorical understanding. When we read a word in the Torah, its specific meaning is enhanced by an appreciation of its conceptual root, deepening the significance of what is being described in the verse.

In the case of Adam's command to eat from the trees of the Garden, the specific meaning in the context is the kind of eating we are familiar with — chewing and swallowing. But conceptually, what are we really accomplishing when we eat? Eating comes in response to hunger. Hunger is a state of inner lack — we need something, we are incomplete. Eating is a process of filling that lack — bringing ourselves to completion.[11] Though we usually associate eating specifically with the consumption of food to fill physical want, in both Torah and Rabbinical literature the term is applied broadly to refer to any act which fills lack and brings us toward completion.[12] If so, the implication of the command to Adam that he must eat is that he must come to completion through eating.

In what area was Adam in need of completion? When we ask this question we are not interested in just any lack. We are trying to

---

11. Maharal, *Netivot Olam* I, *Netiv HaAvodah*, ch. 1.

12. For example, see *Bereishit* 39:6 with *Rashi*. There the term "eating" is understood to mean conjugal relations. Though this is a very different specific meaning, it nonetheless remains faithful to the same conceptual root of filling lack. For a Rabbinic example, see *Bava Batra* 75a which discusses the Meal of the Leviathan. This refers to an event that will occur at the end of time in order to usher in the coming of the Next World. It cannot refer to a barbecue for the righteous — our relationship to physical being will be radically different at that time in preparation for the transition to the Next World. Rather, it refers to an experience that will bring us to the state of completion necessary to enter the Next World. See Maharal, *Gur Aryeh, Bereishit* 1:21.

understand the first command of God to man; we are interested in something essential. What is man's essential lack?

In Torah we look to names when we seek to identify essence, for that is what names reference.[13] A name labels its owner, and labeling identifies essential qualities, not accidental ones. The Midrash tells us that when Adam named the animals, he also named himself.

> [And the Holy One said to him,] "And what is your name?" [Adam replied,] "I should be called Adam, because I was created from the ground [*adamah*]."[14]

Adam called himself *adam* after the *adamah*, the "ground" from which he was formed.[15] The commentaries ask why the ground should specifically give man his name when all the creatures of the world were also formed from the ground. They answer that Adam meant that man and ground uniquely share a characteristic: just as the ground exists to actualize potential — we plant in it seeds so they will grow — so too man's task is to actualize his potential.[16]

When a cow is born it is a cow. When it dies it is a cow. It changes quantitatively through its life, but not qualitatively; its future capabilities are, for the most part, already present at birth.[17] Personal development does not define the task of a cow. On the other hand, when a human being is born he personifies a question: "What will this person make of himself?"[18] Not merely because as an infant he is missing all the capabilities that define our humanity, such as speech and intellect. More so because after developing those capabilities, the possibilities in front of the child remain infinite. On which of his myriad talents will he choose

---

13. See Maharal, *Derech Chayim* 4:14; Maharal, *Gevurot HaShem*, ch. 24.
14. *Bereishit Rabbah* 17:4.
15. Ibid.
16. Maharal, *Tiferet Yisrael*, ch. 3.
17. Ibid. The word for animal is *beheimah*, which spells out *bah mah* — What is in it is what it is.
18. The numerical value of the letters of *adam* are the same as the word "*mah*" — which means the question "what?".

to focus? What path will he choose? How far along it will he travel? This process of developing self defines the human project and therefore determines man's name — *adam*. Man's essential lack, then, is his unactualized potential. When Adam was told to eat, to complete his lack, he was being commanded to actualize his potential.

A MIRROR IN THE WORLD

We have expanded the command to eat to its conceptual base of actualizing potential. But there was also a specific meaning to the command to physically consume fruit. How do we conceptually eat/actualize potential through physically eating/consuming fruit?

Potential that has not been actualized is invisible to us; how can we know what it is that we need to actualize? It must have a concrete expression for us to know what it is; yet, if we can see it, it is no longer in potential!

Though the nature of our potential may not be apparent to us, we can discover it reflected in the world. A creator always creates in his own image[19] — true creation is the recreation of the self in a different form. Thus, man, who is created by God, is created in God's image.[20] The world is also created by God, and therefore the world as a whole must also express His image.[21] Since both man and the world express the same image of God, man can find himself reflected in creation, awakening to himself through knowing the world.[22] In Hebrew, the word for "taste," *ta'am*, also means "reason" or "meaning." By tasting the world, we

---

19. Maharal, *Chiddushei Aggadot* III, pp. 146 and 148.

20. *Bereishit* 1:27.

21. See Maharal, *Chiddushei Aggadot* III, pp. 146 and 148. Man, though only a part of creation, contains the whole image because he is the essence of the entire creation and all of creation is represented in him; man unifies creation into a single entity.

22. See Malbim, *Parashat Terumah, Rimzei HaMishkan* and *Peirush HaMalbim* on *Tehillim* 139:16 that man and the world mirror one another. Rabbi Tzaddok HaKohen, *Sichot Malachei HaShareit* 20b, states that man can understand the world only because he contains it within him. That all of creation gave of itself to the creation of man is also implicit in Maharal, *Chiddushei Aggadot* III, p. 148, cited in the previous note.

come to know it. Thus Adam was commanded to eat from all the trees of the Garden — to taste all the tastes in creation — for through this he encountered the world fully, knew it, and so understood himself.

Adam, due to his extreme sensitivity to his inner potential,[23] was capable of discovering himself directly through the world. We, however, live very much in the world around us, rather than in the self that is viewing the world.[24] Our inner self is foreign to our natural awareness, so we need specific guidance to find and unravel it. The Torah, through its mitzvot, is our guide in this project.

This is hinted at in a strange comment that was made by one of the leading Sages of the Talmudic era. In answer to the question of what verse encompasses the essence of the Torah, Ben Azi cited: "This is the book of the generations of man."[25] His response is odd because the line he quotes says almost nothing. A glance at its context makes matters worse, for the verse introduces little more than a list of names: so-and-so gave birth to so-and-so and died at age such-and-such, etc. What does Ben Azi mean when he says that these words contain the essence of the Torah?

The question is answered by understanding the word "generations" in Ben Azi's chosen line. A later verse states, "These are the generations of Noach. Noach was a righteous man ... who walked with God. Noach gave birth to three sons."[26] The Sages are troubled by the fact that the passage begins with an announcement of the generations of Noach (literally, the births of Noach), but before telling us who his children were, interrupts with a description of Noach's righteousness.[27] The Sages answer this anomaly by stating that the principal "generations" of man are not his progeny, but his good deeds. That is, before anything else, Noach

---

23. Rav Chayim Volozhin, *Nefesh HaChayim* 1:15 and 2:17.

24. As heard from Rav Moshe Shapiro. He based himself on the Introduction to *Mesillat Yesharim*. See Chapter 15.

25. *Bereishit Rabbah* 24:7 from the verse *Bereishit* 5:1.

26. *Bereishit* 6:9–10.

27. *Rashi, Bereishit* 6:9. The word *toldot*, which we are translating as "generations," is from the word *yalad*, "to give birth," and *yeled*, "child."

"generated" his righteousness, or himself as a righteous man. The word "generations" or "births" is appropriate in this context because we affect who we are through every action we perform. The choices we make through the course of a lifetime determine which of the innumerable possibilities that originally lay within us we will actualize. In a sense, we give birth to — or generate — ourselves. This is our principal "generation."

Returning to Ben Azi, the verse "This is the book of the generations of man" now takes on new meaning. The Torah is here being described as the book which guides us in self-generation.[28]

The fact that realizing potential gives us such deep satisfaction confirms its centrality to our humanity. If after running a race a runner feels he did the best he could, then he feels satisfaction regardless of whether he won or not; the important thing was that he gave it his all and brought out of himself what he had. When we write a paper that we feel says what we have to say, or when we genuinely express ourselves through a piece of music — these bring satisfaction.

If our obligation is to develop ourselves, and this is what we are doing by performing mitzvot, then what aspect are we developing? It is not a mitzvah to run marathons or to master Kantian philosophy, yet both of these develop us. We will learn later that creation is for the purpose of giving the greatest good.[29] What is the greatest good? What gives us the greatest satisfaction?

Though any realization of potential brings a degree of satisfaction, the deeper the level of humanity we bring out of ourselves, the deeper the satisfaction we feel. That is why when a woman gives birth, recreating the totality of her humanity in the world, the satisfaction is immeasurable. Greater still is the satisfaction that comes from realizing our deepest self in its purest form, our *tzelem Elokim* (image of God),

---

28. See also *Rashi, Bereishit* 1:1 that the Jewish people are the "produce" of creation while Torah is the "way." The way is the path to get to the goal, which is the produce. Through Torah the Jewish people become realized. That is, through Torah the Jews become who they are supposed to be — actualizing their potential. See also R. Shlomo Wolbe, *Alei Shor* II, pp. 19–20.
29. See Chapter 4, pp. 45–47.

our *neshamah* (soul).[30] A momentary instance of this is the experience of divine inspiration, which is considered the greatest human joy.[31] Through the mitzvot we actualize our *tzelem Elokim* comprehensively.

By saying that man's task is to develop his deepest potential, we are not straying from our earlier conclusion that the defining responsibility of man is to develop *emunah* (faith). Rather, we are understanding that responsibility more deeply. Remember that Adam compared himself to a seed planted in the ground. The metaphor was not chosen lightly. What do the seed and the ground of the metaphor represent in man? We have a dimension of self that is taken from the ground, our body, and we have another dimension of self that was planted in our body, a Divine *neshamah*.[32] Our "seed," the potential that we need to actualize, is that *neshamah*. In actualizing our *neshamah* we are defining and developing ourselves around the part of us that both resembles the Creator — it is our *tzelem Elokim* — and is connected directly to Him.[33] When we talk about *emunah* we usually think about a certain feeling or sense we have of God's existence and our dependence upon Him. But that feeling is meaningful only when and because it arises from an actual connection to God. This connection is the basis and essence of genuine *emunah*.[34] By actualizing the part of ourselves connected directly to the Creator, we develop the foundation that manifests itself in our awareness in the form of *emunah*.

In recognizing that we derive our greatest satisfaction from achieving *emunah*, we return full circle to the opening comments of the first chapter — that man naturally yearns more than anything else for connection to the infinite Creator. We now see that the Torah commands

---

30. The term *tzelem Elokim* refers to a number of different things in man depending upon the level of reality we are relating to. For a source which explicitly links it to the *neshamah*, see *Peirush HaRakanti* on *Parashat Bereishit*.

31. See *Mishnah Sukkah* 5:1, and *Talmud Yerushalmi* 5:1 brought in *Tosefot Sukkah* 50b. See also the discussion of Hillel at the end of Chapter 16, pp. 307–308 and note 36 there.

32. *Bereishit* 2:7.

33. See Ramchal, *Da'at Tevunot* 76–81.

34. See Maharal, *Gevurot HaShem*, ch. 7.

us to achieve nothing other than that which we naturally desire most for ourselves.[35]

GUIDING THE PERPLEXED

By commanding Adam to eat from all the trees of the Garden, God was, in effect, requiring him to fully engage the world. Had he done so he would have actualized himself. But if Adam merely needed to interact with the world to bring himself out, why do we need to be commanded in an array of specific actions — many of which make no clear sense to us — to unlock our potential?

Man has a physical dimension to his being and a spiritual dimension. Adam's makeup was heavily weighted toward his spiritual dimension so he experienced the world through his spiritual root. For example, when he saw a cow, he saw it the way his *neshamah* would view it — as a potential *korban* (sacrifice). Today, however, our center of self is mired in our physical being so as we encounter the world we interpret it through the lens of our body.[36] When we see a cow, we see steak. Thus we cannot intuitively find our essential self mirrored in the world the way Adam could. We require the Torah to represent the *neshamah*'s perspective and identify the actions that give it expression. The Torah's mitzvot are the acts the soul would choose were it given the chance to determine what we do.

The distance of our awareness of self from our soul is the reason the mitzvot often seem strange — we cannot view things from a spiritual perspective. Watching a cow burn on an altar seems senseless when we are hungry and no longer feel closeness to our Source through a dedication.

The skewed nature of our unguided experience of reality can be seen through a simple thought experiment. Let us imagine ourselves as students. When our alarm goes off in the morning our first thought is, "Already?

---

35. See *Mesillat Yesharim*, ch. 1.
36. See Chapters 17 and 18.

Am *I* tired! I really want to sleep more. I'll stay in bed just a few more minutes. My first class isn't that important anyway." Then another voice chimes in, "No, you should get up and go to class. It's the right thing to do." Analyzing this internal conversation reveals three distinct voices: "*I* really want to sleep" — first person. "*You* should get up" — second person. "It's the right thing to do" — the ideal is understood to be defined by a third person.

I think we all intuitively identify our self with our internal, idealistic self and assume that it defines us. However, our experience of our physically based, selfish needs in the first person — their association with our "I" — indicates the true location of our sense of self. When the alarm rings we do not hear a voice cry out, "Yes! I would love to get up to go to class," answered by, "Perhaps you are tired and need to rest more." The physical needs are always first person. Those selfish desires are opposed by higher ideals, but the higher ideals are conveyed to us as if from someone else — *you* really should go to class. This other voice is not totally foreign; it speaks directly to us. But it is not us. The ideal that is being conveyed comes from very far away, a source that is not even present, third person — it is the right thing to do. Our ideals emanate from God, the realm of our *neshamah*. We are not identified with this dimension of our being; it is experienced as third person.[37] For this reason, we cannot view the world naturally from the perspective of the *neshamah*.

We do not, however, need to go all the way back to Adam to find individuals who could find their spiritual core reflected in the world. Our forefathers Avraham, Yitzchak, and Yaakov, though they were never commanded in the mitzvot, intuited them from the world.[38] If they passed a cow, they might see potential phylacteries before they thought about lunch because prayer was more central to them than eating; their self was anchored closer to their *neshamah* than to their bodies.[39] When

---

37. See Rav Eliyahu Dessler, *Michtav Me'Eliyahu* I, p. 143 and R. Shlomo Wolbe, *Alei Shor* II on *Da'at*.
38. *Bereishit* 26:5, *Rashi*, and *Ramban* there.
39. See Rav Yosef Yehudah Leib Bloch, *Shiurei Da'at* I, *Hashgachah*, pp. 84–86.

their "alarm" went off in the morning their first thought was, "Great, I sure do want to get up and do some good."[40] If there was any opposing voice it was along the lines of, "Maybe *you* would like to sleep a bit more?" Their spiritual aspect determined their interpretation of the world, with physical and ego needs experienced as coming from outside their self.

Though the forefathers were close enough to Adam to perceive the world through the prism of spirituality, they were not on the same level as Adam. They saw the necessity of 613 actions to actualize all facets of the *neshamah*, whereas Adam, because of the depth of his spiritual connection, was capable of bringing himself out with only a few commands.

We, however, are distant from both Adam and the forefathers, for we need to be commanded in 613 specific and often inexplicable mitzvot to reach our inner self. Through them we strive to transform ourselves into a being centered around our *neshamah*, with our physical bodies relegated to the role of vessels through which our *neshamah* takes on expression. And since, ultimately, the *neshamah* is a direct — as opposed to indirect — expression of God into the world, creating ourselves in the image of our *neshamah* is synonymous with connecting ourselves to the Creator. This provides the basis for true *emunah*, an awareness that arises from the structure of our being, rather than a feeling, philosophy, or fantasy that merely floats on the surface of our consciousness.

---

40. Similar to David HaMelech, who was awakened at night by the stirring of his soul to arise and learn Torah. See *Berachot* 3b with the commentary of the Gra, *Peirush HaAggadot*.

CHAPTER 3

Faith and
the Social Fabric

It is greater to entertain guests than to visit with the Shechinah
(the Holy Presence).[1]

IN THE OPENING CHAPTER we spoke of our innate desire in all aspects of human experience to reach beyond our isolated ego awareness. We saw in the previous chapter that through the mitzvot of the Torah we build ourselves around our *neshamah*, that part of us that emanates directly from the Creator. This results in a deepened sense of our self, which we experience as emerging from God, and, as we encounter reality outside of our self, an ongoing awareness of God the Creator of all of existence. These two forms of *emunah* satisfy our yearning for connection in two arenas of our experience: that of man with himself and that of man with God.

But there is a third arena of human experience — man with his fellow man. There, also, we hunger to go beyond our isolation, in this case through genuine relationships. If, as we said, all desire to reach beyond ourselves is a consequence of our detachment from God, and the Torah provides the path to recover our connection with God, we expect the mitzvot to help us in this area also. We do find a whole category of mitzvot involved with relationships between people. How does the Torah aid us in our quest to truly connect with others?

---

1. *Shabbat* 127a.

27

This question is particularly relevant today. Human relationships are in crisis.[2] We tend to see others as objects through which we achieve our needs, projections of ourselves, or individuals from whom we are hopelessly cut off. Satisfying connections with people are rare and difficult to form, with a disturbing percentage of attempts falling apart. Why are relationships so problematic in our generation? How does the Torah help us with this situation?

HATRED DESTROYS A TEMPLE

The Talmud states that the Second Temple, the one whose ruins lie before us in Yerushalayim, was destroyed because of *sinat chinam* (baseless hatred).[3] The Talmud tells the story of the specific hatred which directly caused the destruction: "Yerushalayim was destroyed because of Kamtza and Bar Kamtza."[4] There was a man who was a friend of Kamtza but hated Bar Kamtza. He hosted a party and sent his servant to bring his friend Kamtza. But the servant mistakenly brought Bar Kamtza instead. The host, seeing his enemy at his party, publicly humiliated Bar Kamtza. Though there were great rabbanim present at the gathering, no one intervened on Bar Kamtza's behalf, making everyone culpable in his eyes. Bar Kamtza was so incensed that he went to Rome and informed on the Jews in a way that led to Rome's invasion and the destruction of the Temple.

It is understandable that the Talmud blames Bar Kamtza for the disaster since he brought the Romans. But the commentaries ask why Kamtza was held accountable — what did he do in the story? They answer that in a context of baseless hatred, even friendships are alliances against others.[5]

---

2. In truth, our experience of self and God are just as much in crisis. But we have forgotten what it is to experience another level of reality and we have forgotten what it is to be internally connected, so we are less aware of the pain in those dimensions (see Chapter 15). Our inability to connect to others, however, weighs heavily upon us. We need relationships and the evidence of our difficulty forming them confronts us on every side. We are aware that we are lonely.

3. *Yoma* 9b.

4. *Gittin* 55b. See also *Eichah Rabbah* 4:3.

5. Maharal, *Chiddushei Aggadot* II, p. 99.

Kamtza's relationship with the host was less a bond with him than a division from others — he contributed to the fracturing of community that led to the disaster. Where hatred is rampant all relationships are compromised.

The fact that the Temple has not been rebuilt indicates that the problem that caused its destruction has not been addressed.[6] We still suffer from baseless hatred and, therefore, our relationships are also compromised. We can understand, then, why real connections between people are so difficult. But what is the cause of this endemic hatred?[7]

SPLITTING THE SPIRITUAL FROM THE PHYSICAL

We will learn later that any nation that attacks the Jews derives its strength from our shortcomings. The character of our attacker mirrors our internal lack and provides an external representation of what we need to work on.[8] Rome destroyed the Second Temple — if we understood Roman culture we would gain insight into what is causing our social breakdown. The best window into Rome is Amalek, a people who issue from the same source as Rome and express Rome's cultural essence.[9]

What distinguishes Amalek as a people? We spoke earlier about the significance of names.[10] Amalek's name tells us who they are. The word "Amalek" is related to the word "*melikah*," which is the act of slaughtering

---

6. *Talmud Yerushalmi, Yoma* 1:1.

7. Baseless hatred caused the destruction of the Temple because when the Jewish people succumbed to it, they ceased to be a party for revealed relationship with the Creator. The Creator is the source of all existence. He does not relate solely to one part of creation; that could only happen if He were not the source of the rest of it, which contradicts His being One. The Creator relates either to the entirety of reality or to a unit which represents the entirety of reality. The Jewish people represent all of mankind, which is itself a microcosm of existence. But when the Jewish people are broken down into hopelessly warring factions, they are not a unity which is capable of representing humanity or creation. So the revealed relationship with God ceases and the Temple is destroyed. See Maharal, *Derech Chayim* 4:12.

8. See Chapter 14, pp. 243–248.

9. See note 23 of this chapter.

10. See Chapter 2, p. 19.

bird sacrifices in the Temple.[11] The word specifically refers to the severing of the head from the body. The head is the entry point of the *neshamah* (soul) into a person; the body is the instrument through which the *neshamah* takes on expression in the physical world. Amalek's name implies that they, as a culture, sever the connection between man's spiritual being and his physical experience and expression into the world. Our conquest by Rome, then, indicates that we also, on some level, are holding these two realms apart. In what way do we see this with the Jews?

This cutting off of the spiritual from the physical can show itself in several ways. The obvious form is a denial of any spiritual reality, removing God from the picture entirely. This results in an immoral or amoral vision of the world. This expression of Amalek is easy to identify. A more complex form is a denial of the significance of physical reality. In this version a person considers himself wholly spiritual, which is impossible in the context of this world. His connection to spirituality inevitably degenerates into a façade or corrupt fantasy so that he is, in effect, also living only in the physical world.

If we are searching for a corruption in the Jewish people mirrored in Amalek to explain our vulnerability to Rome, neither of these expressions is plausible. The Jews have never lost touch with the existence of morality and ideals. And though there have been movements within the Jewish people that tended toward an unrealistic spirituality, the Torah with its mitzvot has always kept the mainstream of the Jewish people firmly anchored in physical reality. There is, however, an even more subtle expression of the break between the physical and spiritual realms representative of Amalek. This is when the existence of both the spiritual and physical are acknowledged, but the spiritual vision is not genuinely integrated with our day-to-day outlook or conduct. Since the spiritual realm drives what happens into the physical dimension, this lack of implementation indicates that the spirituality lacks reality and, again, the person effectively lives in a physical world disconnected from

---

11. Rama M'Pano, *Asarah Ma'amarot* 5:8; *Vayikra* 1:15.

its spiritual roots. It is in this guise that the Jews find themselves susceptible to influences representative of Amalek.

When the Jews were leaving *Mitzrayim*, Amalek was the first to attack
them, earning the title *reishit goyim* (the first of the peoples), meaning the
first to attack us.[12] When the attack is recounted in *Sefer Devarim* (Deu-
teronomy), the Torah says, "Remember what Amalek did to you as you
left *Mitzrayim*. They happened upon you…"[13] The language of "happened
upon you" is problematic, since the Torah does not recognize anything as
"just happening." This is especially true of this event, as Amalek traveled
far for the opportunity to fight with the Jews.[14] Rather than describing
what actually occurred, the Torah is using language that corresponds to
the way the Jews perceived the event. They saw the arrival of Amalek as
unfortunate happenstance. The Jews were drawn to interpret reality as
directionless chance rather than understanding every event as another
installment in an ongoing relationship with God.[15] They severed the

---

12. *Bemidbar* 24:20 with *Rashi*. We have learned that the first time something appears in
the Torah, that appearance expresses its essence. That Amalek was the first of the peoples
to attack the Jews and that this is emphasized in the Torah indicates that they embody the
essence of the opposition of the nations to the Jews. If so, how can we understand Amalek
to express specifically Rome? We will learn later that the perversity of Roman culture is also
essential and lies at the basis of all of our exiles. See Chapter 14, pp. 243–248.

Since the attack of each nation reflects a corresponding weakness in our pursuit of our
historical mission, Amalek must embody the essence of our weakness — what we need to
work on, our historical challenge. After all, just as Amalek was the first to attack us, the
weakness that provoked the attack was our first and, therefore, most essential weakness.
This would indicate that our fundamental task is to fully integrate our connection to God
with our involvement in physical reality. We will refine our understanding of what this
means in Chapter 8. This does not contradict what we said earlier that our personal task is
to develop all aspects of ourselves as expressions of our connection to God. It is just another
way of framing and phrasing the same idea. See Chapter 9.

13. *Devarim* 25:17–18.

14. *Midrash Tanchuma, Ki Teitzei* 9.

15. Having lived for so long as slaves to a culture that did not recognize the Creator, the
Jews needed to develop the ability to relate to Him. During the actual departure this was
not an issue, for it was accomplished through God's unbridled revelation, which forced the
Jews' awareness of His existence. But this was sufficient only so long as God was in His role
as savior and hero, where He was doing everything. The goal was a mature relationship in

connection between their awareness of God and their reality, which empowered Amalek, the people whose culture is built around a similar separation.

RECOVERING THE CONNECTION THROUGH HONORING OTHERS

This reveals a weakness amongst the Jews to fully include God in their physical reality and perhaps gives us insight into why Rome was able to destroy the Temple, the vessel of our relationship with God. But what does this have to do with the baseless hatred that the Sages identify as the direct cause of the Second Temple's destruction?

In preparation for this first battle with Amalek, Moshe turned to Yehoshua and commanded, "Choose for us men who will go and fight against Amalek..."[16] The Sages take note of Moshe's choice of the word "us" — "Choose for *us* men..." Moshe was the undisputed leader of the Jews. He had recently led his people out of *Mitzrayim*, destroying the most powerful nation on earth in the process. Yehoshua was his assistant and used to arrange the benches in the study hall before Moshe would teach. Why did he say, "Choose for *us*?" He should have said, "Choose for *me*." The Sages derive from this that a teacher should value the honor of his student equally with his own honor.[17]

---

which the Jews were active participants using their free will. Reaching this required the gradual scaling back of God's revelation so that instead of being shown God's existence the Jews were required to take increasing responsibility for recognizing Him, which was synonymous with appreciating His participation in their more mundane, physical reality (See *Ramban, Shemot* 13:16). This was a struggle, as evidenced in the murmuring of the Jews during this period and their difficulty refraining from gathering more than a day's portion of *man* (manna). Eventually, the Jews reached a point where they could develop no further in this matter—at least at this time—and cried out, "Is HaShem in our midst or not?!" (See *Shemot* 16:20, 27–28) They were not yet capable of fully integrating their recognition of God's existence with the reality of their lives. This weakness precisely corresponded to the subtle form of Amalek's worldview we described—recognizing the existence of spirituality but not genuinely integrating it into experience—and brought on the attack.

16. *Shemot* 17:9.

17. *Rashi, Shemot* 17:9 from the *Mechilta*.

Though this is a priceless and noble lesson to learn, why does the Torah choose to teach it to us on the eve of our first battle with Amalek? The Torah is not merely a heap of insights. It is composed of teachings like a regular book is composed of words. In a book, each individual word has its meaning, but the intent of the book only arises from the order of the words. So, too, with the Torah — as important as the individual insights are, the primary meaning of the Torah can only be reached through attention to its order and structure.

Since when we confronted Amalek the survival of the Jewish people was on the line, we would expect the Torah to be focused on issues that were directly relevant to the immediate situation. After all, there are many places in the Torah where learning the importance of honoring others would fit appropriately. So, why teach it here? Since we understand that the battle with Amalek was over the connection of spirituality to the physical world, we could rephrase our question as: what is the relevance of the way we treat our fellow man to connecting the spiritual dimension to physical reality?

Posing the question this way makes the answer obvious: Proper relationships with people are dependent upon our recognition of the honor and value of the other. Without this basic respect there can be no real relationship. The true value of a person lies in his being created in *tzelem Elokim* and possessing an infinite *neshamah*. *Tzelem Elokim* is the most profound expression of spirituality in physical reality. We cannot beat Amalek, those who sever the connection between spirituality and the physical realm, unless we can unite those same realms. We demonstrate that ability in truly honoring one another. The baseless hatred of the Jews during the time of the Second Temple showed they lacked the ability to relate to the *tzelem Elokim* in one another. This was the primary expression of the Jews' lack of integration of spirituality with physical reality that left them vulnerable to Roman conquest and the destruction of the Temple.

AMALEK THE DESPISER OF PEOPLE

That Amalek's essence is expressed in a lack of honoring others and that this disrespect stems from an inability to connect God to the world is made explicit by the Sages.[18] *Megillat Esther* (the Book of Esther) records the salvation of the Jews from the evil plans of the Persian regent Haman, an Amalekite. The event was catalyzed by a confrontation Haman had with Mordechai, the leader of the Jewish people and a spiritual giant of his day. Haman made himself into an object of idolatry, and Mordechai refused to bow to him. Once Haman became aware of this, he "despised destroying Mordechai alone, for they told Haman [who] Mordechai's people [were] and Haman sought to destroy all of the Jews."[19]

The Sages are troubled by the use of the word "despised" in this context. Had the verse said that Haman found killing only Mordechai "too small" an act for someone of his great stature we would have been satisfied that we understood his decision to target the Jewish people as a whole.[20] But the word "despise," which denotes loathing and contempt, tells us that Haman's emotions went far beyond that. From this, the Sages derive that Haman was, "Despicable, the son of one who is despicable."[21] They connect the word used in *Megillat Esther* — *vayivez*, "and he despised" — to the only other place in the Written Torah where the term appears in exactly this form: "And Yaakov gave to Esav bread and cooked lentils, and he [Esav] ate and drank and got up and left, and he despised [*vayivez*] the heritage of the firstborn."[22]

Esav was the grandfather of Amalek, the individual who founded the people of the same name. Esav is the source of everything Amalek represents, and Amalek is the essential expression of everything Esav was in potential.[23] When the Sages describe the Amalekite Haman as

---

18. See also *Shemot Rabbah* 27:6 which identifies Amalek as a *leitz*, or scoffer. The scoffer is one who undermines honor in general, denying the existence of a realm of higher meaning and, consequently, its expression in people.

19. *Megillat Esther* 3:6.

20. Maharal, *Ohr Chadash*, p. 130.

21. *Esther Rabbah* 7:10. We will discuss the switch in the *midrash* from "despise" to "despicable" momentarily.

22. *Bereishit* 25:34.

23. Amalek was the firstborn son of Elifaz, himself the firstborn son of Esav. Elifaz bore Amalek through an incestuous relationship with his own daughter. Amalek is therefore

"despicable, the son of one who is despicable," they identify this characteristic of despising as Amalek's inheritance from Esav. Since Amalek represents the essence of Esav, and this is the trait Haman inherited, this contempt must be the defining trait of both Esav and Amalek. Why does a tendency to feel contempt have the weight and consequence to define a people?[24]

When we despise a person, we see ourselves standing in a category different from him, and we are offended by any implication of connection to him. To feel this way we must be utterly blind to his value. We value ourselves, but we believe that what gives us value is not found in him. For this to be the case, we must identify our value with some aspect of self which resides solely in us, or at the very least with something we share with some others but not with the one for whom we feel contempt. We, then, do not find our value in our shared humanity.

In truth, our joint membership in humanity is built on all people being created in *tzelem Elokim*.[25] For us to despise another, we must be blind to *tzelem Elokim* or value something over it — which is synonymous with blindness since, if we truly recognized *tzelem Elokim*, we could not give anything even comparable value. Moreover, if we miss this aspect of another's makeup we must not have a genuine internal experience of it. For if we did, we would be aware of *tzelem Elokim* coming to us from a place so above our individuality that it includes everyone.

To say that Haman "despised" is to tell us that he did not experience his humanity in the context of *tzelem Elokim* — he certainly did not identify his personal greatness with this aspect of himself. This is all the more telling since Haman was despising specifically Mordechai,

---

Esav concentrate (*Bereishit* 36:15 and *Rashi, Bereishit* 36:12). Here lies the connection between Amalek and Rome, for it is the character of Esav that animates Rome. We will discuss this in the beginning of Chapter 14.

24. Technically, the contempt of Haman was for the act of merely killing Mordechai. But the Sages understand Haman looked down on *merely killing* Mordechai because it was *killing merely* Mordechai — meaning the insignificance of the act derived from the insignificance of Mordechai.

25. *Pirkei Avot* 3:14.

one of the great Sages of his day. If Haman could not see *tzelem Elokim* in Mordechai, he could not see it in anyone, including himself. It is for this reason that the Sages do not describe Haman as "a despiser, son of a despiser," which would be a more direct derivation from the verses, but, rather, "despicable, the son of despicable." That Haman despises indicates that he is blind to *tzelem Elokim*. He can only be blind to it in others if he has not actualized it in himself. Since *tzelem Elokim* is the basis of true human value and it does not define Haman, he is therefore despicable.

ESAV THE DESPISER OF PRIESTHOOD

The Midrash connects this to the fact that Haman's forefather Esav also despised something many generations earlier. In that case, Esav was despising his inherited status as the firstborn — he sold it to Yaakov for a bowl of lentils. What is the connection between Esav despising the right of the firstborn and Haman despising another person?

Yaakov wanted to buy the rights of the firstborn from Esav because they included the right of officiating over the Temple service — our responsibility to maintain the connection of God to physical reality.[26] Yaakov knew that Esav was not on a spiritual level fitting for such a task, and so wanted to wrest this right from him.[27] Esav sold it for the satisfaction of a meal, showing his utter indifference to the honor. In fact, he despised the priestly rank. He gave it no value because, according to him, it had no purpose. The Temple service was to connect God to the world, and Esav did not attribute any reality to such a connection.

Linking Esav's rejection of the priestly service to Haman's loathing of Mordechai reveals that the joining of spirituality to the physical world finds its most intense expression in the *tzelem Elokim* of man. One who is as oblivious to the external connection of God to the world, as Esav's disdain for the priestly tasks demonstrated, cannot experience

---

26. *Bereishit Rabbah* 63:13.
27. *Rashi, Bereishit* 25:31.

the internal connection of *tzelem Elokim* in man, as revealed by Haman despising Mordechai.

This is confirmed by the statement Esav made as he rejected his firstborn heritage: "Behold, I am on my way to die — why do I need the rights of the firstborn?"[28] Esav saw life as a weigh-station between non-existence and death. His goal was only to fill his needs and maximize his pleasures during the interim. Someone who so cheapens life could not have had any genuine spiritual identity, for if he did he would put a very different value and purpose on life. Esav chose a fleeting satisfaction over the honor of connecting the Creator to His world because he didn't recognize the existence of that connection. His inability to see it in the world around him mirrored his inability to find it in himself. That inability to find it in himself was inherited by his descendent Haman, who then could not find *tzelem Elokim* in others.

THE IMAGE OF GOD IN MAN

We learn the proper way of relating to people from our forefather Avraham; of all our ancestors, he stands out as the exemplar for one who had meaningful relationships with others.[29] The Torah teaches us that after Avraham fulfilled the mitzvah of circumcision, he was in pain for several days. God came to Avraham's tent to comfort him and ease the burden of his suffering. At that moment a group of three peasants passed by, and Avraham leapt to his feet to greet and entertain the potential guests. The verses state:

> And he ran toward them from the door of the tent and bowed to the ground. And he said, "If I have found favor in your eyes, my lords, do not pass by your servant. Water will be brought and you can wash your feet and rest under the tree..."[30]

---

28. *Bereishit* 25:32.
29. *Michah* 7:20.
30. *Bereishit* 18:2–4.

There is a problem with the way the word "my lords" is vowelized in the Hebrew text. The Hebrew word in the verse is *adonoi*. The proper way to greet strangers is with the title "lord" — *adon*, using the plural *adonim* when greeting more than one. The *oi* at the end of the word in our verse adds the first person singular possessive pronoun — *my* lords. But the vowelization in the word makes ambiguous whom Avraham was addressing. If Avraham were addressing the leader of the group of peasants, the word *adoni* ending with a *chirik* vowel should have been used — my lord. If he were addressing the members of the group together, the possessive should have been added to the plural *adonim* producing *adonai*, with a *patach* vowel — my lords. But the Torah uses the *kamatz* vowel — a combination of the *chirik* and the *patach* — producing *adonoi*, a form that is normally reserved for addressing the Creator.[31] Was Avraham, then, speaking to God?

The Torah tells us that Avraham left his tent before it tells us he addressed anyone as lord. Thus the order of the verses implies that he was speaking to the peasants, because the revelation of the *Shechinah*, the presence of God, was still back in Avraham's tent. It is still viable to say he was speaking to God because sometimes verses in the Torah are out of chronological order, but it is not a comfortable reading. Yet, the vowel form would require some stretching to read it as addressed to the peasants — we would have to say he was addressing the leader but simultaneously intending that the others in the group hear his words, combining the singular and the plural and therefore saying *adonoi*, using the *kamatz* vowel which combines singular and plural. While possible, this is strange usage. Either reading is, therefore, imperfect. For this reason, the *midrash* offers both readings.[32]

---

31. Maharal, *Gur Aryeh, Bereishit* 18:3 explains that the physical shape of the *kamatz* vowel is a combination of the singular *chirik* and the plural *patach*. Because God has a singular aspect — "*HaShem* is One" — and a plural aspect — "*Elokim*, All powers" (the word "*Elokim*" has a plural ending), when we address God as "*Ado-noi*, my Lord" we are addressing Him as both "my Lord" and "my Lords."

32. *Rashi, Bereishit* 18:3 from *Bereishit Rabbah*.

But there is a bigger problem with the verse than the vowels or whom Avraham was addressing with the word *adonoi*. Everyone agrees that Avraham was leaving the *Shechinah* to greet people! How are we to understand that? One does not, pardon the comparison, excuse himself from the president to give lemonade to passing strangers!

This metaphor obviously does not do justice to Avraham's situation, for we cannot compare the honor of God with that of the president. But mediating against Avraham's decision to leave the tent was not just that God's honor is immeasurably greater than that of the strangers. We have discussed that through mitzvot we create and experience connection to the Creator — that is our purpose in life. Avraham was in the presence of God! Whatever that means, it is certainly an intense connection to and revelation of God in this world. How would Avraham leave that Presence to do anything else?

The commentaries answer that Avraham was not leaving the *Shechinah* at all; he was merely moving from one form of the Presence to another. When Avraham greeted guests he related not to the physical form in front of him, but to the *tzelem Elokim* within them.[33] Refracted through the individuality of every human being, Avraham saw and connected to the Divine spark which uniquely founded that person.

This encountering another as a unique and personal expression of the Divine spark is the foundation of genuine human relationships and the basis of all mitzvot between man and his fellow man. Person to person mitzvot are generally categorized as *gemilut chassadim* (acts of kindness).[34] But the essential *chessed* (kindness) we can show another is our recognition of his Divine greatness — acknowledging the significance

---

33. Maharal, *Netivot Olam* I, *Netiv Gemilut Chassadim*, ch. 4. We still have not completely answered our question. Surely the *Shechinah*, the Presence of God, is a more intense revelation than *tzelem Elokim*, the image of God in man. Maharal answers that sometimes less is more. A little in a digestible form may give us more than a lot in a non-digestible form. If we are thirsty, a glass of water will be more useful than a fire hydrant. Avraham, who as a human being lived through his physical aspect, could relate more to Godliness as expressed in its physical likeness — *tzelem Elokim* — than to pure *Shechinah*.
34. *Pirkei Avot* 1:2.

of his existence.[35] This recognition inspires giving — we wish to be part of such greatness. But it also profoundly affects the way we give. Though we show *chessed* through giving, those acts must all be envelopes to deliver the message that we see the other's life as meaningful and worthy of our support. There is no greater gift for a person to bestow. It was this recognition of divinity that justified Avraham's departure from the *Shechinah*. It is staggering to contemplate how Avraham must have actually related to others to justify his decision to leave the tent.

The Torah brilliantly communicates the depth of Avraham's connection to people in a single vowel. We are told that Avraham said the word *Ado-noi* and we do not know if he was addressing God or a person.[36]

HONOR IN OUR TIME

Although Avraham provides a paradigm for how deeply people can relate to one another, this level of human connection is not only a thing of the past. There are individuals who approach it even in our times.

Rav Mordechai Schwab, who was known as the Tzaddik of Monsey, was sitting in his living room late one night. At the time, he was an elderly man. There came a knock at the door. Like Avraham running out of his tent, Rav Schwab leapt from his chair and opened the door. Someone from the neighborhood was there with a question. Rav Schwab invited him in, sat and spoke with him, and then escorted him out. When the door was closed, Rav Schwab's son said to him, "Pa, I realize that you need to speak with people when they have questions. But why

---

35. R. Shlomo Wolbe, *Alei Shor* II, *Maʾarechet HaAvodah HaMusarit*, ch. 6.

36. The Talmud generalizes from Avraham that entertaining guests is greater than communing with the *Shechinah* (*Shabbat* 127a). Were we to find ourselves in the same situation as Avraham, Rambam in *Hilchot Aveilut* 14:2 obligates us to act as Avraham did. The *Mishnah Berurah* certainly understands the example of Avraham to actually obligate us (333:8). If we would give precedence to guests over the *Shechinah*, however, we would be acting on an externally imposed obligation that is based on the reality of *tzelem Elokim* in man. Since Avraham was not commanded, he must have actually connected with the *tzelem Elokim* in order to react the way that he did. Presumably, in our halachic obligation we hear a need to strive to relate to the *tzelem Elokim* in others as Avraham did.

did you jump out of your chair and run to open the door? It was 11:30 at night. That person's question was not pressing; he could have come tomorrow. It was a chutzpah!"

Rav Schwab looked at him in complete astonishment, saying over and over again, "Eliyahu, Eliyahu HaNavi," as if to say, "His greatness is no less than that of the prophet Eliyahu." Both were, after all, created with the same *tzelem Elokim*. Rav Schwab related to every individual in this manner. When he passed away, among the many people who insisted on coming to the house to give condolences to the family was the repairman who had fixed the washing machine in the house several weeks earlier. He said, "I came to work on his washing machine and he made me feel like I was the king," a theme repeated by visitor after visitor.[37]

*   *   *

The foundation of meaningful relationships between individuals is the ability to see and acknowledge the true honor and value of others, the *tzelem Elokim* within them. The Sages have taught us what blocks this recognition: an inability to integrate our awareness of God with our actual, physical experience. This integration is precisely what the mitzvot of the Torah create.

We are born into the world naturally aware of its material facet. This is because before we invest any effort in developing ourselves, we are anchored in our physical experience and only sensitive to material reality. Through the mitzvot, we strive to shift the center of our personality inward to the point from which we emerge from the Creator. By recovering connection to our root in God while retaining our presence in the physical world, we bridge these two realities. This results in *emunah* in all facets of our awareness.

Emunah is the experience of attachment to God. In each sphere of awareness there is a difference in the mode of that attachment and,

---

37. Both of these stories were heard from Rav Mordechai Schwab's son, Rav Yehoshua Schwab.

therefore, in the nature of the mitzvot through which we build *emunah*. In our awareness of standing directly before God, we are attached through our sense of absolute dependence. The mitzvot in this category (*bein adam l'Makom*, between man and God) are based on *yirat HaShem* (the fear of HaShem) which is the sense of vulnerability that arises from our dependence upon Him.[38] In our awareness of our personal, inner world, we attach through the depth of our self and its resemblance to God. The mitzvot in this category (*bein adam l'atzmo*, between man and himself) are based on deepening ourselves through creatively developing our spiritual potential in emulation of God the Creator.[39] We will explore this in the context of our discussion of free will in the next section of this book. In our awareness of ourselves in community with others (*bein adam l'chaveiro*, between man and his fellow man), we attach to God through encountering the *tzelem Elokim* we see mirrored in the eyes of those who stand before us. The mitzvot in this category are based on emulating God's giving and support, which both actualizes our own *tzelem Elokim* and, in turn, brings it out in others allowing us to experience it clearly.[40]

Regardless of what sphere we are operating in, *emunah* is our goal and the principal accomplishment of the mitzvot. The different avenues merely present us with distinct opportunities and ways to achieve it. Since Torah guides creation to its completion and Torah singularly fosters *emunah*, the purpose of creation, our purpose, is to achieve *emunah*.

Armed with this understanding we can examine our world. Comparing what we find to what we would expect of a creation whose purpose is *emunah*, we will ask some basic questions about why reality functions the way that it does. Through this process we hope to develop a coherent understanding of creation and our place in it.

---

38. For example, through prayer. See Chapter 21, p. 401 and note 23 there.

39. For example, through Torah study. See Chapter 6, pp. 96–97 and Chapter 14, pp. 271–272.

40. For example, through charity. But, as we said earlier in this chapter, the primary gift in any giving is the affirmation of the value of the other. As much as material gifts can be needed and appreciated, they are a means for conveying this affirmation.

THE MEANS:
Free Will

CHAPTER 4

A Worthwhile Investment

His wisdom decreed that for the good to be complete it was fitting that the one who is having the good should be the owner of that good. That is to say, someone who acquired it himself and not like someone whom the good merely accompanies in an accidental manner.[1]

THE TORAH IS OUR guide to actualizing our deepest potential. Through it, we reach beyond the confines of physical reality and encounter the Creator directly, through the self, and through our fellow man. This is the achievement of *emunah* in all dimensions of our awareness, which is our purpose.

It is reasonable to ask, if man was created for this *emunah* why do we need to develop ourselves to achieve it? At this point in our discussion, this question is only a desire for clarification — nothing has been said so far that is contradicted by the fact that we must take charge of completing ourselves. It just requires explanation why a world created by the all-powerful Being was not created finished from the outset. A deeper look, however, turns this anomaly into an apparent contradiction that threatens our whole structure of understanding.

The Torah's vision is built on the idea that God created our reality in order to give.[2] This is a direct deduction from our most basic

---

1. Ramchal, *Derech HaShem* 1:2:2.
2. Ramchal, *Derech HaShem* 1:2:1. See also note 8 of Rav Freidlander at the end of *Da'at Tevunot* 37.

understanding that the Creator contains within Himself all existence. The totality of God's inclusiveness is conveyed by one of the names the Torah applies to Him — *Makom*, or Place.[3] The Sages explain that this name tells us that though, "you might think the world is the place of the Holy One, in fact, the Holy One is the place of the world."[4] This cryptic statement begs extensive meditation. For our purposes, it is enough to realize that place presents the possibility for existence. The Creator's name *Makom* denotes that He is not merely the source of everything — He is even the source of its possibility.

Our unexamined vision of the act of creation is of God filling endless, empty space with His handiwork. But this is heretical, for where did the space come from? God is the creator of space also. This is not just nit-picking, but actually reaches to the essence of what we mean when we recognize God as the Creator. When we search for the Creator, we are not looking for a being who arranged our present circumstances. That is how the term "creator" is used in common parlance — in everyday life a creator is one who takes raw materials from his surroundings and gives them a new form or arrangement. When we search for God the Creator, however, we are looking for the source of being itself, the basis of everything.[5]

The existence of empty space presupposes the possibility of filling it. Therefore, it contains the potential for all that can eventually come into being. God is also the source of that potential. The creation of that potential is God's primary innovation; physical creation is merely actualization of that potential. Thus, each day of creation did not begin with the morning when things were actually made. Rather, it began with evening — a dark emptiness that held the possibility and potential for that which filled it the next morning.[6]

Because the Creator contains within Himself everything found

---

3. *Bereishit* 28:11. See *Rashi* there.
4. *Bereishit Rabbah* 68:9.
5. Rav Chayim Volozhin, *Nefesh HaChayim* 1:2.
6. *Bereishit* 1:5.

in creation, including its very possibility, He cannot receive from creation — the existence of anything in creation requires that it come from the Creator. If God gets nothing from creation, He must have created in order to give.[7]

What is it that He wants to give? The Creator's perfection requires that He desire to give the greatest possible good. The greatest good is the Creator Himself, for He contains everything in its fullest expression.[8] So theoretically God should create us like Him. But this would require that we have a level of being comparable to that of God, for it is in His being that His perfection resides. This is impossible, for God is necessary. I do not mean in the subjective sense that we must recognize His existence to understand our world, though this may be true. Rather, necessity is a characteristic of God's actual being — He cannot not be. His being is profoundly different from ours or, for that matter, from anything we can genuinely comprehend.

Obviously, necessity of being cannot be created — something that is necessary in the sense in which we are speaking already exists and does not need to be created. This is the case with the Creator, not the creation. Since creation itself cannot have the perfection of God, the Creator gave creation the opportunity to cleave to God and participate in the infinite goodness that resides exclusively in Him.[9]

For reasons we will discuss in a moment, the only creature capable of cleaving to God is man. This cleaving is the basis of man's *emunah* and he achieves it through the self-actualization that comes from doing mitzvot. This self-development, then, is not just *man's* purpose, but the purpose of creation.

---

7. We could also say God created to express Himself (see *Bereishit Rabbah* 5:1). But there has to be someone or something to express Himself *to*. That is man. And man's recognition of God's expression is precisely the manner in which man receives good. So God creating to express Himself and to give good are really two sides of the same coin. See Rav Freidlander's introduction to *Da'at Tevunot*. See Chapter 16, note 28.

8. Saying God is everything does not imply that God also contains evil. Evil is not a creation so much as a selective blockage of God's expression.

9. Ramchal, *Derech HaShem* 1:2:1.

This conclusion is problematic because it means that before man develops himself, creation is not merely lacking an element of completion. Rather, it is not fulfilling its purpose. Why would God create the world in such a way that attaining His goal waits on the efforts of man?

But the delay in the achievement of God's purpose is not the most difficult aspect of the situation. The fact that man must take the initiative to develop his connection to God also leaves open the possibility that he will decline to make the effort and, therefore, remain separate from God. As well as preventing God's intended gift of good, this brings evil.[10] The reality is that placing the responsibility on man to develop his connection to God has resulted in a world overrun with pain and suffering, which seems the opposite of what God intended. If the all-powerful God created in order to give man good, what can justify this outcome or even its possibility?

To rephrase the question: God created to give the greatest good possible. The greatest good is connection to God. Why, then, is He hidden behind the thick veil of a dark, seemingly natural world, which both blocks His revelation and opens the world to evil and suffering? Obviously, this is not a new question. But having recognized the centrality of good to the Creator's intention, the question penetrates deeply enough to shake the foundations of our faith.

Just as the question is not new, there is an answer that is not new. We must utilize free will to choose our relationship with the Creator; this requires that the Creator hide Himself. As a result, we begin without the relationship and must make choices that will develop it. However, this allows the possibility that we will turn away from God, cutting ourselves off from His good. The need for free will also explains why man is the only creature fully capable of receiving from the Creator and why man

---

10. Literally, the word *ra*, which is translated as "evil," means "broken off" ("*Tero'eim b'shevet barzel* — Break them with an iron rod" [*Tehillim* 2:9]), meaning broken off from the Creator. Since the way we cleave to the Creator is through emulating the character He reveals to us, which is good, we decline cleaving by acting in a manner that fits the common understanding of evil.

is the centerpiece of creation — for he alone has free will.

But introducing the concept of free will is less an answer to the question posed by evil than a shift in the focus of the question. The basic contradiction between God's purpose of giving good and the realities of existence remain. Free will may explain why evil is necessary, but what explains why free will is necessary? Since the Creator's ultimate goal is the giving of good, free will must be sufficiently important to justify all the pain of history. Considering the march of suffering that makes up much of history, free will cannot merely add positively to creation; it must be absolutely necessary to the accomplishment of creation's purpose. Why is free will so all-important?

*   *   *

The goal of creation is for the Creator to give to man. The greatest gift the Creator can give us is a relationship with Him — to let us participate in all that the Creator is. There are three elements to this relationship: firstly, the actual connection, secondly, we who are relating to the Creator, and lastly, the Creator with whom we are relating. Free will is central to all three of these elements: it intensifies the actual relationship, it allows for our existence as individuals in a relationship with the Creator, and it gives us the capacity to perceive the Creator with whom we are relating. We will begin our investigation by exploring how free will intensifies our experience of relationship with the Creator. But since this relationship is only the means through which the Creator gives, we must first understand what giving is.

LEVELS OF GIVING

There are many levels to giving. Sometimes giving is done solely to get something, like a political donation to gain influence. Usually, however, giving arises out of a mixture of motives, such as writing a check for the building fund of a worthy cause with the promise of a name prominently displayed over the entrance. In spite of the mixed motives, the act is admirable because the desire to do good is present, with the satisfaction of selfish needs only helping to push a difficult decision over the top. So long as there is an element of genuine giving, the act is meritorious and elevates the giver.[11] But even in these cases when personal benefit is only a secondary consideration the giving is imperfect, for it includes some selfishness.

The selfish element in giving can be subtle, such as in what we might term the "grandmother syndrome." When we walk into our paradigmatic grandmother's house her first question is, "Would you like some cookies?" We answer "no," and she responds with a plate heaped with the sweet little diet-killers served with a glass of whole milk. There may be a host of legitimate reasons why we do not want what she is offering, but Grandma is bursting to give to us. Here the giver is gaining nothing more than the satisfaction of giving — and the receiver may even appreciate the unconditional love which is conveyed through the cookies more than he mourns his shattered diet. But as an act of giving, it is again compromised by being motivated at least partially by the needs of the giver.

This highlights the fact that perfect giving is distinguished by being determined exclusively by the needs of the receiver. It is different from Grandma's gift because of its exact fit with the true requirements and potentials of the receiver and usually entails some holding back on the part of the giver. This can be painful; after all, the giver wants to give. But if the giver is truly there for the receiver rather than to gain secondary personal benefit or relieve his desire to give, he will provide only what is best for the receiver — no more and no less.

Sculpting a gift to the needs of the receiver requires sensitivity to what is given — a fine piece of chocolate passed to a diabetic is not helpful. But how it is given is also important. For example, if someone asked a waiter for some water and got a bucket spilled over him he would not be happy. He got exactly what he asked for, and in greater quantity than he dreamed, but in a manner from which he could not benefit. In a sense, because the water was poured *on* him when he needed it *in* him, he did not receive anything.

---

11. *Pesachim* 50b; Rav Eliyahu Dessler, *Michtav Me'Eliyahu* III, p. 115.

The Creator is the perfect giver — He is only interested in our benefit. He does not give all that He could give.[12] Rather, He gives all that we can get, and He gives it in a way that allows us to get it to our greatest benefit.[13] It is this last consideration — the effects of how something is given on what is received by the recipient — which opens the door to understanding the role of free will in our relationship with the Creator. To grasp its relevance, however, we must first understand how we assimilate pleasure.

MAKING IT A PART OF US

Pleasure is the experience of expansion that comes when we join with something beyond us. Generally, this comes in two forms. Either we enlarge our self, such as when we consume food, which is experienced as a selfish pleasure. Or we experience the boundaries of the self dissolving as we merge with a larger reality, such as when we are enraptured by a piece of music. This is a more spiritual pleasure.[14] These two forms of pleasure have very different qualities—the selfish pleasures tend to be clear and sharp, while the spiritual pleasures are more subtle, yet, ultimately, more profound. With either one, however we have the pleasure of a sense of expansion.

Regardless of which kind of pleasure we are experiencing, its intensity is always proportional to the strength with which we connect to that which is giving us pleasure. For example, with the selfish pleasure of eating, food invariably tastes better when we are hungry; even the lowly tuna sandwich that we normally scorn is savored after a long hike. The need for the food, like the suction of a vacuum, attaches us more strongly to the meal, heightening its flavor and the pleasure of our eating experience. Spiritual-type pleasures are also sensitive to the

---

12. Ramchal, *Da'at Tevunot* 26.

13. Ramchal, *Derech HaShem* 1:2:2; Ramchal, *Da'at Tevunot* 18. See also Chapter 3, note 33 about Avraham entertaining guests.

14. See Chapter 9, pp. 144–148.

intensity of our attachment to them. If we go to a sophisticated classical music concert but have no background in the musical theory that underlies the music's composition, we may have difficulty connecting to the music and are likely to fall asleep. If, however, we understand what the composer is trying to do, the particular blending of sounds and the development of harmonic themes, our attention has something to latch onto and we find pleasure in the music.

One of the most powerful ways we have to strengthen our connection to something is by investing ourselves in it. For example, when we eat bread, it tastes good. But if we are the ones who baked it, the bread tastes better. Our exertion is an investment of self in the bread that then bonds us to it. The deepened connection increases the pleasure we derive from it. Investment of self can bond us to every facet of physical experience, even location. One of the best ways to feel at home in a new house or dorm is to clean it. By putting a part of ourselves into the place, we become connected.

This phenomenon is sufficiently universal that it affects halachic practice. If we store wheat for a friend and it begins to rot, even though the quantity of edible wheat diminishes with the spreading rot, we do not immediately sell the wheat. The money from the sale would only buy a bushel of someone else's wheat to replace the bushel our friend worked to grow, whereas, "A person wants his own bushel more than nine bushels of someone else's wheat."[15] Because he put effort into growing his wheat, it is more precious to him and he prefers it, even in a smaller quantity, to someone else's wheat. The ratio of one to nine is understood to be an exaggeration, but the principle is accepted, with the details of how much and when left for the Sages to work out.[16]

The reason bonds are formed through an investment of effort is because our sense of self is largely a consequence of our personal history — the ways we have chosen to expend our energy over the course of

---

15. *Bava Metzia* 38a.
16. See Rav Tzaddok HaKohen, *Pri Tzaddik* IV, p. 236 for the mystical connection of this particular ratio to our discussion.

our lives. Whatever is part of that history is part of ourselves, and the more it is part of our history, the more it is part of ourselves. We feel one with our bodies because whenever we act, we act through our bodies — they are inextricably associated with us. We feel at home in our homes because we have done so many things in them. A craftsman feels attached to his personal tools, someone who fixes his own car often comes to identify himself with his car. Similarly, anything that is part of our expending energy or receives our energy becomes a part of our personal history and, so, of us. The degree and nature of the bond will be dependent upon the quantity and quality of the energy. If we invest with joy, the energy attaching us to the object will be inextricably bound up with joy, and this will affect our relationship with the object. If we labor with resentment, the bond will never properly form, for that resentment will forever affect our sense of connection to that which is the object of our effort.[17]

We now begin to understand the words of Ramchal that open this chapter. The Creator saw in His wisdom that it was better that we acquire good ourselves and not be like "one whom the good merely accompanies in an accidental manner." Compare a wealthy kid whose father gives him a Volvo with the boy who waits tables to buy an old Ford Fiesta. The Volvo, with its leather seats and arctic air-conditioning on a hot summer day is objectively more comfortable. But the kid in his Fiesta, sweating with the window down, has a different level of satisfaction driving down the street. The Volvo *is* more, but the kid with the Fiesta *has* more.

INVESTMENT IN RELATIONSHIPS

Just as we connect to physical objects through investing ourselves, so too relationships.[18] For example, a large part of the initial attachment between a mother and her child comes through the effort the mother exerts in delivery. In the time of the Talmud, when a cow refused to give

---

17. See Rav Eliyahu Dessler, *Michtav Me'Eliyahu* III, p. 17.
18. Ibid., p. 13. There Rav Dessler extends the idea to spiritual matters, but the concept is just as applicable to relationships.

milk to her calf, the farmer placed salt in the womb, reminding the cow of the pain of birth, and the milk began to flow.[19]

An immature person thinks that his love and feeling of connection to another is awakened through receiving gifts from that other — if you give me gifts I will love you. Conversely, he believes he can make another love him by giving that person gifts. In fact, receiving gifts may engender indebtedness — which is a different kind of relationship — or it may awaken gratitude, which may motivate actions that create love. But receiving gifts does not, in and of itself, create love. The emotions move in the opposite direction; it is the *giver* of gifts who develops love.[20] The giver invests a part of himself in the other through the gift, and that part of himself in the other is the basis of his sense of connection to that other.[21] If we want someone to feel connected to us, we invite or catalyze their giving to us.[22]

---

19. *Shabbat* 128b.

20. Rav Eliyahu Dessler, *Michtav Me'Eliyahu* I, pp. 36–37.

21. This is not to say that we place a part of ourselves in the other and then relate to that. Rather, the giving creates a sense of bonding that allows us to recognize and accept the other as a true other, complete with his or her own *tzelem Elokim*, and relate to him or her on that level. Another way to understand this is to recognize that we all contain one another within ourselves in potential (See for example *Tomer Devorah*, ch. 1, *middah* 4). As one gives of himself to another, he awakens and strengthens that part that is from him in that other and then he can recognize an echo of himself in the other, which, again, allows him to extrapolate his sense of *tzelem Elokim* to the other. This is why, in a successful marriage, we see the husband and wife often become similar over time. Not because they imitate each other, but rather the part in the wife that is the reflection of her husband is strengthened through the giving of her husband, and vice versa the husband becomes similar to his wife because of her giving to him. They remain different because each is his own person refracting the other through his or her own unique character.

22. A child's misunderstanding that receiving gifts produces love is a product of his immature focus on the objects of life as ends unto themselves. If having is the goal, then receiving gifts awakens love because love is the greatest bond to another and this other, by giving me what I need most — things — is deserving of my greatest connection, love. Therefore, whatever I feel toward him is, by definition, love. Any society that focuses overly on material wealth is apt to confuse this shallower relationship with true human connection, undermining the possibility of achieving full relationships.

The primary purpose of objects is as a medium for relationships. The goal is connection to other people, which is far more valuable than material objects. I know of a case where a

Our relationship with the Creator is no different. Here, also, the more we invest ourselves in connecting, the more strongly bonded we become.[23] This provides a first-level answer to our question of why free will is so important to the attainment of the goal of creation. The Creator created in order to give good. Good is dependent upon the intensity of our connection to the Creator, and intensity of connection is increased by effort. We need the ability to invest effort in the relationship in order to increase the strength of our relationship with the Creator; therefore, the Creator must be hidden so that we can strive to find Him.

The weakness in this approach is that to truly justify free will, we would need to find some way of measuring the increase in good that is achieved through the hiddenness of the Creator, and to show that it outweighs the suffering of history. But this is not possible. If we want a satisfying answer to our question, then, we must look further.

A DEEPER CONNECTION

To intensify our connection to the Creator we strengthen our involvement in the bridges that connect us to Him — the mitzvot. Our Sages tell us that fulfilling a commandment that requires exertion is more valuable than fulfilling one that is accomplished effortlessly.[24] No inconvenience is too small to make a difference; the example the Sages bring is someone putting his hand into his pocket to give charity and pulling out the wrong change.[25]

As we explained before, this greater investment of effort in the mitzvah

---

father gave his teenage son a car, an apartment, and a credit card on the condition that his son not contact him any more. The story was that the father was a widower, found a woman he wanted to marry, and she made the father's break with his son a condition of continuing their relationship. The child became suicidal until Rav Leff, then in Miami, placed him with a warm family who took him in as their own.

23. Ramchal, *Derech HaShem* 1:2:2, "It is fitting that the one enjoying the pleasure should be the master of that good."

24. *Avot D'Rebbi Natan* 3:6.

25. *Arachin* 16b. See Rav Eliyahu Dessler, *Michtav Me'Eliyahu* III, p. 14.

brings greater connection. But it is clear that the Sages have in mind not merely a quantitative increase in bonding but, rather, a qualitative change. This is hinted at in the statement by the Sages that those mitzvot for which our ancestors risked their lives are ones we continue to fulfill today with strength, commitment, and satisfaction.[26] We understand from here that extraordinary investment in the performance of a commandment can have effects that stretch over history. But how can the sacrifice of a simple Jew 2,000 years ago affect our observance of a commandment today?

The soul is a many-layered entity that emanates from its root in the Creator, descending through dimension after dimension of reality until it finally connects to physical being through our bodies.[27] Its lowest and most distant extension from the Creator vitalizes us physically — this is what we call the *nefesh*. The next level up gives us autonomous aware-ness — this segment of the soul is called *ruach*. Higher still, the aspect called the *neshamah* begins to blur independent self as it touches levels of being transcending individuality. Above the *neshamah* we enter the pool from which the Jewish people receive life. Even higher, we leave the boundaries of time and encounter the fount from which the entire Jewish people throughout history are drawn.[28]

---

26. *Shabbat* 130a.

27. See Rav Chayim Volozhin, *Nefesh HaChayim*, *Sha'ar* 1.

28. Jung's concept of the collective unconscious echoes this reality. His work provides experimental backing for the existence of these levels of self for those who do not find sufficient evidence of this reality through their own inner experience. In prayer we rise to higher levels of the soul — see Rabbeinu Yonah, *Berachot* 22b, *Tzarich*. I believe that this rise is hinted in the text of the *Amidah* (the Standing Prayer). When we say "*Baruch*", which means "increase in the world" (*Nefesh HaChayim*) — our physical being (*nefesh*) is nullified before God as it craves to receive from Him, so we bend our knees. When we say "*Atah*", "You" — we relate to God through our autonomous self, or *ruach*, recognizing God as other to us and therefore bending even more in nullification before the Creator. When we say "*HaShem*" — we relate through our root connection to God, or *neshamah*. It identifies our self with the Creator and therefore we stand up straight. We no longer bend in nullification before Him because we exist only as an expression of Him into the world and, therefore, are not separate. When we say "*Elokeinu*", "our God" — we relate through the *chayah* and lose our individuality (our God). We exist only as an aspect of the nation who represents God. When we say "*Elokei Avoteinu*", "the God of our fathers" — we relate through the *yechidah*,

When a person is willing to give up his life to fulfill a commandment, he invests a level of self that goes beyond his individuality.[29] After all, if he were not connecting to something that transcended his personal existence he would not be able to give up his life — his own life would be everything to him and no cause could justify the sacrifice. Since that person who sacrifices his life for a commandment is motivated from the deepest recesses of his soul, his action impacts the foundations of our being, affecting the spiritual substructure from which we all issue over history. A Jew from 2,000 years ago can thus influence our connection to the mitzvah for which he sacrificed even though we live thousands of years later.

THE EXAMPLE OF TORAH STUDY

From here we see that by investing ourselves to connect more fully to a mitzvah we do not merely become *more* bonded, rather we become more *deeply* bonded, incorporating a different level of self in the observance of the task. This is seen in the study of Torah. There is a verse in *Tehillim* which states, "His desire is in the Torah of God, and he strives day and night in his Torah."[30] From this verse the Sages learn that, though the Torah is originally referred to as "the Torah of God," after a person labors in learning it — striving day and night — the Torah "is called after his name: 'his Torah.'"[31] The Torah becomes so deeply integrated with the individual that he comes to understand Torah through the prism of his personal experience of reality. This variation of Torah is unique to him and is therefore "his Torah."[32]

This explains the switch in the verse from referring to the Torah as

---

connecting to God as a part of the nation throughout history and beyond time. See Appendix 3.

29. See Rav Eliyahu Dessler, *Michtav Me'Eliyahu* II, pp. 111–112. See also Chapter 14, pp. 269–270.

30. *Tehillim* 1:2.

31. *Avodah Zarah* 19a.

32. In another sense it is our Torah in that, by creating it, we possess it. The investment in creation forms a bond and establishes ownership where there is no competing claim.

"the Torah of God" to calling it "his Torah." But the Sages take this a step further: they say that the Torah is "called after his name," meaning the Torah is given the name of the one who is learning it so intensely. Names label essence.[33] We call something by what it is, not by a secondary attribute. To say that the Torah is named after a particular individual is to say that the person, with his unique personality and perspective, has become the animating essence of his vision of the Torah. It is not Torah from his perspective; it is the Torah *of* his perspective. This not only defines the Torah's relationship with him, it also defines his relationship with the Torah. For this individual to become the essential center of his Torah, his Torah must become his essential expression in the world.[34] He and the Torah must become one.

We are speaking here about the Oral Torah, our analytic probing of the prophetic written works through the lens of the oral tradition handed down from Sinai. The Written Torah — prophetic Torah — was communicated directly from the Creator to the prophet, without human perspective. In this sense, prophetic Torah bears the name of the Creator. The inference from the verse that Torah becomes the individual's Torah was made by Rava late in the Amoraic period long after prophecy had ceased. All that remained of prophecy was the record of prophetic experiences — the works of the prophets. Those became the basis of the Torah. But without direct access to the Source, or the prophet who had access to the Source, the Sages necessarily needed to interpret texts — which meant that Torah was now coming through the individual. Thus Torah was named after each individual Sage, for it was refracted through each individual's unique core-self and experience.[35]

---

33. See Maharal, *Derech Chayim* 4:14; Maharal, *Gevurot HaShem*, ch. 24. See also Chapter 2, p. 19. I knew someone who claimed that she had successfully roused people from comas by gently, but repeatedly, calling their names into their ears. We would understand this as the name bypassing the specific biological state of the person, penetrating directly to his essential self.

34. *Devarim* 26:17–18; *Shir HaShirim* 6:3; *Berachot* 6a.

35. See for example Maharal, *Derech Chayim* 1:5 that the *Av Beit Din* (Chief Judge) refracted his Torah through the characteristic of *din* (judgment) whereas the *Nasi* (leader

But Torah is Divine — how can Torah be determined or even influenced by an individual? If we no longer hear the Creator's voice directly in the world, we must access it indirectly through our own inner connection, the *tzelem Elokim*, or image of God, which lies at the heart of each one of us.[36] When prophecy fell silent and the Creator no longer revealed Himself explicitly in the world through open miracles, the last remaining window to Divinity became the *neshamah*, the human soul. The individual integrating the Torah with his deepest being — which itself emanates directly from the Creator — became the "sole" connection of the Torah back to its Divine source in the Creator. The Torah being named after an individual is not, then, an incidental consequence of the cessation of prophecy; it is the very basis of Torah in the post-prophetic period.[37]

This all sounds very inspiring, but these words are empty and meaningless unless we can actually reach so deeply within ourselves that we can hear the echo of the Divine. The Talmud states that though prophecy was taken from the prophets, it was not taken from the wise.[38] The intuition of the Sages is a hidden form of prophecy.[39]

How is this achieved? How do the Sages reach so deeply within themselves? We said earlier that through extreme sacrifice and investment, earlier generations reached a place in the collective soul of the Jewish people that changed our relationship with mitzvot for all of history. So, too, extraordinary sacrifice and investment of self can allow people to transcend their limited individuality and gain access to parts

---

of the generation) interpreted it through *chessed* (kindness), each one based on his own character and experiences.

36. See *Chiddushei HaRamban* on *Bava Batra* 12a and Rav Tzaddok HaKohen, *Tzidkat HaTzaddik*, p. 210. To genuinely reach this place requires a selfless commitment to God and His Torah. See the *Midrash Tanchuma* quoted on the next page.

37. See Rav Yosef Yehudah Leib Bloch, *Shiurei Daat* I, *Chomer v'Tzurah*, p. 28 from *Sanhedrin* 35a that halachic rulings must arise from the level of understanding that transcends intellectual articulation. See also Maharal, *Derech Chayim* 1:1 on *sevarat ha-lev*.

38. *Bava Batra* 12a.

39. *Chiddushei HaRamban* on *Bava Batra* 12a.

of themselves from which the echo of the voice of the Creator is still heard. This is done through the commitment and personal investment that is the cornerstone of the Oral Torah. For those of us who have not undertaken the severe discipline required for greatness in the Oral Torah, our physical beings envelop our souls in a fog that blocks clarity. With extreme effort in the Oral Torah, those who are truly dedicated can cut through that fog.

A passage from *Midrash Tanchuma* describes the sacrifice required to achieve this level of Torah:

> The Oral Torah is vast while the Written Torah is brief. About the Oral Torah it is written, "Longer than land is its measure, and wider than the sea."[40] It is also written concerning the Oral Torah that, "You will not find it in the land of the living."[41] What does it mean you will not find it in the land of the living — will you find it in the land of the dead? This is to tell us that the Oral Torah will not be found with one who seeks the pleasures of this world — desire, honor, and greatness in the world — rather only with one who "kills himself" for its attainment... This is the way of the Torah: you shall eat bread with salt, you will drink water in measure, you will sleep on the ground, you will live a life of difficulty, and in the Torah you will strive. For God did not strike a covenant with Yisrael except in regards to the Oral Torah... The Oral Torah is difficult to learn and only comes with hardship. It is compared to the darkness, for it says, "Those who walk in darkness shall see a great light..."[42] It is as severe as death and its jealousy is as cruel as the grave. No one can learn it except a person who loves God with all of his heart, with all of his soul, and with all of his wealth, for it says, "You shall love HaShem your God with all of your heart, with all of your soul, and with all of your wealth."[43] How do we know this is love of Talmud? For

---

40. *Iyov* 11:9.
41. Ibid., 28:13.
42. *Yeshayah* 9:1.
43. *Devarim* 6:5.

it says afterwards, "And these words that I command you today will be on your heart."[44] What is this? Talmud, which is on the heart.[45]

This passage speaks of three things: (1) that the Oral Torah forms our covenant with God, meaning that which establishes our connection to the Creator, at least in the post-prophetic period, (2) that the Oral Torah is "on our hearts," and (3) that the Oral Torah requires extraordinary commitment and effort. The Oral Torah connects us to God by being connected to our deepest essence — our heart — which is itself connected directly to God (*tzelem Elokim*).[46] We can only reach that level of self because we are working with Torah — which reflects this inner self — and because we are investing a superhuman effort to penetrate beyond external layers of personality. The *midrash* compares this to death — focusing on Torah to the exclusion of superfluous aspects of personality, which have become confused with the self but actually merely hide the true self.[47] In the process, the self that is identified with these extraneous facets of personality falls away, and the "I" that was defined by that self dies.[48] What remains is a deeper self that expresses more purely its Divine root.[49] When this is the self at the center of our Torah, the Torah retains its basis in the Divine Source.[50]

---

44. Ibid., 6:6.
45. *Midrash Tanchuma, Noach* 3.
46. *Shir HaShirim Rabbah* 5:2.
47. See the end of Chapter, pp. 24–25.
48. This is similar to the "death" required for *teshuvah* (repentance) the leaving behind of the old self to make room for the new, which is achieved through embarrassment. We will discuss this in the next chapter.
49. A *talmid chacham*, in his forties yet renowned for the depth, breadth, and integration of his Torah, was asked how such a young man could know so much. After dodging the question a few times he looked up and said, "I didn't eat or sleep for twenty years."
50. The relationship of the Oral Torah to free will is considerably deeper than what we have raised here. In the next two chapters we will learn that free will is the basis of a self that is *tzelem Elokim*, "in the image of the Creator" and therefore capable of acting as a center for Torah in the absence of revealed prophecy.

CONNECTING WITH OUR TRUE SELF

We now see that only through extraordinary investment of effort can we reach certain levels of self. A possible answer to our question of why free will is necessary begins to emerge. It is not just that free will improves the quality of our connection to the Creator — it also forges our relationship with Him on a deeper level, with a more essential self. God can give us a relationship without our contributing to it. But any relationship that is given or pressed upon us is not a relationship with *us* in any meaningful sense of the word. It is more like the example we mentioned earlier of asking for water and getting a bucket dumped on our heads. We get lots of water, but it all drips down our bodies and none of it is absorbed. So, too, if the Creator would allow good to gush toward us without any effort on our part, it would all run off us like so much water. This is the meaning of the distinction made by Ramchal in the quote at the opening of this chapter. Without free will, our joy, our connection with the Creator, would be something that merely accompanied us rather than something that is ours, essentially connected to us, connected to the "us" that is essential.

To bring our selves to the relationship we must invest in the relationship. We cannot do that if it is already given to us; we cannot strive to find God if He is already there. Only because the Creator is hidden can we discover Him — and through the massive effort of discovery unite even our deepest essence with Him. Thus the verse cited in the previous *midrash* states, "Those who walk in darkness will see a great light." The light we come to see — the closeness to God — is great because of the darkness — the distance — from which we emerge.

*　　*　　*

In this chapter we began to explain the need for free will by exploring how it affects the quality of our connection to the Creator. We found that the hiding of God required by free will forces us to invest effort to find Him, which enhances the relationship. But we have no scale that can demonstrate that the gain in quality outweighs the cost in human suffering, leaving this an incomplete answer. Therefore, we began to probe how the effort we invest in the relationship influences the facet of self through which we relate to the Creator. We found that it deepens the aspect of personality through which we connect to God.

But this contribution of free will suffers the same problem of measurement we encountered when we tried to assess free will's influence on the quality of our relationship with God. In order to fully justify free will we would need to identify where the self that is capable of a meaningful relationship with the Creator begins. In other words, how deep do we need to go? And, based on that, how much pain and how much hiddenness is warranted to engage a sufficiently essential self to achieve the goal of creation? Does this match the actual extent of the Creator's hiddenness and our consequent suffering? We do not have the capability to answer these questions.

There is also another difficulty with attempting to justify free will through these considerations. Both the enhanced quality of relationship and the deepening of self we have spoken about are a result of our efforts to overcome the hiddenness of God required for free will. But this hiddenness is not synonymous with free will. God's hiddenness is a prerequisite to the actualization of free will. But free will is not a prerequisite to hiddenness. We could exert ourselves to create a relationship with God without the decision-making that is free will and still enhance the relationship and deepen the connection. When we do not choose to make bread but rather Mom makes us do it, as long as we are not resentful, the loaf still tastes especially good. This is so even though the effort did not involve choice. The pangs of labor are involuntary but still contribute to the depth of the bond between a mother and her newborn child. Choosing is a particular kind of effort. We have not even begun to explain why we need specifically *choice* to achieve the goal of connecting our self to the Creator.

These shortcomings will be addressed in the next chapter, where we will look at a more fundamental effect that free choice has on who we are that relates to the Creator. Rather than focusing on how it deepens our personality, we will examine how it establishes our individuality.

CHAPTER 5

The Making of Self

The Creator is the ultimate good. But it is the nature of good that it gives good, and this is what the Creator desired, to create a creation in order to give it good — for without someone to receive the good, no good is given.[1] However, in order that the good given should be complete, He knew in His wisdom that it was fitting that the receiver of the good should receive it through the efforts of his own hands. For then he would be the owner of the good he received, and he would not be embarrassed to receive it like someone accepting charity from another. Our Sages say about this, "One who eats that which is not his own is embarrassed to look in the face of the one who gave it to him."[2]

WE HAVE ESTABLISHED THAT physical existence was created to allow the Creator to give good through relating to man. We asked: if this is the case, why is the Creator so hidden? We answered: to allow free will to found man's relationship with the Creator. But we were challenged to explain why free will is such a vital element in our relationship with

---

1. The seeming implication that the Creator needs creation is answered by Rav Freidlander in his notes to the edition of *Daat Tevunot*, which he edited and published (Bnei Brak, 1974), p. 4, *iyun* 2.
2. Ramchal, *Daat Tevunot* 18.

the Creator that it justifies all the suffering of history, which is the direct consequence of His hiddenness. We learned that free choice allows an investment of self in our relationship with the Creator that both enhances the connection and deepens the self engaged in the relationship.

We concluded, however, that this does not adequately answer our question. We cannot base our justification of the Creator's hiddenness on the intensification of the relationship that it catalyzes without showing that the added joy it produces outweighs all the torments of history. That, we cannot do. Focusing on free will's deepening of self also yields no solution. If it is a matter of deeper-is-better, we are faced with the same impossible valuation. If, instead, we understand that the deepening moves us toward a particular depth of self that must be reached to achieve creation's purpose, we do not know — and without prophecy cannot determine — where that critical point lies. We, therefore, cannot show how our suffering directs us specifically toward that point. And, in any case, all these answers relate to free will as a means of investing effort into our relationship with the Creator. Free will is a very specific kind of effort, which requires decision making. Why do we need to make decisions in our effort to form a relationship with the Creator?

To satisfactorily answer our question we need to recognize a more profound effect of free will on the self. Freely willed decisions do not merely allow us to deepen our self; they are responsible for there being a self at all. Only through unforced, deliberate decisions can we achieve any individuality or otherness in relation to the Creator, which, as Ramchal says in the opening quote to this chapter, is a prerequisite to a relationship. "The Creator desired to create a creation in order to give it good — for without someone to receive the good, no good is given."

When we receive things without choosing or deserving them, we have no opportunity to define ourselves as individuals. Our self is washed away by the giver. We are not an active participant in the gift, but merely a target to receive the kindness surging out of our benefactor. An example of this is the grandmother's gift we cited in the last chapter, where, after refusing her generous offer of cookies, we are pushed to take them anyway. The gift is not motivated by Grandma's cognizance of our unique individuality — she gives to us against our specific interests. And we certainly do not actualize our individuality in the exchange — we said no. When we discussed the grandmother syndrome previously, we focused on the shortcomings of her act of giving. But the relationship itself is also incomplete. Though the shower of love we get from Grandma is wonderful, we could not tolerate it defining all of our relationships. From a parent, for example, it would be smothering. If our mother would push food on us after we said we did not want it, we would feel our personal space intolerably violated.

The Creator created the world to give. There is no giving without an "other" to give to. Without free will there is no other. By understanding this consequence of free will we begin to recognize its necessity to the accomplishment of the Creator's goal and, therefore, its value, regardless of the complications it introduces.

EMBARRASSMENT AS LOSS OF SELF

In the quote which opens this chapter, Ramchal explains why it is important for us to create our relationship with the Creator rather than merely receive it. He states that by making the relationship we avoid embarrassment: "Then he would be the owner of the good he received, and he would not be embarrassed to receive it." He cites the example of someone receiving charity to illustrate that embarrassment is our natural reaction to receiving something for free. We have already recognized that the free will that allows us to create a relationship brings with it evil and suffering. If the reason why we need to achieve our connection is to avoid embarrassment, why doesn't the Creator simply create us without this emotional response? Then, presumably, there would be no need for free will and evil in creation. Why is embarrassment a necessary part of creation?

The Sages see the emotion of embarrassment as something so fundamental that they impute it to every level of creation, even plants.[3] When a grapevine gets too long, the distant fruit no longer receives

---

3. In *Shemot Rabbah* 28:1, the Sages also attribute this response to angels.

sufficient nourishment from the original roots of the plant. Farmers then take a branch far down the vine and stick it into the ground, where it sprouts roots and becomes a new source of nutrients. This creates a halachic problem, because we are forbidden to have benefit from fruit that grows during the first three years of any newly planted tree.[4] The new root system is considered a new planting, even though the old root system might be long past the three-year prohibition. How are we to identify which grapes on the vine are growing from the new roots and which grapes are growing from the old ones? The Sages answer that we look to the leaves of the vine — they always face away from the source that giving them nourishment. The Sages give us a memory device for this sign: one who eats from another's food is embarrassed to look in his face.[5]

Obviously, there is a physical explanation for why the leaves face away from the root that sustains them — the Sages only reference embarrassment as a convenient way of remembering the halachic implication of the leaves. But the Sages are also hinting here at a point we made earlier, that existence is structured as a metaphor for higher dimensions of reality.[6] Biology is nothing more than an instrument for communicating meaning. There is a (spiritual) reason why there is a (physical) reason for the leaf turning away. The leaf's response echoes our reaction to receiving something unearned.

Why is creation saturated with embarrassment? What is fundamental about it? The experience of embarrassment is an experience of loss of self. When we do something embarrassing we feel that we have acted in a way that is not representative of humanity — or at least of our social group. Our action reflects upon us, effectively testifying that we lack the wherewithal to be included with humanity or our group; the basis of our existence is undercut. The person who is embarrassed turns inwards to avoid contact with those whose very existence reinforces his sense of

---

4. *Vayikra* 19:23; *Shulchan Aruch, Yoreh De'ah* 294:1.
5. *Talmud Yerushalmi, Orlah* 6a, brought in *Tosefot Kiddushin* 36b.
6. See Chapter 2, p. 16 and Chapter 16, pp. 299–300.

inferiority. The Sages consider this withdrawal a mini death experience, for in the context of afterlife, death is primarily a withdrawal from connection to the world.[7]

An illustration of this is seen in the role embarrassment plays in the process of *teshuvah* (repentance). Embarrassment is listed in Rabbeinu Yonah's *Sha'arei Teshuvah* as a necessary step to repentance.[8] Why?

Teshuvah from a transgression is not accomplished by simply apologizing for a misdeed, even when the apology is accompanied with genuine remorse — this cannot bring absolution. Rather, repentance is a process by which we become other to the person who did the offending act. We must be able to honestly declare, "The person I am now could not do this deed that was done." We become a more fundamental expression of ourselves, centered in a deeper place more closely aligned with our root self emanating from the Creator; the more superficial facet of personality that previously motivated the offending act is no longer part of us.[9] This is how *teshuvah* cleanses us of transgression — we do not remove the transgression from ourselves so much as we remove ourselves from the transgression. The reason *teshuvah* requires embarrassment is because we cannot become a new self unless we cease being the old self. Embarrassment is the little death that clears the site for a reconstructed identity.

CREATING SELF THROUGH FREE WILL

How does this relate to free will? How does free will prevent embarrassment? Ramchal is discussing free will as an intrinsic element in man's process of building a relationship with the Creator; he is not speaking of an instance where we did something wrong. Why should there be any embarrassment when we have not done anything wrong to require a loss of self?

---

7. *Bava Metzia* 58b; *Sotah* 10b; *Peirush Rabbeinu Yonah* to *Pirkei Avot* 3:11.

8. 1:21.

9. Rav Chayim Volozhin, *Nefesh HaChayim* 1:18–20.

Our confusion stems from our imprecise description of embarrassment. Although embarrassment usually results from the loss of a preexisting self, embarrassment is less about the loss of self than the experience of a lack of self. It would equally be experienced by someone who never had a self. When Ramchal states that free will is necessary to avoid embarrassment, he means that without free will we would never achieve selfhood. Free will is the capability through which we create ourselves as a self.

The embarrassment of accepting charity illustrates this point. There, also, we do nothing wrong; why should we feel embarrassed? We all need things outside of ourselves to survive. When we earn what we receive, however, it is ours by right, and therefore no dependence on the supplier results. It is not really coming from the supplier so much as *through* him. He does not choose to give it; he is forced by a right that we have created through our effort. It is therefore coming to us, from us, mediated by an externally anchored system of justice.

When receiving charity, however, we sense a lack of self. We are getting something that we have not earned and is therefore not ours. It is a gift from the giver, establishing our dependence upon him. The giver becomes our source — he is sustaining us. We lose our independent base and are transformed into an extension of his root.[10] No longer coming from ourselves, we lose selfhood. We would find ourselves in exactly this situation with the Creator if we did not create and earn our relationship with Him, thus Ramchal's comparison.[11]

---

10. See *Bereishit* 18:8 and *Peirush HaAlshich* in *Sefer Torat Moshe*; *Shemot Rabbah* 28:1 with Rav Tzaddok HaKohen, *Pri Tzaddik*, Rosh Chodesh Sivan, 4; Maharal, *Tiferet Yisrael*, ch. 24.
11. Within the context of a healthy relationship there is both giving and receiving. This builds connection, for mutual dependency and trust are part of any deep bond. But this is true in the context of an established relationship between two existing individuals. Outside the context of an appropriate relationship, or when a person becomes habituated to receiving, there is a loss of genuine, solid self. Shlomo HaMelech thus writes, "One who hates gifts will live (*Mishlei* 15:27)," for the trait of loving gifts fosters the kind of dependence that blocks the formation of a true, independent self. (Maharal, *Netivot Olam* I, p. 21 and *Derech Chayim*, 4:1, *Eizehu Ashir*). We will explore this idea more in depth in the next chapter.

The gift we are specifically interested in is a relationship with the Creator. The contrast between receiving a freely given relationship and a relationship that we ourselves have created is comparable to the contrast between an infant daughter suckling from her mother and, some years later, now married and with her own children, that daughter being taken to lunch by Mom. The infant daughter has done nothing to connect to her mother. The adult daughter's relationship is based on years of building herself in the image of her mother and connecting through the mutual understanding that comes from similar life experiences. At both stages, the daughter is receiving from her mother. In both instances, at least as important as the food, is the emotional connection and support that comes from Mom through the medium of the food. It is true that when the daughter is suckling she has a profound and even enviable closeness with her mother — and were the child not to go through this period of utter dependence and attention she might be emotionally crippled. Still, we instinctively feel revulsion toward anyone who attempts to maintain this level of dependence as life progresses. The hopelessly overprotective parent or hopelessly dependent child strikes us as perverse. Life is to be lived. At its core, this involves developing a self.

The importance of coming from one's self is not just a philosophical concept; it underlies our whole sense of self. This was brought home to me at an early age. Where I grew up, when a child turned seven his birthday party usually consisted of a scoop of ice cream and a piece of cake for each guest, a few games, and a popped balloon or two. In return for sponsoring this simple party, the celebrant expected to receive a cheap dart gun or a cardboard glider from each of his friends. I received a number of such gifts for my seventh birthday, but one child gave me an unexpectedly large and heavy box. When I opened it there was a beautiful, expensive clock radio inside. The complicated reasons why this child's parents chose to give this gift are not relevant to our present discussion. My reaction to the gift, however, is. The sight of this radio took my breath away. Not out of joy. Rather, I felt like I had been kicked in the gut — a certain deep embarrassment. What was I supposed to do with this gift, where did it come from, how was I supposed to possess it? There was no context, no appropriate relationship within which to fit this radio. At that age I could not have articulated the specifics of my feelings, but the sting of the loss of self was sufficiently sharp to be branded on my memory for life. (I did, however, manage to overcome these feelings and use the radio happily for many years.)

One of the abiding features of morning prayers in Yerushalayim is the constant trickle of individuals who pass through the synagogues seeking charity. There are specific individuals who come consistently year after year. One can see their attitude toward their situation clearly reflected in their faces; often it will evolve over time. Ultimately, receiving charity is an unnatural situation, for it undermines a person's selfhood. It takes great inner strength to maintain one's true humanity when need pushes a person to seek charity. People who are in the situation for a long time can lose that humanity — different people in different ways. Some lose the awareness of impropriety that lies at the core of charity and make it into a livelihood or even a business. Occasionally people lose their humanity altogether.

I remember one person in particular to whom this occurred. The first day he came to ask for money, he sat and told anyone who would listen to him why he was collecting. He had begun to experience seizures, lost his job, and needed to support his family. He was a simple, sweet man when he first appeared. Over the years, however, he slowly stopped caring about himself. His appearance changed radically — clothing, beard, hygiene... The stench of tobacco began to overwhelm the rooms he would enter, and all life went out of his eyes. As painful as this process was to watch, his deterioration was a sign of a person with a deep sense of the fundamentally human need to come from one's self, and he was a clear lesson of how corrosive to basic humanity is the loss of that sense.

ACTING FROM OURSELVES RATHER THAN REACTING

How does the freely willed decision specifically create a self? Let us approach the situation from the opposite direction: what is the significance of an action that is not freely chosen? Imagine doing a mitzvah, such as giving charity, because someone forces us at gunpoint. What is the significance of the act? A good result has occurred. The Creator wanted the poor person sustained and it has been accomplished. But the Creator did not create us because He needed something done. The Creator can achieve His desired results without assistance.[12] He also does not need creation to unfold through process — He is above time and can reach His intended result in the instant of creation.

That the world develops over time through actions directed by man must be for the sake of man. What, then, is the significance to us of the action at gunpoint? The action did not come *from* us, it came *through* us. We were effectively a cog in a machine, with our action determined from outside of ourselves. Anyone else could have substituted for us and the same result would have been achieved. In fact, no one needed to be there at all — the gunman could have stolen the money and given it to the poor person himself. Our "I" is effectively not present in the action because it is totally determined from outside ourselves. We function as an interchangeable object with life traveling through us. Forced from without, the action is meaningless to us, for there is no "us" present in the act.[13]

From this thought experiment we realize that for actions to have significance to us, we must have a significant role in the action. It must come from us. Coming from us means we have to make the decision and not be forced from without. Absolute clarity of truth and moral necessity would affect us the same way as a gun, removing our decision, and therefore our personal contribution to our actions.[14] With truth to some degree hidden, however, we need to decide. With free will, we can stand above the causal sequences of nature and initiate action. Through

---

12. *Iyov* 35:6–7; *Bereishit Rabbah* 44:1.

13. Ramchal, *Derech HaShem* 1:3:1.

14. The term necessity in this sentence is meant literally. Presumably, this requires a level of revelation that reveals the link between truth and reality, where turning from the truth is turning from existence. Otherwise, following the truth is an act of choice. Rav Dessler, however, seems to understand that truth intrinsically contains the force of compulsion and that choice lies in recognizing truth (Rav Eliyahu Dessler, *Michtav Me'Eliyahu* I, pp. 111–113).

our decisions we define and develop ourselves as unique individuals.

Let us ask the question directly: Where does our individuality and selfhood really lie? When am I an "I"? In what act do I genuinely actualize myself? It is some indication of how misdirected our society is that we can go through life so distracted that we never ask this most basic question.

The answer is, we are a self and achieve our unique individuality in our moments of choosing. We pass most of our time carried by the various currents that intersect our lives — pulled along by the awakening of this emotion or that inclination. We function as passive nodes through which forces external to our essential self flow. Our actions are reactions, responses unregulated by anything we would identify as our self. The only time we actually exist in our unique individuality is when we stand above the play of various forces and pulls, making a genuine decision.

This does not mean we actualize ourselves choosing between apple pie and pecan pie. That is merely a war of inclinations in which the strongest rules. A dog also occasionally has to pick between two pieces of meat — this is not a decision, it is an instinctual play of forces. Genuine decisions occur when two possible choices arise, each representing different value systems and we must choose which one to submit to — we must define ourselves. Without the involvement of values in the decision, the faculty of choice has nothing upon which to act. We will go into this in more detail in the next chapter.

There are occasions where our actions are a consequence of a prior decision.[15] Then the action is not an actualization of self per se; it is an extension of a previous actualization, a continuing sign of the strength of the original choice. Or it may be the consequence of someone else's choice — the education we received, for instance. Take the example of a person who finds himself with an opportunity to shoplift. If he has

15. This paragraph is based on Rav Eliyahu Dessler, *Michtav Me'Eliyahu* I, *Avodat HaAdam, Kuntrus HaBechirah,* pp. 111–117.

a developed moral sense he would not even consider stealing. If he is a professional thief, on the other hand, he would not even consider not stealing. Prior education or decisions have brought each one of these people to where they are, to the particular set of values they have and the strength with which they hold them. As a result there is no decision to be made in the present moment. Because there is no balance between the attractions, the decision on values is not tested — there is no additional defining of self. It is when there is some level of parity between the two pulls, each representing different ideals, where the possibility exists of going either way, that we can stand above the conflicting influences and make a decision based on how we define ourselves as people. At such a moment we do not need to be determined by the somewhat stronger pull. Rather, we can choose from ourselves. If we take advantage of the opportunity, who we are as individuals is determined by us.

The Creator cannot create our self. Self cannot be given, for then it is not self. We must create it through our choices. Then we come from ourselves and stand as individuals before the Creator, able to relate to Him as an "other." Only in the act of creating from ourselves is there personal being on some level distinct from the Creator,[16] allowing the possibility of the Creator giving, for only then is there someone to give to.[17]

---

16. Since the Creator creates all the circumstances within which we function and sustains our being throughout the whole process, we are "other" to Him only in a relative sense of the word — but it is sufficient for an act of giving to take place. We will investigate more fully the nature of this independence in the next chapter.

17. Rambam, in *Peirush HaMishnayot Makkot* 3:16, states that a single true act of choice is enough to create an entity capable of receiving reward — in our language, establish self. "When someone fulfills one of the 613 mitzvot properly without any ulterior motive at all, but, rather, purely and with love, he merits the Next World. The Creator commanded us in many mitzvot because then it is impossible that a person will not, at some point in his life, perform a mitzvah because he chooses to do the right thing with no ulterior motive." Rabbi Yosef Albo in *Sefer HaIkarim* (3:29), takes this further and says it need not be specifically a mitzvah that is done. Rather, any act that is performed with the intention of serving HaShem — that is, without succumbing to influences external to the essential self — will create some existence in the Next World. See, however, Maharal's discussion of this statement of Rambam in *Derech Chayim* at the end of the sixth *perek*. Maharal suggests a number of

In the previous chapter we attempted to justify free will, and the hiddenness of the Creator that accompanies it, by the effort and investment of self it required in the formation of connection with God. We realized, however, that this alone could not explain the need for free will. The ability to enhance the relationship or deepen ourselves that it provides cannot justify evil, and the contribution of nondescript effort cannot explain the specific need for making choices, which is what free will is all about.

In this chapter we recognized that freely willed choice is the basis of our independent self. This resolves the question of how an all-powerful, giving God would tolerate evil in His world because free choice, which allows for the possibility of evil, turns out to be a prerequisite to accomplishing the goal of creation. As Ramchal states: the Creator created to give, and giving requires an "other." Through free choice, and only through free choice, can we create that other.

We can now combine free will's capacity to actualize individual self, which adequately justifies free will, with our previous observation that free will allows us to invest ourselves in our relationship with the Creator. Choosing is the essence of all of our efforts and colors them. We said earlier that the nature of the bond that is created through investment is determined by the nature of the energy that is invested — if

---

ways of understanding the intent of Rambam, successively rejecting the viability of each of them. A principal problem Maharal has with Rambam's explanation is that Rambam's focus on the positive act seems to imply that he does not hold people accountable for their transgressions. At one point, however, Maharal suggests that Rambam could mean that an individual will suffer for his many transgressions. But since he still gains the Next World from his one pure act, Rambam focuses on the one successful act because any suffering for the other deeds is of secondary significance to the root achievement of the eternity of the Next World. This reading is the one that supports the position we are developing here. Maharal states that this understanding is workable. In the text of *Derech Chayim* presently available, Maharal seems to go on to reject this as the actual intent of Rambam. There are, however, difficulties with the text of *Derech Chayim* at that point and it may need emendation. In any case, since Maharal regards the position as acceptable, regardless of whether it is the position Rambam is presenting in *Peirush HaMishnayot*, we have support for the idea that a true act of choice is the foundation for our true existence.

we strive with joy, we will be bonded in joy. So, also, if we strive from our individual selves, our "I" will be joined, and indeed formed, in the effort. But if we have no choice, if we are forced by an outside source to strive, it cannot be *we* who are bonded, for the essence of our selfhood will be absent.[18]

---

18. Ramchal, *Derech HaShem* 1:3:1.

CHAPTER 6

To Be and Not to Be

The one who is having good should acquire it himself and not be like someone whom the good merely accompanies in an accidental manner. When he does acquire it himself he resembles, to the extent possible, the completeness of the Creator. The Creator is complete from Himself—not accidentally, but as a necessary consequence of His being. This is impossible to find in any other creature. But there is some similarity if the other himself acquires the completion.[1]

IN THE PREVIOUS CHAPTER we established that the reason for free will is to allow us to create a self in order to stand separate and receive from HaShem. Self—at least in the world as God made it—cannot be given directly.[2] That which comes from another is an extension of that other.

---

1. Ramchal. *Derech HaShem* 1:2:2.
2. In Chapter 8 (pp. 132 and 135) we will discuss the fact that God's Oneness—the totality of His omnipotence—requires that He be unrestricted. He could have created the world differently than He did and, even having created it the way He did, He is not bound by His own laws. See Ramchal, *Da'at Tevunot* 36. What we are discussing here is the way God chose to order His creation—the way it works. Self-development is the purpose of creation and, therefore, its process determines the way creation is structured. Though God is not restricted by that, any violation would be exceptional; it would not be representative of the way He established structure (See Maharal, *Netzach Yisrael*, ch. 1 for a discussion of the concept of structure in creation). If God wanted self generally to develop differently He would have created existence in another way, whether we can imagine it or not.

If self is the objective, the only option is to create potential and opportunity, and then leave it to creation to achieve selfhood on its own. The
classic example of this is a mother giving birth to a child. After a period
of nurturing, she must give him space if he is to develop individuality.
Separation and individuation as a means to receiving are the goal of
God's creation. God therefore makes man incomplete, giving him free
will to finish the job and gain self in the process.

But when we create ourselves we do not merely fulfill a technical
prerequisite for the Creator's giving; we achieve existence itself. As we
mentioned earlier the Creator's goal is to give to us — the greatest good
that can be given.[3] This is the good that is in Him, all the being and
reality that He is. Ideally, then, in order for us to receive the greatest
good, He should give us a level of being comparable to His. This cannot
happen: First, He is not created — His existence is necessary.[4] Creation
cannot have this quality for that which is necessary cannot be created
because if it is necessary it already exists — that is Him, not us. Second,
His necessity requires that He be fully actualized — He is all He can be
entirely from within Himself without any other determining Him.[5] We
cannot be given this quality, for if the Creator created us in a manner
in which we automatically come from ourselves we would, in reality, be
coming from and determined by Him and not ourselves.[6]

These are not minor characteristics; these qualities of the Creator
define the unfathomable depth of His being and existence, His absolute
independence. Without at least some equivalent of these qualities we
could not be understood to have received the real good of the Creator,
for our being would lack all significance — effectively, we would not
exist; any existence associated with us would not be our existence. The
point is not that our utter dependence would mean no "I" separate from
God to receive from Him — that we have already said. We are adding

---

3. See the beginning of Chapter 4, pp. 45–47.
4. Ramchal, *Derech HaShem* 1:1:3.
5. Ibid., 1:2:2.
6. Ibid., 1:3:1.

that nothing of real value would have been given. What has any value to us besides self—at least a self that connects to God? What can we possibly have if we lack self?[7]

We mentioned earlier that because we cannot have the Creator's level of being, the actual goal of creation is that we attach ourselves to the Creator and at least participate in the greatness of His being. But these qualities of necessity we cannot share through participation. God's qualities of internally based necessity, by their very nature, cannot be received from or anchored outside the self. These two qualities, which we cannot receive directly from the Creator, we must, to the degree possible within the context of creation, achieve in ourselves.[8]

Free will allows us to accomplish both of them. When we earn what we have rather than receiving it so that what sustains us in existence—that we are—is ours as a just reward for our actions, we approach necessity of being. When our particular qualities — who we become—are a result of our own decisions, we are who we are from within ourselves and are not determined from outside ourselves. We then approach God's quality of necessity of actualization. We not only participate in the greatness of the Creator but, to some extent, can achieve it in ourselves, allowing us to resemble the necessity of the Creator, as Ramchal states in our opening quote.

ACHIEVING BEING:
EMULATING THE CREATOR'S NECESSITY

The Creator is existence itself. We spoke of the need to shed our childish visions of the Creator filling empty space with creation, which pictures God *in* existence. God is not *in* existence; He *is* existence. Not the finite, limited reality that we directly experience. The Creator is necessary, eternal existence, which is the source and basis of finite reality.

---

7. See *Nedarim* 41a and *Midrash Tanchuma, Vayikra* 1: "If you are missing *da'at*, what do you have? If you have *da'at*, what are you missing?"
8. Ibid., 1:2:2.

When we say that the Creator is necessary and eternal, we do not mean what Greece attributed to physical reality (and we tend to attribute to all of reality), that it has always been and always will be.[9] That eternity is a kind of logical inertia. It begins with the fact that in the present moment there is existence. Since any present is a result of its immediate past and that past was once a present, necessarily existence always was because any moment that ever was had a past before it from which it arose. And since the present causes the immediate future, which then itself becomes the present, existence always will be. Through logic we cannot conceive of any change in this pattern; therefore existence is eternal, with eternity meaning an infinite extension of the present into the past and the future.

A spiritual perspective does not make it past the first step of recognizing that there is existence in the present. Rather than taking that existence for granted and jumping to the before and after, a spiritual perspective sees in the present reality not a fact but a miracle begging explanation for how it can be. Where is the greatness of Being necessary to give existence to dust?[10] Certainly not in the dust itself. There must be a Being with sufficient significance to support that existence.[11]

---

9. What is called in Hebrew *kadmut*.

10. This should not be confused with the "first-cause" argument for the existence of God that is a variation on the argument for eternity discussed in the previous paragraph. The first-cause argument departs from the conclusion of eternal physical reality by asserting that the regression into the past cannot go on infinitely — there must be a starting point, a first-cause. The first-cause argument is based on issues of chronology and causality. The process of thought outlined here is based on a metaphysical issue. In a sense, the first-cause argument approaches things horizontally (through a progression of time) whereas we are approaching it vertically (through a progression of depth). We are not asking what is the start of creation but, rather, what is its basis.

11. Rabbeinu Bechaya, *Bereishit* 15:7 brings a *midrash* that Avraham, after spending the first three years of his life in a cave, came out for the first time to see the world and immediately asked, "Who created the heavens, the earth, and me?" This began a quest which did not end until Avraham discovered God. What was Avraham asking in his question, "Who created this?"? Was he asking Who initiated creation or was he asking Who lies at the foundation of reality? The event occurred in a time when the world was filled with idolatry, which meant that, though the worship was misdirected, everyone at least worshipped

Finite reality, by its very existence, testifies to this. Inquiry after the nature of that Being eventually leads to the conclusion that It must possess the quality of necessity.[12] The eternity we attribute to God, then, is not an endless iteration of the present but, rather, derives from the profoundly different level of being required to found existence — He must be, therefore He is eternal. Even without the Torah's guidance, the spiritual searcher would identify this Source of existence with its quality of necessity as the Creator: He is the author of physical existence from

---

something — i.e., recognized that a Higher Reality founded existence. The point that Rav Chayim Volozhin makes in *Nefesh HaChayim* 1:2 — that existence is continually supported from Beyond — would have been intuitive to everyone in Avraham's time. In that case, Avraham's question, "Who created this?" could not have been merely "Who began reality in a chronological sense," for that would be of secondary concern to the more basic question of "Who is the foundation of reality?". Since the two issues are intertwined — for Whoever is the metaphysical foundation is also the Creator in a chronological sense — Avraham's question must have included both ideas, but have been directed primarily at the metaphysical basis of reality. Avraham, then, was expressing the bewilderment at existence that we have described as the basis of the spiritual perspective and is the foundation of the spiritual quest.

Avraham's assumption that the search was for a Being with Whom there was a relationship rather than some Source indifferent to our individual lives was a consequence of his encountering reality through his spiritual self as opposed to observing through his intellect — he was searching for a Giver, not a philosophical concept. The conclusion we draw is always shaped by the question we ask. See Chapter 15, pp. 179–180.

Avraham's defining trait was *chessed*, which means giving that is initiated from the benevolent self as opposed to mercy, *rachamim*, which is caused by an external source, that is, drawn out of the person by a reaction to the needs of the recipient. In keeping with his character, Avraham's search was for the absolute initiator of reality. He was not satisfied in his pursuit of the Giver with the half answers of idolaters, who worship intermediary forces that merely play their part in a larger picture that ultimately controls them. These forces did not initiate creation. He did not rest until he found the true Source and Initiator of existence. It is this search for God the true Initiator that leads to the conclusion that God must have the quality of necessity.

12. This is not meant to be a rational proof so much as a description of the structure of emerging spiritual realization. We will discuss the limits of rationality in Chapter 15. In a person whose spiritual experience is both genuine and more developed, acceptance of the existence of a Creator is not based on a process of thought but, rather, is an integral component of awareness and identity. See Maharal, *Tiferet Yisrael*, ch. 37 in the context of his answer to why the first of the Ten Commandments, which requires that we have *emunah* in the existence of God, is not phrased as a command but, rather, as a statement of fact.

its chronological beginning because He is the metaphysical source of existence.[13] All this greatness stems from God's necessity and to have any connection to this greatness we must emulate that necessity.

As we mentioned, the necessity of the Creator we seek to emulate has two expressions that are relevant to us: His existence and the nature of His existence. Let us focus first on emulating the necessity of His actual existence.

If the Creator related to us through His trait of *chessed*, giving freely of Himself regardless of our merit, we could not gain any necessity deriving from ourselves: what God gives would come from Him irrespective of who we are and what we do. Rather, we achieve personal necessity by the Creator mediating our relationship with Him through *din* — strict judgment.[14] In a relationship of judgment we are given what we have earned according to our actions. We are represented in the relationship because we define and drive it. Furthermore, we are not a passive extension of the Creator's root because He does not give us our support as a gift — it is ours by right based on the system of judgment that He has instituted. We are our own root for we are sustained by what is ours.

Maharal, an important sixteenth-century scholar, explains a *midrash* in a manner that has staggering implications for our present discussion. The *midrash* states:

> The Holy One says, "Of all My creations I love only judgment."[15]

Maharal comments:

> We have already clarified that judgment is something that is necessary. Therefore, judgment in particular is specific to HaShem — for HaShem

---

13. Thus, Avraham's quest for the Basis of existence led to a recognition of the Creator, and our first knowledge of God is as the Creator (See Rambam, *Hilchot Yesodei HaTorah* 1:1, Ramchal, *Derech HaShem* 1:1:1).

14. *Devarim* 32:4. See Rav Yosef Yehudah Leib Bloch, *Shiurei Da'at* I, ch. 10 (*Nissim V'Teva* III, *Mishpat*).

15. *Devarim Rabbah* 5:7.

is necessary existence and not merely possible, and judgment also is necessary.[16]

When Maharal says that judgment is necessary, he means that it is clear truth — its conclusions follow inevitably — and also that the structure of reality that is built upon that judgment must give it expression. When, for example, a Rabbinical court compels us to follow a Torah judgment they are acting as agents of metaphysical reality. For this reason, judgment resembles the Creator. Just as the Creator must be, so, too, justice must be.

Applied to our present discussion, when we earn our existence or that which sustains us in existence — that is, when what we are or have is awarded to us through judgment — we have it and are sustained not by any sufferance, charity, or generosity but by right. It must *necessarily* be given to us because of the obligating force of law and justice. Through justly earning what we have, our existence becomes, in some sense, necessary, echoing the Creator's necessity of being because the necessity of judgment reflects His necessity. We say "echoing" because our necessity is based on a system of judgment anchored outside of us, whereas the necessity of the Creator is not dependent upon anything outside Himself.[17] But since the Creator has established this system of judgment, within the confines of that system our existence attains necessity, and we taste, however distantly, the greatness of necessary Being.[18] On a deeper level, because it is the will of the Creator that creation should be conducted according to judgment, to the degree that we earn our

---

16. *Netivot Olam* II, *Netiv HaDin*, ch. 1.

17. For this reason, Maharal states that man cannot emulate the Creator in the area of *din* (judgment), only in *chessed* (giving), because *chessed* comes from our individual selves, as it does with the Creator. But in *din* we are dependent upon a structure of truth that does not come from us, which is not the case with the *din* of the Creator (*Netivot Olam* I, *Netiv Gemilut Chassadim*, ch. 1).

18. "Within the confines" is an important caveat. The Creator is ultimately not constrained by the system of judgment He created. See Chapter 8, pp. 132 and 135, the discussion of the fourth error from Ramchal, *Da'at Tevunot* 36.

existence through judgment, our necessity is a direct extension of the necessity of the Creator. The necessity is ours, however, for we have catalyzed it through our actions.[19]

Obviously, there can be no concept of judgment and earning unless we are the author of the actions that are to be rewarded. Were we compelled to act, that which compelled us would earn the reward, not us.[20] What we have is ours by right only because we act of our own volition; free will enables us to echo the Creator's necessity of being.

THAT WE ARE AND WHO WE ARE

We mentioned a second aspect of the necessity of the Creator's being in addition to His actual existence. Who He is, His nature, is also necessary. The necessity of the Creator's being requires that He always was and always will be all that He is. He is Who He is out of the necessity of His own being; nothing from without determines Him. We, creation, cannot be what we are with this same forcefulness of existence because we lack necessity, as evidenced by the fact that we had to be created. But at least through free choice we are able to choose who we are so that our nature is self-determined.[21]

When we speak of determining our nature we are not referring to merely adopting philosophical positions. Only when we act upon choices do we genuinely define ourselves.[22] Moreover, our actions develop us in the image of the values implicit in the acts.[23] For example, when we choose to give charity rather than order a third slice of chocolate cheesecake we commit to the importance of giving. When we do so

---

19. If the will of the Creator were to run the world through the trait of *chessed* we would still be connected to the necessity of the Creator, but it would not be our necessity that partakes of His necessity. We would simply be connected to His necessity. This would limit the degree to which His necessity enhanced the significance of our being.

20. Ramchal, *Derech HaShem* 1:3:1.

21. Ibid., 1:2:2, quoted at the beginning of our chapter.

22. Rav Eliyahu Dessler, *Michtav Me'Eliyahu* II, pp. 36–39. See also Chapter 1, p. 3.

23. *Sefer HaChinuch*, mitzvah 16.

consistently we become more giving people. If, instead, we elect to buy the cake, we proclaim the priority of selfishness, internalize it, and make it more difficult to give the next time.

We determine our nature through the same choices that earn our existence. The righteousness of the act merits our existence while its specific content develops us in specific ways.[24] Our nature, as well as our existence, then, echoes the greatness of the Creator to the extent possible within the confines of creation. As Ramchal states in the quote which opens our chapter:

> The Creator is complete from Himself — not accidentally but as a necessary consequence of His being. This is impossible to find in any other creature. But there is some similarity if the other himself acquires the completion.[25]

Through free will we are able to attain significant being, both in terms of our existence and our nature. This is our "otherness" to the Creator, which enables us to receive His good and achieve creation's purpose. This is an astonishing accomplishment — and the opportunity to achieve it is God's ultimate gift to us.

THE NATURE OF BEING OTHER

What do we mean when we say that we achieve significant being and are "other" to the Creator? We cannot mean that we gain existence, which is anchored in ourselves to the exclusion of the Creator. That is impossible, since the only thing that really exists is the Creator.[26] If we achieved actual independence we would be separated from existence and, therefore, cease to exist![27] Moreover, if we impute a separate existence to ourselves,

---

24. In Chapter 9 we will discuss what characteristics we are striving to develop in ourselves through our choices.

25. Ramchal, *Derech HaShem* 1:2:2 quoted in the opening paragraph of the chapter.

26. *Devarim* 4:35,39. See Rav Yosef Yehudah Leib Bloch, *Shiurei Daat* II, *Plas B'Maagal*, p. 105.

27. This is phrased in an extreme manner to keep the ideas clear. In actuality, the issues play out on a more subtle plane since any "independence" we can earn is always by virtue of

we, in effect, equate ourselves with God, Who truly does exist, and compromise God's quality of uniqueness, which is fundamental to His being the Creator.[28]

Yet, if we are not other to the Creator, the Creator has no one to give to, and the purpose of creation is lost. What, then, do we mean when we say that we gain an existence that is, in some sense, other to the Creator? Our stance toward God in *tefillah* (prayer) provides a good starting point from which to understand this idea.

In the *Shemoneh Esrei* (the Standing Prayer), we address the Creator in our capacity as members of the Jewish people; all praises and requests are submitted from the first person plural — "we thank," "we ask." There is one exception, where we address Him from our first person singular "I." That is when we use the name *Ado-noi*, "my Lord."[29]

Whenever we use the name *Ado-noi*, "my Lord," we are relating to the Creator in our capacity as an individual rather than as a member of the community. The fact that this name of the Creator includes within it our relationship to Him — *my* Lord — is not unusual; several of His names share this characteristic.[30] This commonality makes it no less noteworthy; we will return to this point later. What is important for us at the present is that in the midst of the standing prayer, by saying "my" in "my Lord," we are relating to the Creator specifically through our quality of being an "I." We cannot really be said to understand what we are saying when we use this name without understanding who or what it is to be an "I." In this case our job is complicated by the fact that our

---

the system of judgment created and maintained by God. But within the context of creation where, "*Kol derachav mishpat*" (All His ways are judgment [*Devarim* 32:4]) — and therefore, judgment is assumed — independence becomes possible. Even here, however, the concept of independence has its limits because God is not bound by His laws. See Chapter 8, pp. 132 and 135; and Ramchal, *Daat Tevunot* 36, the fourth misunderstanding.

28. See the beginning of Maharal, *Drush L'Shabbat HaGadol*.

29. If we wanted to say "our Lord" we would say *Ado-nainu*. See *Tehillim* 8:2. See Chapter 3, p. 38, for a discussion of the grammatical structure of the name *Ado-noi*.

30. *Ado-neinu* — our Lord, *Elokeinu* — our God, *Elokei Yisrael* — the God of Israel, *Elokei Avraham* — the God of Avraham, *Elokai* — my God, etc.

"I," which identifies our independent self, comes in the context of nullifying self through accepting subservience to the Creator — my *Lord*.

FREE WILL: THE CAPACITY TO ACTUALIZE SELF

We have discussed that our "I," or self, emerges through our freely willed acts; this is free will's purpose. To understand this self we need to investigate free will and the process by which it generates self.

We usually refer to free will as "choice." But this is not exactly accurate, at least as we commonly use the term. When we decide between sushi and tuna salad, we also call it a choice. But the outcome of that "choice" is determined by a war of inclinations because there are no competing values we are selecting between. That decision takes place within us through forces that are distinct from our essential self. There is really no active choice being made and the decision occurs without any dedicated faculty in man. The mere existence of multiple possibilities does not engage our capacity for free choice.

Free will operates when our choices are between actions that represent different value systems and we define ourselves through our choice. Actual decisions in life often involve complex mixtures of moral considerations and competing desires; they are seldom as obvious as the choice between buying dessert or giving the money to charity. For example: we are faced with the choice of moving to the suburbs or remaining in the city. In deciding, we will weigh the comfort of the suburbs against the drudgery of a heavy commute, which is primarily a pleasure issue. But the commute also means less time with the family while the additional space of suburbia contributes to the peacefulness of the home and the education system is better there, which add value considerations to the decision.

Right and wrong in a given situation can also be clouded by the appropriateness of a choice to the chooser. Someone who newly learns the value of charity and jumps to give away a disproportionate share of his money may become resentful, eventually dropping charity completely. Alternatively, he may overpower his hesitations and continue to give the charity but only robotically, unable to engage his full self in the act because he did not take the time to develop his character to contain the sacrifices involved in the deed.[31] These are complications in distilling where the choice lies and what the real issues are in a decision. The point remains that whenever a moral issue is implicated in a choice, free will is operative.

It is not, however, just the introduction of a moral angle that makes the decision an act of free will. Just as a dog deciding between two bones does not make a freely willed choice, a dog faced with the selfless act of saving a child from drowning or the selfish act of chasing a cat is also not choosing. In both cases the dog is a battleground of instincts, albeit in the second scenario more sophisticated ones. In man, however, the Creator placed a capacity to choose, to stand above the pull of various options and — whether he consciously articulates them or not — evaluate their meanings and implications, and decide how to act, thus defining his values and determining himself.

What we call free choice is really a specific capacity given to man through which he actualizes self. Instances of moral choice provide the context in which this capacity can be active. The capability to freely choose is the loftiest element of creation, allowing man — uniquely among all other creations — to achieve being.[32]

The structure of our humanity reflects the fact that our selfhood exists in the act of choice. We arise from the combination of a physical body drawn from the material earth[33] and a Divine, spiritual *neshamah* (soul) directly drawn from the Creator and invested into that body. Our material body is the part of us that is broken off as an individual element in creation and pulls toward our selfish, individual inclinations. The *neshamah* craves return to its source in the Creator and pulls us to fealty and service to the Creator.[34] We are formed out of the very elements that provide the contrary pulls that give a context for our essential self, our free choice, to operate.

---

31. See Rav Yosef Yehudah Leib Bloch, *Shiurei Da'at* II, pp. 109–116, *Plas B'Ma'agal Raglecha*.
32. Rabbi Meir Simcha of Dvinsk, *Meshech Chochmah*, *Bereishit* 1:26, equates man's free choice with his *tzelem Elokim*, the image of God in man.
33. Also a creation of God, but one where the connection is much more hidden.
34. Ramchal, *Derech HaShem* 1:3:1; Ramchal, *Da'at Tevunot* 24.

Since our choice is between the selfish pull of the body (in its various forms) and the obligation of spiritual ideals, we are not creating the choices — they already exist. We only have the option to determine ourselves by choosing which pull defines us. Either we follow our inclinations or we follow our ideals, but either way we are following. Everyone has to serve; it is just a question of what or whom.[35] If we choose to follow the pull of the *neshamah* and serve the Creator, we create our selfhood in the very act of subservience to the Creator, and our independence disappears in its formation. There is enough of a self formed through the choice to receive from the Creator, while there is no real separation to undermine our existence. The concern we raised earlier of our creation of self contradicting our existence in God is thus addressed — the self we create is wedded to God.

But what if we choose to follow our bodies and be selfish? We said that choosing actualizes self. Are we also creating self when we choose to follow our inclinations? Is it possible to create a self separate from God? We may feel that we are serving ourselves when we do so, but in actuality we are subsuming ourselves within physical pleasure, an energy that is ultimately foreign to our essential selfhood.[36]

The root of our being is our *neshamah*; our body is a vessel through which that *neshamah* can take on expression in the world. Though our humanity arises from the melding together of these two dimensions, one is primary and one is secondary. Spiritual reality is the basis of existence; physical reality is its expression. Our physical inclinations, though part of being human, are not definitive or even representative of our humanity. Following their pull is not an actualization of self; it is

---

35. Moshe did not ask Pharaoh to "Let my people go." Rather, he said in the name of the Creator, "Let My people go so they can serve Me." We could not leave our servitude to Pharaoh without accepting the kingship of the Creator. The primary departure from *Mitzrayim* actually came through the offering of the *korban Pesach* (the Passover offering), the first act of service done by the Jewish people to the Creator. See *Rashi, Bemidbar* 41:41, that implies the departure from *Mitzrayim* came on the day the *korban Pesach* was offered, though it was the day before the actual physical departure. See also Chapter 7, p. 104.

36. Ramchal, *Derech HaShem* 1:3:2.

a loss of self. We don't usually feel that way when we are following our inclinations,[37] because when we become subject to our physical being we also enter the skewed worldview of a physically determined world.[38] But our worldview does not change reality — only our understanding and experience of it.

For example, would we say that a person who decides he is a chicken and squats under a table squawking is affirming his unique individuality by making this choice? Presumably we can all agree that such a person is mad. If we had clarity on what we really are, we would view the choice of following our physical inclinations as a similar insanity. Since our body exists to allow our spiritual root to take on expression in the physical world, it is like clothing for the *neshamah*. We don our body to come into the world, but it exists to serve the *neshamah*, not to define it.[39] When we follow the inclinations of our physical being, in effect we come to exist for our body. Metaphorically, this would be the equivalent of thinking we are mannequins, posing and posturing in life for the purpose of displaying our clothing. The image is bizarre, but captures the inversion of priorities that happens when we let our desires take the lead. Following after our inclinations is not a creation of self; it is a loss of self. We cannot create a self separate from God — only its illusion.

From this line of reasoning it is apparent that there is really no such thing as making a bad choice because pursuing the "bad" option does not come from who we are. We are following along, dragged after our inclination. And since our actions express and develop who we are, "choosing badly" signals the disappearance of the true self. Making a choice cannot be understood to be an act whereby we actively choose between two competing possibilities — because there is really only one legitimate possibility.

---

37. The first *shaàr* in Rabbeinu Yonah's *Shaàrei Teshuvah* makes a distinction between the occasional slip and consistent transgression. In the occasional slip, we may maintain our perspective, but if we consistently transgress we usually become party to the warped vision of a physically determined world. We will discuss this worldview in the final section.
38. See Chapter 2, pp. 24–25.
39. See the *Peirush HaGra* to *Sefer Yonah* 1:3.

So what does it mean to choose? Choosing takes place when we are confronted with a moral decision and we act morally, affirming and actualizing our true self. In such a situation we can also be selfish. But being selfish is not "choosing" to be selfish. Rather, being selfish is declining to choose — foregoing the chance to assert our selfhood and instead passively allowing our self to be overwhelmed by elements external to it.[40] In any situation where there is a moral decision to be made, we either choose to be moral, that is, we actualize and create true self, or we relinquish the opportunity to choose and, instead, are washed away by our inclinations.

Since morality is determined by the Creator, the moral choice represents acceptance of the authority of God. Achieving the individuality necessary to accomplish the goal of creation, then, only occurs in the choice to submit to the Creator. It is the achievement of self because the Creator *is* the root of our true self, so accepting His law is experienced as expressing and actualizing our self. "Choosing" in the other direction, following an inclination, though it looks and feels like the ultimate affirmation of self in opposition to the Creator, is actually a resignation from choice and the loss of any truly independent being.

This is graphically illustrated in *tefillah*. We begin the *Shemoneh Esrei* by blessing the Creator and bowing before Him to show our subservience. When we come to the word "*Ado-noi,*" "my Lord," we stand up![41] Standing up is a sign of kingship — the one who rules stands up, the servants bend down. We become a ruler — we reach selfhood, free of any determination by anything foreign to the self — in the very declaration of our dedication and submission to the Creator. This also explains how our "I" can be part of the very name of the Creator — *Ado-noi,* my Lord. Since our "I" only exists in complete nullification

---

40. This passivity can be very active —gorging one's self, overcoming a competitor, giving a complex lecture to impress people, etc. But it is passive in terms of asserting selfhood, since these are acts through which our true self capitulates to an energy that is ultimately foreign to the self.

41. *Berachot* 12a.

to the Creator, our identity is that of a vehicle for His expression. We are part of His name because a name labels His expression into the world, and our very identity is defined by our being vehicles of God's expression.

Someone "choosing" to follow his inclinations can be compared to a governor who serves an authoritarian dictator who is out of sync with the democratic principles of a (hypothetical) free world. The governor appears to rule his province and personally senses himself to be in control. But he is deluded on two levels. First, all the governor's authority derives from the power of a dictator who has no genuine relationship with him; if any political expedience arises that requires the elimination of the governor, he will be killed. Power merely flows through the governor at the convenience of the dictator, without the governor having any intrinsic connection to it. Second, even the power of the dictator is illusory. The dictator controls the press so the governor sees the dictator as all-powerful and, therefore, thinks his own position is secure. But in actuality the dictator's reach is limited to the confines of his tiny country and runs counter to the much larger context within which his country exists and upon which it depends. The dictator clings to his rule only at the sufferance of his neighbors. As soon as the dictator ceases to serve a purpose, he will be washed away — his governor with him.

Someone following his spiritual root, on the other hand, is like the son of the king of the world. When the king gives dominion over a specific area to his son, the rule of the son is real and secure. Though the son's power also emanates from a source outside himself, he is a true representative of that source, for he is the king's son. He is an agent of the king because he himself is an extension of the king. Therefore the king's power is, on some level, the son's power.[42] And the king's power

---

42. The son will fill the place and continue the rule of the king in the next generation (See Maharal, *Gur Aryeh, Shemot* 1:8). In the case of our relationship with the Creator, *our* being is defined by expressing God into the world — we are *tzelem Elokim*, the image or expression of God.

is also real, for it determines the world rather than existing in a context that the king does not control.

INDEPENDENT DEPENDENCE

Have we sufficiently addressed the difficulty posed by selfhood and free will? Anyone who has made a genuine choice in life knows the satisfying taste of selfhood that comes in its wake. This feeling is a consequence of what we have called otherness to the Creator, which is the ultimate purpose of free will. Even if we choose to attach ourselves to our spiritual root and recognize our subservience to the Creator, our problem with free will is this very "otherness"! What does it help that we have submitted to the Creator; there is still an "I" who is submitting. Without this there is no receiver and the goal of creation has not been accomplished. For that matter, even when a person sides with his physical inclinations, what difference does it make if, objectively speaking, he is choosing to be a mannequin? Isn't our concern the sense of independent selfhood we experience? This is created whether or not the root from which it arises is false!

We can easily answer our question regarding the person who follows his inclinations. Internal experience that is not based in reality is meaningless fantasy. The person who "chooses" to follow his inclinations and tastes his being in that choice has defined his reality exclusive of the Creator and is therefore cut off from Him and true reality. In the extreme case where a person chooses this way consistently and this choice characterizes his whole person, it is hard to understand how he even continues to exist. He has made himself into a living cartoon; there may be color but there is no substance. The commentaries tell us that such a person has undercut the basis of his existence and requires special support from the Creator to remain within the framework of physical existence. This support is given to allow him the possibility of repentance or so that he can provide context for others to make real choices.[43]

---

43. See Rav Moshe Cordavero, *Tomer Devorah*, ch. 1, *Mi E-l Kamocha*, that the Creator sustains man to allow repentance. See *Shemot* 10:1–2, that the Creator uses people so that others can learn from them.

The question raised by the individual who is making good choices, however, is more difficult. Through the capacity of free will, he is *genuinely* attaining some level of being—that is the purpose of free will. What is the nature of the righteous individual's existence?

The "I" of the righteous individual is utterly subservient to the Creator, yet it still exists. That is to say, the "I" exists from itself in the context of the Creator's justice by virtue of its righteous actions. Through emulation it achieves a greatness of being resembling that of the Creator to the extent possible within the context of creation. But since, on the deepest level, the only thing with real existence is the Creator, the very reality of the self means it derives its existence from the Creator. We exist from ourselves yet exist from the Creator by virtue of our emulation of Him. How is this possible? How can our existence be supported by the Creator while maintaining its otherness?

Clearly the connection achieved through emulation works differently from the normal method of "cleaving." When we cleave, we participate in the greatness that is the Creator. But that method locates our existence in the Creator and so will not serve us here. By definition, we cannot be other to the Creator while having our existence located in the Creator! Here our existence is located in us—yet it is still derived from the Creator!

When we develop ourselves in emulation of the character and values we see in the Creator—that is, when we become a certain way because the Creator is that way—the qualities that we acquire are actually His qualities expressed through us. We are not copying Him; we are actualizing those aspects of ourselves that come directly from Him. Effectively, we become a branch after His root.[44] In freely choosing whom we become and creating ourselves, we specifically emulate the Creator's quality of creating and self-actualization. This makes us much more than a conduit, for we are a branch after His root where we, too, have become a

---

44. Ramchal, *Derech HaShem* 1:2:3.

root — an initiator and source in our own right.[45] We both resemble God as closely as is possible and the quality we resemble is the one which is His deepest expression in creation. We do not merely express a quality of the Creator. Rather, we become an expression of Him.

If the only thing that truly exists is the Creator, then everything that we perceive as having distinct existence is actually a distinct veil or hiding of the Creator. In the creative moment of the genuinely free choice, as we become a creator in our own right, we achieve self and some level of real existence. We achieve this because by being a true creator we strip to the barest minimum the extent to which our particular existence obscures the Creator. Rather than hiding the Creator, our being, through fully representing the Creator, is a vehicle to convey Him into the world almost unhindered, thus revealing the basis of our true existence. Because of our capacity to achieve this, the Torah describes us as created *b'tzelem Elokim*, in the image of God.[46] In the language of the Sages, the Creator gives Himself to us.[47]

THE METAPHOR OF HARMONIC RESONANCE

The physical world supplies us with a magnificent metaphor for the relationship between the Creator and a creation emulating Him through free choice. It is harmonic resonance.[48] A cellist stands in the back of an auditorium playing a single note on his instrument. The hall is empty of everything save a lone violin sitting on the distant stage. If the note the cellist plays is the same as the note to which one of the strings of the violin is tuned, he will soon find the violin playing along

---

45. This language of becoming a branch that is itself a root was heard from Rav Moshe Shapiro.
46. Rav Chayim Volozhin, *Nefesh HaChayim, Sha'ar* 1.
47. *Shabbat* 105a. The relevance of this source to our topic with its deeper understanding was heard from Rav Moshe Shapiro. See also *Shemot Rabbah* 33:1; *Avodah Zarah* 19a.
48. The metaphor of harmonic resonance is used to illustrate a different aspect of the relationship between man and God by Malbim in *Rimzei HaMishkan, Shemot, Parashat Terumah.*

with him even though no one is touching it.

This sounds mystical but, in fact, the physics behind the effect are straightforward. The cello is played by causing one of its strings to vibrate. There is a characteristic rate of vibration corresponding to each distinct note. We hear the cello because when its string vibrates it causes the air to vibrate at the same rate. The vibration then travels through the air, reaching our ear, which then hears the note uniquely associated with this specific rate of vibration.

The cello can be heard where the violin is, so the vibration is arrives there too. The violin string is tuned to the same note as that played by the cello. Therefore, it can vibrate at the same rate as the air carrying the sound of the cello. The air impinging on the violin string causes it to vibrate. It does this only because it can move in sync with the air disturbed by the cello. If a different rate of vibration was arriving — were the cello playing a different note than that to which the violin was tuned — the violin string would be unaffected, because it would not be able to vibrate at the rate of the surrounding air and so would not be able to absorb the energy from the air. Once the violin's string begins to quiver it sends its vibration to its soundboard, giving forth music from the violin.

A harmonic resonance is like an echo, but the interaction is more sophisticated. In an echo we hear the source's sound; it bounces off a flat surface and is simply reflected back to us. In resonance, however, though the energy is derived from the source and the sound produced resembles the source's sound, the sound is actually being created by the receiver. The violin is playing — the soundboard of the violin is being made to vibrate by the vibrating string of the violin; it is the violin that we hear. Yet all the energy is coming from the cello.

Resonance is also different from an echo because an echo is produced by any flat surface, whereas resonance occurs only when there is fundamental similarity between the source and the receiver — in our case, the string of the cello and the string of the violin are tuned to the same note.[49]

---

49. Emulation does not mean being the same. The violin is not exactly the same as the

Because it mimics the cello, the violin becomes, in a sense, an expression or representative of the cello. It does what the cello did, playing the music of the cello in violin style, powered by the playing cello. We hear an echo of the cello reverberating through the violin's own sound.

The relationship between God and man emulating God through free will parallels the cello with its resonant violin. God reveals an aspect of Himself into physical reality through creation. Existence radiates out from God and takes on expression in the various elements of creation. The reality of each element is the unique facet of God's revelation that it conveys. Man, through the creativity of his choice to serve God, becomes a creator and source, thus establishing self. This selfhood is an emulation of God (what we called earlier a branch after its root, which is itself a root). This emulation maximizes the extent to which man's being is a conveyor of the existence and revelation emanating from God. Because the emulation of God comes in the creation of self, however, it is not God we encounter in man — it is man. But precisely because we meet man we meet God, for it is man's selfhood that so deeply resembles God. Man shines with the Godliness he has attained and, therefore, reveals God. Though man expresses himself in his own words, it is the voice of the Creator that is heard resonating in those words.[50]

---

cello — the length and tension of the violin string are different from the length and tension of the cello string. The note each produces will have a different tonal quality, as one emerges from a violin and the other from a cello — they are different instruments. Still, the violin is tuned in a manner that is the equivalent for a violin of the tuning of the cello — both strings vibrate at the same rate. So, too, our emulation of necessary being is not and cannot be exactly like that of the Creator. We do not have necessary existence. But as we make our decisions, choosing to accept the rule of the Creator, our righteousness gives necessity to our own being as a result of the Creator's justice.

50. In the first four books of the *Chumash* every time we hear Moshe speak Torah it is the *Shechinah* speaking through Moshe's throat (*Zohar, Pinchas*). Moshe was a conduit through which the voice of God spoke. The last book, *Devarim*, is composed of Moshe's words (speaking at the command of HaShem, "like an agent filling the instructions of his sender" — Maharal, *Tiferet Yisrael*, ch. 43). Most commentaries understand this to mean that God commanded the specific words Moshe was to say, but it was Moshe who was actually saying them. *Devarim* is an intermediate stage and precursor to *Torah SheBe'al Peh*, the Oral

It is like meeting a strong-minded, independent young man who closely resembles his father in character. We say to him, "When I look at you I see your father." What we mean by that is not that we see the father; we very much see the son. It is precisely because we see the son so strongly that we think of the father with his forceful character, for we see the father in his son. By creating self, we profoundly emulate God and, therefore, achieve some level of existence; but that existence emanates from God for it is only because we emulate God that we achieve true existence — "God gives Himself to us."[51]

A SECOND PATH

The achievement of selfhood we have described so far is based on emulating God's quality of being from Himself. We do this through our own self-determination. But this can be treacherous for it lies tantalizingly close to the illusion of autonomy that our inclinations dangle before us. The snake tempted Chavah to eat from the Tree of Knowledge with the statement, "You will be [a *creator of worlds*] like God."[52] The temptation was so powerful precisely because of its proximity to what man was truly created to do — to be like God by being a *creator of himself*. We strive to emulate the necessity of God by developing ourselves and establishing our existence upon our own merit, rather than being dependent upon charity. But this is easily confused with a delusion of existence independent of God.[53] The snake seized on this subtlety to lead man to disaster. The Midrash teaches that the snake told Chavah that God ate from the tree to create His world, and she could eat from the tree and create in the

---

Torah, where, in the absence of prophecy, we not only say the words but must also choose the particular words through which Torah is expressed. Yet they remain Torah, God's instruction. *Torah SheBe'al Peh* is the ultimate resonance of God through man. See Chapter 14, pp. 271–272..

51. See note 47 in this chapter.

52. *Bereishit* 3:5 with *Rashi* there.

53. Rav Moshe Shapiro spoke of our attributing necessity to our own being. See Chapter 14, notes 86–87.

same way[54] — in other words, she could be like God to the point where she would become an independent foundation of reality, replacing Him.

In the last section of this book, we will look more carefully at how the snake and our inclinations function. For our present discussion, it is sufficient to recognize how challenging it is to distinguish the energies that motivate achievement from those that bring us to destruction and loss of true purpose.[55] Few are able to maintain the purity of genuine being that is transparent to its dependence upon the Creator and to stand strong against the delusion that we replace God — that, "the strength of my own hands has created this wealth."[56] For this reason, the path to gain connection to the Creator that we have been describing is that of the individual of supreme righteousness who does not fall; we will label this the path of Yosef. Throughout a life of astounding accomplishment, Yosef consistently credited the Creator with his successes, resisting all temptation to see himself as the source of his achievements.[57] This is

---

54. *Tanchuma Bereishit* 8, and *Rashi, Bereishit* 3:5.

55. The inclinations in man are corruptions of internal forces that actually exist (see Chapter 9). If the principal drive in man is to achieve existence through emulating God, then the primary corruption is to think we are existence by substituting ourselves for God. We can only do this because we experience ourselves as, on some level, necessary. In the last section we will discuss how the false experience of necessity expresses itself in the sin of acquiring the Knowledge of Good and Evil and how it founds the cultural medium of the final exile.

56. *Devarim* 8:17.

57. See *Rashi, Bereishit* 39:3, *Bereishit* 41:16. The primary act for which Yosef is renowned is his refusal to acquiesce to the advances of his master's wife. This represented and actualized a tremendous control over his physical desires. According to the emphasis we are placing on Yosef crediting the Creator with his achievements, the fact that his object of desire was specifically the wife of his master takes on added significance. Yosef's relationship with his various masters were each an echo in this world of Yosef's relationship with his ultimate master, God. (This was particularly true with Pharaoh.) Since a man's wife is his expression into the world and his honor, the wife of his master would also represent God's honor in the world. Just as Yosef resisted taking his master's wife for himself, he resisted taking away God's honor — he was constantly praising God and crediting all his achievements to God. There are opinions that Yosef eventually married his master's daughter (*Bereishit Rabbah* 85:2 and 89:2. For an alternative opinion, see Chapter 8, note 23). Continuing our line of reasoning, this would represent achieving the status of *melech b'tachtonim*, kingship in the lower realm as a representative of the Creator, which is man's true role.

the exceptional path. Most of us cannot do this without falling.

There is a second path, another paradigm for achieving relationship with the Creator — that of Yehudah. He provides the example of an individual who falls, admits to his failure, repents, and achieves greatness through his recovery.[58] The Jewish people are called *Yehudim*, after Yehudah, because this is the common and, therefore, the national path. We turn our attention now to understand this path.

---

58. Two of Yehudah's sons in succession married Tamar and died childless. Yehudah refused to give Tamar to his third son in Levirate marriage, fearing that son would die also. Tamar wanted to bear the kings of Israel so she masqueraded as a prostitute before Yehudah. Yehudah, not recognizing that the prostitute was Tamar, succumbed to the temptation and conceived a child with her. When it became obvious that Tamar was pregnant Yehudah was informed and condemned her to death, thinking she had violated her Levirate responsibilities. Tamar then produced signs that Yehudah was the father. Yehudah admitted what he had done under extraordinarily embarrassing circumstances, saving Tamar. David HaMelech issued from the line which came from the child Tamar bore with Yehudah.

CHAPTER 7

Rosh Chodesh and Repentance

R. Shimon b. Pazzi pointed out a contradiction: It says, "And God made the two great lights," but later in the verse it says, "The great light to rule the day, and the small light to rule the night."[1] What happened? The moon said before the Holy One, "King of the Universe! Two kings cannot use one crown!" He answered, "Go then and make yourself small." The moon protested, "King of the Universe! Because I said something legitimate, I had to make myself small?"... On seeing that the moon would not be consoled, the Holy One said: "Bring a sin-offering to atone for My diminishing the moon." This is what R. Shimon b. Lakish meant when he said: "Why is the verse regarding the goat offered on the new month written differently from the verses regarding the goat offered on other festivals? Regarding the goat of the new month, it is written, "A sin-offering for God,"[2] whereas with the goat offered on the festivals there is no mention of "for God!" Because the Holy One said: "Let this goat atone for Me, for making the moon small."[3]

THE CHALLENGE OF FREE will is a daunting one: to emulate God by determining one's self, while resisting the inclination to see one's self as the foundation of reality. Holding on to the clarity that we exist

---

1. *Bereishit* 1:16.
2. *Bemidbar* 28:15.
3. *Chullin* 60b.

only in our service to God stretches man to his limit and beyond. We are all on a level to struggle with this task, but few can be consistently successful. Our inclinations are challenging in their own right. And they arise from our physical being, whose influences are reinforced by our living in a world dominated by its physical dimension.[4] Failure at some point is the more likely outcome.[5] How, then, does free will help the average person and the nation as a whole?

Though the Jewish people cannot survive without fully righteous individuals, the nation itself is named for Yehudah, the person who fell but achieved greatness through his repentance. It is through repentance that the Jewish people as a whole redeem themselves and actualize their free will. To understand the connection between repentance and free will, we need to trace free will, at least as we experience it, back to its origins in the beginning of creation. This requires understanding the commandment of Rosh Chodesh, sanctifying the new lunar month.

THE CONFLICTING ROLES OF THE MOON

The mitzvah of Rosh Chodesh was the first command given to the Jewish people as a nation.[6] This is startling when we remember the significance of being first. Our surprise is increased when we compare it to the next command given to the Jews, by implication one of secondary importance relative to the obligation to sanctify the new moon. This was the obligation to sacrifice the Pesach offering in *Mitzrayim* (Egypt).[7] The Pesach sacrifice was the first act of service performed by the Jewish people to God and was, therefore, simultaneously our recognition of Him as our King and our induction into His service as a people.[8]

---

4. *Berachot* 17a.
5. See Maharal, *Gevurot HaShem*, ch. 60, that exile, a consequence of sin, is the natural state of the Jewish people.
6. *Shemot* 12:2. See also *Rashi, Bereishit* 1:1.
7. The command begins from *Shemot* 12:3. The actual command is *Shemot* 12:6.
8. Maharal, *Gevurot HaShem*, ch. 60. See Chapter 6, note 35.

We have said numerous times that recognition and dedication of self to God are man's purpose and root obligation.[9] We spoke about it in terms of *emunah* (faith). But *emunah* is inseparable from obligation to serve, when we appreciate the true level of our dependence upon God. *Emunah* necessarily includes within it a recognition of God's kingship.[10] The Pesach offering, then, should have been first. How could anything precede it? What is the significance of sanctifying the new moon?

The actual mitzvah to sanctify the new moon is our obligation to search the sky, after the old moon has disappeared, for the first light of the new moon. Those who sight it testify before the high court, who then declares the commencement of the new lunar month.[11] We can look to the prayer that is recited to commemorate the Temple sacrifices of the new month for some hint to its significance.[12] We find there an uncharacteristic concentration on the sin-offering that was brought on Rosh Chodesh. Bringing a sin-offering, in and of itself, was not unusual; every holiday required a sin-offering. But normally the holiday prayers only mention it in passing. On Rosh Chodesh the sin-offering is the focus of our prayer.

The unique significance of the sin-offering to Rosh Chodesh is confirmed by the verse that commands its sacrifice. In contrast to every other holiday, where we are merely told to bring "a sin-offering,"[13] on Rosh Chodesh we are commanded to bring "a sin-offering *for God*."[14] This deviation in the text is explained by the Sages with one of the most obscure statements to be found in the Talmud, cited at the beginning

---

9. In Chapter 2 we discussed that Adam's *first* obligation to eat from all the trees of the garden was, in fact, an obligation to develop himself as a being connected to God. This command to form a relationship with God is primary.

10. See *Mechilta, Parashat BaChodesh, Parashah* 6, and Maharal, *Tiferet Yisrael*, ch. 37 that associate the first of the Ten Commandments, which obligates us in *emunah*, with accepting God's Kingship.

11. See *Sefer HaChinuch*, mitzvah 4.

12. *Mussaf* prayer for Rosh Chodesh.

13. For example, *Bemidbar* 28:22.

14. *Bemidbar* 28:15.

of this chapter: God commanded the sin-offering of Rosh Chodesh to atone for His having shrunk the size of the moon during creation.[15]

To speak of atonement for God awakens a flood of questions, but before we can begin to unravel them we must understand the diminishing of the moon referred to in the passage. The reduction of the moon is hinted at in the *Chumash* in its description of the fourth day of creation. There it states:

> And God made two great lights: the great light to rule the day, and the small light to rule the night; and He made the stars.[16]

The Sages are troubled by the verse initially saying that God created "two great lights" and then saying that He made the "great light" to rule the day and the "small light" to rule the night. If He made two great lights, why does the verse suddenly speak of a small light? The Sages answer that originally God created the sun and the moon the same size, but when the moon found itself equal to the sun it protested, "Two kings cannot use one crown!" so God commanded the moon to shrink itself.[17] As well as an overall reduction in the moon's size, this resulted in its waxing and waning, creating the cycle that produces the regular appearance of a new moon. Thus the connection to Rosh Chodesh.[18]

This Talmudic passage raises many questions. First, what does it mean that the moon protested? How can the moon talk? When we see references in Talmudic literature like this, where something that does not normally speak does speak, generally it means the Sages are giving voice to the perspective on creation specific to the facet of creation represented by that particular element.[19] God orchestrates all the various

---

15. *Chullin* 60b.

16. *Bereishit* 1:16.

17. *Chullin* 60b. For alternative interpretations of the verse and their shortcomings, see Maharal, *Gur Aryeh, Bemidbar* 28:15.

18. See the blessing recited over the new moon.

19. Maharal says this in several places. For example, *Tiferet Yisrael*, ch. 24 and *Chiddushei Aggadot* IV, p. 93.

elements of creation to produce an overall result; in its totality creation is coherent. But each element has its role and perspective, pulling in its own particular direction; as individual pieces, various elements may even conflict with one another.

What was the moon's protest, "Two kings cannot use one crown?" In what sense were the sun and moon kings? At the time of their creation, the sun and moon were clearly assigned roles of ordering creation — they were placed in the heavens "to rule the day" and "rule the night."[20] The sun and the moon jointly establish the most basic structure of physical reality: time. Imposing order is called kingship, for a king rules — he determines the laws and, therefore, the order of the society that forms around him.

But if time was being structured by the light of the sun and moon coming into the world, and the moon was originally the same size as the sun — meaning it perfectly reflected all the light of the sun — then there was only one source determining the structure of time — the sun. Since the moon reflected the source light of the sun perfectly,[21] whatever light the sun produced the moon automatically conveyed to the world. The moon's effect on the world was entirely governed by the sun. The moon had the appearance of ruling, but did not determine anything.

The moon's actual function contradicted its apparent assignment. It was given the role and appearance of a ruler, yet it lacked the essence of leadership. It appeared to rule and yet decided nothing. It was this contradiction that the moon "voiced" to God.

God's response was to command the moon to reduce its size and initiate the lunar cycle of waxing and waning. At first glance, this appears to be something like, "You don't like the way I do things, take that..." But a moment's thought reveals that, in fact, God was answering the moon's principal problem. God introduced a new "decision" into

---

20. *Bereishit* 1:16.

21. See Rabbeinu Bechaya, *Bemidbar* 28:15, that even in the original version the moon was a reflecting light. Any other interpretation would have difficulty explaining why the moon protested and not the sun.

the order of creation, a new kingdom for the moon. Whereas before, the moon was a perfect reflector, which meant the amount of light reaching the world was wholly determined by the amount produced by the sun, now the light reaching the world was a consequence of two factors: how much original source light was available from the sun and how much the moon "decided" to convey to the world.

MAN AS GOD'S MOON

The Sages are not primarily interested in the moon in this discussion. To get to the underlying issue we need to identify the aspect of creation represented by the moon. The moon relative to the sun is what we might call a first receiver. The sun produces light for the world. But the moon receives it first and then conveys it to the world. The moon rules the night when the sun is hidden, but does so as the representative of the sun. In that role, it is pulled between the opposing functions of being a receiver from the sun and a provider or ruler for the world. In the original version of creation, the reality of the moon as ruler was sacrificed to maximize it as a receiver. The benefit was great light; the cost was that an essential aspect of the identity given to the moon by God was overshadowed. The change instituted by God in response to the moon's protest allowed the aspect of the moon as ruler to be more fully expressed, but only at the expense of the amount of light reflecting off the moon.

The Sages teach us here the conflict and resolution inherent in this position of first receiver. In its role as first receiver to the sun, the moon directly parallels man's role in creation relative to God. God is the sole source of light, reality, and sanctity for creation. The infinite God is not directly revealed in the finite physical world. Instead, He created a representative to convey His light to the world — man. Man is God's moon.

In the original creation of the Garden, God was so clearly revealed to Adam that the necessity of unwavering obedience was unquestionable. God's light flowed unimpeded through Adam in the form of the radiance of his *tzelem Elokim*. He was a perfect reflector, which gave Adam immeasurable glory — the Midrash states that before his sin the angels bowed to Adam, mistaking him for God.[22]

But man plays a double role: receiving from God and ruling over the physical world as God's representative. Adam, like the moon, found himself caught in a contradiction. The very clarity of God's omnipotence which propelled God's majesty through Adam unhindered, giving Adam regal splendor, precluded Adam making any decision about how to rule. In his role as king, Adam felt he lacked the essence of kingship — he seemed to decide nothing. The singular truth of God's reality was too compelling.

Echoing God's command to the moon, Adam chose to "make himself small."[23] He ate from the Tree of the Knowledge of Good and Evil and clouded his awareness of the Creator.[24] That very clouding blocked the free flow of *tzelem Elokim* through Adam, drastically reducing the glory emanating through Adam.[25] But at the same time, with God revealed to him less obviously, Adam gained a broadened capability of choice and, so, the essence of kingship.

The question of whether or not Adam was "supposed" to do the sin, or whether it was, in the overall scheme of things, good that it happened, is beyond our discussion.[26] For our present purposes, however,

---

22. *Bereishit Rabbah* 8:10.

23. See Ramchal, *Daat Tevunot* 72, for the connection of the moon to man in this *gemara*. It is worth noting that in the case of the moon also, the Talmud does not state that God made it small, but rather God said to the moon, "Make yourself small." However, in the continuation of the passage God seeks atonement for "making" the moon small. The language of "make yourself small" maintains the parallel to Adam.

24. See Chapter 16 for a full discussion of the sin.

25. *Chagigah* 12a.

26. Any change in the nature of Adam's kingship not only reflected upon himself. It also affected the accomplishment of his purpose, which was to convey the kingship of God. Before the sin, God's kingship showed directly through Adam — Adam's individuality disappeared in the flood of *tzelem Elokim* that emanated through him. Since our relationship with God was experienced through self-nullification it was based on the trait of *yirah* (fear). After the sin Adam, with his broadened scope of choice, made decisions that determined the world around him. He was a genuine ruler and, therefore, *represented* God's kingship. As we discussed in the previous chapter, this allowed man to echo the significance of God's being — that He determines Himself. Since the relationship was achieved through Adam

it is enough for us to recognize that in eating from the tree, Adam was disobeying God; he was explicitly told not to do it. The underlying content of all of God's commands is that we should "choose life,"[27] meaning connection to God, the source of life. Adam, in eating from the tree, was consciously disobeying God and, therefore, moving away from Him — which is moving toward death. Furthermore, in justifying his decision to eat contrary to God's command, Adam was equating his understanding of reality with God's understanding, for which the Sages declare him a heretic.[28]

God, however, is the source and ruler of everything. Nothing exists outside of His creation, including evil.[29] Necessarily, if the sin happened, it must eventually lead to good. Creation is like a circle: whether we run toward God or we run away from God, we are always running toward God. It is merely a question of how indirect a path we take. God commanded a relationship of limited free will, roughly equivalent to that of a mother with her suckling infant where connection is based primarily on the merging of the child with the mother through the child's lack of distinct self.[30] Adam chose instead a relationship based on a broadened capacity for choice, roughly equivalent to that of a mother with her adult daughter, now a mother in her own right, who connects through emulation.[31]

CHOOSING SELF, THE ESSENCE OF KINGSHIP

Let us return to our passage from the Talmud. After the moon was reduced in size it again protested to God, saying, "Because I have said

---

establishing himself as an individual in relationship with God, it was accomplished through *ahavah* (love). In a moment we will see that in some ways Adam's sin actually increased his nullification to God through *yirah*.

27. *Devarim* 30:19.

28. *Sanhedrin* 38:2.

29. See *Yeshayah* 45:7.

30. A connection based on *yirah* — fear and self-nullification.

31. A connection based on *ahavah* — love, connection of two distinct entities through emulation. See note 26 in this chapter.

something legitimate, I needed to make myself small?" The moon's original problem was a contradiction in its position. It was given all the glory possible in kingship, shining with the intensity of the sun. But it lacked the essence of kingship, the ability to determine. God responded by giving the moon the ability to determine, but only at the price of the full glory of kingship. Since the moon was originally created with the glory of the sun, this must be its due.[32] The moon therefore protested, effectively saying, "Why should I have to sacrifice in order to right an imbalance not of my own making?"

The Talmud then records a series of attempts by God to console the moon, all of which are rejected, until God finally states, "Bring a sin-offering to atone for My diminishing the moon." What shocks us about this statement is that we understand the term "atone" to mean a wrong has been committed that requires amends, and such a thing makes no sense in association with God.

Though this is the way the word "atone" — *kapparah* — is used in common parlance, both Torah and Rabbinic literature give the term a broader meaning of "cleansing" or "removal."[33] In fact, the commentaries explain that this is its meaning even when used in relation to sin.[34] Atonement is not a process of making up with an offended God. Rather, sin creates a lack in the transgressor — lack is the true meaning of *cheit*,[35] which we translate as "sin." Atonement is removing that lack.[36]

When God says "Bring a sin-offering to atone for Me," the meaning is: bring a sin-offering to remove the claim against Me by the moon. Somehow the sin-offering on Rosh Chodesh is an answer to the moon's protest.

---

32. Maharal, *Gur Aryeh*, *Bemidbar* 28:15.
33. Ibid.
34. Ibid.
35. *Bereishit* 32:39. Yaakov said to Lavan, "I never brought you a *treif* animal, *anochi achateinu*, I bore the loss..."
36. This interpretation, including the proof texts, is taken directly from Maharal, *Gur Aryeh* on *Bemidbar* 28:15.

In establishing an offering on Rosh Chodesh, God is endowing the day that resulted from the diminution of the moon with a unique sanctity.[37] We can understand better how this directly "atones" for the loss incurred by the moon's shrinking if we return to Adam's parallel situation. Adam also began with the glory of ultimate kingship. But, because he lacked the opportunity to make decisions due to the clear revelation of God's truth, he distanced himself from God to obscure that truth. This necessarily reduced the intensity of the light of God flowing through him. But he gained the essence of kingship. The moon's protest against its diminution parallels Adam's complaint that he was placed in a contradiction and needed to act. He chose to broaden his choice in order to gain the essence of his kingship — the ability to determine his world. Why should he lose his glorious resemblance to God, which his original creation revealed is appropriate to him?

God's answer was the sin-offering of Rosh Chodesh. Though the Talmud sees an implication in the verse that the sin-offering "atones" for God, the sacrifice is actually brought to atone for the sins of the Jewish people.[38] Somehow our atoning for our sins "atones" or fills the loss incurred by dimming the moon and, by implication, the glory and resemblance to God lost from Adam due to his sin.

A sin-offering is an act of repentance. Repentance is a process where we look at our deeds and realize we have become someone who is not really us. We reject the self we have become; we push it away so that a new self can emerge, one genuinely representative of who we are in essence.[39] When we choose self through repentance we are not choosing to be someone else; we are choosing to be more ourselves. The root of our being emanates from the Creator and desires to reconnect to Him. The inclinations that lead us to transgression are not really us as much as they are attachments to us to allow free choice to be actualized. Following after the pull of the inclinations defines the self around

---

37. Ibid.
38. *Rashi, Bemidbar* 28:15.
39. See Chapter 5, p. 69.

something disconnected from its root; it is a loss of true self.[40] Repentance is reconnecting ourselves to our root through centering ourselves in an aspect of self that is still fully connected and subservient to the King.[41] When we become defined by that facet of self, we can look back at our deeds and truly say that the person we are now could not have done those things — the fellow who did that has nothing to do with us. We are servants of the King, not transgressors. Repentance, then, is a process of choosing self.

We explained earlier that man was given free will to provide the possibility of resembling God.[42] God is not externally determined. He is who He is from Himself. We approach this quality when we decide who we are in the world. From all the potentials and possibilities that lie within us, we choose what to actualize. Who we are, to the extent possible, comes from us. Whenever a person makes a choice, he is in some small way choosing and determining himself — we are formed through every decision. But when the choice is to repent, the entire content of the act is a choice of self. Repentance is the essence of choice, the fullest actualization of the potential to choose self.[43]

The consolation to man for his loss of external resemblance to the glory of God is the chance to repent, the opportunity to resemble God on an internal, essential level. This is all linked back to the moon because the waxing and waning of the moon represents man's choice to sometimes convey the light of God to the world and sometimes to block that light from the world. Adam's sin compromised his awareness of the Creator's omnipotence, giving us the capacity to turn away. This is represented in the diminishing moon; just as we "choose" to convey less and less of God's light, the moon conveys less and less of the sun's light. But because we can turn away we can also change and turn toward. This is the act of repentance. It is marked on Rosh Chodesh, for this is the

---

40. See Chapter 6, pp. 91–92.
41. Rav Chayim Volozhin, *Nefesh HaChayim* 1:18.
42. See Chapter 6.
43. Thus Rambam discusses free will in *Hilchot Teshuvah* (ch. 5).

day the moon turns around and begins to bring more and more of the sun's light to the world, representative of man finally putting the brakes on his pattern of blocking God's revelation through sin and instead beginning to reveal more and more of his Godliness. As we repent we bring a sin-offering.

We began this chapter by asking how the majority of the Jewish people can benefit from free will if, in general, it leads to failure. The answer is through repentance — like Yehudah, for whom we are named. Because we sinned, we can repent. In a sense, repentance is the ultimate act of self-creation. In a single act we fulfill all the potential of our free will to be who we are from ourselves. Whereas the purely righteous person builds himself painstakingly, choice by choice, the one who repents creates himself in a moment.[44]

We can ask, if repentance is so powerful, why do we value the righteous individual who does not fall — the Yosefs of the world? Though the one who repents has done in a moment what it takes the righteous a lifetime to accomplish in terms of emulating the Creator's quality of determining Himself, the repentant also lacks something. We spoke of another characteristic of God which free will allows us to emulate. God's existence has the quality of necessity. We can achieve an echo of this when we earn our existence through judgment, which also has the quality of necessity. The repentant lost this resemblance to God's necessity when he sinned, for his existence became supported by God's desire to show mercy rather than by the necessity of judgment.[45] Since resembling God's necessity is the foundation of our otherness to God which allows Him to achieve His goal in creation to give and the *ba'alei teshuvah* (those who repent) lack this, we return to our question, how does the repentant connect to God?

---

44. *Avodah Zarah* 17a: "There are those who acquire the Next World over many years, and there are those who acquire it in a single moment."
45. *Yalkut Shemoni, Tehillim* 25, *remez* 702. Repentance does not work through God's attribute of justice or *hanhagat ha-mishpat*. It is dependent upon the revelation of a higher level of God's relationship with creation.

Repentance does not achieve connection with God by establishing the *ba'al teshuvah* as other to the Creator, able to receive reward in the same manner as the righteous. Rather, repentance profoundly nullifies the *ba'al teshuvah* to the Creator because of his dependence upon God's mercy. Adam sinned to mask God's omnipotence so that his responsibility and the autonomy of his kingship would be increased by expanding the reach of his choice to determine himself. In this sense he became more independent and able to emulate God. But, paradoxically, the relationship became based on his dependence on God for his existence by requiring His mercy to blunt strict judgment. This accentuated the relationship of nullification represented by the suckling child.

At first glance it looks like the *ba'al teshuvah*, while connected to God, is certainly connected in an inferior way. After all, Adam's goal in sinning was to increase his independence and in some ways he seems to have achieved the opposite! But after more consideration it is not so clear. After all, though Adam chose to give priority to a relationship mediated through his independence, God, however, had commanded a relationship of nullification.

Furthermore, if we restrict our attention to the *ba'al teshuvah*'s connection to God we are only seeing half the picture. God's revelation in the world is also the goal of creation, as we will discuss in the next chapter. This is not to say that there are two unrelated goals to creation, for God's revelation and man's connection to God are flip sides of the same coin. Man connects to God according to how God is revealed in the world. The *ba'al teshuvah*, though he has fallen, catalyzes a new level of God's revelation that the completely righteous cannot reveal precisely because they are completely righteous. Through the process of repentance and forgiveness, the evil of sin becomes a cause for new closeness to God demonstrating that evil only serves God's purpose, revealing the totality of God's control of reality.[46]

---

46. Rav Chayim Freidlander, *Siftei Chayim, Mo'adim* I, *Tikun al Yedei Teshuvah*, pp. 291–300.

By this we do not mean to put the *ba'al teshuvah* ahead of the righteous. As we will learn in the next chapter, the righteous man's ability to stand above all the inclinations that compete for his attention and decisively choose service to God allows him to uniquely appreciate the singularity of God. The point is that the *ba'alei teshuvah* and the righteous use choice in distinct ways, leading to different relationships with God and different revelations of His unity. Both are necessary to the full achievement of God's purpose.

CHAPTER 8

Free Will and Our Perception of the Creator

"And Yaakov remained alone..."[1] R. Berekia said in the name of R. Shimon, "There is none like God, Yeshurun,"[2] should be read, "There is none like God. But who is like God? Yeshurun," referring to Yisrael Saba [our forefather Yaakov]. Just as it is written about God, "And HaShem will be exalted alone,"[3] so too in respect to Yaakov it is written, "And Yaakov remained alone."[4]

THERE ARE THREE ELEMENTS to our relationship with God: the relationship itself; we, who are trying to create a relationship; and God, with whom we are trying to relate. We began our discussion of free will with the statement that its actualization affects all three of these elements. Thus far we have learned how free will profoundly deepens the relationship we form with God and is the basis of our existence as individuals striving to develop a relationship with Him. But what about God, with whom we are trying to relate? Obviously we cannot change

---

1. *Bereishit* 32:24.
2. *Devarim* 33:26.
3. *Yeshayah* 2:11.
4. *Bereishit Rabbah* 77:1.

God Himself in any way, through our free will or otherwise. How can our free will affect this element of the relationship?

Free will does not affect God Himself. But it does affect how we perceive Him. If we are trying to develop a relationship with God we must, on some level, know Him. The only characteristic of His that we can comprehend is His Oneness — that He alone controls all of reality. Free will drives the process through which we achieve this comprehension.

The *midrash* that opens our chapter establishes that man can emulate God's characteristic of being "alone." When we acquire a characteristic in emulation of God, that characteristic is, for us, an extension and expression of its source in God. We are thus attached to Him through the characteristic we are emulating like a branch is attached to its root. Our emulation of God's "standing alone" allows us to connect to God's quality of being alone. What does it mean for man to be alone and what does it mean for God to be alone?

The verse cited in the *midrash* to establish that Yaakov stood alone describes the moment before Yaakov wrestled with the *malach* (angel) of Esav — the spiritual force that is his basis. On a simple level the verse tells us that when Yaakov fought with this *malach*, he was alone — he had no assistance. On a deeper level, we are only truly alone in a moment of genuine choice, for then we stand beyond all of the many forces external to our essential self that buffet us and choose solely from ourselves.[5] Moreover, as we clarified earlier, through the actions we choose to do we earn our existence, standing alone on our own merits rather than being supported from outside ourselves by God's mercy.[6] According to this understanding, when the verse states that Yaakov stood alone it means that he reached the point where he was truly from himself before wrestling with the *malach*.[7] Therefore, when the *midrash* speaks about

---

5. See Maharal's explanation of why matzah, the bread of poverty, is symbolic of freedom in *Gevurot HaShem*, ch. 51.

6. See Chapter 6, pp. 84–86.

7. The simple understanding of standing alone — that Yaakov fought the *malach* without aid — and the deeper understanding — that he was existentially alone — are two facets of the

Yaakov connecting to God's attribute of standing alone through emulation, it is speaking about Yaakov fully actualizing his free will. But what does being "alone" mean with respect to God? To what trait of God is Yaakov connecting?

The verse that the *midrash* cites to support that God is alone is "And HaShem will be exalted alone." This refers to the final revelation that God is unique in having true existence and, therefore, is the sole Author of all that happens in creation, having no partner, competition, or opposition. This is what we call His unity or Oneness. God is the one and only in terms of truly existing, supporting existence, and controlling existence.[8] In effect, God's Oneness attests to the fact that He stands outside of existence and contains it and everything in it.[9] The *midrash* is telling us that when we stand alone *in* the context of creation we connect to God's standing alone *outside* the context of creation.[10]

---

same reality. It is against the inclinations personified in Esav that we must choose to serve God in order to stand unto ourselves and merit our existence. We are able to do battle with those inclinations only because we stand alone — we act independent of any of the influences he represents, and we come with the weight of existence that this independence earns. According to the simple reading of "alone" as unaided, the continuation of the verse to the battle with the *malach* makes obvious sense. According to the deeper reading of "alone," the transition to the battle means that the *malach* attacked Yaakov *because* Yaakov reached this level and was ready to face the *malach's* challenge. The *malach* attacked to fulfill its purpose of pushing Yaakov to actualize the potential he had within him to overcome the *malach* and all that it represented. See *Rashi, Bereishit* 32:26 that the angel had to sing to God after the wrestling match. This indicates it had achieved its purpose by being bested. See also *Bava Batra* 16a that the intention of the *Satan* (who is the spiritual force of Esav) is to further God's will. Therefore the *Satan* would only attack when Yaakov could overcome him.

8. Ramchal, *Daat Tevunot* 36.

9. See also Chapter 4, p. 46 and Chapter 17, p. 318 where we discuss God's name *Makom*.

10. When we declare the Oneness of God in the *Shema*, we are accepting the yoke of the kingship of Heaven. So singularity and kingship are synonymous. See *Midrash Tanchuma, Bechukotai* 3 that just as God is the King in the upper realm, he gave man the opportunity to be king in the lower realm. This is equivalent to saying that just as God is One above, we are one below, unifying creation. See Maharal, *Chiddushei Aggadot* III, pp. 145,146 *adam nivra yechidi*, that man gives form to the world and thereby unifies it like a king unifies his people. A king unifies his people by providing vision, purpose, and structure around which everyone can both organize and unite. Man does this for creation, for without man physical

This oneness of God, with which we resonate through our own self-creation, is also the only quality of God that our conscious understanding can approach. We spoke in the beginning of the book about the need to bring our bodies into our relationship with the Creator in the form of deeds — mitzvot.[11] But including our bodies was in addition to the obvious need to include our minds. Our awareness is not synonymous with our self but it is certainly central to who we are and is essential to achieving attachment of our selves to others. If we are creating a relationship with God we must, on some level, know Him. The only attribute of God we can know is His Oneness.

Since God created existence to achieve a full relationship with man, creation must allow for the involvement of our understanding in that relationship. Since Oneness is the only quality of God to which our understanding has access, the purpose of creation is to reveal this attribute of God.[12] Therefore, when man actualizes his free will to stand alone and come from himself — which we explained earlier was man achieving his purpose[13] — he connects to the ultimate expression of God for which the world was created — God standing alone revealing His unity. But what do we mean when we say that man's intellect grasps this Oneness?

UNDERSTANDING GOD'S ONENESS

The primary way we use our minds in relationships is to understand whom we are relating to, which is problematic when talking about God. We cannot directly comprehend God or anything about Him, for He is

---

creation is a heap of disparate parts. Man, by uniting the physical world with its spiritual source (Maharal, *Chiddushei Aggadot* III, p. 148) connects all parts back to their unitary purpose. On another level, through man's understanding, the disparate parts of creation are unified into a cohesive whole. Truly connecting to the spiritual realm and truly having a personal vision to unify creation both require the exercise of free will.

11. See Chapter 1, p. 3.
12. Ramchal, *Da'at Tevunot* 34.
13. See Chapter 6, especially pp. 96–97.

infinite and we are not.[14] The commentaries state, however, that though we can never comprehend God, there is one aspect of Him that our understanding can at least approach, and that is His Oneness — that He is the singular Source and Basis of reality, and nothing but God exercises any form of independent control over any facet of existence.[15] This aspect is distinct from all others in that we do not perceive it directly but, rather, by negating its opposite.[16]

The process of understanding God's Oneness is roughly comparable to telling a child that his father is strong. To the child, that means Dad can pick up toy blocks easily. Because the child can barely do so, this is his only frame of reference for strength. When a third person comes and picks the child up, the child is overwhelmed by the person's strength, and his appreciation for what strength means is greatly enhanced. When he sees his father wrestle with the stranger and dispense with him effortlessly, the child is really impressed. The child does not directly comprehend his father's strength. Rather, he understands the stranger's strength and then realizes that his father's strength is not that but, rather, something immeasurably greater.

In the case of our effort to understand the Oneness of God, however, we must go beyond this because the point is not merely that God

---

14. When the Torah describes God as kind or powerful, for example, it is not describing God Himself. Rather, it is talking about the way God expresses Himself in relation to creation — the character of His revelation. Though this revelation is infinite and we cannot fully comprehend even this, what we can understand is useful for connecting to God, for it allows us to emulate God, modeling our expression into the world after His expression into the world (see Ramchal, *Daat Tevunot*, note 2 from Rav Freidlander; Rav Chayim Volozhin, *Nefesh HaChayim* 2:2; *Shemot Rabbah* 3:6). Ramchal in *Daat Tevunot* is the standard source for highlighting man's focus on God's unity. Some understand Ramchal to mean that the unity we strive to recognize is that of His expression into the world. Others understand him to mean the actual unity of the Creator Himself rather than merely that of His revelation into creation. The implications of this distinction are staggering. But we need not enter our head between these two mountains because, regardless of the conclusion on this point, the issue discussed in this chapter would be expressed in exactly the same words.

15. Ramchal, *Daat Tevunot* 36.

16. Ibid., 34, 38.

is infinitely more powerful, but that He is the *only* one with power. This requires a much fuller negation of the other. To achieve this we also, like the child in the metaphor, begin with a delusion that something has power to oppose God. After we appreciate how powerful this other thing is, we watch it collapse before God. The process then goes a step further, however, when, retroactively, we understand how the other's existence only served God's intentions. In this negation we appreciate that everything that is and all that happens comes directly from God, and whatever seems independent is no more than a disguised agent of the Creator.

We cannot have complete clarity of this reality as long as evil continues to exist, obscuring God's complete omnipotence.[17] But even while evil remains, we can approach this clarity by realizing how illusory is anything that appears to work against God. And if we have a series of successively more powerful experiences of seeming opposition to God disintegrating before Him, our understanding is projected beyond any appreciation of God's unity available in this world to a level that is beyond this world and our direct grasp.

YAAKOV'S RECOGNITION OF GOD'S ONENESS

Comprehending the Oneness of God, or even approaching it, stretches our understanding to its limits and beyond. From where do we get the capability to achieve this? Like all our other spiritual talents, our Forefathers — Avraham, Yitzchak, and Yaakov — are our source. All the challenges that the Jewish people have faced or will face were confronted by one or another of them.[18] As they dealt with their challenges these forefathers created the internal strengths that we draw on throughout

---

17. Maharal, *Gur Aryeh, Shemot* 17:16.
18. This is the concept *maaseh avot siman l'banim*, that the deeds of the forefathers portend the experiences of their children. See Ramban, *Bereishit* 12:6 from *Midrash Tanchuma, Lech Lecha* 9.

history to face ours.[19] Where do we see our forefathers achieving recognition of God's Oneness and, thereby, creating this capacity for us?

The *midrash* that opens our chapter makes clear that Yaakov had a special affinity for this mitzvah. The *midrash*, however, speaks of Yaakov emulating God's Oneness, as opposed to actually recognizing it. We would expect that the resonance that emulation produces would prime Yaakov to recognize it also. But we need not speculate on this point, as the Torah makes clear that Yaakov, at the end of his life, achieved the deepest possible recognition of God's Oneness.

From the moment Yaakov became the sole root from which the Jewish people would arise, his life was an unceasing succession of exiles and trials.[20] He was chased out of Israel and his father's home by Esav.[21] He ran to the house of Lavan, where he was oppressed for twenty years. And upon his eventual return to Israel, his daughter Dinah was violated.[22]

---

19. See Chapter 4, pp. 56–57 for an explanation of how the efforts of someone in the past can affect others in later generations.

20. Yitzchak intended Yaakov and Esav to jointly found the Jewish people. Rivkah recognized that Esav had lost the ability to play his part and that, therefore, Yaakov had to assume Esav's responsibilities. She instructed Yaakov to take the blessings needed to fill what had been Esav's role. From the moment he took those blessings, Yaakov became the lone source of the Jewish people and his life of trials began. We can understand those difficulties as a consequence of Esav's failure and all that it implied and augured for human immersion in physical reality — the natural arena of Esav. Had Esav become the person Yitzchak envisaged, things would have been different. That is to say, theoretically, a path exists that does not require the suffering of which history is composed. But that is not the actual, expressed world. Esav's job does get done — by David HaMelech and his descendants . They are the children of Leah, Esav's natural wife. But they only succeed in doing it in the context of a world of extreme darkness and suffering.

21. Though the Written Torah makes no obvious reference to it, the Oral Torah derives that Yaakov spent 14 years in the house of Eiver, where he was able to build himself through Torah study in preparation for the times to come (*Megillah* 17a, *Rashi, Bereishit* 28:11). This was a reversion to his original identity as "a dweller in tents." But, in the context of his new responsibility of involvement in the world, this was its own kind of exile.

22. *Bereishit Rabbah* 84:3 enumerates these three trials along with the disappearance of Yosef as Yaakov's principal pains. The *Yalkut Shemoni* brings a version of this *midrash* that puts the test of Esav after the test of Lavan, which switches the focus from Yaakov's flight from Israel to the threat of his annihilation by Esav and his soldiers when Yaakov returned

When it appeared that he had passed all the tests that life required of him and a well-earned tranquility had finally set in, Yaakov's beloved son Yosef disappeared and was presumed dead. It is beyond our scope to trace the detailed development that Yaakov achieved as he underwent each of these trials and their parallel to the historical experience of the Jewish people.[23] It will suffice for our purposes to examine how Yaakov emerged from his final ordeal of the disappearance of Yosef with utter clarity that God is One.

Yaakov selected Yosef from among his twelve sons to receive the totality of his wisdom and to lead the new generation.[24] Yosef's half-brothers became jealous of Yosef and sold him into slavery. They concealed their act from their father Yaakov by feigning that Yosef had been killed by a wild animal. Yosef was lost to Yaakov for twenty-two

---

to Israel. The version of *Bereishit Rabbah* is more consistent with paralleling Yaakov's suffering to the Jewish people's history of exile. We can bring the two versions of the *midrash* together by understanding Esav's chasing Yaakov from Israel and Esav's opposition to Yaakov's return to Israel as parts of one process of depriving Yaakov of the Land of Israel.

23. The *maaseh avot siman l'banim* (see note 18 of this chapter) of Yaakov's four principal trials and how he grew from them to the four exiles of the Jewish people and how we grow from them is hinted to in the Midrash. See *Bereishit Rabbah* 84:3 and *Shemot Rabbah* 26:1. The parallel is seen most easily between the last sorrow of Yaakov — the twenty-two-year disappearance of Yosef — and the long fourth exile of Rome. See *Ohr Gedaliyahu, Likutei Vayishlach* 4 and *Likutei Vayigash* 1. See Chapter 20, note 66. But the exile of Greece and our reaction to it also obviously parallels the despoiling of Dinah by Shechem and what came from that experience. Though what happened to Dinah was a tragic blow, her brothers achieved an unprecedented *azut l'kedushah* (fierceness in defense of sanctity) in response when Shimon and Levi destroyed the city of her violators. Yaakov protected the daughter, Osnat, who resulted from Dinah and Shechem's union (*Pirkei D'Rebbi Eliezer* 37; *Yalkut Shemoni, Bereishit* 34:134; *Peirush Baalei Tosefot, Bereishit* 34:1). Osnat eventually made it to *Mitzrayim* where she married Yosef (*Pirkei D'Rebbi Eliezer* 37; *Targum Yonatan, Bereishit* 41:45). She thus, as well as becoming the source of two tribes and eventually *Mashiach ben Yosef*, was the grandmother of Pinchas the warrior priest (*Sotah* 43a), who fought to preserve the sanctity of Israel. This parallels the violation of the Jews by the Greeks — both culturally and physically — and the emergence of the Maccabees as warrior priests along with the achievement of a new kind of zealousness in our service to God.

24. *Rashi, Bereishit* 37:2 and Maharal, *Gur Aryeh* there; *Bereishit* 37:3 and *Rashi* there.

years, during which Yaakov assumed that Yosef was dead.[25] The loss of
Yosef was devastating to Yaakov. In addition to the profound grief that
normally attends the loss of a child, the disaster was compounded for
Yaakov by a prophecy he had: if all of his sons lived he would not see
Gehinnom (Purgatory), but if any died he would not even make it to the
Next World.[26] The imagined death of Yosef, then, meant to Yaakov that
he had also failed and lost his role in history.[27]

Twenty-one years later a famine forced the sons of Yaakov to go
down to *Mitzrayim* to seek food. The regent of *Mitzrayim* imprisoned
one of them, Shimon, and a year later threatened to take Binyamin, the
only full brother of Yosef, and Yaakov's remaining link to his deceased
wife Rachel. This sadistic ruler was dragging what was left of Yaakov's
life into complete collapse by threatening his children who were his only
hope for the future. When the breaking point was reached, news arrived
that not only were Shimon and Binyamin out of danger, but Yosef was
alive and he was the regent who was running *Mitzrayim*.

Yaakov journeyed down to *Mitzrayim* with his remaining family to
settle there and to see Yosef. Their reunion was an emotionally charged
affair. The Torah writes that when they finally met, Yosef broke down
and wept.[28] It is strangely silent about Yaakov's reaction to the meeting, implying that he did not cry. Why did Yaakov not cry? The event
certainly meant more to him than to Yosef. The Midrash answers that
he was not crying because he was busy reciting the *Shema* — the declaration that God is One.[29]

How do the Sages know that Yaakov was saying *Shema*? There is no
direct indication of this in the text. If he was saying something why do

---

25. *Bereishit* 37:23–35. See *Rashi, Bereishit* 37:34.

26. Ibid., 37:35 and *Rashi* there; *Midrash Tanchuma, Vayigash* 9.

27. This seemed to be confirmed by the fact that Yaakov had no prophecy during the entire
period of Yosef's disappearance — he was plunged into a depression by the loss of Yosef, and
without joy there is no prophecy (*Bereishit* 45:27; see also Rabbeinu Bechaya on that *pasuk*
based on the *Targum*).

28. Ibid., 46:29.

29. *Rashi, Bereishit* 46:29.

they assume that it was specifically *Shema*? If Yaakov's intention was to thank and praise God, why not *Hallel*? The *midrash's* statement implies that there was something in particular about this moment that made the declaration of God's Oneness singularly appropriate.

The key to understanding this *midrash* lies in remembering what it means to say that God is One. It is the declaration that God is absolutely everything; there is no other power but Him. With this in mind it is not difficult to understand how the Sages draw their conclusion that Yaakov was reciting the *Shema*. Yaakov had spent twenty-two years suffering with the knowledge that his chosen son was dead and that he, Yaakov, had lost his purpose. The life of his family then became threatened by what appeared to be a madman in *Mitzrayim* who seemed determined to destroy the future. The ruler of *Mitzrayim* was for Yaakov, in that moment, the personification of evil. Then the news arrived that this cruel despot was none other than his missing son, Yosef. Suddenly, all of Yaakov's sufferings were seen in their proper light. The threat to his children was needed to actualize the dormant love of the sons of Leah for the sons of Rachel, without which the Jewish people could not survive.[30] Yosef's exile brought Yaakov's family to *Mitzrayim*, where they needed to be to develop into a nation and earn the Land of Israel.[31] Yaakov's pain over the loss of Yosef was necessary to spur the brothers to action. His sense of purposelessness provided a context for his own personal challenge of remaining true to God despite God's apparent indifference or absence.[32]

The absolute personification of evil turned out to be the savior himself; all of Yaakov's suffering was exposed as the only vehicle by which he could achieve the goals set for him by God. God's unity was revealed. Yaakov reached an unsurpassed clarity that everything is from, and for, God. At that moment, the only appropriate thing to do was recite the *Shema* — declaring that God is One. The Midrash states that Yaakov effectively lived in the Next World — had complete awareness of God's

---

30. Hinted at in Maharal, *Gur Aryeh*, Bereishit 45:14.
31. *Bereishit* 15:8–16, *Bereishit Rabbah* 82:13; Maharal, *Gur Aryeh*, Bereishit 45:23.
32. *Ohr Gedaliyahu, Likutei Vayishlach* 4 and *Likutei Vayigash* 1.

presence — for his remaining seventeen years on earth, despite the fact that he was in exile in *Mitzrayim*.[33]

It is important to note that Yosef did not recite the *Shema* when he met Yaakov, even though he was also aware that the person who appeared to be all-evil was actually an agent of God. Knowledge alone was not enough. It was the experience of misunderstanding and the upending of evil's convincing control that energized the clarity. This is possible only with free will, which requires us to interpret our world and allows us to make mistakes. The resulting contrast, as we move from darkness to light, catalyzes a deepened attachment to God's singular unity. That attachment intensifies our awareness to a qualitatively different level of clarity.

NATIONAL RECOGNITION OF GOD'S ONENESS

Though recognizing God's Oneness is the purpose of creation and Yaakov reached a clarity that defined human potential for that recognition, history had not yet reached its conclusion. It is not enough for a single individual to gain it, even one as great as Yaakov. All of mankind must come to this understanding, and that can only come through the leadership of a nation that has achieved this awareness.

Yaakov attempted to give his clarity to his children so that, through them, it would reach the Jewish people. Before he died he assembled his sons to reveal the future. But when the moment arrived, his vision was taken from him. Yaakov suspected that his children did not merit the revelation. They reassured him, declaring, "Hear (our father) Yisrael, HaShem is our God, HaShem is One. Just as in your heart there is only One, so in our hearts there is only One."[34]

Yaakov's sons recited the *Shema* using the same words we do. But when they said the word "Yisrael" they intended it to refer to their father, whose name was also Yisrael. This confirms what we said earlier in the

---

33. *Tanna D'Bei Eliyahu Rabbah* 5.
34. *Pesachim* 56a.

chapter about Yaakov's special relationship to the mitzvah of recognizing God's Oneness. The sons added, "Just as in your heart there is only One, so in our hearts there is only One." This was to reassure Yaakov of their righteousness. But though this statement revealed what the sons had in common with Yaakov, it also highlighted the difference between them. While Yaakov's sons connected to God's Oneness in their hearts, the seat of *emunah* (faith), Yaakov himself also had God's oneness in his head, the seat of understanding. Yaakov succeeded in giving his children the potential to perceive God's Oneness, but the actual clarity could only be achieved through the kind of process that Yaakov himself had gone through.

To fully appreciate the Oneness of God, we as a nation must go through a series of experiences where we witness evil rise to power, then watch it evaporate before the Creator, serving Him in the process. Nationally we face this in the form of a sequence of empires. As each nation conquers us, we see the awesomeness of its strength. When it acts in a way that seems to go against God — for example, destroying His Temple — we are convinced that it operates outside the confines of God's will. Eventually, the conquering nation serves its purpose of pressing the Jews to repent and its power crumbles. The nation then disappears from history, revealing that it was no more than an instrument of God.

Our understanding of strength is expanded by our experience of the conqueror. Our appreciation for God's strength is enhanced by our realization that God's power is far greater than the conqueror's. Moreover, as the enemy resolves into a tool of God, we are left with a sense of the uniqueness of God's control. Our original illusion that the challenger following his selfish desires was as an independently existing force is the very illusion that, as it collapses in on itself, gives rise to a profound conviction that there is nothing but God. The stronger the foe and the greater our certainty of his independent, unassailable power, the deeper our clarity about God once the enemy disappears.[35] Free will, which

---

35. Ramchal, *Da'at Tevunot* 40.

allows for the initial error, is a prerequisite to the conviction created by moving from misunderstanding to clarity.[36] We will discuss in the next section how free will is also instrumental in creating the situations out of which our clarity arises — the process by which our sins bring the conquering nations upon us in the first place.

Our experience in *Mitzrayim* provides an example of how this works.[37] When Moshe first approached Pharaoh to demand the release of the Jews, Pharaoh's response was, "Who is God?"[38] When told that God is the all-powerful Source of being, Pharaoh countered, "The Nile is the source of *Mitzrayim's* existence. In this generation I am the personification of the force represented by the Nile. Therefore, I created myself."[39] Pharaoh revealed that his understanding of power was limited to the strongest thing he knew, which was himself. The Jews, as slaves to Pharaoh, were subject to Pharaoh's distorted view. That Pharaoh exercised total control over their lives with no conceivable escape from his grasp bolstered the illusion.

The destruction of *Mitzrayim* followed, with the Egyptians themselves, the grand defiers of God, playing their appointed part in the script by running of their own accord into the raging sea to drown before the stunned silence of the Jews.[40] The Exodus culminated in the Song of the Sea, where the Jews sang: "I will sing before God, for He is exalted above all those who are exalted."[41] The verse means: We thought *Mitzrayim* was exalted, but God is even more exalted than that. This verse makes clear

---

36. Ibid., 36. Ramchal states that the possibility of recognizing an alternative to God and intellectually rejecting it is enough to appreciate the unity of God. So *actually* suffering under the power of the seeming alternative—which only happens as a consequence of transgression — is not necessary to the process. Once we fail to recognize intellectually the falseness of the alternative to God, however, we are forced to experience its falseness, which is the process of exile and redemption.

37. See Rav Yosef Yehudah Leib Bloch, *Shiurei Daat* I, *Hashgachah*, p. 87.

38. *Shemot* 5:2.

39. *Shemot Rabbah* 5:14.

40. *Rashi, Shemot* 14:27.

41. *Shemot* 15:1.

that the greatness we recognized in God was a consequence of it being more than what we had attributed to the Egyptians.[42]

But the revelation of God's power during the Exodus went beyond vanquishing the Egyptians. We added in our song, "He has thrown the horse and its rider into the sea."[43] Not only did God destroy the people who rose against Him, He even threw down their source of strength — their horses.[44] The totality with which God showed His superiority indicated that there is nothing but God. The ten plagues prepared us for this recognition by revealing that every facet of existence — every means of sustenance, every power, every potential haven — is under God's sway and is nothing more than a means by which He expresses His will in the world.[45]

The revelation during the Exodus was particularly deep and sweeping because it inaugurated the relationship of the Jewish people with God. But as potent as the experience was, it was not complete.[46] The

---

42. See *Shemot Rabbah* 21:11. The formula we are developing here is: Our relationship with God is a consequence of the greatness we can recognize in Him. The greatness we can recognize is a function of the greatness we attribute to His enemy before God vanquishes it — the greater the enemy, the greater our subsequent appreciation of God. In Appendix 2, A Modern Gathering of Straw, we take a subtly different approach. There we say: Our closeness to God is definitive of us. When we are pulled away by subjugation to an enemy, a need to return to God is created in us. When the enemy is vanquished releasing us, we return to God. The greater the enemy, the greater the subjugation and distance from God. The greater the distance, the greater the need and, therefore, the greater the subsequent closeness. These two approaches are really the same process viewed from different angles.

43. *Shemot* 15:1.

44. See *Shemot Rabbah* 21:5 that the horse in the verse refers to the spiritual force of *Mitzrayim*.

45. The ten plagues undid the hiding of God resulting from *Mitzrayim*'s corrupt understanding of the ten statements through which the world was created. See Maharal, *Gevurot HaShem*, ch. 57.

46. During the Exodus, God revealed Himself through overwhelming miracles. The strength of the revelation was its weakness, for by utterly nullifying the natural world we could not see that nature is also an expression of God's will — and God's oneness requires that everything that exists serve Him. The salvation in Persia commemorated on Purim contrasts with this. There, we had a similar pattern of a seemingly invincible enemy who threatened the Jews. He pressed us to repent and was suddenly vanquished by God, with all his wealth and power transferred to us. But on Purim the salvation occurred without any visible disturbance of

cognizance we could reach of God's oneness was a function of the strength we attributed to the Egyptians before God washed them away.[47] The Jews in *Mitzrayim*, emerging directly from slavery, could survive an illusion of only limited independent power in the Egyptians before God had to invert the situation and reveal Himself.[48] That could only produce a limited appreciation of God's strength. The full revelation of God's singular omnipotence could only emerge from the destruction of a more complete power of opposition, which we could only face once we gained the strength to survive its onslaught.[49]

The internalization of Torah has given us the ability to maintain our identity and commitment to God, regardless of the power demonstrated by enemies blocking our recognition of God.[50] With that internalization has come a succession of kingdoms to conquer us that, taken together, constitute full opposition to God's singular control and that, therefore, provide the precursor and means to reveal God's absolute Oneness.

ILLUSIONS OF INDEPENDENT POWER

The commentaries identify five possible illusions we can have about forces or powers that affect reality independently of God; all of these illusions must be dispelled before we can have a full appreciation for God's oneness.[51] The illusions are:

(1) That forces exist that serve God, but have independent authority.
(2) That an independent source of evil exists that opposes the source of good.

---

natural causality, demonstrating that nature also exists to serve God. The commentaries look to Purim for an echo of the final redemption that will fully reveal that God is One.

47. *Seforno, Devarim* 16:3.
48. See Appendix 2, A Modern Gathering of Straw. We became obligated in the modern exiles by the sin of the golden calf. The calf was created by Michah. Michah was the part of the Jewish people that needed to be cleansed by the experience of enslavement in *Mitzrayim* but could not be because we did not at the time have the strength to survive it.
49. *Ohr HaChayim, Shemot* 3:8.
50. Ibid.
51. Ramchal, *Da'at Tevunot* 36.

(3) That nature is an array of forces that function independently of God's direct oversight and control.

(4) That laws exist outside of God to which He must conform.[52]

(5) That the forces and laws created by God to structure the functioning of creation can be manipulated by man for his own selfish purposes.

From the time of the destruction of the First Temple onward the Jewish people have faced a series of conquering nations, each of whose strength was or is founded on one of these illusions. As each nation's strength is broken, the illusory nature of its power is exposed. After they have all fully passed, God's Oneness will stand revealed.

The kingdoms were: Babylon, Persia, Greece, and Rome.[53] Babylon worshipped idols.[54] Yet, Babylon recognized the omnipotence of the Creator — Nebuchadnezzar, the king of Babylon, praised the God of Daniel, calling Him the God of gods.[55] The idolatry of Babylon was, then, a worship of agents of God.[56] The idols were worshipped because

---

52. Rav Freidlander in note 23 to *Daat Tevunot* 36 understands this fourth illusion to be that God is constrained by His own laws. Rav Zevulun Shwartzman (heard directly from him) understands Ramchal to view this fourth illusion as an extension of Greek *kadmut*, that there are laws that exist outside of God that constrain Him. We are following Rav Shwartzman here.

53. The word exile is typically used to translate the Hebrew term *galut*. The word *galut*, however, applies as much to being subjugated by another as to physical banishment — exiled from one's true identity, so to speak. The Sages thus apply the term to the Greek "exile" even though the Jews were not expelled from the land.

54. See *Daniel*, ch. 3.

55. *Daniel* 2:47. This was in the second year of Nebuchadnezzar's rule. This is evidence but not a proof, since we see Daryavesh (king of Media) also praising God in *Sefer Daniel* 6:27 after Daniel was saved from the lions and we are specifically contrasting Babylonian worship to that of Persia-Media. Persian (Median) idolatry, while recognizing one supreme god, thought that good and evil had independent sources (see note 58 in this chapter). But Nebuchadnezzar praises the God of Daniel repeatedly in *Sefer Daniel*, and the Midrash (*Vayikra Rabbah* 13:5) states that he included in a single verse the praises of God which David HaMelech scattered throughout *Tehillim*.

56. Nebuchadnezzar's destruction of the Temple was a means of controlling the Jews, not an attack on God. See Maharal, *Ner Mitzvah*, p. 17.

they were attributed independent authority. The success of Babylon seemed to confirm the existence of these forces. The Jews suffered the overwhelming strength of Babylon and learned to respect it, only to see it swept into oblivion by God through His agent, Persia.[57]

The idolatry of Persia was much more extreme than that of Babylon. Rather than recognizing independence in a servant of the One God, Persia recognized two sources of reality — that of light and that of darkness.[58] Through the strength acquired by worshipping these deities, Persia vanquished the mighty Babylon and built an unprecedented empire reaching from Africa to India.[59] There was nothing that seemed able to challenge Persia's power. Its control of, and disregard for, the representatives of God, the Jews, is recorded in the beginning of *Megillat Esther.* But the *Megillah* also testifies to the miraculous, yet quiet, way in which God utterly neutralized the might of Persia and steered it to His purpose. Haman was killed and Mordechai inherited his political and economic power. Esther became queen and bore Achashverosh a son, Daryavesh, who supported the return of the Jews to Israel to build the Second Temple in Yerushalayim.[60]

Eventually, Persia was overrun by a surging Greek army led by Alexander the Great. Alexander was a student of Aristotle and brought with him a vision of a natural world governed by laws that function independent of any relevant influence from God. Though Alexander consciously desired to impose this understanding upon the world, his success on the battlefield was seen by the Sages as an expression of Divine will. They state in the Talmud that when Alexander passed through Israel on his

---

57. See *Yeshayah* 14:22; *Megillah* 10b; Maharal, *Ohr Chadash*, pp. 62–63.
58. *Sanhedrin* 39a. This presumably refers to Zoroastrianism. This was the state religion of the Sasanians (see *A History of the Arab Peoples* [London, 1991], p. 9, by Albert Hourani), a Persian-based empire that controlled the area in which the Talmud was assembled throughout the Talmudic period. In Zoroastrianism, the Sasanians were reviving the ancient Persian religion that was current during the time of the Jewish exile to Persia-Media. Though believing in one supreme god, they attributed a separate source to the existence of evil (Wikipedia, Zoroastrianism).
59. *Megillat Esther* 1:1.
60. See *Rashi, Chaggai* 1:1.

way to *Mitzrayim*, Shimon HaTzaddik approached him in the clothing of the high priest. Upon seeing Shimon, Alexander got off his horse and bowed. His generals were alarmed and asked for an explanation. Alexander answered, "Before each victorious battle, a vision of this figure appears to me in my dreams."[61]

Alexander's dream revealed that Shimon HaTzaddik, or what he represented, was responsible for the success of Greece. The time had come for the Jews to meet the challenge of reaching toward God from the spiritual desert of a secular world. Alexander's victories were needed to provide that secular backdrop; he swept away the idol worshipping world of Persia and replacing it with a world dominated by the secular philosophy of Aristotle. But that revolution was only appropriate once the Jews could work with the new situation constructively. In effect, Shimon HaTzaddik led Alexander to victory because Shimon HaTzaddik personified this capacity to succeed in the challenge of finding God from within a darkened world. In his generation, as prophecy was disappearing, he provided the leadership to replace it with the Oral Torah as the primary medium of relationship with God.[62]

But after Alexander's death and the fracturing of his empire, Israel and the Jews became pawns in the jockeying for position between the resulting kingdoms. The secular culture of Greece changed from an ideological backdrop to an oppressive imposition. Cowed by a superior army and swept away by the thrill of the new Greek enlightenment, the Jews felt the overwhelming power, both physically and culturally, of Greece's scientific and philosophical advances. Vast numbers of Jews discarded their faith for the immediacy of Greece's rational vision and the physical abandon that accompanied it. The future of the Jewish people was in doubt to an unprecedented degree until the sudden rise of the Maccabees. With their 10,000 partisans, the Maccabees faced down 65,000 troops

---

61. *Yoma* 69a.

62. As heard from Rav Moshe Shapiro. The second *mishnah* of *Pirkei Avot* is the first recorded instance of an individual presenting Torah in his own name. Shimon HaTzaddik is the author of this *mishnah*.

and cavalry of the best trained and equipped army in the world.[63] In what was a staggering and miraculous victory, the irrelevance of nature when confronted by genuine faith was demonstrated. The hand of God was clearly evident. And for anyone who could still doubt the Divine origin of the victory, the obvious miracle of the Menorah was there to establish Who was revealing Himself at this time.[64]

Rome, who the Maccabees invited into Israel as a counterweight to Greece, soon gobbled up the country and its people. Originally pagan, the Roman conversion to Christianity transformed its brutal imperial rule of Israel into intensive religious persecution of the Jews. This stretched, with varying degrees of violence, over almost two thousand years. Erecting the New Testament upon the foundation of the Torah, the mantra of the Christian overlords was that, though God had loved the Jews, they were guilty of sin and God, therefore, was not allowed to forgive them by virtue of some rule of strict justice that obligated Him.[65] This limitation on the freedom of God effectively contained God within a context that stood outside Him, and, therefore, was prior to Him. This indicated a residual commitment to the Greek concept of *kadmut*, the eternity of existence — that is, with no beginning and, therefore, no absolute Creator.[66] The monotheistic influence of Torah that formed the basis of Christianity was reaching Rome distorted by Rome's Greek cultural roots.

The miraculous survival, development, and occasional flowering of the Jewish communities through two thousand years of sometimes horrific oppression and slaughter gave ongoing testimony to the inadequacy of this Christian critique. The recent, miraculous emergence of the modern State of Israel provided a decisive repudiation from Heaven of their doctrine.[67]

---

63. *History of the Jewish People; The Second Temple Era*, p. 71.
64. Maharal, *Ner Mitzvah*, p. 22.
65. Ramchal, *Da'at Tevunot* 36.
66. In *Physics* 1:7 Aristotle argues for the eternity of matter. See note 52 in this chapter.
67. For a neutral account of the inexplicable manner that the State came into being, see *The Siege: The Saga of Israel and Zionism* (New York: Simon & Shuster, 1986), by Connor Cruise O'Brian.

The final illusion of control separate from the Creator is man imagining that he can use the instruments by which God directly administers His world to achieve selfish ends. As opposed to the illusion of nature, where man sees himself manipulating neutral physical forces independent of God's oversight, in this illusion man thinks he can directly manipulate God. This represents the most extreme compromise of God's singular and total omnipotence. The example of this cited by Ramchal is of individuals during the Babylonian siege of Yerushalayim who thought to repel the enemy by invoking names of *malachim* (angels). They wanted to use them, God's immediate servants, to surround the city with walls of water and fire to protect it in spite of God's decree of destruction.

In our time, this example would most directly parallel the appropriation of *kabbalah* (mystical practice) by individuals who divorce it from the context of tradition and attempt to use it for selfish ends.[68] Though clearly representing a distinct category of violation of God's Oneness, if this were the only example, this fifth of five obstructions would be somewhat obscure. Presumably this category also includes any situation where we as Jews leave ourselves vulnerable and effectively rely on the covenant between God and the Jewish people to force Divine intervention to save us.[69] When we do so outside the context of any sense of meaningful identification with the covenant and its reciprocal obligation to God, or sense of gratitude, we are attempting to selfishly manipulate God.

The first two of the five illusions we mentioned — the idolatries of Babylon and Persia — have passed;[70] the idea that an idol would represent an independent power seems to us an absurdity. To some degree, then, the Oneness of God has been revealed. But the last three illusions remain. Though the ancient state of Greece is gone, its natural vision still has defining influence over the way we look at the world, so Greece has yet to be fully overcome. The implied limitation on God endemic to

---

68. Heard from Rav Zevulun Shwartzman.
69. See, for example, *My Mission in Israel 1948–1952* (New York: Simon & Schuster, 1951), p. 291, by James G. McDonald.
70. See Chapter 14, pp. 257–258.

the Christianity of Rome is also deeply intertwined with our thinking, as we will discuss in detail later.[71] So, though the Caesars have passed, along with, at least for the moment, overt religious oppression, Rome is still present. And we continue to identify ourselves as Jews — with all the expectations of God that come with that identity — without feeling a reciprocal sense of obligation.[72] These illusions of power independent of God continue to compromise our *emunah*. Still, our connection to Torah allows us to remain Jews committed to the service of the One God despite the harsh cultural context within which we operate. We continue to strive for a true relationship with God and to move history away from its present distorted view of power in order to bring the revelation of God's total control over existence.

*   *   *

The purpose of creation is to bring us to recognize the singular omnipotence of God. Our free will operates against the backdrop of history to achieve this. But what of the development of self we spoke about in previous chapters as the purpose of creation? Which is our true purpose?

Identifying two intentions is not a contradiction — both can be goals and both can be pursued simultaneously. In the next section, however, we will conclude that just as we must develop individually, we must also develop as a corporate national entity. Whereas individual development occurs over a lifetime, national development can only unfold through history. History is not merely a span of time. It has specific content through which we grow. That content could either catalyze our national development or reveal God's unity. But we have only one history — which goal is history structured to facilitate?

In the next section we will describe how national development, just like the revelation that God is One, requires that we experience a sequence of conquests by empires. These two goals, therefore, are achieved through the same historical context.

---

71. See Chapter 18, pp. 359–360.
72. See note 67 in this chapter.

On a deeper level, they are actually one and the same process. We concluded earlier that the true self we are developing is defined by its commitment to serve God.[73] Jewish nationality is no different — we are a nation centered on commitment to God.[74] In its full expression, that commitment requires our recognition that God is One. Conversely, deeper understandings of God can only be comprehended by deeper facets of the self — recognition, therefore, requires internal development.

The equivalence of these two processes is the message of the *midrash* that opens our chapter — through standing alone we emulate and resonate with God standing alone — the process through which we attain self is the same as the process through which God is revealed. We shed the exiles through which God's unity is revealed as we develop self because our development of self is synonymous with deepened acceptance of God's mastery. As we saw in *Mitzrayim*, it is this acceptance that frees us from all yokes based in this world.[75]

It is now time for us to examine the process of personal and national development and see how they progress in parallel with our emerging recognition of God.

---

73. See Chapter 6, pp. 91–93.

74. We became a nation through offering the Pesach sacrifice, which was our acceptance of the unity and kingship of the Creator. See Maharal, *Gevurot HaShem*, ch. 60.

75. See Maharal, *Gevurot HaShem*, ch. 36 and ch. 51; *Pirkei Avot* 3:5. In the next section, as we trace our internal development, we will discuss the parallel evolution in our ability to conceive of God and His relationship with reality. But it is easy enough even at this point to recognize how these two processes meet in the end. Our ultimate achievement of self comes through identifying that which is most deeply us — our "I" — with God. But before that "I" is recognized to emanate directly from God, we experience ourselves as independently existing through our egos. This sense of autonomy, which is the basis of the self before it is fully developed, is also the most profound challenge to the unity of God — if I exist, there is someone other than God. And, at least as the historical process winds down, there is nothing clearer to us than our own individual existence. We will see that to achieve our true self — to become a resonance of God — we must struggle against the desolate autonomy of our ego that fills our experience of self in our final exile to Rome. Until we achieve God's unity within, we will not perceive God's unity without.

THE APPLICATION:

Exile
and
National
Development

CHAPTER 9

The Structure of Our Choices

Jealousy, lust, and the desire for honor remove a person from the world.[1]

THROUGH FREE CHOICE WE create self, becoming a receiver of God's goodness and fulfilling the purpose of creation. There are two aspects to this self-creation: 1) through our chosen actions we merit our existence, rather than being dependent upon the Creator's charity, and 2) we decide how to develop our self rather than our nature being determined from without. In other words, that we exist and who we are both come from us.[2]

We must face concrete decisions in order to exercise the free choice through which we achieve these. As far as earning our existence is concerned, the determining factor is the morality of the choice. Since the

---

1. *Pirkei Avot* 4:21. The approach taken in this chapter and the next is similar to the one I used in *The Jewish Self* (Jerusalem, Feldheim, 1998). Some of the material may, therefore, seem familiar to those who have read it. I have, nonetheless, included it here because of important changes that have been made to the original material and as the proper introduction to new material that adds significantly to the approach used in *The Jewish Self*. The Sages tell us that it is much more difficult to concentrate on familiar Torah than on unfamiliar Torah, but both the depth of understanding attained and the reward received are greater (*Yoma* 29a; R. Eliyahu Dessler, *Michtav Me'Eliyahu* III, pp. 124–125).

2. See Chapter 6, pp. 80–87 from Ramchal, *Derech HaShem*.

Creator defines virtue through His commandments, this translates into obedience to the mitzvot. The details of the mitzvot are not relevant to this calculation. The righteousness of the act gains us merit and builds justification for our being, regardless of its specific content.

With regard to developing our unique character, however, it is the particular content of our choices that determines who we become. What are the choices through which we develop self? Who is the self we are trying to become?

We concluded in the first section that the root mitzvah, and therefore the essence and basis of all mitzvot, was the positive obligation to eat from all the fruits of Gan Eden. Combining the broader conceptual implications of the act of eating — that it fills a lack — with our awareness that the primary lack of humanity is our unfulfilled potential, we determined that the essence of all mitzvot is to actualize our deepest self. The mitzvot, then, as well as meriting our existence, are also the actions through which we develop our unique self, and choosing to do the mitzvot are the choices through which we create self.

The self we actually create has structure and detail as a consequence of the specifics of each mitzvah we perform. Each mitzvah is directed at a particular facet of our total person. Full development requires actualizing all our different facets through all the mitzvot.[3] The mitzvot, then, would seem to be our guide to understanding who it is we are striving to become.

Most of us, however, have not reached the point where we understand all of our choices within the framework of Torah and mitzvot. And even for people who have, the deterioration in our spiritual acuity resulting from our increased integration with our physical being long ago

---

3. See *Makkot* 23b that there are 248 positive commandments in relation to the 248 limbs that the Sages identify as composing the body. The body is the physical expression or shadow of the *neshamah*, each limb giving expression to a distinct facet of the *neshamah*. Each limb is, in turn, associated with a specific mitzvah through which the facet of *neshamah* connected with that limb is actualized. The whole self is actualized through doing all the mitzvot.

extinguished our ability to focus on the uniqueness of each mitzvah while we do it.[4] As we mentioned earlier, the prophet Chavakuk, coming at the end of the era of revelation, identified *emunah* as the basic purpose underlying all mitzvot and directed us to concentrate on this general intention when doing any mitzvah.[5] So even though the self we are trying to create is built through the mitzvot, the mitzvot themselves can tell us little more than that we are attaching ourselves to God and becoming faithful.

But though our identification with our physical being blurs our vision of the spiritual self we are moving toward, it allows us to clearly resolve the detailed structure of the physical self we are striving to overcome. Every meaningful choice is made against an opposing option, or rather, against an inclination that pulls us toward an opposing option. Otherwise, our capacity to choose is not active in the decision for the decision comes naturally.[6] The composite of all our inclinations, like a photographic negative, forms an inverse picture of the person we are trying to become. The opening *mishnah* of our chapter itemizing our primary inclinations therefore holds the key to understanding, albeit indirectly, the structure of the self toward which we are striving.

THE MIRROR OF OUR INCLINATIONS

Why do our inclinations neatly form an inverted picture of our true self? Though as we create self we must push against opposing forces to make our accomplishments meaningful, what is the mechanism that so precisely sculpts our inclinations to play this role?

We were formed by God as unfinished beings to give us an opportunity to create ourselves. Inclinations are born out of lack. So the very lacks within us that we must complete create our inclinations. Because those inclinations pull to reinforce our existing deficiencies, it is

---

4. *Makkot* 24a. We mentioned this spiritual slide in Chapter 2, p. 17 and will go into it in detail in the coming chapters.

5. *Chavakuk* 2:4.

6. Ramchal, *Derech HaShem* 1:3:1–2.

precisely against them that we must struggle to build our selves.[7]

How do our lacks give rise to inclinations? Before we are born, our *neshamah* has no association with physical reality and is, therefore, free of physicality's limitations, experiencing only the boundlessness of connection to its infinite Source.[8] When it is joined to our body before birth, it becomes party to the restrictions of physical being and can no longer maintain its full integration with infinite reality.[9] The *neshamah* experiences something akin to what a student feels when he arrives at boarding school and is first shown his dorm room, which is roughly the size of his closet at home; when he asks where the rest of his room is, he is politely informed that he will have two roommates. The sense of constriction or suffocation he feels at that moment, but on a vastly larger scale, is what our *neshamah* feels at the loss of its expansive boundlessness, generating a profound hunger to return to the Creator. This hunger powers the spiritual pursuits by which we reach back to God throughout our lifetime.[10]

But this yearning to return is prone to corruption, for it is not the only consequence of cutting the *neshamah* off from its infinite Source. We also lose clarity about where we are deficient and what will satisfy our need. Though ideally our physical aspect should merely serve the *neshamah* by providing a medium through which the *neshamah* can strive to recover its spiritual connection, initially our physical being pulls in its own direction. It co-opts the *neshamah*, or at least the attention of the self that arises from the *neshamah*, and directs it toward physical being in one form or another. We come to view our lack as one that can only be satisfied within the finite sphere of physical reality.[11]

---

7. See Maharal, *Gur Aryeh, Bereishit* 8:21.
8. *Niddah* 30b, and see Maharal, *Chiddushei Aggadot* IV, pp. 158–159.
9. Ibid.
10. *Yalkut Shemoni, Kohelet, ch.* 6, *remez* 972. See Chapter 1, pp. 1–2.
11. The term "physical" is not used here in its limited meaning of "material" but, rather, to contrast with spiritual. Physical refers to that dimension of reality that obscures its dependence upon the unitary Creator. This is the *hester panim* of reality, that which "hides God's face." In this context the expression "physical aspect" does not refer exclusively to the body

In the next section we will examine more precisely the structure of perception that our physical aspect presses upon us that creates this illusion.[12] For now, it is enough to recognize that our physical being's diversion of our awareness toward physical reality causes the self to interpret its desire for expansion as a physical, as opposed to spiritual, need.[13] This is what we experience as an inclination, and it comes in various forms, depending on the facet of self through which the desire is focused at the time.[14] Overcoming our inclinations through developing our self involves transforming each facet of our personality from one that commandeers the attention of the *neshamah* to one that serves as the *neshamah*'s vehicle of expression. This frees us to experience our longing to expand in its true form as a desire to return to God.

As our opening *mishnah* points out, our principal inclinations are lust, a desire for honor, and jealousy. There is a fourth — a sense of inadequacy. We will discuss in a moment why it is not listed in the *mishnah*. What are the components of self that, in their unfinished state, generate these inclinations? What is the proper role of these components in achieving our purpose of relationship with God and how do we bring them to completion?

THE DEVELOPING SELF

Lust is a desire for sensory pleasure revealing a component of self directly associated with our bodies that is in need of development. Honor is a desire for recognition and respect. We can desire to receive honor for various things and within specific limits this is legitimate; respect

---

but includes any facet of personality through which we can experience ourselves as independent entities broken off from the Creator. Even intellect, when not guided by a spiritual source and perceiving reality as self-contained, would be, in this sense, physical.

12. See Chapters 15 and 16.

13. This understanding is certainly true after the sin of Adam, when good and evil become mixed. The implication from the *Gur Aryeh* cited in note 7 in this chapter is that it is even true of the root inclination to evil prior to the sin.

14. For the connection of the various inclinations to specific facets of self, see Maharal, *Derech Chayim* 4:22.

that acknowledges our *tzelem Elokim* brings out our true identity and provides the basis for proper social interaction. In the context of our *mishnah*, however, honor refers to the need for recognition of our independence, power, and control that results from a corrupted sense of identity. Jealousy is a craving for some quality or thing that we could imagine possessing but belongs to someone else. In its most fundamental form it is our jealousy to usurp God's role of defining reality, demonstrating that the facet of our personality that holds the capacity to define — our intellect — requires taming.[15] A sense of inadequacy expresses a loss of self indicating that, beyond all these facets of personality, there is an essential self that takes on individual existence through them but can be lost and needs recovery.[16]

Our bodily energy, identity, and intellect are all physical aspects of personality — meaning they are anchored in the dimension of reality that hides our dependence on God.[17] They have expression in the world, as do their corruptions, the inclinations. Our essential self is not physical and only has expression in the world through these physical aspects. So also, the essential self's corruption – inadequacy — is only experienced through our physical inclinations, which is why inadequacy is not mentioned explicitly in the *mishnah*. It is, however, a distinct corruption because its source is different from that of the other three, and though we experience this inadequacy through the other inclinations, our experience of those other inclinations is radically different when it stems from inadequacy. With lust, honor, and jealousy in their simple form we identify and experience our *self* as these inclinations. When

---

15. See *Bereishit* 3:5 with *Rashi* there.

16. Maharal, *Ner Mitzvah*, pp. 11–15. Maharal in his commentary on this *mishnah* in *Avot* (*Derech Chayim* 4:22 cited in note 14 in this chapter) is also an important source for this discussion. But in *Derech Chayim* Maharal focuses on slightly different aspects of the inclinations as he divides them among the various facets of self. In *Ner Mitzvah* he is interested in how the connection of the inclinations to facets of our personality translates into the kingdoms that conquer the Jews. Since we will also develop this relationship in subsequent chapters we will rely here on Maharal's division in *Ner Mitzvah*.

17. See note 11 in this chapter.

the inclination begins from inadequacy, however, we experience a *lack of self*. These inclinations then fill the void because we have no alternate center through which to filter our reality. The passion and intensity of the inclinations is much less for our experience emerges from an underlying sense of emptiness.

These four aspects of self that we intuit from our inclinations — bodily energy, individual identity, intellect, and a root self — are identified by Maharal as the four basic facets of human personality.[18] Each was created for a purpose, playing a specific role in our overall task of making a relationship with the Creator. But each is originally encountered by us in an incomplete state and must be developed to fulfill its part in our humanity.

Our bodily energies are a consequence of our having material being. Material being allows us to exist as an entity separate from God — a prerequisite to relationship — and to perform mitzvot through which we cleave to God. We have already discussed how physical actions are essential to our relationship with the Creator, as our primary connection to reality comes through the material world.[19] Through doing mitzvot, we are also able to reach beyond the limitations of our understanding in connecting to the spiritual realm, for mitzvot performed out of obedience contain the Creator's intentions for the act, building us spiritually.[20]

Through our sense of autonomous identity we act upon and determine our environment. This lends us a quality of *malchut* (kingship) and allows us to cleave to the Creator through emulating His quality of kingship, as we explained in the previous section.[21] This is the aspect through which we experience our individuality and exercise free will, so it is primary among our physical aspects.[22] But it does not unto itself

---

18. See note 16 in this chapter.
19. See Chapter 1, p. 3.
20. Ibid., pp. 3–4.
21. See Chapters 6–8.
22. Both Maharal, *Derech Chayim* 4:22 and the Gra (*Peirush L'Shir HaShirim*) state that this facet, the *ruach*, is an individual's primary identity.

define us, for without our root connection to the Creator we would not have free will and our sense of individuality would necessarily be illusory.[23] And without our physical and intellectual aspects, we could not exist or function.

Our intellect is a tool that can allow us to see beyond the physical world we occupy and connect our consciousness with God.

Our root self is the point from which we emanate from God and through which we return and actually cleave to Him. Because of its freedom from physical causality, our connection to this point, combined with our sense of identity, allows for a capacity of free will and also provides the upward pull that is a necessary component to free will expressing itself. Our root self is our essence. But we are not synonymous with that root connection to God, for if there were only that connection we would disappear into the Creator and have no distinct being.[24] Our other three aspects, which are all physically based, make possible individuation, because physicality is a medium of division, in contrast to the unity of pure spiritual reality. They also provide a basis for the inclinations that pull away from the Creator. This pull balances the influence of our root self, enabling us to actualize our free will and achieve true selfhood.

Achieving true self — the one that echoes the Being of the Creator we spoke about in the previous section on free will — is dependent upon our prioritizing these four aspects of self. The three physically based aspects need to serve the root connection to God.

When we are first born, none of these facets of self have distinct definition. As we mature, they each develop in us in a characteristic order, with different aspects dominating at different stages in life. Since our anchor in this world is our body, and life begins when the *neshamah* is invested into that body, the *neshamah* is initially only a guest and we are defined by our physical being. Over time the *neshamah* strengthens

---

23. See Chapter 6, pp. 90–92.
24. See Maharal, *Chiddushei Aggadot* IV, p. 132, on *Arachin* 15a, that *tzurat adam* is *sechel ha-divri*.

and the body weakens.[25] Because of this, the aspect of self that defines us at any given point in our life ascends from the most physical to the least tangible, as the influence of the *neshamah* intensifies.

In our early years we are dominated by the influences of our material being. We have some sense of individuality and intellect, and even a spiritual sense — but only within the framework of our experience of bodily needs. As we first encounter our body with its energies it does not serve the higher purpose of providing a means for connection to the Creator through the root self. In its raw state we experience it as an end unto itself. As the dominant force in our personality, it centers the self in our material needs; our *neshamah*'s desire for expansion is directed toward the material realm, so that we strive to bring the world to us and consume it. This is the inclination for pleasure.[26] It serves as the first challenge we must choose to overcome in actualizing ourselves as a being connected to God. We must constrain our bodily self to its proper role as a means to actualizing our root self in individual connection to the Creator.

We are aided in this task by the continual weakening of our physical side with age and the corresponding strengthening of our spiritual side that slowly elevates the anchor of our personality. At a certain point along the way we gain enough strength to overpower the pull of our bodily needs and contain them so that they no longer control us.

Though it is the pull of the root connection to God that energizes this effort to contain bodily attractions and achieve self, when we succeed we do not suddenly become focused on our connection to God. Rather, our center shifts to our individual identity, the next facet up the ascending ladder of our personality. In this second stage our sense of individuality gains full potency.[27]

---

25. Maharal, *Ner Mitzvah*, p. 19.

26. See Chapter 4, p. 51 that pleasure comes through the expansion of self. For the concept that pleasure is a desire to swallow the world, see Maharal, *Ner Mitzvah*, p. 11.

27. If we do not directly master our bodily desires while we are still centered in our bodies, our development may become distorted by fixation on pleasure (a possibility we will discuss

As we first encounter this aspect, once again it is uncontained or quickly deteriorates into its untamed state once it becomes our center. It does not naturally experience itself as an emissary and emulator of the Creator in service of the actualization of the root self's connection to God. Rather, our sense of being an individual with power to determine our environment takes precedence, centering us in our awareness of self and presenting our desire to expand as a craving to expand the self through the exercise of power — to rule over others and gain the honor that is normally associated with domination. The root self generally lacks the force of being to stand up to an inclination in its moment of full strength.[28] This new inclination assumes the leadership of the self.

We are challenged to develop our sense of individuality. We must use our free will to contain it within its proper boundaries and role of emulating the Creator's *malchut*. Again, as our center continues to shift toward ever-more-rarefied aspects of self, the intensity of our awareness of self wanes, and we gain the ability to rein it in and experience awareness of genuine self in the context of our relationship with the Creator. But once again, just as the continuing ascent of our center eventually weakens our sense of individuality to the point where we can take charge of it, that same ascent also strengthens another aspect of self — the next one up in our personality — our intellect. Though intellect was created to connect beyond the immediacy of physical experience to the spiritual essence that lies hidden behind it, we first encounter intellect in its unrestrained state — or it quickly becomes unrestrained once it becomes the center of our personality. Though even less tangible than identity, it is still a consequence of our physical, detached being and naturally pulls toward itself, dominating rather than serving. Instead of providing

---

in the next chapter). But when our center shifts to our individuality, our physical desires may simply become less relevant. We can "grow out of it" without forcefully exercising our free choice directly against the inclination. Then the act of choice comes in the decision to grow up and move to the next stage. This is an alternate path to develop which we will discuss in Chapters 12 and 14.

28. See Maharal, *Ner Mitzvah*, p. 18, for a hint to this idea.

a bridge to our root self and spirituality, uncontained intellect seeks to define reality from its detached perspective without reference to God.

This is a more profound separation from God than the previous corruptions. Defining life around pleasure and power is a distortion of our relationship with God but is not a direct contradiction to that relationship. In the pursuit of pleasure and power, we can still recognize the preeminence of the transcendent realm — we just funnel our connection to a higher source through selfish energies. This is idolatrous — for the service is then ultimately self-serving; but at least there is service. Centering ourselves in the intellect, however, puts us in direct competition with the Creator. We appropriate to ourselves the role of God — we place ourselves in the position of the Creator by defining reality.[29] This inclination is most appropriately termed jealousy — wanting for ourselves what is rightfully God's. We will better understand the implications of this corruption when we discuss the Knowledge of Good and Evil in the next section.

The jealousy of the intellect highlights an important point. Though under the influence of the increasing strength of the *neshamah* we move continually to less physical aspects of the personality, this does not mean we become more spiritual. We are approaching closer to our final goal of becoming spiritual, but at each intermediate step we are actually farther from a spiritual self. This is because as the corrupt center of personality becomes more refined, our sense of autonomous significance increases, which inclines us to experience ourselves as existing independent of the Creator. Ultimately, our spirituality is a consequence of our dependence on the Creator,[30] so the naïve trust in God of a child relishing his chocolate bar is actually deeper than the sophisticated rebelliousness of a college student pouring over Nietzsche. But it is also true that a college student is closer to the life experiences that can eventually teach him real wisdom. This process will become clearer in the last section of the book.

---

29. This will be discussed extensively in the next section.
30. See Maharal, *Tiferet Yisrael*, ch. 24.

As our center rises further, we eventually gain the strength to contain the intellect and relegate it to its true status as a vehicle for connection to God. Rather than defining the world, we use it as a vessel to receive higher understanding. This frees us to occupy and identify with our root self.

THE STRUGGLE FOR OUR ROOT SELF

As we initially encounter our material aspect, identity, and intellect their significance is exaggerated, causing us to confuse these mere facets of self with the actual self. We confuse a servant with the king, leading to all-consuming experiences of pleasure, power/honor, and jealousy. What inclination initially corrupts the root self? What distortion can it suffer? The root self cannot be excessive in its appropriation of significance. It is *supposed* to define us; it is *supposed* to be king!

The perversion of the root self comes when its existence seems to dissolve. The root self emerges directly from the Creator and is anchored in unitary, spiritual reality. We experience it as melded with the Source of being. But even as we come to identify our self with this spiritual connection, our physically based aspects continue to pull us to locate reality in the physical realm and in our sense of individual detachment — a process that only intensifies with time as we explained regarding the intellect. Their pull is reinforced by our primary experience of reality coming through physical experience. These influences together undermine our emerging sense of a spiritual self, lending it a fictitious and illusory air. After having worked through all the other levels and finally reached our essence, that which should define and rule us seems not to be there. It is like going through the trials of the yellow brick road, finally reaching Oz, and pulling back the wizard's curtain only to find his room empty. This results in a profound sense of inadequacy.[31]

---

31. This answer is sufficient for our present purposes. We currently lack the background needed to more thoroughly explain the origin of this sense of inadequacy. On pp. 269–273 of Chapter 14, however, we will understand that we can only occupy the spiritually based

This is our most painful corruption, bringing a sense of meaninglessness and inclining us to bitterly slander life and everyone around us.[32] The inadequacy that is its result can also produce an almost psychotic pride and arrogance as we strive to compensate for and protect our empty core. A kind of fragile paranoia pervades the self that leads to responses of extraordinary destructiveness when challenged.[33]

This corruption reaches more deeply into us than the others.[34] In each of the previous three we are distracted from our essence by

---

root self through active and continuous self-sacrifice. Since all other facets of our personality are no longer options, when we falter in this self-sacrifice we are left in complete limbo, which we experience as utter emptiness.

32. Maharal calls the essential self the *sechel ha-dibri*, literally, the speaking intellect or speaking soul. This is essential man because through speech we combine all elements of our being (See *Chidushei Aggadot* IV, p. 132 and p. 138, on *Arachin* 15a). The centrality of speech to our identity is confirmed by the fact that the moment man gained his uniqueness in creation by receiving a spiritual soul, he gained the ability to speak (*Targum Yonatan, Bereishit* 2:7). By speech Maharal means specifically communication that expresses a spiritual content — such as Torah or prayer; in *lashon ha-kodesh* the term for speech, *dibur*, is specific to this (heard from Rav Moshe Shapiro). Mere symbolic communication is attainable by animals and is not unique to or expressive of man. Thus, just as man's being combines spiritual reality with physical reality, and his purpose is to actively join these two dimensions, so, too, the speech that defines him connects spiritual reality to physical reality. The inverse is also true. We only lose true speech and instead utilize verbal communication as a weapon to destroy through slander when we lose our humanity—when contact with our *tzelem Elokim* is lost; our emptiness becomes reflected in the emptiness of our speech as we try to protect our bankrupt self through slandering others. See Chapter 15, pp. 289–290. In the next chapter we will draw the parallel between the inclinations that characteristically arise in man outlined in this chapter and the kingdoms that conquer the Jewish people through history. That parallel associates Rome with this fourth inclination to slander and destroy that arises from the dissolution of the inner self. Rome is represented in Midrashic literature by the pig — the animal that to all external appearances is kosher but in actuality is not, for it is lacking the hidden, inner sign of *kashrut*: chewing the cud. (See *Vayikra Rabbah* 13:5.) Rome develops a wholly external man who possesses all the external characteristics of humanity — one who uses speech — but lacks his defining spiritual connection — he speaks slander instead of Torah. We will analyze Rome thoroughly in the final section of the book.

33. We mentioned in the previous note that Rome is associated with this inclination. In *Daniel* 7:7 Rome is signified by a nameless, destroying animal.

34. See *Vayikra Rabbah* 29:2 from *Ovadyah* 1:4.

overindulging our expression. But at least the essence is still there exercising its influence. In the case of the pursuit of pleasure and power, our connection is tainted, but there is a connection. And even with the intellect, though it positions us in competition with God and effectively denies the existence of transcendence, its intangible nature leaves us open to spiritual influences. Experience retains a transcendent depth even as we attack the legitimacy of transcendence.

But when corruption reaches our root self, the connection to God and any genuine sense of that connection are undermined. Rather than struggling to recover our focus on our root self from the distracting pull of our other elements, as is the case when dealing with the first three inclinations, this corruption seems to require that we create the connection. We will discuss in the next section how we can achieve full relationship with the Creator from the midst of this precarious situation. For now, we have at least identified the natural process through which we make the choices that give form to our self and have gained some sense of the self we must create.

CHAPTER 10

From Individuals to a People: Free Choice and History

And the earth was formless, and chaos, and darkness was upon the face of the deep, and the spirit of God hovered over the face of the waters.[1] "And the earth was formless," this is the Babylonian exile... "and chaos," this is the exile of Persia... "and darkness," this is the exile of Greece... "upon the face of the deep," this is the exile of the evil kingdom [Rome]... "and the Spirit of God hovered," this is the spirit of the Mashiach... And in what merit will he come? "Hovered over the face of the waters," in the merit of teshuvah, which is compared to water...[2]

MAN WAS CREATED BY God to serve as that being with whom He would have relationship. Every facet of man's character was created for that purpose. These facets in their raw state pull man toward selfishness, but once developed, they each provide a unique avenue of connection to God. Until man fully actualizes all aspects of his character, complete relationship between man and God will not have been achieved.

There was a time when the totality of man was embodied in a single unit of humanity—the couple Adam and Chavah. Because of their exalted spiritual level, their personality was centered in a depth of soul that included all the potential of humanity, and they could, through a

---

1. *Bereishit* 1:2.
2. *Bereishit Rabbah* 2:4.

few actions, have achieved everything that is incumbent upon man. But their sin brought human personality to a more physical place, forcing its breakdown into numerous individuals and shattering the human task into a myriad of component parts.[3] So, though we have spoken about an individual's process of actualizing himself as a way of connecting to God, no single person is any longer capable of completing by himself man's purpose of achieving total relationship with God.

After Adam's sin the limitation of an individual is twofold. First, the point at which each individual's personality is focused includes only a part of human potential. And second, with the distinct facets of character separated out from one another, the development of different traits often requires incompatible circumstances. For example, we must choose the priority of the Next World over this one — i.e., the service of God over immediate physical pleasures. Only someone who has access to worldly delights — a wealthy person — is fully confronted with this choice. A destitute individual is never given the option of seeing his experience here as an alternative to defining life around God, for this world is, for him, wanting. On the other hand, we need to learn to be satisfied with what we have. Someone who is wealthy enough to pander to his every whim is not faced with the challenge of finding genuine satisfaction in his portion. Only a person who suffers lack faces this difficulty and can grow through his decision to be content.[4]

Because no single human life can present all the required scenarios that would allow for the complete development of all human potential, and because no individual personality encompasses all human potential, God's relationship with man is necessarily not with an individual per se, but with mankind as a whole through individuals. Across the breadth of a generation, every combination of strengths and challenges confronts

---

3. Pure spirituality is unitary. Physical reality is the medium of separation and breaks all aspects of existence down into their component parts. The deeper the center of human personality is thrust into our physical dimension, the more it breaks down into distinct individuals, each expressing less of the totality of what it is to be human.

4. Ramchal, *Derech HaShem* 2:3:1.

someone, somewhere, at some time, allowing for all the choices necessary to perfect every possible facet of our humanity as instruments for reaching God. God's relationship with man is a composite of all the partial connections achieved by individuals, and we individuals form a single collective entity connecting to God through the root of our souls, all of which emanate from Adam. In effect, God continues His relationship with Adam; Adam merely exists through mankind.[5]

MAN THROUGH HISTORY

Adam and Chavah's failure required the transformation of humanity from individuals to a multitude. After Adam, man first existed as a homogenous mass of people. In the end this also led to disaster with the Flood in Noach's generation and the dispersion of mankind from Bavel after the building of the Tower. Humanity was then further broken down into distinct peoples, each representing specific facets of Adam's character. God's relationship remained with all of mankind. But His direct relationship was channeled through the Jews who, while only one people among many, were representative of man because they were drawn from Adam's root spiritual core. By isolating the more spiritual part of man from the rest of him, the relationship with God could be distanced from the pitfalls of the past, reach completion, and then be conveyed to the rest of humanity. In this final version of man's relationship with God, the Jews as a people are the ones who must face the challenges necessary to catalyze the full development of humanity.[6]

---

5. Each one of us must play his part by facing a "hiding of God" tailored to press him to actualize the specific facet of personality that is his unique focus and therefore his unique responsibility. And though each of our tasks fits each of us perfectly, generally we do not know ourselves with sufficient depth to be able to understand why we were given the task that is ours. The distribution of responsibilities is based on the nature of our root *neshamah* and we have not had direct knowledge of this level of self since prophecy passed from human experience. We must accept the appropriateness of our situations and assignments on faith.

6. See Ramchal, *Derech HaShem* 2:4.

We have moved the focus of man's task from an individual to a generation, and from a generation to a generation of the Jewish people. But history also has a role to play here. The choices we face are not only defined by our unique combination of talents, resources, and challenges; the specific nature of the choice is also affected by the context in which we must make it. For example: achieving true faith in a world of idol worship is very different from achieving faith in a meaningless world. In the idolatrous world we must choose between faiths, in a meaningless world we must create faith. Or another example: learning to give in the midst of a pleasure-based society is a different challenge than learning to give in a power-based society. In a pleasure-based society our own desires are reinforced by our surroundings and we must struggle against our inclination to keep what we have for our own gratification. In a power-based society, on the other hand, giving can enhance influence. The challenge of giving is quite different in these two contexts.

To fully actualize all aspects of human potential, then, we must experience every choice against every backdrop, which means facing each of our inclinations against cultural settings dominated by each of those very inclinations. This requires incompatible social contexts. Therefore, just as one person cannot face every test because different tests require contradictory circumstances, so, too, no single generation can face the full gamut of tests because different tests require conflicting cultural settings. So to face every permutation of test and achieve full relationship with God, the composite relationship with the Jewish people must be assembled across the length of history.

THE CULTURAL CONTEXT OF THE KINGDOMS

The various cultural contexts the Jewish people must face to fully actualize humanity are supplied by a succession of conquering empires. How do these various empires provide backdrops specifically animated by different inclinations? We mentioned a moment ago that mankind was broken down into distinct peoples. The individuals who form a particular people share an underlying trait, which then defines the collective entity of the people and its culture. We spoke in the previous chapter of the inclinations that confront an individual during the course of his development. If an individual does not master any one of the inclinations as it awakens within him, though he will continue to develop, his experience of himself and his world can become refracted through that inclination.[7] Fixation on a particular inclination, then, can define a person and supply the shared characteristic that unites a people and energizes their culture. It makes sense that those peoples dominated by an inclination should be conquerors. We spoke in the last chapter about the superior power these inclinations often have over the true self when they are at full strength.

Babylon, Persia, Greece, and Rome were each cultures mired in one of the four root inclinations we find in individuals: Babylon in power, Persia in pleasure, Greece in jealousy, and Rome in inadequacy and the arrogance and destructiveness that grows out from it. Across historical time these kingdoms sequentially conquer civilization, and with it the Jewish people, providing us with the cultural context necessary to fully actualize all facets of ourselves and our relationship with the Creator.

Rather than viewing the process of exile as individual Jews experiencing their lives within the context of foreign nations, the Sages guide us to view the process as happening to the Jewish people as a whole. Any true people have some degree of collective existence. Just as our conquerors are a collective entity of individuals sharing a defining similarity, so too we, the Jewish people who are experiencing the conquest, are an organic unit. Obviously each one of us also experiences his individual being and faces his own personal challenges. Even that, however, occurs within the national context, which profoundly affects and influences our individual experience. But on another level we also exist as a unified entity. This entity has a *neshamah*. It is the spiritual pool out of which all individual Jewish *neshamot* flow, and its

---

7. See Chapter 9, note 27.

expression in the world — its body, so to speak — is through all the Jews that are, have been, and will be.[8]

Just as individuals go through a process of growth and development, so, too, this collective entity of the Jewish people goes through a process of growth and development. The development of individuals is catalyzed by the inclinations we face and against which we choose relationship with the Creator, thereby actualizing our personality. So, also, the entity of the Jewish people must struggle against forces that pull us away from our connection to God. The equivalents of the inclinations on the collective level are the kingdoms that conquer us and, by introducing their foreign visions of what it is to be human, pull us away from service of the Creator. In the same manner that, as individuals, we eventually master our inclinations and confine them to their proper roles, so, too, as a nation we eventually overcome the cultural influences of these kingdoms and push them out of our lives, confining them to their proper boundaries. In the process we create ourselves on a national level as a people profoundly connected to God.

FOUR FACETS OF DEVELOPMENT

Modern Jewish history, beginning with the destruction of the First Temple almost 2,500 years ago, has been a back-to-back succession of four exiles — to Babylon, Persia, Greece, and Rome. The First Temple was destroyed by the Babylonians in 423 BCE,[9] and the Land of Israel

---

8. The *Mishkan* (Tabernacle) and Temple served as collective expressions of this "body." See *Malbim, Parashat Terumah, Rimzei HaMishkan*.

9. There is controversy over when the destruction of the First Temple occurred and, as a result, over any date that is calculated from the destruction. 423 BCE is the generally accepted date amongst Rabbinic sources; 586 BCE is the generally accepted date by academics. Dates help us orient ourselves, which is why I mention them. But the actual moment is not significant to anything discussed in this book — 423 BCE effectively means "a very long time ago" and it does not much matter for our present purposes whether it was 2,400 years ago or 2,600 years ago. If anything, since we will be emphasizing our distance from the First Temple and everything it represents, the academic date only strengthens our point. Subsequent

was all but emptied of her inhabitants, who were sent to Babylon. Persia eventually gained control of the Babylonian Empire, and the Jews were transferred to Persian sovereignty. Seventy years after the destruction of the First Temple, in 353 BCE, the Persian King Daryavesh, son of Esther, gave permission to complete the Second Temple, and a modicum of Jewish autonomy returned.[10] But it did not last long, as eighteen years later Alexander took the throne of Greece and was soon racing through Israel on his way to *Mitzrayim*. Though he himself was fairly lax in his supervision of the Jews, his death in 323 BCE brought us under the authority of the generals who inherited his empire and Greek pressure intensified, eventually leading to the Chanukah rebellion in 168 BCE. This brought a brief respite of sovereignty to the Jews, but soon the rule of our own leaders turned oppressive and was little different from foreign domination. The Romans then arrived, eventually destroying the Second Temple in 70 CE. That began an exile in which we still find ourselves today — Western culture is a direct extension of Roman culture.

The *midrash* that opens our chapter hints at the parallel between our history of exile and the process of self-development. In the *midrash* the Sages analyze the second verse in *Chumash*:

> "And the earth was formless, and chaos, and darkness was upon the face of the deep, and the spirit of God hovered over the face of the waters."[11]

They see in it a veiled reference to our exiles:

> "And the earth was formless," this is the Babylonian exile... "and chaos," this is the exile of Persia... "and darkness," this is the exile of Greece... "upon the face of the deep," this is the exile of the evil kingdom [Rome]... "and the Spirit of God hovered," this is the spirit of the *Mashiach*... And

---

dates based on the destruction are used here to understand sequence so the only concern is that we retain consistency in the dating system we use. A discussion of the date controversy is beyond the scope of this book; we will use the Rabbinic dates.

10. *Yirmeyahu* 29:10, *Megillah* 11b.

11. *Bereishit* 1:2.

in what merit will he come? "Hovered over the face of the waters," in the merit of *teshuvah* (repentance), which is compared to water...[12]

When the Sages find an allusion like this, it is not because of some superficial similarity, such as four words in the verse, four exiles. Rather, there must be an essential connection between the straightforward meaning of the verse and whatever the Sages find referenced there. When the verse states that the world was "formless, and chaos," it is speaking about stages that creation went through as it came into physical being. The word *tohu* in the verse, which we translated as "formless," refers to creation when it was raw matter, with no form whatsoever.[13] *Bohu*, "chaos," refers to the first introduction of form.[14]

That creation began as raw matter to which form was then applied is significant. Had creation actually come with form and matter unified, there would be no possibility for individual development — change would require the elimination of the original object to be replaced by a new one.[15] But the fact that matter had form applied to it in the context of creation means that there can be a process of evolution where there is a conserved entity that "throws off one form and clothes itself in another form."[16] The world evolves through process, passing through successive

---

12. *Bereishit Rabbah* 2:4. The whole text is: "And the earth was formless," this is the Babylonian exile, for the verse states, "I saw the land and it was formless and chaotic" (*Yirmeyahu* 4:23, prophesying the Babylonian destruction); "and chaos," this is the exile of the Medes: "and they were in a confusion to bring Haman" (*Megillat Esther* 6:14. The Medes and Persians ruled jointly, so the reference to the Medes is synonymous with Persia, as evidenced by the verse cited from *Megillat Esther* that describes a time of Persian rule. The proof comes from the word for confusion *vayavhilu*, which shares the same root as the word *bohu* translated as chaos); "and darkness," this is the exile of Greece that darkened the eyes of Yisrael with their decrees. Greece said to them: "Write on the horn of the ox that you have no portion in the God of Yisrael"; "upon the face of the deep," this is the exile of the evil kingdom for which there is no measure, just as there is no measure to the deep.

13. *Ramban, Bereishit* 1:1.

14. Ibid.

15. As heard from Rav Moshe Shapiro.

16. This phrase is commonly used in the commentaries. See for example Rambam, *Moreh Nevuchim* 3:8.

levels of completion that lead to the spirit of God hovering over the waters and, by implication, redemption. Connecting the exiles to this verse implies that they also represent a process by which creation — or more specifically, the Jewish people who have come to represent creation — suffer a succession of exiles through which they evolve from an unfinished state to a finished state.[17] The *midrash* identifies in the verse four distinct stages, revealing that the process of creation has, on a fundamental level, four stages. That the Jewish people suffer four exiles and that an individual develops in reaction to four inclinations merely echo this fundamental structure of development.

DIFFERENT FACETS OF OUR HUMANITY

This *midrash* conveys only the general role of the exiles as vehicles or engines of development. For the specifics of what kinds of changes they

---

17. Since we brought a proof from the simple understanding of the verse to the underlying meaning of the *midrash*, we interpreted the verse conservatively according to the classical commentary of Ramban — that the relevance of process to creation is learned from the terms *tohu* and *bohu*. But once we understand the intent of the *midrash*, we can return to the verse and see that the *midrash* is reading it a bit differently — that process is also learned from *choshech* and *tehom*, "darkness" and "deep," that they also refer to successive stages in the development of creation. According to the *midrash*, the verse teaches that creation began with amorphous matter. Form was then added, but initially it remained too general to have any actual definition. Darkness then followed, which was the stage when creation first became comprehensible, so that the hiding that darkness brings became relevant in that there was something to hide. "The deep" refers to another level of hiding — when physical creation developed to the point where it was an almost impenetrable barrier blocking man's ability to perceive reality as God's creation. "Darkness" and "deep" refer to the increasing articulation of creation as an object understandable unto itself without reference to God. In the previous chapter, we explained how, in the process of development, man increasingly experiences himself as a self-contained reality separate from God. Historically, the hiding of a transcendent source to reality began under Greece — who is thus referred to as "darkness" — but reaches its height under Rome. See also Chapter 12, note 14. Eventually, the vacuousness of Rome will become so great that it pulls God back into the world through the arrival of *Mashiach*. This is the continuation of the *midrash* — "'The Spirit of God hovered,' this is the spirit of the *Mashiach*." (See Maharal, *Ner Mitzvah*, p. 18.)

mediate, we must jump to the first explicit reference to the full set of exiles, which is found in *Sefer Daniel*. After exiling the Jews, the king of Babylon, Nebuchadnezzar, had a dream that so terrified him that he could not remember it when he awoke; all that remained from it was a profound sense of foreboding. The king demanded that his counselors tell him both the dream and its interpretation or die. Daniel, who had become an advisor to the king after being brought to Babylon, prayed to God for insight and the matter was revealed to him. He came before Nebuchadnezzar and told him the dream:

> You, O king, saw a great image. This great image, which was mighty and of surpassing brightness, stood before you and its form was terrifying. The image's head was of fine gold, its breast and arms were of silver, its belly and thighs of bronze, its legs were of iron, and its feet were partly of iron and partly of clay. While you looked, a stone was cut out by no hand, which struck the image on its iron and clay feet, and broke them in pieces. Then the iron, clay, bronze, silver, and gold were all broken in pieces together, and became like the chaff of the summer threshing floors — the wind carried them away and they found no place to rest. And the stone that struck the image became a great mountain that filled the whole earth.[18]

Daniel then went on to give Nebuchadnezzar the dream's interpretation:

> This is the dream, and we will declare its meaning to the king: You, O king, are a king of kings, to whom the God of Heaven has given the kingdom, the power, the strength, and the glory. Wherever live the children of men, the beasts of the field, and the birds of the sky He has given you dominion. He has made you ruler over them all. You are this head of gold. And after you another kingdom shall arise inferior to yours, and then a third kingdom of bronze, which shall bear rule over all the earth. And the fourth kingdom shall be strong as iron, for iron breaks in pieces and subdues all things. And like iron that

---

18. *Daniel* 2:31–35.

breaks, so shall it break and crush all things. And as you saw the feet and toes, partly of potters' clay and partly of iron, that fourth kingdom shall be divided. But as you saw the iron mixed with clay so shall this kingdom have the strength of the iron. And as the toes of the feet were partly of iron and partly of clay, so this kingdom shall be partly strong and partly brittle. And as you saw iron mixed with muddy clay, the people of this kingdom shall mix themselves with the seed of men. But they shall not cleave one to another, just as iron does not mix with clay. And in the days of these kings the God of Heaven will set up a kingdom that shall never be destroyed. And this kingdom will not be left to other people, but it shall break all these other kingdoms into pieces and consume them all. And it shall stand forever.[19]

This dream occurred in the second year of the rule of Nebuchadnezzar,[20] which meant there remained another sixty-eight years to Babylonian domination before the Medes and Persians came to power.[21] This was years before the outbreak of the Peloponnesian War, when Greece was still a loosely defined ethnic group of rival city-states.[22] Divided against itself, Greece was far from any capability of becoming an empire. And it would be hundreds of years before Rome would pose a threat to the Near East.[23] So the identities of the three kingdoms that were destined to succeed Babylon were not yet evident, nor were they revealed prophetically through the dream or its interpretation.[24]

---

19. Ibid., 36–44.

20. Ibid., 2:1.

21. See *Megillah* 11b.

22. Based on the date 423 BCE for the destruction of the Temple. Since the destruction occurred in the nineteenth year of Nebuchadnezzar's rule (*Megillah* 11b), the dream would have been in 441 BCE. The Peloponnesian War began in 431 BCE. According to the academic date for the destruction, which is earlier, Greece would have been even further from becoming an empire at the time of the dream.

23. Rome defeated Antiochus III, the ruler of the Syrian third of the Greek Empire, in 190 BCE.

24. Sixty-eight years later, after the end of Babylonian rule in the first year of Daryavesh the Mede, Daniel explicitly prophesied the succession of Persian kings and the coming of Greece (*Daniel* 11:2–4). Rome was still not mentioned by name.

However, the dream does hint at something far more important — the nature of the societies that formed these conquering kingdoms. In depicting the kingdoms as different parts of a human form, the dream was revealing that these kingdoms would express unique cultural visions distinguished from one another by centering on distinct aspects of our humanity.[25] This is significant to us because in addition to conquering and controlling civilization militarily, these kingdoms dominated civilization culturally, making it over in the image of their particular vision. It was that aspect of the kingdoms that was conveyed in the dream because it was specifically this cultural domination that presented the Jews with their primary challenge.

To be subjugated militarily and politically is degrading and prevents the expression of certain facets of nationality. But by pressing upon us their alternative vision of man and society, these kingdoms threatened our existence as a nation. It is through Torah's understanding of these that we form the distinctive relationship with the Creator that defines us as a people. Without Torah's vision we have no center and our identity dissolves. The threat was serious, for the culture of each of the kingdoms was motivated by a powerful inclination that also pulled at us and was framed in the trappings of glory that conquest brings.[26] In response, we as a nation had to strengthen the facet of personality that each kingdom corrupted, integrating it into our connection with God, and grow, just as an individual must grow in response to the awakening of his inclinations.

How did this process work? Just as a poet looking at a flower will see beauty while a scientist will see biochemistry, so we all see the world as a mirror of our interests. The Babylonians filtered their understanding of the world through a corrupt form of the aspect of self that dominated their psyche — Nebuchadnezzar's dream associated this with the head — and created a society that reflected their vision. When Babylon

25. Maharal, *Ner Mitzvah*, p. 10.
26. *Berachot* 17a.

conquered us we were necessarily thrust into their world.

Just as the world we see is a reflection of ourselves, we are a reflection of our world. If our sight is focused by the dominant culture on specific aspects of our surroundings, it will affect how we experience ourselves. Entering Babylon's world pushed our internal center toward the aspect of self that defined Babylon—our head. But Babylon's world reflected the perspective of a corrupted head. We were under pressure to assimilate that vision, which necessarily entailed the corruption of our head. This required us to sanctify this aspect of our humanity. We had to forcefully choose to create relationship with God in direct opposition to the contrary pull of Babylonian corruption.

In another parallel to the process of individual development, when we succeeded in sanctifying the aspect of self dominated by Babylon, there was no respite. Persia took over the world and made over civilization in the image of reality and humanity as seen from the corrupted aspect of self in which they were centered — the equivalent of the chest of man. This placed us in their world and challenged us to sanctify the aspect of personality Persia represented—one lower in spirituality than Babylon's and further from God. The process continued until we were eventually conquered by Rome, when we entered the virtual feet of our humanity, the part of the body farthest from God and least sensitive to spirituality. There we remain still, challenged to recover spirituality from within the desert of Rome.

THE KINGDOMS AND THEIR INCLINATIONS

This understanding of the process of growth forced upon us by exile is still, however, very general. Nebuchadnezzar's dream told us that the societies that tested us represent the head, chest, thighs, and feet of humanity. But what are these aspects of our humanity? This was clarified in another dream in *Sefer Daniel*, this time a dream of Daniel himself.

> I had a vision by night, and, behold, the four winds of heaven stirred up the great sea. And four great beasts arose from the sea, one different from the other. The first was like a lion, and had eagle's wings; I looked till its wings were plucked off, and it was lifted up from the

earth and made to stand upon its feet like a man, and a man's heart was given to it. And behold another beast, a second, like a bear; it raised itself up on one side; it had three ribs in its mouth between its teeth and was told, "Arise and devour much flesh." After this I looked, and lo another, like a leopard, which had upon its back four wings of a bird; the beast had also four heads, and dominion was given to it. After this I saw in the night visions, and behold a fourth beast, dreadful and terrible, and extraordinarily strong with great iron teeth; it devoured and broke in pieces, and stamped the residue with its feet; it was different from all the beasts that were before it... I came near to one of those who stood by, and asked him the truth of all this. He made known to me the interpretation of this matter. These great beasts, which are four, are four kings, which shall arise out of the earth. But the holy ones of the most High shall take the kingdom and possess it forever and ever.[27]

In Daniel's dream the four kingdoms are each represented by an animal. The Torah views animals as embodying specific character traits in a purified form, which can be found in people in a more blended manner. For example, a goat is offered as a sin-offering because the basis of any sin is stubbornness, and stubbornness is the trait that goats exemplify — the Hebrew term for goat is *eiz*, which also means brazen. We offer the goat as a sin-offering because we are giving back to God that aspect of ourselves that strayed and led us away.[28] Whenever animals are mentioned in the Torah, they represent a trait. When Yaakov blessed his sons he compared many of them to animals.[29] In each case he was identifying the central characteristic of his son and blessing him that his unique strength should come to full expression.

When Daniel was shown the kingdoms represented by animals, he was seeing the primary character trait that was the foundation of each of their various societies. A lion embodies the quality of ruling — lions

---

27. *Daniel* 7:2–7, 16–18.
28. *Peshuto shel Mikra, Shemot* 35:26.
29. *Bereishit*, ch. 39; *Rashi, Bereishit* 39:28.

broadcast a sense of authority and assurance, a consequence of their control of their environment — thus lions are frequently used as symbols of kingship. Yehudah, who founded the line of kings in Israel, was compared by Yaakov to a lion,[30] there was a picture of a lion on Yehudah's flag,[31] and there were lions carved on Shlomo HaMelech's throne.[32] Babylon was represented by a lion because its society centered on a desire for power and the glory of ruling over others. The act that distinguished Babylon from all the other kingdoms was its destruction of the First Temple; this was done as a means to rule over the Jews by removing a potential focus for rebellion, not because of any intrinsic opposition to the Temple.[33]

Nebuchadnezzar had recognized the greatness of God long before he destroyed the Temple. In the second year of his rule, after Daniel interpreted the dream we cited earlier, Nebuchadnezzar bowed to Daniel and said, "It is true that your God is a God of gods, and a Lord of kings, and a Revealer of mysteries, seeing that you could reveal this mystery."[34] Nebuchadnezzar did not destroy the Temple until the nineteenth year of his reign,[35] and then only in response to the rebellion of King Tzidkiyahu.[36] That he would destroy the Temple of God for the sake of power in spite of his recognition of God's greatness clearly indicated his priorities. This inversion of values is particularly pointed when we remember that the goal of personal development is to harness our traits as vehicles to connect to God. In destroying the Temple, Nebuchadnezzar instead used his trait of power to destroy man's ability to connect to God, giving primacy to what should have been a means.

The second animal in Daniel's dream, a bear representing Persia,

---

30. *Bereishit* 49:9.
31. *Bemidbar Rabbah* 2:7.
32. *Megillat Esther, Targum Sheini* 1:2.
33. See Maharal, *Ner Mitzvah*, p. 17.
34. *Daniel* 2:47.
35. *Melachim* II 25:8.
36. Ibid., 24:20, 25:1.

signified a society focused on the pursuit of bodily pleasure: "Arise and devour much flesh."[37] Persia's infatuation with pleasure is clearly evident in *Megillat Esther*, which begins with King Achashverosh making a 180-day drinking party for his officers and servants that is followed immediately by another week-long bash for the citizens of the capital.[38] The Talmud derives from the text that Achashverosh intended more than just drunkenness at these parties when he put men and women together along with all the wine.[39] In the midst of the second party, Queen Vashti offended Achashverosh by refusing to appear unclothed before his guests and was put to death.[40] Achashverosh's subsequent method of choosing a new queen makes clear the dominant force in his life and, by extension, in Persian society.[41] Achashverosh collected all the most beautiful women of the realm and the one who satisfied him he took as his queen.[42]

The dream's third animal, a leopard, represented Greece. The leopard is renowned in Rabbinic literature for its determination. "Be brazen like a leopard," it says in *Pirkei Avot*, meaning be undeterred from your goal.[43] The leopard represents intellect, which is unyielding in its pursuit of understanding.[44] Determination is not an accidental quality of intellect, but rather is an expression of its detachment from material being; intellect acts upon its environment whereas material reality is acted upon.[45] The Greeks identified themselves with their intellect. The relentless

---

37. *Daniel* 7:5.

38. *Megillat Esther* 1:3–5.

39. *Megillah* 12a.

40. *Megillat Esther* 2:12–14; *Megillah* 12b.

41. See also *Megillah* 11a, that the bear in Daniel's dream represents Persia, for the Persians eat and drink like a bear and are fleshy like a bear.

42. *Megillat Esther* 2:1–4, 12–14.

43. *Pirkei Avot* 5:20. See the commentary of the Bartenura there. *Peshuto shel Mikra, Shemot* 35:26.

44. Ibid. One who is embarrassed and holds back his questions will never grow in learning (*Pirkei Avot* 2:5).

45. See, for example, Maharal, *Derech Chayim* 6:3.

character resulting from this identification revealed itself in the extraordinary speed with which Alexander spread the Greek Empire across the ancient Near East, swallowing up Syria, Israel, *Mitzrayim*, and Persia in the thirteen short years he ruled Greece before his death.[46] The Greeks used their intellectual focus to reject any received tradition and set out to define the world from the perspective of man's understanding.[47] This was an expression of jealousy for in this they took what was not theirs, usurping God's role of determining reality.[48]

The last animal in Daniel's dream was a nameless destroyer with iron teeth to match the iron feet of Nebuchadnezzar's dream. Iron was the material of destruction in the ancient world; from it the swords of war were forged.[49] Iron implements were not allowed in the construction of the altar of the Temple, for the altar existed to bring life to the world, and iron was used to bring death.[50] As opposed to the prior kingdoms that were represented by specific animals, implying they were each defined by a specific human characteristic however corrupted, Rome was

---

46. Maharal, *Ner Mitzvah*, p. 16.

47. Maharal, *Ner Mitzvah*, pp.12, 16. See Ramban, *Vayikra* 16:8 quoted in note 69 in this chapter.

48. See Maharal, *Ner Mitzvah*. Maharal associates Greece with several qualities. One is that of taking importance away from others, which seems to be a rephrasing of jealousy, but our approach may be a slight departure from his explanation. In *Ner Mitzvah*, Maharal also associates Greece with honor. These both represent facets of the motivating energy of the Greek personality. See *Sanhedrin* 109a for the different intentions of those building the Tower of Bavel. (The experience of the Tower is relevant for, like Greece, they sought to displace God using human intellect.) Among them were those who sought honor, saying that God could not have Heaven to Himself (honor) and those who made war on God, seeking to displace His Heavenly status and, in effect, take it for themselves (jealousy). See Maharal, *Chiddushei Aggadot* III, p. 260, on *Sanhedrin*. The jealousy aspect is the most appropriate one to emphasize for our eventual focus on the issue of control at the end of this book. Maharal in *Ner Mitzvah* also associates Bavel with both jealousy and honor. But obviously a feeling of jealousy is defined by what one is jealous of, just as a desire for honor is defined by the kind of honor one desires. The power focus associated with Bavel makes its jealousy and honor completely different from the jealousy and honor of Greece.

49. Ibid., p. 17.

50. *Shemot* 20:22, and *Rashi* there.

not represented by any recognizable animal. Rome does not embody a characteristic that is corrupted. Rome personifies the force of corruption itself.[51] Rome is the heel, the sensationless part of the body farthest from our spiritual center.

DECLINING HUMANITY

It is strange that Babylon would be depicted as the head and Greece as the thigh in Nebuchadnezzar's dream. Babylon was a barbarous idol-worshipping society whereas Greece gave us philosophy, science, and advanced culture — all activities centering in the mind. We might think that this is because Nebuchadnezzar had the dream, adulterating the vision according to his arrogance.[52] But Yaakov had an equivalent dream, which paralleled Nebuchadnezzar's relative valuations of the kingdoms.

> Yaakov's dream of a ladder with angels going up and coming down upon it[53] foreshadowed the dream of Nebuchadnezzar. "Angels of God going up" implies two "and coming down" implies two. These are the representative angels of the four kingdoms that will complete the rule of the nations. "Going up and coming down" is written in the verse and not "coming down and going up." They will go up and it will be an ascendance for them, but each will be less than his successor.[54]

As we move through the succession of kingdoms, we are moving further and further from our spiritual connection to God, which defines humanity. Babylon is the golden head because, for all its barbarity, its dedication to idol worship was at least a dedication to worship. The

---

51. See *Bemidbar* 24:20. Thus Rome is viewed less as a specific nation than as a force that corrupts other nations (*Bereishit Rabbah* 42:4).
52. All dreams have aspects that are irrelevant or untrue (*Berachot* 55a).
53. *Bereishit* 28:12.
54. *Bereishit Rabbah* 68:14.

worship was corrupted by a selfish slant, therefore Babylon was the head and not the essential spirit of a human being,[55] but it was still higher than the subsequent empires. Greece's focus on the intellect was actually a reflection of its lowliness and distance from God, for intellect was for them a substitute for spirituality. Therefore, Greece was represented by a less valuable metal and a less honorable part of the body.

We are building here the parallel between the individual development of a person over a lifetime and the development of the Jewish people over history. Yet, when describing our individual growth we spoke of man's center rising through the development process to increasingly ethereal aspects of self, whereas here we talk about successive kingdoms being less spiritual. With individual development, we also observed that as man's center becomes less physical he himself becomes less spiritual. We explained this paradox by recognizing that the self is actually a composite of the individual and his connection to the Creator. As our individual being becomes more significant, we increasingly sense ourselves as independent of any connection to God. Our overall level, therefore, declines. Greece's substitution of human intellect for dependence on God is a classic example of this. Their very greatness resulted in their lowliness.

We see here illustrated the fundamental point we made at the end of the last section: there is a connection between the aspect of self we are focused on and working on in a given kingdom and the clarity we can have of God while under its dominion. A shift in one results in a change in the other. Our two goals of developing ourselves personally and recognizing the complete unity of God are inseparable — the challenges against which we must work to achieve each of them come in tandem and take place within one integrated process unfolding through the medium of the exiles.

---

55. Maharal sees the shortcoming of Nebuchadnezzar's vision in the fact that the kingdoms were represented in a statue with focus on its material composition, giving significance to the physical vessel over its spiritual essence (*Ner Mitzvah*, p. 10).

NATIONAL DEVELOPMENT AND THE
REVELATION OF GOD'S UNITY

The four exiles compose a single great process with successive stages of increasing difficulty, squeezing out more and more of the potential that lies within us to create relationship with God — both in terms of our development and in terms of recognizing God's unity. Our first exile — to power-based Babylon — while extremely painful in terms of its slaughter and destructiveness, was a comparatively soft introduction to the hiddenness of God.

The desire for power is a body-based energy. We dominate through physically overpowering our opponent. The satisfaction it brings is an almost sensual experience — picture the football player raising his fists in triumph after a successful tackle.

The material reality from which our bodies are drawn is in its purity substance without form and requires the imposition of form from without to achieve definite existence.[56] Therefore, people who are governed by a physical energy like the desire for power while needing satisfaction of their desire, are not defined by it. The power seeker still needs to be personally defined from outside himself, just as matter needs form. Therefore, the pursuit of power does not contradict service of a transcendent source; in fact it requires that service. But it perverts selfless service of God to idolatry.

As physical desires go, Babylon's affinity for power was also less severely opposed to pure spiritual values than the other bodily-based inclination, lust. Despite the visceral satisfaction associated with a sense of power, it is still not a direct physical experience in the manner of sensual pleasure. Power resembles the kingship through which we emulate and connect to the Creator. It is experienced together with glory, which is a consequence of relationship with others and resembles the honor that comes with spiritual attainment. Lust, on the other hand, is experienced directly through the material world and isolates the one

---

56. Maharal, *Gevurot HaShem*, ch. 4.

who experiences it within himself. There is no honor in lust.

Of the exiles, then, the Babylonian worldview and psyche were the closest to those associated with the pure spirituality of Torah — thus Babylon was the golden head. We hear Nebuchadnezzar recognizing and declaring the glory of God. His last words recorded in *Sefer Daniel* are: "Now I, Nebuchadnezzar, praise and extol and honor the King of Heaven, all of Whose works are truth, and ways judgment. He is able to abase those who walk in pride."[57] God was hidden under Babylonian rule in the sense that the Temple was destroyed and the Jews exiled to a foreign land and culture. But just as Nebuchadnezzar was able to recognize and praise God in his Babylonian context, so we could pierce the relatively thin veil that Babylonian idolatry placed over a true understanding of God's workings in the world, and create relationship within the context of Babylonian society.

We could only do this by mastering the desire for power that perverted the Babylonian vision. We said in the previous chapter that this inclination is contained by channeling our sense of identity and control — the basis of the urge to power — toward emulating God's Kingship. In Babylon we did this, taking responsibility for our collective identity by developing it into a vehicle for achieving relationship with God and, through this, recovered clarity of God's omnipotence.[58] Once that was done our purpose in Babylon was accomplished. We left for Persia to enter a cultural context governed by the pursuit of physical pleasure within which we could take on the task of containing that energy.[59]

---

57. *Daniel* 4:34.

58. In the third chapter of *Daniel*, Chananiah, Mishael, and Azariah were thrown in a furnace because they refused to worship the idolatry that resulted from Babylon's perversion of power. This is weak as a proof that nationally we mastered this inclination. But at the end of this chapter we will ask questions which will lead to the refinement of our model and tighten its association with the known details of our historical experience.

59. On a national level we face the inclination for power before the inclination of lust while as individuals we face lust before power. We explained in the previous chapter that the order of the inclinations for individuals is determined by our being born primarily physical and becoming more spiritual over time — so the more physical inclinations dominate us

The desire for pleasure that dominated Persia was also a bodily desire. So, again, there was no direct opposition to recognition and relationship with a higher authority under Persian rule; Persia, like Babylon, was an idol-worshipping society. It was represented in Nebuchadnezzar's dream by the chest of man — which is still one of the higher parts of the body, located above the diaphragm that separates our crude physical functions from our more elevated ones. The chest was made of silver, a precious metal. But Persia was still a step down from Babylon in the sense that Persia's lust was baser than Babylon's pursuit of power and glory. Pleasure is a desire to receive; receiving is not a spiritual quality but, rather, a characteristic of material existence.[60] Because pleasure is a more base experience than power, its perversion of man's spiritual connection is more extreme. Though Persia's pleasure was still experienced as a connection to a higher source, that connection was shunted down a path that more deeply compromised the true nature of spirituality than had Babylon's desire for power.

True recognition of the spiritual Source of reality must recognize the unity of that Source — that nothing truly exists but the Creator, as we discussed earlier.[61] Even our awareness of ourselves as a distinct existence must be subtle, as we concluded in our discussion of free will.[62] The more one is aware of the distinct existence of his ego, the more the transcendent source he recognizes must be diminished and distant from true unity. Thus even the desire for power, since it also to some extent accentuates the experience of the "I," must bring in its wake some form of idolatry; for we cannot possibly relate to the unitary Source when we experience a pronounced self.

Pleasure, which speaks to a much baser facet of our humanity, gives

---

first. On a societal level, however, because we are not starting off as purely physical beings, the order of inclinations is determined by their forcefulness of expression rather than their degree of physicality (See Maharal, *Ner Mitzvah*, p. 11).

60. See, for example, Maharal, *Derech Chayim* 6:3.

61. See Chapter 8.

62. See Chapter 6, pp. 100–101.

rise to a much thicker experience of self. This requires that someone under the sway of lust must more deeply compromise his concept of Source to something even more removed from the unity of the true Creator than was the case under Babylon. Thus, unlike Babylon, where idols represented agents of the One God, Persian idolatry recognized good and evil as two distinct realities with two distinct sources—a much more extreme and debilitating form of idol worship.[63] Persia's more prominent experience of the "I" also provided a transitional form of awareness to the full ego-focused sense of man separate from God that was the basis of Greece's man-centered world.

But in spite of the extreme perversity of its idolatry, Persia was still a worshipping society and, as such, was sufficiently in accord with the Jewish worldview for the Jews to retain their cultural cohesion within its context.[64] The eventual release of the Jews from Persia signified the achievement of some mastery over the inclination toward lust and repudiation of the idolatry that characterized Persia. When exactly to mark this moment is not clear, as when the Jews started to return to Eretz Yisrael they did so only with the permission, protection, and financing of Persia. Once Nechemiah arrived in Israel, however, all the Jews there sent away their foreign wives[65] and a decisive break was made with idolatry.[66]

Having completed the task of containing our bodily energies and taking possession of the physical facet of our national character, it was time to move to the next stage of development. Under Nechemiah the Jews built the Second Temple. We will learn later that the primary purpose of this Temple was to provide a haven for elaborating the Oral Torah, our

---

63. *Sanhedrin* 39a; Ramchal, *Da'at Tevunot* 36. See Chapter 8, note 58.
64. Though the Jews needed to fight for their survival while in Persia, as recorded in *Megillat Esther*, that battle was initiated by Haman, an Amalekite, for reasons unconnected to Persia and its idolatry.
65. *Nechemiah* 13:23–30.
66. *Yoma* 69b. See Chapter 14, pp. 257–258, and *The Jewish Self*, ch. "A Moment of Favor".

analytic probing of the prophetic Torah.[67] Since our relationship with God defines us as a people, the increasing importance of the Oral Torah meant the anchor of Jewish personality on a national level was shifting to the intellect. It was only a short time before Greece arrived to challenge the Jews with a corrupted intellect and force us to take responsibility for this facet of character also.

As much as the Persian world obscured genuine relationship with God, the Greek exile represented a darkening of reality of a completely different order. Daniel in his dream of Greece depicted it as a sleek, swift leopard representing intellect. We mentioned that, paradoxically, Nebuchadnezzar pictured enlightened Greece as the relatively lowly bronze thigh of man. Daniel's dream focused on the elevated quality of the source of corruption. Nebuchadnezzar's dream, on the other hand, reflected the diminished quality of humanity experienced under Greece. Greece was the first exile where the corruption lay in our very connection to spirituality — in the intellect that bridged to the spiritual soul. In contrast to Babylon and Persia, where corruption was centered in a physical place and merely compromised our spiritual connection, under Greece that connection was, on some level, cut. As we said earlier, corrupt intellect will not accept definition from beyond itself, which is the very basis of the spiritual relationship.[68]

Though raw intellect has no material component, it is a quality of physical reality — that dimension of existence that hides its dependence

---

67. *Pirkei HaHeichalot*, ch. 27. See Chapter 14, pp. 259–260.
68. Obviously Greece was a diverse, multifaceted culture with many strains. We speak now of the specific facet of Greek culture that was brought to the world through the conquests of Alexander and became the foundation of Western intellectualism. This was predominantly Aristotelian, as Aristotle was Alexander's private tutor. This is not to deny the existence of discussions about God even in Aristotle. But for Aristotle the realm of spirit was understood by the intellect and therefore controlled by it. See note 69 in this chapter. Though the gods of Greek mythology still played a role in Greek society, they were considered an anachronism by many Greek intellectuals even before Greece became an empire. And for those that recognized them, the gods were a force in the world to deal with rather than a connection to true Transcendence.

on God. In order to focus self in the intellect, one must separate from the spiritual realm. The self may be experienced under intellect as existing as part of a larger context, but that context is a dimension of the physical realm — the intellectual or aesthetic — something that man can understand and contain within himself rather than emanating from a realm that is beyond his reach.[69]

The Greek loss of spiritual connection required that Greek society reject the God-centered world they had inherited from prior civilizations. The vacuum created by that rejection brought after it the birth of philosophy, where the Greeks applied their intelligence to defining the world from and for man. The cultural context that Greece imposed upon the Jews was a secular one. To the extent that there was any reference to God, it served as a conceptual element in man's understanding of reality, with God having no real relationship, involvement, or interaction with man.

This put the Jews under an unprecedented kind of pressure. The idol-worshipping societies we had encountered practiced an alternative form of connection with transcendence, at least respecting the value of our overall concept of developing relationship with God. But Greece denied the legitimacy of the project altogether. Moreover, the inevitable effect of living in Greece's world was a shift of our center of self toward the intellect, which was so clearly mirrored in the society and culture the Greeks constructed. This resulted in our suffering the same internal

---

69. In terms of Greek intellect, the Ramban says about Aristotle in *Vayikra* 16:8: "That Greek denied the existence of anything he could not sense and had the arrogance... to think that anything he could not comprehend was not true." In terms of aesthetics, Greek aesthetics relate to forms that take on direct expression in physical objects. This contrasts to Torah aesthetics, where the primary source of beauty exists in the unity of the spiritual realm, with merely its emanations entering physical reality. For example, in *Bava Batra* 58a it states, "Everyone next to Sarah appeared like a monkey standing before a man" referring to the clarity with which her *tzelem Elokim* beamed through her. See *Peirush HaGra, Shir HaShirim* 1:5 *yafeh mareh*, which is the beauty of the emanations of the *neshamah* as opposed to *yafeh to'ar*, which is the beauty of form. Even the beauty of physical form in the verse in *Shir HaShirim* that the Gra is explaining is not referring to a physical shape but, rather, to the precise accomplishment of mitzvot.

detachment from transcendence that was characteristic of the Greeks and intrinsic to an intellectual center. In the world outside the self also all connection to transcendence was lost under Greece with prophecy and miracle, our direct contact with the Creator, disappearing under their domination.[70] Greece pulled us into their darkness. Our experience of reality became so empty of that which we professed to be the basis of reality, that for the first time some Jews adopted the ruling culture and actively worked to undermine Torah.

Greece forced us to exercise our free will on a more profound level than we had before. We now had to find within ourselves the capacity to *initiate* relationship with God from the midst of His silence. Battling against the contrary pull of Greek philosophy, we harnessed our intellect in the service of God through the Oral Torah. Analyzing our tradition and the prophetic documents we had inherited from previous generations, we were able to extrapolate from them into the new circumstances in which we found ourselves. Though the Oral Torah was received on Sinai, it took on a new role and significance with the disappearance of prophecy under Greek occupation.[71] By overcoming the pressure of Greece while

---

70. This is technically true since vestiges of miracle and prophecy lasted into the time of Greek dominion (See *Yoma* 39a that some miracles continued in the Second Temple through Shimon HaTzaddik's tenure as Kohen Gadol and see Chapter 14, p. 260 that the last of the prophets died forty years after the completion of the Second Temple). For the most part, however, these had disappeared before Greece's arrival. We will discuss on page 263 that Greece was as much an effect as a cause. The Jews were moving toward a less intuitive, intellectual relationship with reality and Greece came to actualize this in the world, accelerating the process and intensifying the challenge. In any case, under Greek rule the world became a spiritually barren place. The prophet Zecharyah refers to that world as a pit, a place below the surface of genuinely human reality (*Zecharyah* 9:11–13). See also *Shabbat* 22a, which implies a connection between being in an empty pit and being subject to Greece (as heard from Rav Moshe Shapiro).

71. The Oral Torah was given on Har Sinai along with the Written Torah as a commentary providing all the details of the laws given in the Written Torah. As long as prophecy continued, the Oral Torah had only limited need of creativity — for if a new situation arose, the prophet could receive answers directly from the Source. With the loss of prophecy, the Oral Torah needed to fill these gaps and went from being an adjunct to prophetic Torah to being the basis of our relationship with the Creator. We will discuss the Oral

developing the Oral Torah into our primary mode of connection to God, we took responsibility for our intellect as a means of relating to God. Greece's purpose was served and its forces were ejected from *Eretz Yisrael*, paving the way for our final challenge — finding our root connection to God from the midst of subjugation to the vacuousness of Rome.

The Roman world looked very similar to the Greek, at least initially and on the outside. Reality was defined by man, and there was no genuine place for God. There was, however, a subtle but devastating change — under Rome, man lost all inner sense of the greatness of our humanity, which gives the instinct and impetus for real faith.

Greece had lived off an inherited sense for the greatness of spiritual reality while denying its basis. It spent its principal without making any deposits. Rome, the society that followed Greece, lacked the luxury of the spiritual legacy that Greece had enjoyed, and therefore could not attribute any undue greatness to intellect. Rome was left with the emptiness of man contained in physical reality, where even understanding and beauty were perceived as nothing more than a by-product of material existence.

The spiritual vision of the past had seen the reality of an object in its meaning and purpose, with its material substance the means by which its purpose could be achieved; purpose was determined by the transcendent Source of reality. The Greek intellectual and esthetic vision had seen the reality of an object in its form and understanding, with its material substance the means by which the form and understanding took on expression. The intellectual vision was limited in that its intangible dimension — the form and understanding of the object — were completely grasped by the mind and contained in man. But at least, like the spiritual vision, it retained an intangible dimension which was given priority. Rome entirely lacked the intangible as a separate dimension, attributing all the reality of an object to its material substance, with its form nothing more than the shape in which the material arrived, and its

---

Torah more extensively further on. See Chapter 14, pp. 261–273 and Chapter 21, pp. 399–400.

understanding an arbitrary imposition. Greece's worship of philosophical understanding and artistic appreciation gave way to Roman respect for the power of engineering and the organization of law.

With no access to anything beyond the physical world, man himself was reduced to little more than a cow with sophistication.[72] If all that exists is material reality, then man can never be greater than that world, which is finite, particular, and accidental. The debilitating emptiness of this finite human experience bred a deep sense of inadequacy. Someone who feels so inadequate cannot tolerate the competition of another presence, for he feels nullified before any significant being beyond himself. Therefore he must destroy everything that he cannot incorporate into himself. This was conveyed in Daniel's dream of Rome as a nameless animal of destruction. That is to say, Rome was depicted as a destroyer because Rome's violence was not an accidental trait but, rather, a necessary consequence of its defining characteristic — spiritual emptiness.

To this emptiness, Rome eventually added a superficial spirituality borrowed from the Jews, a nation with roots stretching back to when honest connection to transcendence was intuitive.[73] For Rome, however, this spirituality only served to add religious conviction to their devastating slaughter. Spirituality could be no more than a veneer for Romans, for, as we mentioned, they lacked genuine sensitivity to the greatness of being that they needed for true connection to transcendent spirituality.[74] Rome's inadequacy in this area was clearly evident in its ability to confuse man with God, a perversion to which the descendants of Esav were susceptible as we will see later happened with Haman.[75] This was not like the ambiguity we spoke about earlier regarding Avraham's use

---

72. Nietzsche would say an ape.

73. *Midrash Rabbah Shir HaShirim* 1:41. None of the mud bricks in Rome would hold together until water was brought from the Euphrates. A unifying source had to be imported from the Middle East.

74. *Vayikra Rabbah* 13:5.

75. Haman was an Amalekite, descendent of Esav, the progenitor of Rome. See Chapter 20, p. 378.

of the word *Ado-nai*.[76] There the ambiguity elevated man by recognizing the Divinity that flows through man. Rome diminished God to the point where He could be contained in man — the logical next step after Greece identified transcendence with the intellect contained in man.

Babylon and Persia forced us to choose between faith in God and faith in an idol. Greece, retaining a sense for the greatness of being necessary for true faith, forced us to choose between faith in God and faith in ourselves. Rome, having lost all sense for the greatness of being, forced us to choose between faith in God or no genuine faith.

THE INSENSITIVE HEEL

Finding God from within the spiritual isolation of an unrelentingly physical reality is the final challenge. When we succeed, the collective historical entity of the Jewish people will have utilized its free will to create relationship with God with every aspect of our humanity: our head, chest, thighs, and feet. Thus the Midrash states:

> Says God to Yisrael, "My son, do not think that I have made you like a slave to be sold by his master to the highest bidder. [No! This is not the reason for exile.] Rather, I bring upon you troubles until you fully prepare your heart for Me."... God vows that He will never abandon Yisrael. Until what point will the troubles continue? Until the heel... until you keep the mitzvot till the heel.[77]

When we are pushed down into the heel of our humanity — the aspect that is as insensitive to spirituality as the heel is to touch — and we manage to carve out relationship with God even from there, then our task of creating relationship with God will be complete.[78] Rome, the foot of Nebuchadnezzar's statue, is God's instrument for driving us into that heel. Thus the *midrash* continues by interpreting the verse

---

76. See Chapter 3, 37–39.
77. *Devarim Rabbah* 3:2.
78. See *Sefat Emet, Ekev* 637. See also *Tehillim* 35:10.

in *Tehillim* in which God states, "Regarding Edom, I will cast off My shoe,"[79] to mean:

> Everything is prepared for repentance, and I will tread the wine-presses of Edom with the heel of My foot. When? When you will listen to My mitzvot till the heel.[80]

When we sanctify our heel, God will tread with His "heel" on Edom — the heel of mankind — bringing redemption.

It is logical to recognize Rome as the heel of humanity, the culture that leaves man the least sensitive to spiritual experience. And it is logical to say that once we sanctify our subjugation to Rome by choosing God from the midst of this desolation we will have completed the task of humanity. But if the thick fleshy spot on the bottom of our feet — designed specifically to be impervious to feeling — accurately captures the nature of our relationship to spirituality under Rome, how exactly are we supposed to genuinely turn to God? We will save this question for the last section of this book.

*   x   *

Our history of exile is the history of struggling on a national level to create relationship with God against the cultural backdrop and accompanying inner experience created by the domination of foreign powers. The worldview of each of these societies skewed our relationship with the Creator. It was our task to actualize our deeper self to overcome their pull and, in the process, to create the equivalent aspect of ourselves as vehicles of relationship with the Creator. This process culminates with the Roman exile in which we find ourselves today. Against the background of Rome's extreme materialism, we must create spirituality itself.

This explanation gives us a coherent picture of the structure and

---

79. *Tehillim* 60:10. The translation is based on *Bemidbar Rabbah* 14:1.

80. *Devarim Rabbah* 3:2. In Midrashic literature Edom and Rome are virtually synonymous. Both are descendants of Esav.

direction of modern Jewish history. Viewed as an extension of our individual task of self-actualization through free will, we understand why exile is the appropriate framework within which to advance history. This also clarifies why we experience subjugation to the specific four cultures that have conquered us.

The weakness in this model is that, though we see definite acts on the part of the Jews to bring an end to our exiles, those actions do not correspond in an obvious way to directly containing the inclinations and aspects of self that define the conquering cultures. For example, Persia was a pleasure-based society that should have forced us to contain our bodily energies and direct them toward cleaving to God. We mentioned that the Jews sent away their foreign wives and repudiated idolatry at a time that might be considered the end of the Persian exile. But it is the events that we commemorate on Purim that ended the pressure of the Persian exile. Though the Jews also demonstrated self-control at the end of the Purim story when they refused to take spoils from their Persian foes,[81] the salvation actually came about as a result of national repentance and recognition of dependence upon the Creator — which is very different from containing an inclination toward pleasure.[82]

Chanukah is similarly difficult to understand. It commemorates the salvation from Greece, an intellectually based society. According to our model, we should have ousted the Greeks by taking control of our intellectual energies and channeling them toward Torah. Even though under Greek domination we did harness our minds to the service of God through the development of the Oral Torah, the actual salvation came as a direct result of the self-sacrifice of the Maccabees in battle against the Greek armies.[83] The containment of inclinations that our model predicts was occurring during these exiles. But the fact that energies not directly connected to the process we have described played so

---

81. *Megillat Esther* 9:15–16. Mordechai received the estate of Haman, but Mordechai had not been guilty of partaking in Achashverosh's offensive feast.
82. See Chapter 20, pp. 382–384.
83. Bach, *Tur Orach Chayim* 600; *Megillat Antiochus*.

significant a role in moving beyond these societies indicates that something else is also involved in the succession of the exiles.

Moreover, according to what we have said, exile is built into the structure of creation as the necessary instrument of national realization. Yet, numerous Torah and Rabbinic sources make clear that exile is also a direct consequence of our transgressions and turning away from God — meaning we are responsible for exile. History is not something that just happens to us — an inflexible curriculum waiting for us to learn our lesson before it moves automatically on to the next assignment. There is a more sophisticated interaction taking place between the Jewish people and their historical circumstances that we now need to probe.

CHAPTER 11

Alternate Understandings of Tests

"HaShem tests the righteous, but the evil and lovers of vio-lence His soul hates."[1] Rebbi Yonatan said, when the potter checks his kiln he does not check the rickety pots, because if he taps on them even once they will break. Which ones does he check? The strong barrels, because even if he taps on them many times they will not break. So too the Holy One does not test the evildoers. Rather, He tests the righteous... Rebbi Yosi ben Chanina said, when the flax worker sees that his flax is of high quality, he beats it repeatedly because it improves continually. When he sees that it is imperfect, he will not beat upon it even once because it will break. So too the Holy One does not test the evildoers because they cannot stand up to the test...[2]

OUR PURPOSE IS TO create relationship with God. We achieve this by developing the potential for relationship inherent in each facet of our character, with each facet capable of connecting to God in a differ-ent way.

Because we cannot create something we already have, God's revealed relationship with us, what we refer to as His face, must be hidden. This

---

1. *Tehillim* 11:5.
2. *Bereishit Rabbah* 32:3 and 55:2.

hiding is called a *nisayon*, or test. We become centered in an aspect of personality that is undeveloped and thus detached from God, and we are tested to recover connection by properly developing that aspect of personality.

We are tested in this manner both on a personal level and on a national level. But on a national level the refocusing of personality that presents the test is accomplished through exile.[3] The exiles of the Jewish people are to kingdoms anchored in distorted facets of character. When each nation conquers us, the center of our personality is drawn toward that nation's corrupt character, obscuring our connection to God. To recover our relationship we are forced as a nation to properly develop that facet of our personality in a process directly parallel to that of individual development.

Our opening *midrash* compares tests, and therefore God's subjecting us to the kingdoms, to a potter tapping on his pot to demonstrate its hidden strength.[4] We have capabilities for forming relationship with God, but there is no reason to develop them as long as relationship is already given to us. When relationship is removed, however, we suffer the pain of God's distance and actively strive to recover our connection by actualizing those potentials. So, too, the strength of the pot is unrealized until it is tapped.[5] Tapping represents the pain that comes

---

3. *Devarim Rabbah* 3:2.

4. See Maharal, *Derech Chayim* 5:3.

5. The metaphor is a strange one to convey the essential idea of Rebbi Yonatan that tests come to actualize an individual's potential. Tapping the pot does not actualize the strength of the pot; it merely reveals that the strength exists. An accompanying *midrash* which we will mention in a moment states that tests come only to satisfy the quality of strict judgment (*Bereishit Rabbah* 55:1), meaning that we earn what we get from God and justify His giving it to us. Maharal emphasizes that the actualization spoken of here is for the sake of strict judgment. But when tapping the pot, what have we actualized that metaphorically we should earn something? Nothing has changed but our knowledge of a preexisting quality of the pot!

Rebbi Yonatan is expressing this idea in the context of recognizing that God tests only the righteous because the evil break under pressure. This double meaning severely limits the choice of metaphor. The pot-tapping example captures this second dimension. But still, this additional consideration does not justify the selection of a metaphor that does not accurately convey the

from the hiddenness of God, the vacuum that forces action.

Another *midrash* explains that the reason for tests is to justify God's gifts to us:

> "And it came to pass after these things that God *nisah* (tested) Avraham."[6] It is written, "You have given a *neis* (test or banner) to those who fear You, that they might *lehitnoseis* (be raised up) because of the truth, Selah"[7] This means, trial upon trial, greatness after greatness, in order to raise and exalt them in the world like a ship's *neis* (banner). And what is the purpose of all this? "Because of the truth" — in order that the righteousness of God's trait of strict judgment will be demonstrated in the world.[8]

We explained in the previous section on free will the importance of our actively building our relationship with God.[9] We act in a way that, according to strict judgment, deserves relationship, and the Creator then rewards us with the desired result.[10] Because we earn reward through

---

desired meaning — metaphors are intended to make things clearer, not to confuse.

The simplest answer to this question requires noticing that Rebbi Yonatan's metaphor is cited numerous times in the Midrash and often with a specific reference to the binding of Yitzchak at the *Akeidah*, even when the *midrash* has nothing to do with the *Akeidah* (see *Bereishit Rabbah* 32:3). The *Akeidah* was an instance where, though Avraham was asked to sacrifice Yitzchak, HaShem never intended for Avraham to actually do it. Rather, he needed to actualize and reveal his *willingness* to do so. Revealing the strength to do something without doing it was enough to profoundly change Avraham and corresponds to tapping the pot to know its strength. But why did Rebbi Yonatan select the *Akeidah* to determine his metaphor if this case is so unusual? The *Akeidah* defines what God ultimately demands we actualize. This was Avraham's final test, and the magnitude of his accomplishment is unfathomable. The *Akeidah* is, therefore, the paradigm for actualizing potential. Perhaps we also see here a hint to a deeper level of understanding of the whole functioning of strict judgment in creation, but this discussion is beyond our present scope.

6. *Bereishit* 21:1.

7. *Tehillim* 60:6.

8. *Bereishit Rabbah* 55:1.

9. See Chapter 6.

10. We cannot, however, cause or control the formation of relationship. As we will discuss in the next section, we cannot *directly* create anything. Only God determines what happens. Our goal is to put in the effort and work through his trait of strict justice as much as possible.

God's system of judgment, we gain a quality of necessity that echoes that of the Creator.[11] We said all this about individuals in our discussion of free will; it applies equally to our national experience of exile.

Understanding the exiles as God "tapping on our pot" views them as a necessary and natural part of the process of our national development. Since we need exile to achieve our purpose, it is built into creation's structure. Exile is understood to occur regardless of our actions. Our influence is restricted to determining the speed with which the process unfolds. By developing in whatever way we need to develop, we bring an end to the exile we are in and open the way for the next to begin. But as we pointed out in the previous chapter, understanding tests as a pure process of actualizing potential is incomplete. It cannot fully explain Jewish history when we examine it on a detailed level. More importantly, the Torah speaks of exile as a direct consequence of our transgressions.[12]

Our *midrash* also supplies a second metaphor to explain tests, comparing them to a farmer who beats his flax. Flax has a hard shell that covers the soft and shiny material underneath. To bring out the quality of the flax, the farmer must strike it to break up the shell. Unlike the pot-tapping metaphor where what is revealed must be created or actualized, when whacking flax all the positive qualities already exist but are cut off from us by a shell. "Shell" is a code word among the Sages for a blockage — generally one that we have created.

In other words, according to this flax metaphor we already have the developed character traits that connect us to God but we have covered them over with layers of corruption. This creates a need for a test — some jarring experience that will remove the obstruction. If we understand the exiles as this kind of test, a very different picture of the process emerges than what we have described up until now. Rather than foreign nations centering us in distorted facets of character to cause us

---

11. See Chapter 6, pp. 84–85.
12. *Vayikra* 26:15–44; *Devarim* 4:25–31; *Devarim* 28:15–68 and many others.

to develop our potential, we have corrupted ourselves and the kingdoms come as a consequence — what we call punishment.[13] We will see later

---

13. Alshich can be cited as a source for understanding the flax-whacking metaphor as punishment. He notes (*Torat Moshe, Bereishit* 22:1-2) that in contrast to the *midrash's* association of the pot-tapping metaphor with Avraham's binding of Yitzchak (*Bereishit Rabbah* 32:3), it connects flax-whacking with the test Yosef endured with Potifar's wife (*Bereishit Rabbah* 55:2). Alshich derives from this that just as Yosef was tested to control his inclination, flax-whacking refers generally to tests that purify the righteous from an inclination— the inclination is awakened in them, forcing them to subjugate it. This confirms our specific identification of flax-whacking with punishment because Yosef's inclination was awakened because of his transgression (*Tanchuma, Vayeishev* 8 brought in Rashi *Bereishit* 39:6). We can generalize this to understand that the inclinations which caused our exiles were each awakened to overwhelming strength by our transgressing in relation to that inclination.

Understanding the shells of flax as blockages created by us and the consequent whacking as punishment is, however, open to dispute. The Talmud in *Berachot* 5a explains that there are three reasons why God brings suffering on man. They are: as punishment to repair the consequences of transgression, to actualize hidden potential, and *yisurim shel ahavah*, sufferings of love that purify us from the natural limitations imposed by our being also physical (See Maharal, *Derech Chayim* 5:3). Maharal identifies the suffering of flax-whacking tests with the third category of *yisurim shel ahavah* (ibid.). This seems to run counter to our interpretation of flax-whacking tests as punishments.

In *Netivot Olam* (*Netiv HaYisurim* 1), however, Maharal repeatedly states that *yisurim shel ahavah* come in response to transgression, which returns us to the idea of punishment. This need not be a contradiction in Maharal, for some transgression is intrinsic to the human condition — "For there is no righteous man on earth that does (only) good and does not sin." (*Kohelet* 7:20. See also *Sanhedrin* 46b on the need to bury the righteous.) The Talmud also states, "There is no suffering without transgression" (*Shabbat* 55a). Maharal could then understand flax-whacking tests as *yisurim shel ahavah* and still associate them with punishments, just restricting them to punishments for transgressions that result naturally from the human condition. This fits well with our approach to the kingdoms as expressions of our inherent inclinations. It also answers a serious difficulty with our interpretation. The shells of flax develop naturally. They presumably connote inherent lacks. How can they then represent blockages created by sin, which are presumably artificial additions? Combining the interpretations of Maharal in *Derech Chayim* and *Netivot Olam* we can answer that flax shells refer only to those blockages that result from transgressions that actualize lacks intrinsic to being human. This approach reveals a deeper synthesis between our first approach to the exiles as actualizing potential and the approach we are beginning now of viewing them as punishment because, even viewed as punishment, the exiles are seen to be a necessary part of the structure of creation. Understanding Maharal this way raises a number of issues that are beyond the scope of our discussion.

Alternatively, we could take Maharal's delineation of the categories of suffering in

that as well as a different causality, understanding exile as punishment also implies a different process of growing beyond it. This alternative view will help us fill in the gaps in our understanding of history.

According to this way of relating to tests, the meaning of the *midrash*'s statement that we experience tests to satisfy strict judgment seems obvious. We did something wrong, and accounts must be settled. Upon further consideration, however, things are not so simple. Since we understand that God needs nothing and created only to give good, in His relationship with us there is no place for the retribution we normally associate with punishment. We will address this in the next chapter.

Of immediate interest to us is the *midrash*'s description of tests as "trial upon trial, greatness after greatness, in order to raise and exalt" us in the world. No distinction is made in the *midrash* between pot-tapping tests and flax-whacking tests — apparently even tests that are a consequence of our transgressions are to raise us spiritually.

The details of the flax-whacking metaphor make this clear. According to the metaphor our transgressions create a barrier — the shell — that obscures the part of us that connects to God — the flax. The pain of God's hiddenness — the punishing whack of the flax — is the very thing that removes the barrier, thus repairing the damage of transgression. Like a pot-tapping actualization, a flax-whacking punishment is constructive.

The parallel between the two forms of test runs even deeper. The

Berachot 5a at face value and exclude any reference to the suffering of punishment from the metaphor of flax-whacking. The two metaphors provided by the *midrash* to explain tests (the third metaphor is not relevant to our present discussion) — pot-tapping referring to actualizing potential and flax-whacking referring to purification by *yisurim shel ahavah* — would then imply that suffering as punishment is not designated a test. The concept of test would then be understood to apply only to processes that are geared to move us forward, as opposed to punishment that recovers ground lost through sin. Had we followed this interpretation, the title of this chapter would be "Alternative Approaches to Suffering" instead of "Alternative Approaches to Tests" and we would build our chapter around *Berachot* 5a instead of *Bereishit Rabbah*. This would have no effect on our subsequent discussion other than how we categorize punishment. I have used the first approach because of the emphasis we will place on the progressive nature of the process of punishment.

metaphor of flax-whacking assumes that we had some level of connection to the Creator, represented by the flax's soft fibers, that was set
back by transgression, and we need to recoup our loss.[14] Recovery from
transgression, however, always requires *teshuvah* (repentance) and at
least one consequence of the whacking of the flax must be to motivate
that *teshuvah*. Whenever we repent from distancing ourselves from God
we cannot merely return to our starting point; we must advance the
relationship to a new level. The Talmud states:

> Why was this world created with the letter *hei*, "ה"? Because it is shaped
> like a three-sided hut so that anyone who wishes to exit reality by
> transgressing has the opportunity [to leave through the bottom]. And
> why does the left leg not reach the top? So that anyone who wishes to
> return in *teshuvah* can do so. Why doesn't he return the way he left
> [and come back through the bottom]? Because it won't work.[15]

We will explore this statement in detail in the coming chapters. The
relevant point for now is that the world — reality — is identified with relationship with God. It is easy to "step out" by transgressing. Recovery
requires reentering the *hei* to reconnect with God; but we can only do that
through a higher portal than the one through which we left, signifying a
different and higher relationship. Transgression and *teshuvah*, then, are not
a process that just recovers loss. Rather, like development of potential, they
are an engine for net growth, advancing us toward our goal of actualizing
our full potential.

---

14. In the metaphor, it is the flax that is whacked. The flax, therefore, represents us, not the
relationship, for we are the one getting punished. How, then, do we understand the revealing of the flax to be the recovery of relationship? We learned earlier that our relationship
with God comes through the actualization of those elements of ourselves which are connected to the Creator. Our relationship, then, comes through our character. The soft flax
represents the pure elements of our character through which we are connected to God.
Covering over those traits — focusing ourselves in a superficial layer of personality disconnected from our spiritual root — is the equivalent of blocking the relationship with God.
Breaking that blockage and vitalizing those traits of connection once again is synonymous
with a recovery of relationship.

15. *Menachot* 29b.

This helps us understand how these two very different processes are grouped under the same term, *nisayon*. Though we translate it as "test," the word comes from the root *neis*, which means "banner." Just as a banner is raised high, so tests press us to achieve new heights — in the words of the *midrash*, to reach "greatness after greatness." This is as true when a test is flax-whacking as when it is pot-tapping.[16]

*   *   *

The metaphor of flax-whacking implies that punishment directly brings growth. But we have not yet explained how this works. We must now explore the Torah concept of judgment and consequences. We can then reexamine the process of exile and see how our broadened vision of tests affects our understanding of that process.

---

16. The *midrash* brings a third metaphor: "Rebbi Elazar said, when a farmer has two oxen, one strong and one weak, on which one will he put the yoke? Will he not put it on the strong one? So, too, the Holy One only tests the righteous." This third metaphor is different from the first two. In the first two, the test is for the sake of that which is being tested — tapping on the pot actualizes something in the pot and striking the flax fixes the flax, whereas an ox plowing a field benefits the owner. Normally, we are tested to actualize something in us that we need in order to achieve our personal purpose in life. This comes in two forms, as captured by the first two metaphors in the *midrash*. But sometimes God wants something done in the world that requires an individual to go beyond the needs of his own development — He wants the individual to grow for the sake of the nation. This comes in both of the forms we have described; it is not so much a new kind of test as one applied on another scale. A flax-whacking example of this third type is found in *Yechezkel*, chapter 4, when Yechezkel suffered to absorb some of the punishment that was coming to the Jewish people at the time of the destruction of the First Temple. The *tzaddik*, because of his depth of personality, reaches to the spiritual wellsprings of the nation, and his personal experiences therefore have the same effect as actual national suffering. A pot-tapping example of this third type of test is Avraham at the *Akeidah*. Avraham was pushed to a level of service to God beyond what could normally be demanded of an individual. Because of the depth of Avraham's spiritual reach, his accomplishments affected the Jewish people for all of eternity. Avraham created the possibility of a person achieving the level of dedication he demonstrated at the *Akeidah*, which is needed for the Jewish people to complete the task of history.

CHAPTER 12

The Nature of Divine Judgment

*[Why are we judged on Rosh Hashanah?] It was taught in the name
of R. Eliezer: The world was created on the twenty-fifth of Elul...
From this we conclude that [man was created] on Rosh Hashanah.
In the first hour the idea of creating man entered His mind; in the
second hour He consulted the Ministering Angels; in the third hour
He gathered Adam's dust; in the fourth hour He kneaded it; in the
fifth hour He shaped it; in the sixth hour He made it into a lifeless
body; in the seventh hour He breathed a soul into it; in the eighth
hour He brought him into Gan Eden; in the ninth hour he was commanded [against eating from the Tree of Knowledge]; in the tenth
hour he transgressed; in the eleventh hour he was judged; in the
twelfth hour he was pardoned. The Holy One, may He be blessed,
said to Adam, "This will be a sign to your children that as you stood
before Me in judgment today and came out with a pardon, so will
your children in the future stand before Me in judgment on this day
and be pardoned."[1]*

T HE SAGES GUIDE US to view the hiding of God's face as a test — a process of raising us up. Tests can come in two ways, as a natural part
of the process of creation to actualize our potential and as a punishment
in consequence of our transgressions — pot-tapping and flax-whacking.

---

1. *Vayikra Rabbah* 29:1.

While it is easy enough to understand how being pressed to actualize our potential elevates us, it is less simple to understand how punishment directly accomplishes this same task.

Before we answer how punishment raises us up, we need to ask why punishment plays any role at all in God's relationship with man. We concluded earlier that God created with the singular intention to give us good.[2] This is fundamental to our understanding. How, then, do we explain Divine retribution?

We have explained that man was given free will in order to create himself and earn what sustains him in existence. The concept of earning means that actions bring about consequences. We cannot have what we earn (receiving reward, meaning *because* we earn it) unless there is a possibility to not earn and, therefore, not have (that is, experience lack, which we associate with punishment). Both reward and punishment — God's connection to those who act righteously and the painful lack of connection with those who do not act righteously — are inextricably linked. They are equally a result of a relationship of judgment, where our actions generate meaningful consequences.

But if we look at the first instance of Divine justice we see that this explanation of punishment — a lack of connection to God due to a lack of active creation of relationship — is incomplete.

When Adam transgressed and ate from the Tree of the Knowledge of Good and Evil, God's response was immediate and devastating. He punished the collective Adam with the pain of pregnancy, the pain of birth, the pain of child rearing, increased dependence of women on men, responsibility for and difficulty in gaining sustenance, exile from Gan Eden and, finally, death.[3] Apart from the challenge of grasping why Adam got precisely these penalties, which is beyond the scope of our present discussion,[4] we need to understand the overall nature of God's reaction. We understand that the flip side of our responsibility to create

---

2. See Chapter 4, pp. 45–47.
3. *Bereishit* 3:16–19.
4. See notes 14 and 18 in this chapter.

our connection with God is that failure will leave us without relationship. But what is all this pain and harshness being actively inflicted on man — why the apparent vindictiveness of God's response? How does this fit into our overall vision of God's relationship with man?

EVALUATING WHAT WE NEED, NOT WHAT WE OWE

In our opening *midrash* the Sages ask why God established Judgment Day on Rosh Hashanah. They answer that on the first Rosh Hashanah in history Adam was created, sinned, judged by God, and pardoned. In order that his favorable outcome should be a merit for us as we stand in judgment before God, He tries us on the same day as Adam was judged.[5]

This *midrash* is strange. What does it mean that Adam was pardoned? He was condemned to die![6] Why would we want Adam's judgment to serve as a precedent for our own on Rosh Hashanah?

We think of judgment in general as a process to determine what we owe for our actions. A favorable verdict means we did not do anything wrong, or at least nothing warranting punishment, so we get off without having to pay anything. If we are found guilty, we must pay for our crime through punishment, a term we understand to encompass all the consequences of our unfavorable judgment.

The word "punishment" has the same root as the word "punitive,"[7] and both concepts are inextricably bound up with one another in our minds. Punitive awards are what the offender pays out after damages, pain, suffering, lost income, and medical expenses are accounted for.[8]

---

5. *Vayikra Rabbah* 29:1.
6. The commentaries do not see in the fact that Adam did not immediately die a commuting of the sentence of death. They understand the original warning to Adam was that he would immediately become subject to death, not that he would immediately die. Before the sin, Adam would have lived eternally. See, for example, *Ramban* and Rabbeinu Bechaya, *Bereishit* 2:17.
7. Both are from the Latin *poenre* (American Heritage Dictionary of the English Language).
8. Ibid.

In other words, after the guilty party has, to the best of his ability, made right all that he made wrong, the punitive assessment is added to cause him sufficient pain that he will never consider repeating his action, and neither will anyone else. Punitive damages do not fix anything. They have no positive function; they do not build or rebuild. Even the fear they inspire, though serving a function for society, is not a real change in the wrongdoer. Fear of punitive damages merely puts a barrier between the wrongdoer and the offensive action, but his original desire to transgress persists. He is not changed.

We intuitively associate the consequences of our judgment with something punitive. Therefore judgment, which at best will not take anything from us and at worst will result in suffering, is something only to be avoided — nothing good can come from it. Anyone who views judgment this way and still craves it associates pain with the absolution of guilt, revealing a certain warped self-hatred. His suffering may quiet his shame, but nothing is really accomplished.

This view of judgment is especially absurd when projected into the realm where it is most often applied, that of Divine justice. Inflicting purposeless pain would be a complete inversion of God's true relationship with man where He desires only to give good. Yet God does judge and God does punish. In fact, the Torah even proclaims the Day of Judgment a holiday, with the requisite obligations of joy. How are we to understand this?

God's judgment does not result in "punishment" with all the associations tied to the word in English; judgment in the Torah sense is not a determination of what we "owe." It is rather an evaluation of what we need. On Rosh Hashanah, God judges us to determine what we require to fulfill our role in creation.[9] For example, if an individual's appointed task is to give charity, God might conclude that he needs money. If, however, he has allowed himself to become greedy — if he has formed a

---

9. The more fundamental determination of whether or not a person has a role and, if he is judged to have a role, what role he will play is also being judged on Rosh Hashanah. See Rav Chayim Freidlander, *Siftei Chayim, Moadim* I, pp. 102–105. See also note 19 in this chapter.

shell around his giving spirit so that were he to have money he would not give it in the proper amount or in the proper way — God could determine that he needs to experience privation to open his heart to compassion. The positive decision to give the individual money and the decision to impose the pain of want are both outcomes of judgment. But even the apparently negative, certainly more painful, evaluation that the individual needs to experience lack is not punitive. It is what the person requires to accomplish his personal task in life. It is the "whack" that will expose his pure inner fibers once again.

The Hebrew term that we normally translate as "punishment" is *onesh*. The root is *nash*,[10] which forms a group of words meaning to fall away.[11] *Onesh* is a process by which impurities that we have introduced into ourselves that interfere with our relationship with God fall away, or at least their power to block our achieving relationship with God falls away.

ACTUALIZING THE REALITY OF DISTANCE

The response to Adam's sin is a clear example of this process of Divine judgment and consequent *onesh*. We will examine in detail the sin of Adam in the next section. For our present discussion, it is enough for us to know that Adam ate from the Tree of Knowledge to distance himself from God. His conscious justification was to expand his free will to make his service to God more meaningful.[12] But his motivation could not have been purely righteous for he acted in direct violation of God's command. Adam's decision was skewed by a desire for significance independent of God.

In light of Adam's sin, his punishment seems paradoxical. Adam

---

10. Heard from Rav Baruch Weiss.

11. For example, the nerve that the Angel pulled from its place in Yaakov's thigh was called the *gid hanashe*, the nerve that "jumped away" (see *Rashi, Bereishit* 32:32). Also, Yosef named his son Menashe because God had allowed Yosef to *nashani*, forget — the memory had fallen away — all the toil of his father's house (see *Bereishit* 41:51). The verb *nashar* means drop, like fruit from a tree.

12. Rav Eliyahu Dessler, *Michtav Me'Eliyahu* II, pp. 137–144.

was ejected from the Garden, which profoundly diminished his aware-ness of God's singular greatness. Adam was also required to work to sustain himself.[13] This new responsibility shrouded his utter dependence upon God and opened the possibility that Adam could delude himself into believing that he supported his own existence — that what sustained him was the work of his own hands.[14] Why was Adam being punished with exactly the independence he sinfully appropriated to himself?

An experienced parent is familiar with this form of education. If a child badgers his mother for more and more chocolate, Mom will stave off his requests, knowing that the child will become sick if he eats too much. But if the kid pushes hard enough, eventually the mother gives in, telling him, "Eat what you like!" The child then eats to his heart's content and becomes sick. An evening's nausea teaches the child that he himself does not want so much chocolate.[15]

Sometimes, to really change, a person must be allowed to have what he thinks he wants.[16] Only then will he find out that his desire was mistaken. God's goal is not that man merely adheres to His rules but, rather, that man as a whole individual relates to God — including

---

13. Before the sin, man did not work for his sustenance. Though in *Bereishit* 2:15 it states that man was placed in the Garden to "work and keep it," the Midrash and commentar-ies understand this to be referring to the service of God rather than agriculture. See *Pirkei D'Rebbi Eliezer* 11; *Bereishit Rabbah* 16:4; *Ohr HaChayim, Bereishit* 2:15.

14. *Devarim* 8:11–17. The creation of physical existence was to obscure God sufficiently from man to allow for free will (Ramchal, *Da'at Tevunot* 40). In order to do this the world was created through ten statements (*Rosh Hashanah* 32a), meaning ten layers of physical creation, each further thickening the veil covering the Creator behind the creation (Ram-chal, *Da'at Tevunot* 40; Maharal, *Gevurot HaShem*, ch. 57). The tenth, the final hiding of God, was when God gave man the plants of the earth for sustenance. As soon as man could support himself from the produce of the world, the impression that physical reality was a self-sustaining whole was complete, and God became sufficiently hidden to allow for ex-panded choice. The added punishment after the sin of Adam was that, not only would man get his sustenance from the world, he would also be responsible to make it grow, consider-ably deepening man's sense of independent control.

15. This is different from a punitive consequence for the pain is the true, intrinsic conse-quence of the action rather than a pain artificially associated with the action as a penalty.

16. *Shabbat* 104a. *Ba l'tamei potchin lo.*

with his desires. Punishing man in a way that he refrains from forbidden activity out of fear of further punishment does not accomplish this. Therefore, man is allowed to achieve his false visions in order to experience their true reality. This brings pain — but not as an end unto itself. It reveals to the individual that what he thought he wanted is not his real desire.[17] This is the most effective means for changing aspirations, which is genuine growth. In Adam's case, he thought he wanted distance from God for the sake of independence. He was granted that distance only to discover its painful reality.

On a deeper level, man was originally created as a being already in relationship with God; his only obligation was to bring that relationship to completion. Man's sin broke the original relationship. To achieve the same goal of complete relationship, man could no longer merely develop a preexisting relationship, for none existed anymore. Man needed to create relationship from scratch, which is a very different task, requiring a different set of acts, and therefore different tools and a different environment. Phrased another way, man was originally created close to God. All man needed to do to achieve his goal was to develop that closeness. But Adam, through his sin, changed himself into a being who was internally distant from God. To have relationship, he now needed to *come* close. One cannot come close if he already is, or appears, or thinks he is close; his distance must become a reality for him. Therefore, the response to Adam's sin was to manifest Adam's internal distance from God by ejecting him from the Garden. But this was only for Adam's sake; it established the circumstances that were necessary to allow Adam the possibility of achieving his defining goal in life of gaining a true relationship with God — it allowed him to *come* close.

Adam's sin had made him far from God in the internal reality of who Adam had become — a being detached from God. Gan Eden was an environment reflecting a close relationship — that is, full revelation

---

17. Ramchal, *Daat Tevunot* 40. Ramchal explains that this concept underlies the process of history.

of God's greatness. The reality of Adam's newly created distance would not have been apparent there, because it would have been artificially masked by the overwhelming power of God's revelation in the Garden. Adam would have been held close, rather than being close. The relationship would have been completely powered by God and would have had nothing to do with whom Adam had become — Adam certainly could not have developed it further since he was already closer than was appropriate for him. Adam's distance had to be actualized into reality so that he could begin the process of constructing a new relationship built on the foundation of who he had become.

A mundane example that illustrates this is a bride and groom happily married for a month. The groom decides that he wants to work on the marriage so that it will be even better, so he starts reading pop psychology books about relationships. He comes to the conclusion that he and his wife are too close, which blocks their flowering as individuals able to give their complete uniqueness to the relationship. He tells his bride that he feels they are growing too close too quickly and that they each need more individual space. Her response, through thinly veiled shock, hurt, and tears, is "Uh, okay." Our ambitious groom then reads the next chapter in his book and finds that in the early stages of marriage, or at any stage for that matter, this is an inappropriate thing to say to his bride. He returns to her and tells her that he just read in the book that he should not have said it, adding, "I take it back, pretend it was never said." Her response, through blank eyes that have lost their luster, is "Uh, okay."

This couple now has two possible paths in front of them. They can pretend that nothing was said, in which case their relationship will never grow beyond an empty caricature of marriage: "Pass the salt, dear. Thank you dear. Would you like your toast burnt or burnt, dear." The alternative is for the groom to approach his bride on his knees with flowers in hand for the foreseeable future as they attempt to create a new relationship. They must accept the break that has occurred and allow it to reveal itself in the hurt and distance that has opened up between them, so that they can enter the process of bridging this new gap. If the couple is externally close but internally distant, if they outwardly pretend to be close when in actuality they are not, they will not be able to do the things that are necessary to create a new relationship.

What hurt the bride so deeply was the groom's distance from her, which was revealed by his statement, "We are too close." To make this metaphor more applicable to Adam's situation in the Garden, let us assume that our groom was conflicted about the issue up until he spoke to his bride. By verbalizing this statement, he then chose his distance from his bride as the truth about himself and defined himself as other to her. This established the reality that he was not, on a fundamental level, connected to her. Similarly Adam, through his decision to defy the command of God, made himself into a being who was broken off from God. Adam made himself far, and his only path forward was to bridge the divide. But in order to do that, the distance had to become a reality in the relationship. He had to leave the Garden.[18]

Punishment, *onesh*, is the process of allowing the reality of distance that sin causes between man and God to manifest itself in the world so that we can deal with it openly. As painful as it is, it is the only way forward based on the new parameters we have established through our transgression. Having changed our location, the path to arrive at the same goal is now different.

But since relationship with God is our goal — the only goal that is worth pursuing — *onesh*, when appropriate, is our chosen outcome from judgment; it is the only remaining path to our cherished goal. The Sages refer to the judgment received by Adam as a pardon because, in fact, a much more fundamental judgement than what Adam needed to continue his relationship with God was being made at the time — the

---

18. As for the other punishments, the purpose of creation was the birth and development of man as a being in full relationship with God. The sin of Adam had fantastically complicated this process, introducing many barriers to its smooth achievement. The complication in the base process of birth and development was reflected in all expressions of birth and development in creation, resulting in the pains of pregnancy, birth, and child rearing. Understanding the increased dependence of women on men would require a full treatment of the Torah's view on gender differences.

decision on whether or not there would be any further relationship.[19] Adam's *onesh* was the necessary compliment to the positive outcome — a pardon — in that more important judgement. It was actually the proof of that positive outcome.

We are willing to accept pain in this world when it is necessary to achieve relationship with God. We do not want to sail through life comfortable but directionless; we prefer the jolt and the pain involved in redirecting ourselves. If we have become lost we want to know it. Though ignorance of that fact may allow serenity, we prefer the fear of knowing the reality along with the pain of recovering our path, for then we eventually reach home.[20]

A FUNDAMENTAL JOY, A SUPERFICIAL SADNESS

We enter judgment with anxiety, but voluntarily. Moreover, we enter it with joy. Rosh Hashanah is the day of our judgment. The stakes are higher than we can imagine. Yet the Torah, which does recognize the seriousness of the moment, declares Rosh Hashanah a holiday. We are even obligated to be joyous, as we learn from the Jews who returned to the Land of Israel after the Babylonian exile. On Rosh Hashanah they wept as they viewed the destruction of the Land and confronted the consequences of their actions. Their leaders, Nechemiah and Ezra, said to them: "Go your way, eat fat foods, drink sweet drinks, and send portions to those for whom nothing is prepared; for this day is holy to our Lord; do not grieve, for the joy of the Lord is your strength."[21] We are

---

19. See note 9 in this chapter that on Rosh Hashanah judgment is also taking place on these two levels.

20. This is the way mercy, *rachamim*, functions. God wants connection to man — *chessed*. Man himself chooses distance. God allows that distance to manifest itself in the relationship — *din*. But instead of letting man turn away, which was the original intention of the inclination that motivated man to distance himself, God requires that man sanctify the distance and turn it into a new kind of relationship — God will meet us wherever we are. This is relationship through distance, a combination of *chessed* and *din*, which is *rachamim*. See Appendix 3.

21. *Nechemiah* 8:10.

being judged! How are we supposed to be joyful at such a momentous time with the potential for so much misfortune?

Understanding the joy of Rosh Hashanah requires understanding the particular type of joy that we are obligated to experience.[22] There are many words for "joy" in Hebrew, each with its own unique shade of meaning. The word for "joy" that Ezra and Nechemiah used was *chedvah*.[23] We can get a sense for the specific meaning of *chedvah* by looking at the first time the term is used in the Torah.

When Yitro, the father-in-law of Moshe, came to meet the Jews in the desert after they departed from *Mitzrayim*, he was coming to convert.[24] When he arrived, Moshe shared with him the story of the Exodus, culminating in the miraculous events at the sea, which completed the escape of the Jews and destroyed the Egyptian army. The Torah tells us that Yitro was "*vayechad*" over all the good that God had done for the Jews.[25] The simple interpretation of the word *vayechad* in this context understands it to stem from the root *chedvah*, meaning "joyous." This is the meaning that fits most naturally into the verse; the Torah is telling us that Yitro was happy to hear about the salvation of the Jews.[26]

But *vayechad* can also be from the root *chad*, which means "sharp." Thus the Talmud interprets the verse as hinting that Yitro reacted to the news by his skin becoming covered with sharp points — goose bumps.[27] Why does the Torah use here a word for joy that also implies discomfort or sorrow? Yitro had been a high-level minister to Pharaoh in *Mitzrayim*. He eventually fled because of a dispute over how to handle the Jews.[28] But a lot of his past was tied up in *Mitzrayim*, and the drowning of the Egyptian army would have claimed the lives of

22. This discussion of *chedvah* is based on material from Rav Berel Gershenfeld.
23. *Nechemiah* 8:10.
24. *Midrash Tanchuma, Parashat Yitro* 1.
25. *Shemot* 18:9.
26. *Rashi, Shemot* 18:9.
27. *Sanhedrin* 94a and *Rashi, Shemot* 18:9.
28. *Sotah* 11a.

many of his old friends. The news of the Exodus, then, must have also entailed shock and pain for Yitro.

What, then, *was* Yitro's reaction to the news? We must remember that Yitro was coming to Moshe to convert. This means that, though Yitro had a past that was associated with many different peoples and religious practices,[29] he had recognized that his future lay with the Jewish people and Torah. Yitro's past expressions of self were indicative of facets of his personality. But his present decision to convert indicated that he had identified his essence as being with the Jews. The destruction of *Mitzrayim* was the only means by which the Jews, Yitro's future, could be freed. This brought Yitro profound joy, which emerged from the deepest recesses of his being. The death of *Mitzrayim*, a prerequisite for the saving of the Jews, took with it a piece of Yitro — but a secondary, more superficial aspect. The news of *Mitzrayim*'s destruction stirred both emotions in Yitro: pain and joy. But the joy came from a much deeper place in Yitro than the pain. That does not mean that Yitro ignored the pain — it was real. To have pretended there was no sorrow would have been hypocrisy and made theater out of his emotions toward God. Yitro accepted the pain. But it was a thin layer of tears over an ocean of joy.

One of the commentaries describes *chedvah* as, "an internal spiritual joy that overpowers a superficial sadness."[30] It is like coming to the end of a movie where the hero has saved his girl but his close friend died along the way. Something is irretrievably lost, and yet what matters far more has been saved. We cannot keep back the tears and yet we feel an overpowering joy welling up through the tears. Yitro had lost something that hurt — deeply — but it could not be compared to the gain, which was far deeper.

This is our approach to Rosh Hashanah and judgment in general. We enter with a certain anxiety that something to which we are strongly attached may be taken away — which means pain. But we recognize

---

29. *Midrash Tanchuma, Parashat Yitro* 7.
30. *Malbim, Shemot* 18:9.

clearly that whatever is decided by God is for our good on the most profound of levels. Our present direction, which is comfortable if only by virtue of its familiarity, may need to be sacrificed. But we know that if it has to go, it is for the sake of the only thing that we truly hold dear, which is our full relationship with God.

The term *chedvah* also captures God's attitude toward judgment. The Talmud states that God cries on an outside level over the destruction of the Temple, but in His inner chamber He is joyous — in a state of *chedvah*.[31] Something valuable is sacrificed — the expression of God's glory in the world through the Temple, and therefore man's immediate recognition of, and connection to, the Creator. God "does not want" the destruction of the Temple — meaning on an immediate level it runs counter to his long-term goal; God created existence for revealed relationship, which occurred through the Temple. But if the Temple has become a façade of relationship, its very existence lulls us into satisfaction with the present and blocks real attainment of the goal. The continued existence of the Temple would be the equivalent of Adam remaining in the Garden after the sin. Its destruction became necessary to force our awareness of our shallowness and redirect us toward the goal of true, complete relationship between man and God. Here God reveals Himself as the perfect giver, holding back even when it is painful because it is appropriate for the overall good of the recipient.[32]

Judgment can bring an external loss, but that very loss is the path — as a result of our prior actions, the only path — that can lead to our true goal of relationship with God. Therefore, beginning that path is a cause for joy, even though if we are honest with ourselves it is a somewhat mixed joy. Ultimately, however, the process of judgment is only positive, forward looking, and for our benefit — even those elements that are, in the short term, painful.

*   *   *

---

31. *Chagigah* 5b. There are conflicting versions of this text. We are using the version quoted in the comment of Malbim cited in the previous note.

32. See Chapter 4, pp. 49–50. This is in contrast to what we called the grandmother syndrome.

Before each Rosh Hashanah we read the Torah portion that describes the curses that will befall the Jewish people if we turn away from God. The section is extremely disturbing to read; our recent past has made clear their potentially literal character. Still, say the Sages, we always read the curses before the New Year because "Let the year end with its curses."[33] Why would the Sages want us to end the year with curses? It seems like an ominous sign coming right before the Day of Judgment.

"Let the year end with its curses" means incorporate whatever distance has been introduced into our relationship with God. Let reality reflect the true state of our connection so that we can move forward in a genuine fashion.[34] We do not want the appearance of relationship with God to get us through life. Life has no purpose or meaning but to create real relationship with God. With God there is only truth, there is no room for pretending.

The Sages sum this up with the following phrase: "When the wise say to destroy and the young say to build, you should destroy, for the destruction of the wise is building whereas the building of the young is destruction."[35] A wise person recognizes that even if a lot of energy has been invested in setting a foundation for a building, if the foundation is faulty it cannot be used. Building on an inadequate foundation only spells the eventual loss of a greater investment. The wise have the maturity to accept that the labor invested in the faulty foundation must be sacrificed; the foundation must be destroyed to make room for the construction of a new foundation that is strong enough to carry the intended building. The young cannot stomach the loss of the prior work and therefore cry out to build upon the faulty base. But such construction will lead to the eventual collapse of a skyscraper with all its attendant loss — their building is destruction.

Judgment is always building. Even when it leads to *onesh*, it is building through destruction, the preparation of a new foundation that can

---

33. *Megillah* 31b.
34. This interpretation of the *gemara* was heard from Rav Moshe Shapiro.
35. *Megillah* 31b. The *gemara's* interpretation that follows was heard from Rav Moshe Shapiro.

carry our relationship with God to the end. The pain of *onesh* actualizes the distance from God we have created. God does not shield us from that pain, for it is the pain of actually experiencing the distance we have created. That is the only pain that can sap the desire for distance that started the problem in the first place. Through this pain we redirect our inner desires; through this pain we are motivated to return. The hiddenness of God, the pain of a test, thus directly breaks down shells we have created around ourselves, exposing the soft inner fibers of our true relationship with God.

ADVANCING THE PROCESS

Thus far we have demonstrated how a flax-whacking test, like a pot-tapping one, improves our relationship with God. But when the Sages choose flax-whacking as their metaphor for punishment, where a shell is removed to reveal a preexisting soft fiber, they imply that the process brings us back to the point from which we initially turned away from God. Yet the language of test, *nisayon*, is a language of raising up and advancing us to new heights of connection to the Creator. How does this apply to the flax-whacking *nisayon*?

In the coming chapters we will see that the division between pot-tapping tests and flax-whacking tests is more conceptual than actual. Rather than being distinct frameworks of experience, they are different stages and facets of one process through which creation is eventually brought to its completion. The Talmud states that God does not bring suffering upon us unless we transgress.[36] Maharal points out that though our actions cause the punishment, there need not be equivalence between the seriousness of a transgression and the severity of the response that it generates. Sin can catalyze a process that presses for far greater accomplishment than mere recovery or repair.[37]

For example, the Talmud states that the Jews were sent into exile in

---

36. *Shabbat* 55a.
37. Maharal, *Gevurot HaShem*, ch. 9.

Mitzrayim because of a mistake made by Avraham. When God promised Avraham that his children would inherit the Land of Israel, Avraham asked, "My Lord God, how will I know?"[38] This question is followed in the *Chumash* by prophecy of the Egyptian exile. The simple understanding of this succession of verses is that Avraham's question revealed incomplete faith; rather than unquestioningly accepting God's assurance, he asked for proof. God reacted with the decree of the exile.[39]

But how much fault can we find with Avraham for this statement? For one thing, Avraham was not questioning God's ability to give the Land as much as the Jewish people's reliability to continually deserve the Land through eternity.[40] Granted, the deepest appreciation of God's unity and omnipotence would recognize this, too, as coming within the purview of the Creator's control.[41] But producing that level of faith in man is the endpoint of creation.[42] How much could Avraham be held responsible if he had not reached it at this early point in history? Furthermore, the Talmud sees in Avraham's use of God's name "My Lord God" when he asked, "How will I know," an acceptance of God's Kingship so profound it merited the eventual building of the Second Temple.[43] Yet this question sent the Jews into exile in *Mitzrayim*!

A detailed analysis of this meeting between Avraham and the Creator is beyond our present scope, but at the very least we recognize that whatever lack of faith Avraham had, it was subtle. How could it cause hundreds of years of horrendous Jewish subjugation to *Mitzrayim*? Maharal answers that Avraham's sin functioned as a catalyst to initiate a test that was needed in any case for the long-term development of the

---

38. *Bereishit* 15:8.
39. In *Nedarim* 32a, Shmuel attributes the exile in *Mitzrayim* to Avraham's question. Maharal in *Gevurot HaShem*, ch. 9, gives as one of the explanations for this that Avraham revealed a lack in his faith.
40. *Ta'anit* 27b.
41. Ramchal, *Da'at Tevunot* 36.
42. Ibid., 40.
43. *Berachot* 7b.

Jewish people.[44] Here we see a classic example of how flax-whacking and pot-tapping can partner — an *onesh* rather than merely leading us to recover ground lost through sin instead pushes us to advance the overall process of history.

This concept of punishment initiating a process which leads to change stretching beyond repairing the damage of the initiating sin must be combined with an insight that we mentioned in the previous chapter. Recovery from sin requires repentance, and repentance requires that we achieve relationship with the Creator on a different plane from the one on which the original transgression occurred. As the Sages put it: the world was created with a "ה" so that those who wish to sin can fall out of the bottom and those who wish to return have a route by which to reenter through the opening on the upper left. They cannot, however, reenter through the same opening through which they exited because it doesn't work.[45]

An example from personal growth can be helpful to understand this process. Imagine a simple person, focused in his physical experiences, whose relationship with the Creator is a naïve one. He is aware of the many gifts he receives as he lives day-to-day in the material world. When he eats he recognizes God's generosity in the food and revels in His kindness, genuinely thanking Him for it. At a certain point his desire for immediate physical pleasure strengthens, and his eating becomes an end unto itself. He stops thanking God for his food and starts concentrating on maximizing his pleasure from meals. When he feels the loss of God from his life he repents. But he cannot simply stop eating greedily. That wall was broken down and once down it doesn't go back up; because of his past, the taste of food has become too strongly associated with his physical desires, and eating will always pull him back toward selfishness. To recover relationship with God, he must focus his life differently, for example, in a more intellectual sphere by connecting

---

44. Maharal, *Gevurot HaShem*, ch. 9.
45. *Menachot* 29b, quoted in full on page 193 of Chapter 11.

to God through Torah study. He will continue to eat, but eating must cease to be a defining event in his life, which can happen only if his center of self shifts to his more intellectual facet.

This provides us with a new way of understanding the process of personal development. When we framed tests as pot-tapping opportunities to actualize potential, we explained that we are confronted with an inclination in order to subjugate it directly as it arises. After we succeed we are free to move our center of self to a higher facet of personality. In the flax-whacking mode of test, the pain of God's hiddenness comes in response to our succumbing to an inclination. This forces us to ascend to a higher facet of personality *in order* to contain that lower inclination. This same process of shifting our center to outflank inclinations that have overwhelmed us also operates on the national level with regard to the exiles and provides us with an alternative model for understanding that process.[46]

We will see later that this will explain the manner by which we overcame certain experiences of exile that we could not understand using the pot-tapping model. This also demonstrates how punishment does not merely achieve recovery from sin, but actually pushes the development process forward and can act as the catalyst and engine to actualizing potential.

*   *   *

In light of this new model of tests we must revisit our discussion of exile as a process of national development. Previously, as evidence that exile is a natural process, we cited the fact that the Sages see a hint to exile in the second verse in the Torah.[47] That verse speaks of the developmental process of creation. Since the Sages associate our exiles with that verse we see they understood that the exiles, too, are a process of development. Because the verse records a time before the Jews even

---

46. See Chapter 9 note 27.
47. See Chapter 10, pp. 161–163.

existed, let alone before they transgressed, we know that the exiles are intrinsic to the process of creation.

Recognizing the interaction between punishment and actualization of potential requires a more sophisticated reading of the *midrash*. The fact that creation occurs through a process of development tells us that development is intrinsic to creation. The fact that the verse indicates four distinct stages in the developmental process implies that processes of development in creation have four stages — thus we find four fundamental aspects of personality that an individual must develop and four exiles for national development. But that the medium through which those four stages of national development actually occur is one of exile — this is something for which we must bear responsibility. In retrospect, once we see exile occurring, we know that it is the avenue through which the stages will travel and, therefore, that is what we see hinted at in the verse. But it could have been otherwise. Had Adam not sinned, for example, four stages of development would still have taken place, but not through exile. Whatever process we actually experience would have been imputed to the verse. The verse only specifies that there will be stages and that there will be four — that is intrinsic to creation. But it does not tell us what they will be. The Sages see specifically the exiles in the verse after the fact.

This is comforting on one side and disheartening on the other. It is comforting because it answers an otherwise very difficult question. If the exiles are intrinsic to creation, we can ask how God could create the world in such a way that the cruelty and pain of exile are built into its necessary structure. We can accept, however, that the pain is a consequence of our own decisions. According to our present understanding, exile is built into the structure of creation, but only because of our choices.

Recognizing our responsibility for the exiles is disheartening because it gives the sense that our increasing distance from God is our own doing. It is one thing if the experience of exile is built into creation — this is the process we must go through and eventually it will be finished. But if we are responsible for our distance from God, we are faced with a question: how can we hope to ever complete the task of history when we get further from our goal of relationship with God with each passing generation?

In response to this question there are two things that need to be said. First, as we mentioned in the beginning of our discussion of development, each generation's specific cultural context presents a unique opportunity to work on a particular facet of our overall relationship with God. Completing all aspects of that relationship requires various and contradictory settings. No generation, therefore, can complete the whole relationship; each can only add its part. Over the totality of all generations, the entire relationship in all of its facets is accomplished. God's obscurity in our times tells us nothing of the actual state of our overall relationship with God. Rather, it provides the specific opportunity to achieve the growth that is the unique responsibility of our generation — because God is so distant faith does not come to us naturally, therefore we can and must create it.

Second, we might think that the fact that we must achieve relationship with God from such distance — that is, through exile — indicates that we are failing. Otherwise, why would we require such distance to succeed? But we cannot grade our achievements in advancing the process of creation because we have no vantage from which to know what the alternate possibilities are. Though theoretically Adam need not have sinned, in which case there would have been no exile,[48] it is also true that exile might have been much harsher than it is. The Midrash notes that, in Daniel's dream of the succession of animals representing the kingdoms, the animals arise out of the sea.[49] This is strange because animals live in the forest. The *midrash* explains that the animals issue from an unnatural place in the dream to symbolize that the kingdoms will be weaker than they could have been. It cites other verses that describe the animals representing the kingdoms coming from the forest, indicating more strength to those who conquer us. From where they

---

48. Ramchal, *Da'at Tevunot* 40.
49. *Vayikra Rabbah* 13:5 interpreting *Daniel* 7:2–7 (quoted on pages 167–168 of Chapter 10). See Maharal, *Ner Mitzvah*, p. 10.

actually issue, continues the *midrash*, is dependent upon our merits. In other words, even if we understand that we have caused the exiles, we must also understand that we may have succeeded in reducing their strength. We cannot know how well or poorly we are doing.

*   *   *

We have explained how punishment for our transgressions pushes us to recover the relationship with God that our sins have compromised. It is not, however, a return to our original state. We were changed by our actions and so must develop a new mode of relationship. Rather, punishment brings us to a new place, one from which we can still reach our goal of connection despite our changes. But we have claimed further that punishment actually serves as an engine of growth. The new place from which we reach toward God represents an advance in our overall project. We have given an example of how this process works in individual growth. It is now time for us to examine the actual history of Jewish exile from the perspective of punishment and see how the process appears from this vantage. We will begin by examining the root experience of Jewish exile.

CHAPTER 13

The Roots of Exile

*"And HaShem said to Moshe, 'Until when will this people an-
ger Me, until when will they not believe in Me?'"[1] The Holy
One said, "I have sighed twice because of you. In the end you
will sigh four times through enslavement to the kingdoms."[2]*

W E ARE NOW PREPARED to apply the metaphor of flax-whacking to
understand the Jewish experience of exile. Just as a farmer strikes
his flax to remove hard shells that obscure its soft interior, so God, by
implication, subjects us to trying circumstances to break through the
shells that we have introduced into our personality that block full relationship with Him. This approach understands that we are responsible
for our difficulties because our choices and actions have necessitated
exile; it is punishment. This view is supported by many statements in
the Torah, the Prophets, and the Sages identifying the transgressions
that caused exile and the destruction of the two Temples.[3]

---

1. *Bemidbar* 14:11.
2. *Bemidbar Rabbah* 16:22.
3. See *Vayikra* 26:33–43 (According to Ramban this refers to the destruction of the First
Temple and its associated exiles) and *Devarim* 28:58–64 (According to Ramban this refers to the destruction of the Second Temple and its associated exiles). The works of
the prophets are rife with lengthy sections connecting exile with transgressions, see for

But it is punishment in the Torah sense of *onesh*, which is a process of repair. God manifests in the external world the internal distance from Him we have created through our transgressions. Though painful, this allows us to honestly confront our situation and grow toward a new form of relationship appropriate to who we have become. As we examine our actual history of exile, we want to be particularly sensitive to this aspect of the process, how it pushes us to develop and advances our overall project of achieving complete relationship with God.

We begin by examining the first and, therefore, the root expression of Jewish exile and the sins that caused it to get a sense for the essential structure of this process. We might think that was the time we spent in *Mitzrayim* before the Exodus. But, technically, that was not an exile of the Jewish people as much as an exile out of which the Jewish people was formed. Although there are important structural similarities and anteced-ents found in our Egyptian experience,[4] the first true exile of the Jewish people was the forty years we spent in the desert after leaving *Mitzrayim*, prevented from entering the Land of Israel by the decree of God. This created the reality of a generation of Jews not living in the Land of Is-rael. And since it was the first generation, it weakened the essential link between the Jewish people and their Land, establishing a proclivity for exile.[5] The transgression that caused that first exile is therefore the root cause of all our subsequent exiles.

The direct cause of that decree is clearly laid out in the Torah.

---

example *Yirmeyahu* 9:11–12. The works of the Sages are also filled with this — *Yoma* 9b is perhaps the most famous, but also much of *Midrash Eichah*.

4. See for example *Shemot Rabbah* 1:12 that the Egyptian exile was composed of four de-crees. These decrees parallel the four exiles (See *Shemot Rabbah* 26:1). See also *Rashi, Berei-shit* 15:14 and *Ohr Gedaliyahu, Likutei Shemot* 1 that the redemption from *Mitzrayim* in-cluded within it the eventual redemption from the four kingdoms. See also *Sanhedrin* 111a brought in *Rashi, Shemot* 6:1, *Shemot Rabbah* 5:22, and *Rashi, Sanhedrin* 101b that because the four decrees in *Mitzrayim* did not cleanse us fully, the golden calf occurred; as a result of the golden calf we must go through the four modern exiles.

5. See *Maharal, Netzach Yisrael*, ch. 19. See also *Maharal, Gevurot HaShem*, ch. 60: "If the Jews merit greatness in this world this is unusual and a thing with no consistency. It is as if exile is in the Jewish people's nature and freedom a novelty."

Seventeen months after the Exodus, having spent a year at Har Sinai learning Torah, the Jews stood at the Jordan River with instructions to enter and possess the Land.[6] They requested to first send spies,[7] ostensibly to evaluate the enemy's defenses and determine the best path for attack,[8] but really because they had doubts about the quality of the Land and their ability to conquer it.[9] When the spies returned, they gave an unflattering description of Israel and proclaimed that the Jews would be unable to penetrate the defenses of the Canaanites.[10] Though Yehoshua and Kalev, two of the spies, argued forcefully against this report,[11] the Jewish people accepted the majority version, complained against God, turned their backs on the Land, and prepared to return to *Mitzrayim*.[12]

God responded with the decree that this generation would wander in the desert until they died and their children would inherit the Land in their stead.[13] From this it would appear that understanding the cause of exile involves understanding this transgression of the spies. However, God also stated that the exile would last forty years, one year for each of the forty days that the spies scrutinized the Land with an unfavorable eye.[14] This is in contrast to a statement in *Devarim* that the Jews wandered the desert for only thirty-eight years after the sin of the spies.[15] *Rashi* proves that the forty year decree began retroactively from the sin of the golden calf which technically occurred two years prior to the sin of the spies.[16]

---

6. *Devarim* 1:19–21.
7. *Devarim* 1:22.
8. Maharal, *Gur Aryeh, Bemidbar* 13:2.
9. *Rashi, Bemidbar* 13:2; Maharal, *Gur Aryeh, Bemidbar* 13:2.
10. *Bemidbar* 13:28.
11. Ibid., 14:6–9.
12. Ibid., 14:3–4, 10.
13. Ibid., 14:21–31.
14. Ibid., 14:33–34.
15. *Devarim* 2:14.
16. *Rashi, Bemidbar* 14:33. Since a partial year is counted as a whole year, the golden calf occurred two years before the sin of the spies.

Why would a decree of exile, which came directly in response to the sin of the spies, begin from the sin of the golden calf? The punishment must be a consequence of both sins together. *Rashi's* language is, "From the moment they made the calf this decree came into His thoughts but He waited until they filled their quota."[17] This implies that the sin of the spies somehow completed a transgression that began with the golden calf.[18]

This relationship between the two events is confirmed indirectly by a *midrash* that discusses the days on which these two events occurred. The golden calf was worshipped on the seventeenth of Tammuz, the day when the walls of Yerushalayim were breached before the destruction of the Temple.[19] The Jews rejected the Land of Israel on the ninth of Av, the day when both Temples were destroyed.[20] Yirmeyahu, prophesying before the destruction of the First Temple, had a vision of a rod of almond wood.[21] The rod connoted that God would strike down the Jewish people and raze the Temple,[22] an image in keeping with Yirmeyahu's appointment as the prophet of destruction.[23] But why was Yirmeyahu shown what the rod was made of? What was the significance of almond wood?

The *midrash* answers that almonds are the fastest ripening fruit, maturing twenty-one days after they blossom. This hinted at the twenty-one

---

17. Ibid.

18. Rav Moshe Shapiro emphasized the fundamental nature of these two sins and their relationship to one another. The line of development followed here is broadly based on his approach.

19. *Mishnah Ta'anit* 4:6. The *Talmud Bavli* states that this was the date of the breaching of the walls only in the time of the Second Temple (*Ta'anit* 28b). According to an opinion in the *Talmud Yerushalmi* (*Ta'anit* 4:5), however, even in the time of the First Temple the walls of Yerushalayim were breached on the Seventeenth of Tammuz. Rebbi Elazar in the *Midrash Rabbah* (*Eichah Rabbah*, Proem 23; *Kohelet Rabbah* 12:7) seems to follow the line of the *Yerushalmi*.

20. Ibid.

21. *Yirmeyahu* 1:12.

22. *Malbim, Yirmeyahu* 1:12.

23. *Yirmeyahu* 1:10.

days between the two events that bracket the destruction of the Temple: the seventeenth of Tammuz when the walls of Yerushalayim were breached and the ninth of Av when the Temple was burned.[24] But this prophecy does not just convey the time interval of the disaster; it also implies that the events of these two days are linked like the blossoming of a fruit is to its maturation. This is obvious in the case of the destruction of the Temple. The breaching of the walls was a beginning — the loss of protection that made destruction likely if not imminent. It was not unto itself destruction but, barring some remarkable intervention, devastation would be the natural outcome — it was the budding of a catastrophe that came to fruition on the ninth of Av.

Though Yirmeyahu's vision was specifically in reference to the destruction of the First Temple, this relationship between the seventeenth of Tammuz and the ninth of Av is constant over the years. Time is cyclical; each day has a unique energy that is expressed consistently from year to year. So if the events that took place on these two days were connected like a blossom to its mature fruit in the time of the first destruction, the events that occur on these two days must be connected in the same way when the Jews were in the desert. The golden calf was, then, the beginning of a process that developed into a full break between God and the Jewish people on the ninth of Av when the spies led the Jewish people to turn their backs on the Land. These two transgressions *together* bring about the first exile — and are the root cause of all exile. We need to understand these two sins, how one develops from the other, and how this structures our experience of exile today.

THE GOLDEN CALF — REPLACING MOSHE

The worship of the golden calf took place forty days after the Jews heard the Ten Commandments at Har Sinai. Immediately following that revelation, Moshe went up the mountain to learn the details of the Torah and to receive its concrete expression in the form of tablets. He was

---

24. *Eichah Rabbah*, Proem 23.

supposed to return forty days later. There was some confusion over how to calculate the date. The Jews became convinced that Moshe was late and must be dead and, therefore, built the golden calf.[25]

Even given their assumption that Moshe was gone, the decision of the Jews to build an idol is bewildering. They had just heard the Ten Commandments; at that time all the veils of physical reality were drawn back to reveal God's unity.[26] To this day we are able to recite the Shema, declaring God's unity, only because of that experience.[27] How could the Jews build an idol so soon afterwards?

The commentaries prove that the intention behind the construction of the calf was not to provide a substitute for God but, rather, a substitute for Moshe. As their leader, Moshe acted as an intermediary to God, and Moshe was missing.[28] They needed someone or something else to take over that role and the calf was chosen. The obvious difficulty raised by this understanding is why, if the Jews wanted to replace Moshe, did they choose to build an inanimate idol? Why not replace him from amongst the greats who remained, such as his brother, Aharon?

Suggesting that Moshe's leadership could be replaced by that of Aharon misunderstands who Moshe was and what his leadership represented. The Midrash teaches us that when Moshe was with God on Har Sinai he heard all the Torah insights that would be uttered by all Jews for all of history.[29] This means that Moshe, as a single individual, personified the full spiritual potential of the entire Jewish people.[30] A hint to Moshe's extraordinary greatness came when God first revealed Himself to Moshe and appointed him leader of the Jews. At that time, Moshe attempted to convince God that he should not be the one to bring the Jews out of *Mitzrayim*. There, Moshe argued that he was unfit

25. *Rashi, Shemot* 32:1 from *Shabbat* 89a.
26. *Rashi, Devarim* 4:35 from the *Pesikta Rabbah*.
27. *Devarim Rabbah* 2:30.
28. *Ramban, Shemot* 32:1.
29. *Vayikra Rabbah* 22:1.
30. *Rashi, Shemot* 18:1 from the *Mechilta* and Maharal, *Gur Aryeh* on *Rashi* there.

because he could not speak properly.[31] Speech is the consequence of combining the *neshamah* with the physical body and is unique to man.[32] Other creatures may have an ability to verbally communicate, but the Torah concept of "speech" is specifically the verbal expression of an inner, spiritual reality.[33] Moshe could not speak because his combination of soul and body was so heavily skewed toward his *neshamah* that it pushed the limits of what it is to be human.[34] He was so deeply rooted in his spiritual experience that he could not express it.[35]

In the first four books of *Chumash* when we hear Moshe speak, it is actually God speaking through Moshe.[36] The first time we hear Moshe himself speak is in *Devarim*, the last book of *Chumash*. It was only after forty years of teaching Torah in the desert that Moshe gained the ability to formulate his thoughts in a manner where he could express them fluently. The Midrash generalizes from here that Torah heals speech — that is, everyone's speech.[37] But the process works differently for us than for Moshe. For Moshe, the intensity and depth of his spiritual reality defied containment in particular, distinct words — he needed Torah to integrate his spiritual self with his physical reality. In our case, without Torah we can say words — we simply have nothing to express that is worthy of the title "speech" because we are too detached from our spiritual root. Torah heals speech by connecting physical reality to the spiritual realm. But whereas for us Torah raises us up to spiritual experience, Torah allowed Moshe to connect down — it gave him a voice.

Moshe was a singular individual in history; that he merited bringing Torah to the world indicated that he reached the greatest spiritual heights attainable by man and so was the appropriate person to act as an

---

31. *Shemot* 4:10.
32. *Targum Onkelus, Bereishit* 2:7.
33. As heard from Rav Moshe Shapiro.
34. Maharal, *Gevurot HaShem*, ch. 28.
35. Rav Tzaddok HaKohen, *Sichat Malachei HaShareit* 17b.
36. Zohar III, p. 231, Rav Tzaddok, *Resisei Lailah* 52.
37. *Devarim Rabbah* 1:1.

intermediary to God.[38] This allowed Moshe to provide a kind of leadership that could not be replaced. As the head of the Jewish people, he dramatically shifted the spiritual center of the nation and established our connection to the Creator at a depth of being far beyond the constraints of physical reality. Thus Moshe's leadership was synonymous with a relationship with God that expressed itself through miracles.

Under Moshe's supervision, the Jewish nation was born through the miraculous process of the Exodus, beginning with the plagues and culminating in the splitting of the sea. As they crossed the desert they were sustained by the falling *manna* and water from a rock. Moshe led them to Har Sinai where God gave them the Torah, revealing Himself and the spiritual underpinnings of reality to an unprecedented degree. Since the Jews were also physical beings, these experiences strained them to their limit and seemed only survivable because of Moshe's presence.

The experience at Har Sinai illustrates their dependence upon Moshe. The Midrash states that the intensity of revelation on the mountain was such that when God expressed the First Commandment directly to the Jews, their *neshamot* were drawn out of them and pulled back to their source in God, to the point where they had a deathlike experience. They only survived because it was God they were connecting to, Who is the source of life. The same thing happened with the Second Commandment.[39]

For all its wonderous exaltedness, the experience must have been quite wrenching. After all, the Jews were still physical beings. Following the Second Commandment, the Jews turned to Moshe and asked that he be the direct recipient of the remaining commandments and relay them to the people.[40] Direct revelation was too much for the Jewish people, but Moshe could be counted on to bridge the gap.

As long as the Jews had Moshe to lead them, they were confident that they could maintain this relationship of revelation with the Creator.

---

38. Maharal, *Tiferet Yisrael*, ch. 21.
39. *Shabbat* 88b.
40. *Shir HaShirim Rabbah* 1:15.

However, after forty days without Moshe, as they contemplated their future, the Jews thought that he was gone forever. They were convinced it was unrealistic to think that without him they could sustain the loftiness that had characterized their relationship with God until that point. We can imagine, as they stood in the shadow of the mountain where only days before they had experienced such an overwhelming encounter with the Creator, that the thought of moving forward without Moshe would be terrifying.

THE SIGNIFICANCE OF THE OX

The Jews did not build the calf to replace God. Once we understand the role that Moshe played, we realize that they also did not really build it to replace Moshe. Rather, the purpose of the calf was to replace the prior mode of relationship with God that had been so dependent upon Moshe. Now, in what they thought was his permanent absence, such a relationship seemed untenable.

The key to understanding what the Jews were doing lies in understanding their specific choice of an ox calf.[41] The ox was the animal that interfaced man with nature in the ancient world, for it pulled the plow.[42] Its form, representing harnessed power, symbolized the trait of God through which He creates nature.[43] They nullified themselves to this idol to receive from God as He flowed into the world through this particular trait — their relationship to God was to be mediated through physical reality. Instead of breaking through all the boundaries of nature to reach directly to their infinite Source, as had been the way under Moshe's leadership, the Jews wanted to remain within the familiar boundaries of nature and relate to God indirectly through the physical world He created. The Jews were consciously choosing to diminish the directness,

---

41. See Maharal, *Gur Aryeh, Shemot* 29:1 for a discussion of why a calf and not an adult ox.
42. Rav Chayim Friedlander, *Siftei Chayim* II, p. 60.
43. Nature expresses God's power contained within the strictures of natural law. This contrasts to the uncontained expression of God's power through miracle. This is symbolized by the lion, who is both more powerful than the ox and unrestricted.

intensity, and clarity of their relationship with God. This understanding is supported by the use of oxen in the imagery of the prophets. One of the faces of the angels holding up the throne of God in Yechezkel's vision of the heavenly court was an ox. These faces represent character traits through which God relates to the world.[44] What trait was associated with the face of the ox? Yechezkel gives us a hint when he specifies that the angels' ox face was on their left side.

In Torah and Rabbinic literature the left is identified with the weak side and associated with means as opposed to ends. When we are making something with our hands, the right hand does the primary work with the weaker left hand providing the assistance and support needed to bring the project to completion. For example, if we have to tighten a bolt the right hand turns the bolt — the actual goal and most strenuous task — while the left restrains the nut from moving, providing necessary support. Nothing can be accomplished without the assistance of the left, but it is the right that does the real work. This characterization of left and right in the context of creation associates *din* (judgment) with the left, and *chessed* (giving) with the right. God's purpose (the right) is to give good. Pure giving is unlimited, for it is without specific cause or measure. But the good that is received is greatest when earned, which requires that God hold Himself back, giving through a system of precisely calibrated rewards rather than the unrestricted giving of unadulterated *chessed.* The means (the left) to accomplish the greatest good, then, is through the limited, restricting character of judgment. Thus, the left is associated with the restriction of God's infinite flow and revelation.

Worshipping the ox — the face on the left side in Yechezkel's vision — was striving to focus God's expression in the world through His trait of *din*, which is a force of restriction.[45] This would hide Him behind the mask of nature, channeling the relationship through measured, causal reactions, rather than through His trait of *chessed*, which is free of the

---

44. Malbim, *Yechezkel* 1:10.
45. *Shemot Rabbah* 42:5.

restrictions of natural law and directly reveals God's presence through miracles. The Jews were seeking indirect relationship — to appreciate God through His works of nature — rather than receiving from Him directly. This was a hard and painful choice — to knowingly distance themselves from God and His goodness — but it seemed like the courageous thing to do. Let God be less apparent, even if it meant that the Jews would have to work harder to maintain a connection, so that the relationship could be sustained.

Like Adam before them, the Jews were consciously distancing God from themselves for apparently noble reasons. And like Adam before them, the Jews were deluding themselves.[46] Their choice of the calf revealed their purported motivation to be no more than a justification. The ox mediated man's relationship to nature in a specific manner. Man did not sit on his ox, admiring the beautiful forests that God had made; he hitched his ox to a plow and uprooted the trees to plant wheat. The ox was the animal through which man took control of nature and made it over in the image of his own selfish needs. This is not prohibited; it is part of what man does in the world. Man's task requires him to direct creation on some level. But worshipping this capability defined man by his independence rather than containing it within its proper context as an emulation and service of God.

The choice of an ox revealed that the real purpose of the Jews in diminishing the revelation of God was to take control of their world. As long as God's revelation was clear, the Jews were restricted to relating to the world as He intended it. Everything existed solely as a stepping stone to relationship with the Creator in its purest form. But if they reduced God's expression in the world — if they clouded their awareness of Him and how He defines reality — they would have to be responsible for defining reality and all its contents. This would provide the latitude

---

46. Adam justified eating from the tree because it would expand his free choice and, therefore, his responsibility for his relationship with God. Though this represented an alternate path of service, he was inclined to favor it against the explicit command of God because of pridefulness. See Chapter 12, p. 199. For a detailed discussion of Adam's sin, see Chapter 16.

to understand the world in a manner that supported and idealized living however they chose.[47] Not that they wanted to end their relationship with God — such an idea was out of the question in the world of revelation that the Jews occupied at that time;[48] God's existence and involvement in their lives was undeniable. The calf was for worship — they wanted connection. But they wanted idol worship, or to translate more precisely from the Hebrew, "strange worship." Hiding God's face would allow them to determine the nature of their relationship, providing an opportunity to mix in their own selfish agendas.

IDOLATRY

Even though the Jews intended to maintain relationship with God, their attempt to focus on a particular Divine trait through the worship of the golden calf was idolatrous. The Sages say about idolaters that they "stand upon their gods." The Sages cite as evidence the verse, "And Pharaoh dreamt and behold he was standing on the Nile."[49] The Nile, *Mitzrayim*'s source of sustenance, was worshipped as a god; Pharaoh, in dreaming that he was standing on the Nile, was imagining himself standing on his god.[50] We stand upon that which serves as our platform for being in the world. How can idolaters imagine themselves standing on their god? This implies that their god serves them — presumably gods are to be served, not to serve!

With this image, the Torah conveys the idea that idol worship is a sophisticated form of self-indulgence and self-worship.[51] An idol

---

47. We will explain further on in Chapter 16 (pp. 303–310) that the foundation of the Knowledge of Good and Evil is knowing the world from the perspective of the self. This is why the commentaries understand the sin of the calf to be a repeat, within the context of the era in history in which it occurred, of the sin of Adam in the Garden.

48. In a time of idol worship, man's consciousness of his connection to a transcendent source is central to his awareness. This is far from us today, as we mentioned in Chapter 10, pp. 257–258. We will explain this historical process in more detail in the next chapter, and we will explore its basis and implications in the last section of the book.

49. *Bereishit* 41:1.

50. *Bereishit Rabbah* 89:4.

51. This interpretation of the *midrash* was heard from Rav Moshe Shapiro.

worshipper does not directly serve God, the unitary Source of reality. Instead, the idolater takes a particular force through which God connects to the world and frames it as an independent authority. The force he chooses is the transcendent projection of a particular energy in himself, around which he has come to center his life. An aspect of the idolater's personality, which exists to provide a means to connecting to God, becomes an end unto itself, thus corrupting it.[52]

For example, the trait of *malchut*, the ability to rule, was given to man as a way to emulate God. If it becomes alienated within him from the overall project of connection to God and is elevated to an end unto itself, it warps into a desire for power and comes to dominate the idolater's personality (as we explained in our examination of individual development).[53] In direct parallel to this internal corruption of *malchut*, the idolater alienates from God the Divine trait of *malchut*, the rulership, authority, and power through which God expresses Himself into creation; the idolater elevates it to the status of an independent and dominant force. He worships this force as the center of reality in parallel to his elevation of its internal equivalent to the center of his personality.[54] His service of his god through emulation then leads the idolater to feed his dominant inclination for power with religious zeal instead of nagging guilt.[55] The idolater stands upon the god he effectively created to serve himself.[56]

---

52. See Chapter 9, pp. 148–151.

53. Ibid.

54. In the ancient world when man encountered existence on a more symbolic level the idolater selected the object that most purely embodied this trait for him. In our example of corrupted *malchut* perhaps he would use a lion or ox. He then created physical idols to provide nodes through which to relate to this force.

55. In Chapter 10 (pp. 176–177) we also explained that the thickening of our awareness of self caused by the domination of an inclination forces us to move away from awareness of a truly unitary Creator — for our prominent selfhood contradicts that unity. This results in an idolatrous concept of transcendence.

56. In a context of revelation, where the finite world's dependence upon transcendence is obviously experienced, worship is necessarily built into our reality. In such a world, a person cannot be selfish or egotistical in a vacuum; that would be at such odds with reality as

Idol worship only becomes possible once God and His actual intention for creation become obscured. There can be no confusion about alternate sources of control when God is revealed. Our inclinations, which are the real basis of our identification with an idolatrous force, are held in check as long as we are clear that the true existence of our energies is only as a means to serve God.[57] Thus, whereas the idolaters stand upon their gods, the Sages tell us God stands upon those who have clarity of God's omnipotence — the righteous. They cite Yaakov's dream of the ladder where "God was standing upon him" — meaning upon Yaakov.[58] The righteous do not pervert their vision of transcendence to their self-interests; rather, they make themselves conduits for the expression of God — God stands on them. Their clarity of God allows them to give proper priority to their various aspects of self, channeling all facets of themselves toward the ultimate purpose of relationship with the Creator, rather than letting individual aspects railroad the self to false realities. It was this constraint born of clarity that the Jews subconsciously sought to remove through worshipping the ox.[59]

Our world is an extreme example of this where people attaining glory, power, and pleasure are considered the most successful and to be emulated. If they add some religious practice or community involvement we see it as a complete life. When service is sufficient as a mere added spice to life there is a confusion of goals. We use God to add a façade of meaning to our lives. We make Him a means to our end.

CHANGING TABLETS

Response to the building and worship of the calf was swift — the tablets Moshe had received on Har Sinai were broken.[60] This was not merely

---

to constitute insanity. Instead, selfishness must be reflected in and refracted through our perception of what the source of reality is and our relationship with that source.

57. Rav Yitzchak Izak Chaver, *Siach Yitzchak*, sec. 1, *Drush l'Shabbat Teshuvah*.
58. *Bereishit Rabbah* 89:4.
59. See Rav Yitzchak Izak Chaver, *Siach Yitzchak*, sec. 1, *Drush l'Shabbat Teshuvah*.
60. *Shemot* 32:19. The calf was worshipped as the tablets were being given to Moshe. In

the loss of a choice object. The tablets were a material expression of our relationship with God and their shattering represented the shattering of that relationship.

The Talmud states that the tablets were six cubits long and that when they were being given to Moshe on Sinai there was a moment when two cubits where in God's "hands," two cubits were in Moshe's hands, and there were two cubits in between.[61] This language is used because according to the Talmud when there is a dispute in ownership whatever is in one's hand is considered his.[62] Thus the two cubits in God's "hands" represented an aspect of Torah that is totally "His," meaning beyond our comprehension, the two cubits in Moshe's hands were entirely Moshe's, representing a part of Torah that is accessible to man, and the two cubits in between were jointly owned, referring to a facet of Torah that we can grasp to a degree, but when we try to probe its full depth our understanding fades into an inarticulate blur. In this area of Torah our understanding merges into God's understanding.[63] Torah is the medium through which the Jews connect to God.[64]

The tablets gave this connection material expression. There is a tradition to depict the tablets as rounded on top, even though there is no mention of this in the Talmud. This tradition derives from the verse, "Write them (Torah) on the tablet of your heart"[65] — rounded tops suggest the image of a heart. The stone of the tablets signified the collective

---

response, the Talmud teaches that God resisted letting the tablets into reality, but Moshe pulled them in (*Yerushalmi Shekalim* 6:5). Once Moshe came down the mountain and saw the idolatry he broke the tablets himself (*Shemot* 32:19). A *midrash* states that the letters flew off the tablets and the empty stone became too heavy to carry, so Moshe threw them down (*Midrash Tanchuma Ki Tisa* 30). In response to the sin, God, Moshe, and the Torah itself (reality) all aligned to deny the Jews the tablets.

61. *Yerushalmi Ta'anit* 23a; *Midrash Tanchuma Ki Tisa* 37.
62. *Mishnah Bava Metzia* 1:1.
63. See Maharal, *Tiferet Yisrael*, ch. 48.
64. Maharal, *Netzach Yisrael*, ch. 2.
65. *Mishlei* 3:3. Radvaz quoted by Rav Eliyahu Dessler, *Michtav Me'Eliyahu* II, p. 27.

heart of the Jewish people,[66] and the writing represented God's Torah, which is one with God. The tablets with the writing on them therefore embodied the connection between the Jewish people and God. Shattering them was a shattering of that relationship.

This was not, however, the end of all relationship. After much repentance, God gave the Jews a second set of tablets, signifying the renewal of the connection. But there were significant differences between the first set of tablets and the second set, implying significant differences between the nature of the original relationship and the new one. In the first set, the writing was miraculously cut entirely through the stone.[67] The significance of this was that the tablets did not have writing on stone. Rather, the stone itself formed the writing where the writing and the stone were one entity.[68]

This represented the total integration of the Torah with the Jewish people. Had these tablets been received by the Jews, the Torah would have been so much a part of our being that we would have been unable to view the world in any manner other than the Torah's vision — we would have been totally one with our Torah.[69] These first tablets signified a relationship of absolute revelation — like that which Adam experienced before his sin. All of the Torah was written on them; nothing was left out or hidden.[70] The stone of these first tablets was from God,[71] representing that our heart or anchor of selfhood was located in an aspect of our being that emanated directly from God — our root self, as opposed to our intellect, identity, or physical being. Because the center of self through which we related to God was from the same place as the Torah, we could achieve the total integration of Torah and self.

---

66. As heard from Rav Moshe Shapiro.

67. *Shabbat* 104a; *Shemot* 32:15 with *Rashi*. The miracle lay in the fact that they could be read from either side and that in those letters that were cut all around, the *samech* and *mem*, the unconnected stone in the middle hovered.

68. Heard from Rav Aharon Feldman.

69. This is the level of knowledge called *da'at*. See Chapter 16, pp. 292–293.

70. *Beit HaLevi*, Drash 18.

71. *Shemot* 31:18, 32:16.

The second tablets were cut out of the ground by Moshe,[72] signifying that, as a result of the sin of the calf, our center of self had descended to an earthly, physical place from which we now needed to form the primary bond to the Torah. But unlike the higher center we occupied before the sin, this "heart" was not from the same realm as the Torah, so the integration between the two could not be complete. That is to say, the Torah is a spiritual, unitary vision, but we had come to be defined by our fractured, physical being. In the second set of tablets, the Torah was written on the tablets rather than through them, lacking the integration of material and content — self and Torah — found in the first set. And not all the Torah was revealed in writing; most of the Torah was kept off the tablets, accompanying it as a hidden, oral tradition, signifying that our relationship with God would not be entirely revealed.[73]

We see that though relationship between God and the Jewish people was recovered, it was a totally different kind of relationship. On Har Sinai, God had offered us absolute revelation and closeness. By worshipping the golden calf, we rejected that closeness and separated ourselves from the Creator. The underlying motivation for distancing ourselves was selfish. God would not accept a relationship that was diluted with selfishness, for it would reduce worship to a cover for indulgence. So the original relationship established on Har Sinai could not continue after the calf. And even though we repented, repentance could redirect our goal from selfishness to a desire for full relationship, but it could not undo the distance we had opened up between ourselves and God. But, God also would not compromise on the need for relationship — this was the purpose of creation.

The only available path was to offer a new kind of relationship, one which emerged from distance, to replace the close relationship that had been given and that the calf had made irrelevant. The attentive reader will see a direct parallel in all aspects of the Jewish people's worship of

---

72. Ibid., 34:1.
73. Ibid., 34:27 with *Rashi*; *Gittin* 60b.

the golden calf and Adam's eating from the forbidden tree — the nature of the prior state, the newly created reality, the justification, and the motivation.

A relationship forming from a distance is very different from one in which closeness is already present. When closeness is there, the focus of the relationship is on perfecting our expression of that closeness — acting upon it and deepening it further. But when there is distance, the emotional content of the relationship is the longing for that which we do not have, demonstrated in our uncompromising pursuit of the other.

In a developed relationship we do not exist as an individual who is other to our partner — we are defined in and through the relationship. The symbol of the formation of a covenant is cutting an animal in half[74] to signal that, as a result of the bond, we as individuals are only halves of a greater whole.[75] That was our situation before the worship of the calf. But after the calf our starting point was distance — we no longer had integration with God. That is precisely what we needed to create. This was symbolized in the second tablets where the writing of the Torah was on the stone rather than through it — the integration did not yet exist, which challenged us to create it.

But to form relationship from a distance, the reality of our distance had to take on expression. God had to be hidden. The desert, however, was necessarily a place of revelation. Regardless of how much things changed after the sin of the calf, the Jews could only exist there through constant miracle and revelation — the falling of the *manna*, the miraculous well of water. The opportunity to fully hide God's face came only once the Jews stood on the banks of the Jordan poised to enter the Land of Israel.

THE SIN OF THE SPIES

Relative to the desert, entering the Land of Israel represented a transition to a more natural state; this would have been true even had there never

---

74. *Rashi, Bereishit* 15:10.
75. As heard from Rav Moshe Shapiro.

been a golden calf. But after the golden calf, that transition became more extreme. We had demanded — and created internally — distance from God. Entry into the Land was the time for that distance to be realized in the world and to test whether we could achieve relationship under the new circumstances we had established. Would we desire our connection to God with sufficient strength to search for Him when He was concealed behind the veil of nature that the Land would introduce? The difficulty of the test lay in the fact that God's obscurity was a consequence of the sin of the calf. That act shifted our center of personality to more physical aspects of self. Nature, which laid its claim to being the locus of reality, resonated powerfully with the aspect of self which, after the sin of the calf, seemed most real about us.[76]

The Jews requested that spies be sent ahead of them to scout out enemy defenses. Those spies would be the first to face the test. Moshe understood the challenge and prepared them. He instructed them to look for fortifications, which made sense according to the Jews' stated intention for sending the spies. But he added that fortifications would be a sign of weakness — the opposite of what we would normally think. For, Moshe added, strong people rely on their merits rather than walls.[77]

Moshe's message to the spies was, in effect: "You have been in the desert for two years, where nature has constantly been abrogated; you have been shown the deepest truth of reality, that God runs the world. You are about to enter the Land of Israel that will present itself as a natural environment — you are leaving the protective womb of revelation. Do not forget the clarity you achieved here: nature is just a veil. Be strong to impose the deeper vision you hold within yourself upon your world — do not passively accept the world as it will present itself to you. People derive their strength from God. If they need walls to protect themselves, they are weak." Moshe continued this theme when he told

---

76. The fact that we, through our actions, located ourselves in this aspect of self made our identification with it that much stronger. See Ramchal, *Derech HaShem*, 1:3:8.

77. *Rashi, Bemidbar* 13:18.

them to be especially attentive to trees.[78] The Talmud explains that he was referring to the righteous. He called them trees to emphasize their significance to the spies, whose job was to evaluate the true strength of the enemy. Just as the shade of a tree protects its surroundings, so the merits of the righteous protect their neighbors.[79] Look out for any righteous individuals who might complicate matters. He was principally concerned that Iyov (Job) might still be alive.[80]

When the spies returned, the majority of them reported that the Land was indeed beautiful, but that its beauty was useless — the Jews could not defeat the Canaanites, as their cities were heavily fortified.[81] The spies saw the Canaanite walls and were struck with fear, drawing exactly the opposite conclusion from the one Moshe told them to draw. Upon entering the natural world, they became lost in it, seeing strength in physical objects rather than relationship with God. They passively accepted the world as it presented itself — an internally complete, self-contained, natural environment isolated from its Creator. The spies revealed that they lacked the burning desire for relationship with God that was needed to actively search for God's now hidden connection to reality.

This is seen in the ensuing debate between the ten spies who said the Jews could not conquer the Land and the two spies who dissented, Kalev and Yehoshua. "The cities are fortified," cried the spies. "But Iyov is dead," answered Kalev.[82] These two camps were not talking to one another, for they were living in different worlds. The ten spies were saying that the Canaanites were physically strong and therefore impossible to defeat, for the spies were living in a natural world. Kalev, who was living in God's world, replied that the Jews had no real opposition to face in the Land because no righteous individuals remained to protect the Canaanites. The one person Moshe was concerned about — Iyov — was

---

78. *Bemidbar* 13:20.
79. *Rashi, Bemidbar* 13:20 from *Bava Batra* 15a.
80. Ibid.
81. *Bemidbar* 13:28.
82. Ibid., 14:9, with *Rashi* there.

no longer alive. The Canaanites would be so much fodder for the Jews, who represented God.[83]

The Jews sided with the report of the ten spies, revealing that they, too, accepted a natural vision of the world.[84] With this they failed to actualize the last possible form of relationship that was left after the golden calf fiasco. Through complete revelation, God had defined the world for the Jews as a place of relationship with Him that they merely needed to accept. Through the calf, the Jews rejected that world and any other that was imposed upon them from without. They chose to define the world for themselves. In doing so they changed themselves into beings distant from God, to whom He could no longer reveal Himself and still have genuine relationship.

So God granted the Jews the distance from Him they had chosen. His revelation was hidden, requiring the Jews to understand the world themselves. The purpose of the hiding was not to fulfill their original intention of mixing their selfish inclinations into reality, but to give them responsibility for creating relationship from a distance. This was synonymous with requiring them to actively impose on a darkened world an understanding that recognized the connection of man to God. But when the test came, when they entered a world where God was hidden, they shirked the responsibility they had taken upon themselves through the calf and passively accepted the natural world that presented itself to them. With the calf, when they should have accepted understanding they chose to impose it. With the spies, when they should have actively imposed understanding they chose to passively accept it.

Accepting God's absence was equivalent to not really wanting relationship with Him. The Midrash conveys this idea when it states that one of the complaints of the Jews about the Land of Israel was that, as

---

83. In Chapters 16 (p. 293), 17 (pp. 313–321), and 18 we will discuss occupying the same physical space but living in these two completely different worlds.

84. *Bemidbar* 14:1–4,10. The culpability of the nation is emphasized in *Devarim*, ch. 1 where the Jews rejected entering the land in verse 26 before we read about them hearing something negative from the spies, which does not come until verse 28.

opposed to *Mitzrayim* where water was regularly and reliably supplied by the Nile, the Land of Israel was dependent upon rain for its water.[85] Rain comes as a consequence of prayer. The Jews preferred the natural regularity of the Nile to direct dependence on God. This was roughly comparable to an infant rejecting an opportunity to suckle from his mother and preferring instead to drink from a bottle. A healthy infant craves intimacy with his mother as much as he wants milk and is resentful when he is first weaned. For a baby, the milk is not merely an end unto itself but also an opportunity to be close. The time does come when separation is the appropriate choice. But even when it does, the push to independence is to change the quality of our relationship — not to cut us off from all connection.[86] The Land of Israel was being given specifically as a medium for a new relationship. Though the *manna* would cease and we would become responsible to grow our own food, our need to ask for rain retained enough transparency to our ongoing dependence on God for continued, full relationship. This was the worst possible situation to want more independence and reliance on nature for it was an embrace of God's distance in the very place we needed to prove that we longed to overcome it.

THE EXILE OF A GENERATION

The sin of the golden calf was the equivalent of a breaching of the walls of Yerushalayim; a process that would eventually culminate in a break in our relationship with God had budded. Before the calf, God was revealed to the Jews so that they were prevented from losing relationship with Him by the protecting wall of His obvious involvement in their lives. They could corrupt that relationship, but they could not destroy

---

85. *Rashi, Devarim* 1:27 from *Midrash Tanchuma.*

86. The metaphor is not perfect because we did not have the status of infants at the time of the spies. At any age, however, there is a fine balance between appropriate dependence and appropriate independence. Under the circumstances, this was a desire for an inappropriate level of independence. See also Chapter 4, note 22.

it. It was God's withdrawal in response to the calf that introduced the possibility that the Jews could lose sight of Him entirely. The wall was down, their protection gone; the separation that could grow into the bitter fruit of the end of relationship had blossomed. The fruit matured when God's distance was actualized in the natural environment of the Land and the Jews failed to search after Him, ending all possibility of relationship and bringing exile.[87]

Exile is not one punishment among many; it is destruction. Exile

---

87. That which destroys is an inversion of that which creates. If these two sins accomplish complete destruction they must also correspond to our fundamental obligations.

Man has two primary tasks. He was created to receive good. That good is synonymous with connection to God; therefore, man was given the responsibility and capability of experiencing closeness to Him. The greatest good, however, is not received — it is created. Therefore, we were also given the task of creating relationship. These are two different obligations — in one we are receivers and in one we are creators.

These are experienced through the two modes of connection we have to God. We can relate through *yirah* (fear), where we merge into God by disappearing as individuals. And we can also relate through *ahavah* (love), where we create ourselves as individuals in emulation of God and connect through resonance.

At any point in time both *yirah* and *ahavah* are components of our connection with God but the proportion each contributes varies over time. In the case of the root generation of the desert we see the two extremes of *yirah* and *ahavah*. The relationship that was originally given to us at Har Sinai was one where God was as clearly revealed as He ever was in history. This was the equivalent of receiving relationship, for the essence of our relationship with God is our *emunah* (faith). The intensity of God's revelation on Sinai forced our nullification to Him in worshipful *yirah* and made the active development of our *emunah* almost superfluous. Our primary responsibility was to receive with only minimal obligation to create. (See Maharal, *Gur Aryeh, Shemot* 19:17 on the centrality of the nullification of our free will during the Har Sinai revelation.)

There was enough distance, however, to corrupt the relationship of worship through idol worship. That was the sin of the golden calf. That sin created a much greater distance between God and us that amounted to independence. We could only redeem the resulting independence by becoming responsible for the relationship. The Creator actualized that distance by becoming more obscure and we were forced to take the creative initiative in a relationship of *ahavah*, accentuating the role of our free will as we developed ever deeper parts of ourselves. (Thus the centrality of the hiddenness of God during the reacceptance of Torah in Persia.)

This shift from *yirah* to *ahavah* provides another perspective on how the consequence of sin — which distances us from God — functions to press growth.

represents the end of relationship with God for the generation that experiences it. It is not, however, the end of relationship entirely, for the Creator is permanently committed to His special connection to the Jewish people.[88] The world was created for man to achieve relationship with God; that must happen.[89] After the Tower of Bavel, when the facet of human character directly connecting with the Creator was concentrated in the Jewish people,[90] the accomplishment of creation's purpose was tied to God's relationship with the Jews and it therefore became a permanent fixture of history.

When exile ends relationship with one generation it is to make way for relationship with another generation.[91] What is the significance of a shift from one generation to the next? We have explained that as individuals we have various aspects in which our personality can be focused and through which we can develop distinct facets of our relationship with God. This expresses itself on a national level in different generations finding the anchor of their personality in these different aspects of personality, each with its unique potentials and limitations for building a connection with God.

Exile results when there is no longer any possibility of a generation developing its aspect of personality and furthering its associated facet of relationship. The exile comes to close off an era in Jewish history and make way for another. A new generation will arise to return to God through the distinguishing aspect of personality that is its unique focus. It will develop a new connection to God centered on the facet of relationship relevant to its personality type. This new generation will

---

88. *Ta'anit* 3b; *Berachot* 32b.

89. "As the rain and the snow fall from the heavens and do not return there but, rather, wet the ground so that it bears and sprouts, giving seed to the planter and bread to eat. So also the words that leave My mouth will not return empty until they have accomplished that which I desired and succeed in their purpose." (*Yeshayah* 55:10–11)

90. See Chapter 10, p. 157.

91. *Bemidbar* 14:29–31. The Creator states it explicitly in the case of the generation of the desert. But like all other aspects of this exile, it is part of the basic structure of the process and presages our future experiences.

either complete the project of history or develop relationship as far as it can within the confines of its form of connection. If it doesn't complete history, things will eventually break down and exile will lead to the emergence of yet another generation that will pick up the thread with its own new focus, possibility, and hope. As in personal development, the evolving focus of the generations is toward more elevated aspects of personality that lead to greater independence from God. This independence results in a self that is overall more physical and a relationship with God that is more distant.

The exile that ended the era of the first generation of the Jews, however, was a transition of a different order of magnitude. Rather than moving from one particular facet of personality to another, the two sins that brought this exile represented a failure of the entirety of personality on one level of humanity to complete relationship with God and the need to move to another level of humanity. The switch from the first generation to those that followed was roughly comparable to the change in humanity that occurred after the sin of Adam. The failure of Adam to complete relationship as a single couple resulted in the breakdown of his task into its component parts and his personality into many individuals and peoples to complete those many parts. Similarly, the failure of the generation of the desert to complete relationship with God resulted in the process of building relationship with God being broken down into its component parts and the distribution of those parts to the many generations of Jews that would now arise, each dealing with a specific piece of the overall bond.

*   *   *

The sin of the golden calf and of the spies together brought exile to the first generation of the Jewish people because, between the two of them, all possible versions of connection with God that were open to that generation were shut off. They rejected participating in a close relationship; they declined creating a distant relationship. As the root generation of the nation, their experience contained all the elements that would re-emerge later in the modern exiles of the Jewish people to the kingdoms, where it would be played out in finer detail over historical time.

The connection of these root transgressions to modern exile is made explicit in the *midrash* which opens our chapter. After the sin of the spies God sighs, "Until when will this people anger Me, until when will they not believe in Me."[92] Angering God in this verse refers to the sin of the golden calf — idol worship awakens the trait of jealousy and anger in God.[93] Not believing in God refers to the spies, who failed to recognize God's control of the world.[94] The *midrash* interprets this verse as God saying, "I have sighed twice because of you. In the end you will sigh four times through enslavement to the kingdoms."[95] We made God sigh over the golden calf. As a consequence we will sigh over two exiles to idol-worshipping Babylon and Persia caused by the idolatrous echo of the golden calf that destroyed the First Temple. We made God sigh a second time over the sin of the spies. As a consequence, we will sigh over two exiles to secular Greece and Rome, caused by our passivity toward God's hiddenness in the Second Temple, echoing the lack of faith of the spies when God was hidden from them and they did not seek Him.

It is now time to turn our attention to these modern exiles.

92. *Bemidbar* 14:11.
93. In *Shemot* 20:5 idol worship awakens jealousy. In *Devarim* 9:16–18 the sin of the calf is explicitly connected to God's anger.
94. *Devarim* 9:23 explicitly connects the sin of the spies to a lack of belief in God.
95. *Bemidbar Rabbah* 16:22.

CHAPTER 14

The Process of Exile

*Regarding Keisari (Caesarea) and Yerushalayim: If one says
that both are destroyed, do not believe him; if he says that
both are settled, do not believe him; if he says that Keisari is
destroyed and Yerushalayim is settled, or that Yerushalayim
is destroyed and Keisari is settled, you may believe him, as it
says, "I (Tzur, Tyre)[1] shall be filled from her (Yerushalayim's)
destruction,"[2] meaning if this one is in all its glory, that one
is laid waste, and if that one is in all its glory, this one is laid
waste. R. Nachman bar Yitzchak derived the same lesson
from this verse: "And one people will draw its strength from
the other people."[3]*

THE EXILES THAT THE Jewish people face throughout history
are not a consequence of random shifts in the balance of power on
the world stage. According to the flax-whacking model we are presently
developing, they come to heal specific wounds within us. The medicine
is matched to the wound by the wound creating the medicine.

---

1. The verse speaks about Tzur while the Sages learn from it concerning Keisari. Both were
fortress cities of Rome. The Talmud in *Megillah* 6a seems to equate the two places. In *Be'er
Mayim Chayim, Beshalach* 13 it states that they were the same place. In *Ohr HaNeir, Yevamot* 63a it is suggested that Keisari took over the role of Tzur and therefore one is equated
with the other.
2. *Yechezkel* 26:2.
3. *Megillah* 6a. The last verse quoted is from *Bereishit* 25:23.

The Torah describes this process in a single verse. When Rivkah was pregnant with Yaakov and Esav she felt a great struggle taking place in her womb. She consulted the prophet Shem, who told her that two nations were in her belly, "And one people will draw its strength from the other people."[4] Since the Jews descend from Yaakov while Rome comes from Esav, this prophecy led the Sages to state that Yerushalayim and Keisari, a major Roman fortress-city in the Land of Israel, would never stand simultaneously. "If he says that Keisari is destroyed and Yerushalayim is settled, or that Yerushalayim is destroyed and Keisari is settled, you may believe him."[5] The commentaries explain that whether Yerushalayim or Keisari is on top is determined by the actions of the Jews — if our commitment to God is complete no one can touch us; but when we turn away from God we give our power to Rome, who then comes to destroy us.[6]

Many nations have laid waste to Yerushalayim and exiled the Jewish people. Why does the Torah hint specifically to Rome? Reflecting its cultural inheritance from its forefather Esav, Rome is the antithesis of Yaakov and the Jewish people. The Jewish people center reality in the spiritual realm and see physical being as only the expression of essential reality. Rome, on the other hand, locates reality in the physical world as demonstrated by her modern variant, Western culture. Today's Rome understands science to have access to what truly is, while philosophy is something to take a course on in college.[7] Rome's emphasis on

---

4. *Bereishit* 25:23.
5. *Megillah* 6a cited in our opening quote.
6. *Rashi, Bereishit* 25:23 read according to the *Gur Aryeh* there. Rashi speaks of Tzur rather than Keisari because he is interpreting the verse from *Yechezkel*. See note 1 in this chapter.
7. The Sages actually credit Rome with tremendous knowledge. This would also include the more esoteric branches. But because Rome is so profoundly cut off from the spiritual realm, reality for her takes on a starkly physical character — much more so than Greece. Ultimately, this excludes the purely intellectual sphere as well as the spiritual, and thought, which is respected, centers increasingly around the analysis of the purely physical — science and engineering. The modern marginalizing of philosophy is just an uncluttered expression of the extreme nature of Rome's anchor in physical reality.

physical reality, the dimension through which man attains his awareness of separation from God, leads to an experience of self as the center and basis of existence.[8] Inseparable from this is a belief that, to the degree that man can manipulate the laws of nature, he governs fate; to the degree that he cannot, the world is rudderless.[9] For Rome, man's goal is control, both for its material benefits and for its confirmation of the primacy of the self.

The Jews, however, focus on the deeper reality that God is One — the basis of all being, with reality emanating from Him and constantly dependent upon His ongoing support to exist. God alone controls what happens in the world.[10] Our impact is limited to any influence we have over how God chooses to uphold His world.[11]

God connects to the world as He connects to us and He connects to us in a way that reflects the way we connect to Him — as in other relationships His attitude mirrors ours.[12] As Jews, we strive to lead our day-to-day lives in a manner that reflects our genuine recognition of the Creator as the foundation of existence. In this way, we crown Him King, and He reciprocates by acting as King, giving form to the world as a place that is openly under His auspices. Yerushalayim, the seat of God's Temple and the capital of His representatives, stands in all its glory while Rome, whose culture is based on the self-rule of man, is left powerless. If, however, we turn away from God and live as if we determine our own destiny, then God creates the world as a place that seems to run naturally, subject to the will of man. This empowers Rome, the society that truly embodies the cultural principle of human mastery and control, and allows it to overrun Yerushalayim, the locus of the

---

8. See Chapter 17, pp. 318–321.
9. Ramchal, *Daat Tevunot* 36, the third misunderstanding. These characteristics of Rome will be extensively discussed in the coming chapters.
10. See Chapter 8, pp. 121–122.
11. *Nefesh HaChayim*, 1:3-8.
12. *Mishlei* 27:19.

philosophical and cultural ideal that opposes Rome.[13]

There are really only two perspectives on reality. Either it is God's world run by God or it is man's world controlled by man. These perspectives can be applied with more or less consistency, which leads to a multiplicity of worldviews (and exiles). But at essence, there are only two. The desire for control and its necessary compliment, attributing centrality to the self, are the underlying cause of all exile. Man's first exile — Adam's expulsion from the Garden — and the root exile of the Jews in the desert were both a consequence of man attempting to define reality for himself.[14] Determining meaning is the deepest control and any attempt to seize that privilege indicates a critically inflated sense of self. Rome personifies exile because it is so extreme in exactly these matters: it explicitly understands reality as a neutral object to be controlled and exploited by man[15] and implicit in its culture is the ultimate distortion of man's significance, as evidenced by Rome's ability to confuse man with God (as we will see later happened with Haman).[16] Yerushalayim and Keisari will never stand simultaneously for they each represent a pure form of one of these two diametrically opposed versions of reality. Their worldviews have no overlap; since there is only one world, they cannot both take on expression. If Yerushalayim remains true to its ideals so that existence reflects Yerushalayim's vision, then Keisari has no place; if Yerushalayim adopts Keisari's view, then Yerushalayim undermines its own standing and is soon destroyed and sent to exile.[17]

---

13. *Bereishit Rabbah* 65:20.

14. See Chapter 13, pp. 227–228 and Chapter 16, p. 310.

15. See Chapter 18.

16. See Chapter 20, pp. 378–379.

17. Rome plays this role because it is the cultural inheritor of Esav, so for Rome or Keisari we can read "descendants of Esav." Yet, the Sages say elsewhere that the survival of the Jewish people is dependent upon the descendants of Esav. After the Jewish people left *Mitzrayim* and completed their forty years in the desert, the time came to enter the Land of Israel. Edom, a land populated by descendants of Esav, lay between them and their promised land. When Edom denied Moshe's request to cross through their land, Edom massed in anticipation of war (*Bemidbar* 20:14–20). Though future events revealed that the Jews could have

Nations whose cultures were centered on other inclinations also exiled the Jews. We have already mentioned that Babylon was consumed by power, Persia by pleasure, and Greece by jealousy of the intellect.[18] But this does not compromise the primacy of Rome to the process of exile. Domination by each of these other inclinations required an accentuation of self—albeit one unique to each inclination—and a vision of reality determined by man. So each of these nations expressed, at least indirectly, the corruption of Rome and was, to an extent, a representative of Rome.[19]

---

easily defeated Edom in battle, God forbade the Jews to fight. (See *Bemidbar* 21:21–35 that the Jews subsequently destroyed the armies of both Sichon and Og. See *Rashi, Bemidbar* 22:2 that these were the dominant military powers in the area.) He told them that destroying Esav's descendants would bring the destruction of the Jewish people, implying that the survival of the Jews is actually dependent on Esav's descendants! (*Devarim Rabbah* 1:18. Nothing said in the *midrash* is particular to the Edomites other than their identity as descendants of Esav.) We can understand this when we remember that this meeting between the Jews and Esav's descendants was taking place as the Jews emerged from the desert, a time when God held us close to Him through the intense revelation which characterized our experience in the desert. His immediacy gave us the strength to destroy Edom. But we had not earned that strength. We had not faced the tests of creating our relationship with God so our closeness was not yet a part of us and could be lost. We need the line of Esav—and the threat of exile that it carries—as long as turning away from God remains possible. Destroying the line of Esav prematurely would have threatened our long-term relationship with God by removing a critical corrective force ready to return us to our path when we lose our way. This incident with Edom highlights the necessity of exile to the process of history. Esav can only be destroyed by force at the end of the historical process. (See *Devarim* 25:19; *Rashi, Devarim* 2:5; *Yalkut Devarim* 2:807.)

18. See Chapter 10, pp. 167–172.

19. The Midrash identifies Esav, the forefather of Rome, as the personification of the force of exile in general—see *Bereishit Rabbah* 75:1. See *Bemidbar* 24:20 that Amalek is the root of all the nations of the world in their identity as being other to the Jews; Amalek expresses the essence of Esav and, therefore, of Rome (see Chapter 3, p. 34) making Roman culture the root of all the nations. See the beginning of Chapter 14. (Though Rav Tzaddok HaKohen quotes on numerous occasions the Zohar that Amalek combines the internal quality of both Esav and Yishmael (*shor v'chamor*)—murder and lust—he still states explicitly in *Likutei Maamarim* (16) that Amalek is the essence of Esav. This implies that Esav, and so Rome, lies at the essence of even those nations who arise from the root of Yishmael.)

CREATING OUR OWN ANTIDOTE

Though uncovering the Roman root of these other kingdoms gives us perspective that is important to our larger project, exclusive focus on this level would blur important details of our interaction with them. We experienced each of these kingdoms expressing its definitive inclination rather than as a featureless gradation of the Roman megalomania that underlay them all — with Babylon power, with Persia pleasure, and with Greece jealousy.

Conquest by each kingdom followed the pattern we laid out with regard to Rome. Just as Rome's dominion mirrored our choice to adopt Rome's focus, so too the kingdoms of Babylon, Persia, and Greece were given power by our adoption of their priorities. Babylon, for example, only gained the strength to conquer us when we as a society became enamored with the impulse that determined them as a people, the desire for power.

God gives us exile to force our recognition of the full implications of where we are headed before it is too late. When we become co-opted by an inclination, we experience our fling with it while at the same time continuing to enjoy the intimate connection to God that our ancestors painstakingly developed. But that connection is incompatible with what has become our corrupt focus and the basis of the relationship is slowly eroded. Were we to continue our direction we would eventually undermine our ability to connect to God. The onset of a kingdom compels us to confront what a life based on its characteristic inclination genuinely looks like while enough of our spiritual assets remain to be able to recover our true identity.

When we are destroying what is dearest to us — our true selves and relationship with God — the Creator awakens us with sufficient strength that we must pay attention — He sends us into exile.[20] This is a gift — what we genuinely want — for His tough love saves us from the unthinkable. Imagine a person ambitious for success in business. He

---

20. *Vayikra* 26:44 and see Rav Chayim Freidlander, *Siftei Chayim* I, p. 5.

readily proclaims that his family is his first priority, but he doesn't notice that his fleeting and distracted moments at home are slowly destroying his marriage. There are warning signs — ugly outbursts and a sense of detachment. But he is able to ignore them because of his obsession with work. When his wife leaves him, he is broken. He weeps over the fact that nothing happened earlier to compel his attention to what was happening and would give up all that he has gained to turn the clock back. God, in His loving kindness, does not allow our relationship to reach the point of divorce. Through exile, He forces us to wake up to our situation before a permanent break becomes necessary.

Our present interest, however, is less the rise and fall of individual empires than the process that emerges from our repeated encounter with exile. The history of exile has a definite structure, direction, and purpose. We never repeat an exile; we always proceed to one founded on a new inclination; the inclinations with which we struggle appear in a noticeable order. When we first submit to an inclination it gains decisive strength over us. This becomes mirrored in the world by our being conquered by the associated kingdom. We then come to genuinely regret turning away from God. But when we try to directly contain the inclination and move beyond our corrupted cravings, priorities and actions, it does not work.[21]

Each inclination is limited, however, in that it corrupts only a specific facet of personality and we are subject to the domination of that inclination only as long as we are anchored in its target facet of personality. Therefore, instead of trying to fight an inclination head on, to recover relationship with God in the midst of exile we actualize a higher aspect of personality, centering ourselves there. This shift frees us from the inclination that was subjugating us and eventually leads to freedom from the associated conquerors. But it also leaves us vulnerable to a new inclination, the one that attaches itself to this new aspect of personality we have come to occupy. When we succumb to that inclination, a new

---

21. See Chapters 11 and 12.

nation comes to conquer us and we go through another cycle. Every advance in the process of exile therefore creates the possibility of a new cycle of exile and development. We are thus continually pressed to develop ever higher aspects of ourselves.

Since the direction of our movement is always to higher, more significant facets of our personality, the associated inclination which eventually corrupts us is characterized by an intensifying sense of independence. This leads to increasingly severe exiles. The process therefore leads inexorably toward the unadulterated experience of the preeminent self characteristic of Rome and the final challenge of the Roman exile.

With this outline in mind we can now examine the process of exile on a more detailed level.

A WORSHIPPING CONTEXT

We saw in the previous chapter that the roots of Jewish exile are two sins committed by the Jewish people in the desert: the golden calf and the spies. The sin of the calf was a transgression in the context of a world broadly experienced as ruled by God. With God apparent, we intuitively felt the need to worship. But through the idolatry of the golden calf, we diverted that worship to a veiled service of our physical inclinations, distancing God. After our repentance from the calf, the distance remained. We were challenged to seek God when God and His kingship were hidden. But through the sin of the spies, we instead accepted His seeming absence for the sense of autonomy it allowed.

Over the course of the last 2,500 years the energies that instigated these two root sins reappear to lead us again into exile. Since there are two forms of energy at fault, we expect there to be two exiles. Or, if there are more, we expect them to break down into two groups reflecting these two sins. This was, in fact, the case. The First Temple, which stood in an era when God was close to us, was destroyed because of idol worship and led to the exiles of Babylon and Persia — both idol-worshipping societies. In the time of the Second Temple, when God's presence was hidden, we were first conquered by the non-worshipping Greeks, who overran us because of sluggishness in our effort to reach back to God from the darkness.[22] This led eventually to a complete breakdown in our connection to God and exile to Rome, a society that achieved supremacy while still pagan, lacking genuine connection to transcendence.

These exiles are elements in one lengthy process. Understanding how that process unfolds must begin with a clear grasp of the pull of idol worship, the transgression that caused the destruction of the First Temple. This would require us to project ourselves back in time to an era in which we spontaneously experienced God's immediacy — which is impossible because it is so far removed from the mode of our awareness today. We can, however, at least understand conceptually what it was like.

Reality for the early generations of the Jewish people, from the Exodus until the destruction of the First Temple, was characterized by a sense of God's presence. This was the natural complement of a world in which God expressed Himself openly through miracles and communicated directly with man through prophecy.

In this period, our relationship with God was focused around our worship in the Temple. The Hebrew term for "worship" is *avodah*, which is related to the term *eved*, which means "slave." That these two words share the same root is instructive. A slave expresses no individual identity, for he has no opportunity to act on his choices — his master determines all of his deeds. A slave is a virtual extension of his owner, an instrument through which the owner's will is effected. By implication, service to God is the same thing, with the difference that it is directed toward our transcendent Source. We yield our authority to God and make ourselves a conduit for God's expression into the world.

There is, however, another significant difference between worship and slavery. Though a slave cannot give expression to his choices, he still knows what he wants to do; it is only because of external force that the slave acts on his master's commands. Since our choices define us as individuals, the inner life of a slave maintains his individuality. Worship,

---

22. *Peirush HaBach, Tur Orach Chayim* 670:4 speaks about the expression of this laziness in the Temple service. We will focus more on the effects on our connection to Torah.

however, is voluntary. In worship we not only relinquish control over expressing our choices, we yield the choices themselves. God does not merely tell us what to do; He tells us what we want to do.

It is difficult for us to imagine someone submitting himself to an outside force to this degree, because the surrender of choice is synonymous with a loss of individuality.[23] Since we identify our self with our individuality, we associate such surrender with suicide. Intellectually we may understand the need for this level of submission to God, and our Sages admonish us to strive to reach it: "Make His will your will."[24] Still, in our times, only spiritual giants approach this as an integrated reality. In the ancient world, however, everyone dedicated their whole being to worship: when it was to God they left their fields fallow for years on end during the Sabbatical and Jubilee years; when it was idolatrous, they sacrificed everything they had to their idol including, when necessary, their children.

We must conclude that in those times this submission was not experienced as a loss of self. In fact, the ubiquity of idol worship indicates that this surrender was understood to be necessary to life. We can comprehend this only if we assume that in the ancient world man experienced selfhood in a manner completely different from today. In the era of worship, when we were in the early stages of the historical development of personality that we discussed previously,[25] our self was much less concrete and delineated, remaining transparent to its higher Source.[26] This would have resulted in clear and constant awareness of our dependence upon our Source and a need to be attached to It in a manner similar to a tree's need for its roots. Losing that attachment would have felt like death. We are not talking here about a philosophy of

---

23. See Chapters 5 and 6.

24. *Pirkei Avot* 2:4.

25. See Chapters 9 and 10.

26. In the early stages of history, during the era of worship, our clarity of and attachment to God came through our lack of fully developed self. In the last stages we seek to recover that awareness through the full development of self, that is, through identifying our self with the highest aspect of our being — the root from which our individuality emerges from God.

being; we are talking about an experience of being. Only if man's awareness of his existence was tied intrinsically to a sense of emergence — only if he experienced himself as a stream issuing from a vast reservoir — can we understand the pervasive and unstinting dedication to worship that characterized the ancient world.

This sense of connectedness to Source framed all of human awareness, for our understanding of the world is necessarily modeled after our experience of self.[27] We do not know what anything *is*, only what it looks like. The only exception to this is our self — we not only look at our self, we also *are* our self. We naturally and necessarily extrapolate our experience of self to the rest of creation in formulating our world, for it is our only window on being.[28] If, in the ancient world, we experienced our self as emerging from our transcendent Source, we saw the rest of reality that way also. Separation from that Source, then, would not have seemed like death as much as a violation of the nature of existence. We did not worship to survive, we worshiped because to not worship was inconceivable.

Though we may be able to gain a conceptual picture of this mode of experience, we cannot expect any genuine, visceral appreciation for it because it was so radically different from today's experience. Our perception is filtered through our awareness of distinct individuality; ego is our first reality. While in the age of worship man's primary awareness was of God, with any sense of individual being a secondary consequence of that awareness, today our first truth is, in the famous words of Descarte, "I think, therefore *I* am (and only after that realization can we even ask if there is God)." Because we experience ourselves as detached and independent, we project that self-supporting autonomy on the world and everything in it. Such a reality does not need God, the

---

27. Thus in Hebrew the term for reality is *mitziut*, which means "that which is brought forth." It is related to the term *motzi* like in the blessing on bread *ha-motzi lechem min ha'aretz*, "the One Who brings forth bread from the earth." The connection between inner experience and outer perception is discussed in Chapter 15, pp. 279–280.
28. We will discuss this idea in detail in Chapter 15, pp. 283–284.

source of existence, nor does He have a natural place in it. Our experience even contradicts the existence of what we conceive of as God. God is everything; yet we experience our existence independent of Him.[29]

THE PULL OF IDOLATRY

Man in the ancient world cleaved naturally to God, experiencing joyful return to Source and unification with the totality of reality. Though his sense of individuality was much thinner, in its place he experienced the significance of being that came with his seamless attachment to the necessary Source of all being. From such a starting point, the path forward was to focus more and more on attachment to God. But how could man in such an environment have free will? Where was he confronted with any choice that would present itself as a competing alternative? Mere physical pleasure could not possibly match the expansiveness of spirit that was available.

Such a question misses the point that all human experiences then occurred within the context of transcendent attachment, including physical ones. Pleasure, for example, was not the isolated sense awareness we have today, where we turn inward and reality collapses to the self and its sensation. Pleasure was another mode of attachment to a larger reality, where the experience of connection was funneled through the physical dimension. It was not the individual with his private pleasure, but a transcendent source coursing through the individual, giving cosmic intensity and significance to the experience.

Pleasure was placed in creation for the purpose of attaching us to God; power, and the honor that goes with it, was to attach us through emulating and representing God. The challenge in the midst of these various physical experiences was to remain centered in God. But since they were mediated through the aspect of our humanity that is the basis

---

29. We will analyze both ancient and modern experience in greater detail in the next section.

of our individual being — our physical part — these experiences exerted a strong pull to lower the center of our personality from a point above individuality and, instead, to experience them through an "I" and "for me."

Even if we succumbed to the "I," our ego sense was not exclusive — this was occurring within the worshipful context of the ancient world, where all experience was attached to transcendence. But lowering ourselves to our "I" necessarily shifted the source of reality upon which we could focus. We could not turn directly to the absolute transcendence of God, which is completely removed from physical reality, for it left no place for the "I" that we were experiencing. We had to turn to a lower level of transcendence that was enough in the world to include and reflect the existence of an egotistical self. Once we centered ourselves in the "I," the transcendence that related to that "I" became our object of worship, for it both allowed for and defined us. Focusing on and eventually worshipping this lower aspect of transcendence is what we call idolatry.

When this was a corruption of power and honor — which, though physically based, are relatively spiritual inclinations — the transcendent aspect we related to was not removed from absolute spirituality to the point that it excluded God. Therefore, the idolatrous god was experienced as a servant of God, and the idolatry lay in the attribution of independent authority to this spiritual agent. The transgression here was not only in the attribution of independent capability to the idol but also in the significant reduction in the omnipotence of God that this independence implied. When we succumbed to this idolatry we made ourselves vulnerable to the Babylonians, who were defined by their desire for power and therefore practiced this form of idol worship.

When our inclination deteriorated to the baser physical desire of lust — a more self-centered and spiritually isolating energy — the transcendence that mirrored our self was so much a part of physical reality that it excluded God and was perceived as a locus of existence independent of and in opposition to Him. Though worship of a spiritual source continued, it was accompanied by worship of a separate source of physical existence.[30] This was a much more extreme form of idolatry, profoundly diminishing God by recognizing a competitor, and was the next step in a process that would eventually lead to the rejection of God. It was this form of idolatry that eventually brought us to exile in Persia, a society defined by lust and worshipping two distinct sources of reality.[31]

REPENTANCE FROM IDOLATRY

Though Babylon and Persia were different societies with distinct focuses, they were both variations on the theme of idolatry and therefore the two exiles were linked. Through the combined experience of both of these exiles we were able to fully understand where idolatry was taking us as a nation and we recoiled in horror, recovering our focus on our unadulterated relationship with God. But we could not simply go back to our past form of relationship. As we mentioned before, repentance requires an advance in the mode of our relationship with God.[32] We repent of the essential core of sin, which is turning away from God, and recover our desire to come close to God. But we cannot undo the effects of transgression. We are changed by it, and therefore the manner of relationship with the Creator that we can achieve afterward is different.

Physical experience, intensified by its integration with transcendent awareness, had been our medium for relationship to God. But in the time of the First Temple we co-opted that energy for selfish purposes eventually leading to the destruction of the Temple. Once corrupted in this way, physical experience could never again be safe as the basis of our connection to transcendence. It would always awaken the memory of personal pleasure and draw us back to transgression with strength that we would not be able to resist. The intensity of physical experience would have to be diminished and a new medium for connection to God found. In the language we used earlier: we could not go back the way

---

30. *Sanhedrin* 39a; Ramchal, *Da'at Tevunot* 36.
31. See Chapter 10, p. 177.
32. See Chapter 11, p. 193 and Chapter 12, pp. 211–212.

we came — it would not work. We had to reenter the "ה" of relationship with God through a higher gate.[33]

NULLIFYING THE INCLINATION TO WORSHIP

The idolatry which directly caused the Temple's destruction reflected the thickened sense of ego which accompanies submission to an inclination. We became centered in a shallow layer of personality distinguished by a clear awareness of self. While we remained conscious of our internal transcendent root, we were not connected to it strongly enough for it to define our experience of reality.

To remain at this halfway point, where we retained acute awareness of transcendence but were deeply identified with our physical being and ego, was an invitation to disaster. This heady mix had created the powerful allure of idol worship that destroyed the First Temple. And we had less strength now than before to resist it, for our attraction to God was significantly reduced by the shift of our center away from Him. Yet a return to the self fully connected to the Creator was not possible — through our choices and actions the reality was that we were distant from God.

Having experienced exile, we would not tolerate a situation that would lead to a recurrence of idolatry and a return to exile. If we could not move closer to God to avoid idolatry, we would have to move further away. Based on verses from *Sefer Nechemiah*, the Talmud derives that after the Jews returned from Persia to build the Second Temple they collectively petitioned God to nullify the inclination for idolatry, and their request was granted.

> "And they cried to HaShem their God with a great voice."[34] What did they say? Rav said, and some say it was Rebbi Yochanan, "Oy, oy (the evil inclination to worship idols) that destroyed the Temple and

---

33. Ibid.
34. *Nechemiah* 9:4.

burned the hall and killed all the righteous and exiled Israel from their land is still dancing among us. It was only given to us to earn reward; we don't need it and we don't need its reward." A tablet fell from the Heavens upon which was written the word, "True"... They fasted for three days and three nights and their prayer was answered. A lion-cub of fire ran out from the Holy of Holies. The prophet said to Yisrael, "It was the inclination to worship idols."[35]

The Talmud here records a singular event in history — the elimination of an inclination in man. The desire to worship idols, which so characterized the ancient world and led to the destruction of the First Temple, was no more. But since idolatry grew out of our experience of ourselves as emanating from a transcendent source, ridding ourselves of this inclination could only come through abolishing this aspect of our experience. In effect, when we asked to be free of this inclination we were asking that our identity slip even more deeply into those aspects of self which separate us from God than our transgressions had already brought it; we sought to lose our intimacy with transcendence by intensifying our sense of autonomous individuality and entering more fully into our egos. Since the motivation behind the request was genuine, it was granted.[36]

The blunting of our awareness of a higher source snuffed out the instinctual need for connection to transcendence, marginalizing idol worship. With idolatry out of the way, we could pursue God without danger of that distraction. The problem was that this spiritually barren landscape also lacked any natural sense of connection to and dependence on God — both the motivator for and basis of our relationship with Him.

---

35. *Yoma* 69b. See *The Jewish Self*, ch. "A Moment of Favor."

36. Their request for less connection to the spiritual realm parallels what the Jews did in building the golden calf. But in this case their true intention as opposed to their justification was for the sake of their relationship with God, which is evident in the manner they went about things. Here they requested that God make the change; in the case of the golden calf the Jews took matters into their own hands. There was precedent for the Jews legitimately asking God to distance Himself from them in *Devarim* 5:21–25.

We destroyed idol worship by destroying worship.[37] Thus the Talmud states that the inclination for idol worship — a lion-cub of fire — left from the Holy of Holies — the locus of our worship of God.[38]

A new basis for relationship was needed. Our natural sense of spirituality and its corruption into idolatry had been a consequence of being centered in our more physical aspects of personality — those that craved definition from outside themselves.[39] These were our bodily energies and our sense of individual identity. When we talk of "losing our intimacy with transcendence by intensifying our sense of autonomous individuality," we refer to the center of our personality shifting to intellect. Though a more refined aspect of self, intellect does not naturally connect to spirituality and, therefore, tends to isolate us in our selves, producing overall a more physical experience of reality. Despite this, intellect would have to provide the basis for our new relationship.

A NEW FORM OF CONNECTION

The Second Temple was built in the midst of all these changes and was radically different from the First Temple. When the structure was finished, it so lacked the spiritual radiance of the First Temple that the celebratory shouts from the young men who built it were drowned out by the crying of the elders who still remembered the glory of the first one.[40] The Jews were informed before its construction that God's presence would not dwell there — man was no longer capable of that kind of closeness. At first the Jews refused to build it — what was the point? Only when they were assured that it would provide the focus for developing

---

37. In a sense, we traded an inclination to worship idols for an inclination to not worship at all. Once we no longer felt compelled to nullify ourselves before a higher source, it was only a matter of time before our fundamental inclination toward independence would lead to a forceful rejection of the idea of worship. Rav Moshe Shapiro calls this an inclination to *minut*, usually translated as heresy.

38. For a source that our worship is centered in the Holy of Holies, see *Berachot* 30a.

39. See Chapter 10, pp. 173–176.

40. *Ezra* 3:12. The constant miracles that had characterized the service of the First Temple were also missing in the Second Temple. See *Yoma* 39a and Maharal, *Derech Chayim* 5:4.

a new relationship with God, one mediated through Torah rather than worship, did they agree.[41]

Obviously, there had been Torah during the First Temple. But the Torah of the First Temple was primarily prophetic. It was received as a direct gift from God, with man acting as little more than its receptacle.[42] Such Torah was part of a revelational, worshipping relationship with God. But our awareness of God's immediate presence failed as the Second Temple was being constructed, and prophecy disappeared with it. The last three prophets were Chaggai, Zachariah, and Malachi. Chaggai's recorded prophecy was from the second year of King Daryavesh's reign, when the Jews began the last phase of construction of the Second Temple.[43] Zachariah's recorded prophecy stretched into Daryavesh's fourth year, still two years shy of the Temple's completion.[44] Malachi, who was the last of the prophets,[45] did not tell us the dates of his visions. He seems to have been a contemporary of Ezra — one opinion in the Talmud is that he was Ezra.[46] Ezra came to Yerushalayim in the seventh year of Daryavesh's rule, one year after the completion of the Second Temple. Chaggai, Zachariah, Malachi, and Ezra all died in the fortieth year of the Second Temple.[47] With their passing, prophecy was no more.[48]

---

41. *Pirkei HaHeichalot*, ch. 27.

42. See *Beit HaLevi, Drush* 18.

43. *Chaggai* 1:1.

44. *Zechariah* 7:1.

45. See *Ibn Ezra, Radak*, and *Malbim* on *Malachi* 1:1.

46. *Megillah* 15a.

47. Raivid HaLevi, *Sefer HaKabbalah*.

48. Ibid. This is also quoted in the *Kuzari* 3:39. The abolition of the inclination to worship idols cited earlier took place in the twentieth year of the rule of Daryavesh. See *Nechemiah* 2:1 when Nechemiah left for Yerushalayim and *Nechemiah* 9:4 that records the gathering where the annulment took place. It is clear in *Nechemiah* that these events took place in the same year. See *Peirush HaGra* on *Seder Olam* 30 that prophecy ended after this inclination was removed. That would give us a slightly different date from the forty years we cited. The Gra may not mean that prophecy stopped on the very day of the abolition but, rather, in that general time. Alternatively, the *Sefer HaKabbalah* may not be counting the forty years

God was no longer revealing the truth of reality — prophecy was gone; and we no longer had a natural instinct of God's presence — intuitive worship was a thing of the past. We will see later that during this period obvious, revealed miracles also ceased.[49] Reality presented itself as a wholly material place. We were faced with the modern equivalent of the test of the spies in which we were required to take responsibility for our relationship with God. It was through the Torah of the Second Temple that we reached through this darkness to recover that relationship.

The Torah that emerged from the Second Temple was a different kind of Torah. Because there was no prophecy, we needed to understand Torah from ourselves by extrapolating from our record of the prophecies of the past — the Written Torah — to the current situation in which we found ourselves. We had the tools and skills needed to extend the Torah in this way from the Oral Torah.

The Oral Torah was a portion of the Torah given at Sinai that, for reasons discussed by the Sages and commentaries, we were prohibited from writing.[50] It was to remain an oral tradition to compliment the Written Torah. This Oral Torah contained the detailed instructions for joining the general principles recorded in the Written Torah to the specifics of experience. Of particular interest to us, it also included a methodology for using intellect to work out the proper application of Torah principles to new situations.

But the Second Temple period was new in a way that required a broadening of the responsibilities of the Oral Torah. Beyond determining the proper application of specific halachot, the Oral Torah was now also called upon to guide us in generally reconstructing what had become an empty world into a place centered upon God. There was an even more significant change in the Oral Torah's functioning. It had

---

from the completion of the Temple. Regardless of these specific details, however, the point remains that the Second Temple period was characterized by a lack of prophecy.

49. See Chapter 21, p. 398.

50. See *Gittin* 60b; *Shemot Rabbah* 47:1.

been a mere assistant to the direct prophetic relationship with God; with the cessation of prophecy the deliberations of the Oral Torah became the foundation of Torah. Torah, however, is the will of God. It cannot be determined by human intellect alone, even when based upon prophetic material. Without some channel to God, our insights could be nothing more than the musings of a finite human mind. Without prophecy, where could that come from?

In the era of the Second Temple, instead of Divine guidance coming explicitly from beyond the self as it had to the prophets, it rose up within us from the root connection of the self to God.[51] The goal was to be a pure instrument for investigating the Torah we already had. But the intellect alone did not perform the analysis; that could only produce human understanding. Instead, through purity of intention the intellect acted as a clean lens through which the aspect of our self connected directly to God — our *tzelem Elokim* — could inspire our interpretation from above.[52] The Second Temple was both the external manifestation and the touchstone for this hidden connection to God.

THE ORAL TORAH AND THE CHALLENGE OF GREECE

The changes in awareness we have been speaking about were not specific to the Jews but, rather, were happening to mankind as a whole. The loss of intuitive connection to transcendence which ended idolatry among us also undercut its viability for everyone else. While idol worship continued among the nations, it came to rest more on habit than commitment,[53] severely weakening those societies whose cultural identities were tied to idolatry. The beneficiaries of this process were the Greeks. Their identification with intellect had brought them to reconstruct reality from man's perspective, resulting in a vision of the world

---

51. Rav Tzaddok HaKohen, *Likutei Ma'amarim* 116b; *Pri Tzaddik* I, Chanukah 4.
52. *Bava Batra* 12a with the *Peirush HaRamban al HaTalmud*.
53. See *Chullin* 13b.

as governed by physical law in which God was irrelevant;[54] their vision now became man's spontaneous stance toward reality. As the Jews were expanding the Oral Torah — striving to retain relationship with God in spite of the increasing barrenness of human experience, the Greeks were riding that same barrenness to conquer their idolatrous neighbors powered by the superior strength with which they held their convictions.[55] This set the stage for our next exile.

Greek dominion spread at the beginning of the Second Temple period. Alexander, who brought Greece to the world, came to power a few years after the completion of the Second Temple and was dead thirteen years later, having already conquered the entire Near East, including the Jews.[56] But his arrival in Israel did not mark the full brunt of the Greek exile. Alexander respected the Jews because of their profound intellectual tradition and gave them a great deal of autonomy, allowing the *kohen gadol* (the high priest) to act as governor over the Land. Though the Greek rise to power was a consequence of our distance from God, that distance was not the result of a new transgression; rather, it

---

54. Though there was idolatry in Greece, it was residual, lacking the compulsion that had characterized worship in an earlier age. Same intellectuals in Greece openly proposed the abolition of the gods, something inconceivable in a truly worshipful context.

55. *Seder Olam* 30 states that Alexander's rise to power came at the time that prophecy passed. Daryavesh became king in 355 BCE. Alexander became king in 335 BCE. He thus acceded to the throne in the twentieth year of Daryavesh's rule, which is when the inclination for idol worship was nullified, bringing with it the end of prophecy. See note 48 in this chapter.

56. *Sefer HaKabbalah* of the Raivid HaLevi dates Alexander's arrival in Israel to the fortieth year of the Temple — the year the last prophets died — but he may not have been counting from its completion. See note 48 in this chapter. Rebbi Yosi in *Seder Olam Rabbah* 30 seems to date Alexander's arrival to the thirty-fifth year of the Temple, but, again, it is not clear if that is counting from the Temple's completion. *Yoma* 9a states that the Second Temple stood for 420 years. That would place Alexander's arrival in the eighteenth year of the Temple (the Temple was destroyed in 70 CE while Alexander came to Yerushalayim in 332 BCE). The specific date is less important than that his arrival early on meant that Alexander and all that he represented characterized the period of the Second Temple. Even according to the academic dating system, the vast majority of the Second Temple's existence was in a Greek or post-Greek world.

was a part of our repentance from our prior transgression of idol worship. Rather than forcefully threatening us, the spread of Greece initially provided the cultural backdrop of spiritual obscurity against which the future tests of the Jewish people would occur.[57]

Greece evolved from a cultural context into a domineering aggressor over the 150 years that followed the death of Alexander. What caused the change? It is difficult to understand why we were vulnerable to Greece because, as we explained at the beginning of this chapter, our susceptibility to conquerors is always a consequence of our giving them power by assuming their values and imitating their corruptions. Greece represented man using his intellect to define reality, eliminating God from the world. But at the time of Greek belligerence, we were rapidly developing the Oral Torah, constructing a vision of the world built around the Creator. We would expect this to have protected us from them.

We can look at how we were saved from the Greeks and what the rabbis chose to emphasize in our commemoration of that salvation for a hint as to what we had been lacking. The primary deliverance from the Greeks came through a staggering military victory, whereby a small group of Jewish partisans led by Yehudah HaMaccabee defeated a trained, experienced, and heavily armed Greek force of tens of thousands of soldiers. The odds against the Jews were impossible. Yet, they declared their faith in God, attacked, and, miraculously, were victorious.[58] Though the primary problem with the Greeks was their cultural influence over the Jews, and this was removed by the war, surprisingly the miracle that we focus on when remembering the event is not the war but the one involving the Temple Menorah.

After the defeat of the Greeks, when the Temple was recovered and its service renewed, only enough pure oil was found to light the Menorah for a single day. The Jews needed eight days to make new oil, and the lights of the Menorah burned for those eight days on one day's worth of

---

57. *Yoma* 69a. See Chapter 8, pp. 133–134.
58. *Megillat Antiochus.*

oil. We commemorate this every year by lighting the Chanukah menorah for eight days.[59] The commentaries explain that the rabbis directed our primary attention to the miracle of the Menorah rather than to the miracle of the war because with the Menorah the miraculous character of what happened was undeniable.[60] A victory on the battlefield, on the other hand, can always be ascribed to strength, skill, and daring.[61] The significance of the number eight to the holiday supports this, as this number always hints at a connection to the realm beyond nature.[62] It appears that the repair accomplished on Chanukah was achieving clarity of our dependence upon support from God — implying that this was what had been lacking.

Combining this insight with our awareness that nations are able to oppress us only when we empower them by mirroring their corruptions, we would conclude that we were vulnerable to conquest by the intellectual Greeks because we were using our intellect while oblivious to our dependence upon Divine inspiration — we related to our Torah constructs as products of our own brilliance. The Oral Torah is only Torah if we have the humility to recognize that it comes from beyond us and that the origin of our insight is the Creator.[63] The moment we attribute our Torah to our own intellect, our pridefulness immediately cuts us off from Divine inspiration and our Torah becomes spiritual philosophy. Greek persecution indicated that we did exactly this and, rather than protecting us, our Torah was the very thing that empowered the Greek philosophers to oppress us.

Why was it so challenging to maintain clarity of the Divine origin of our Torah under Greece? In the time of Greek domination, we lived

---

59. *Shabbat* 21b.

60. They did not ignore the miracle of the war. The insertion of *al ha-nissim* to the *Shemoneh Esrei* is focused on the military victory. But the only mitzvah we have is the lighting of the Chanukah menorah.

61. Maharal, *Ner Mitzvah*, p. 22. See also Rav Chayim Freidlander, *Siftei Chayim* II, *Neis HaShemen Mei'id*, pp. 13–20.

62. A theme often repeated in Maharal, for example *Gevurot HaShem*, ch. 47.

63. Rav Tzaddok HaKohen, *Likutei Ma'amarim Sefer Yehoshua.*

in a world where we had no immediate awareness of or encounter with spirituality. Greece institutionalized this denuded experience into a complete and consistent vision. According to the Greek worldview that swept the world, reality was effectively a self-contained, natural place.[64] It had always existed and always would, moving from before to after by the ceaseless march of physical law. Any recognition of God functioned as a conceptual element in a philosophical system — God's existence had no direct, practical involvement or impact on actual living. In such a world, every object had its place and understanding consistent with the Greek picture. Our job was to face down this vision with a painstaking reformulation of reality, placing the Creator at its center, redefining every element of existence within the context of spiritual awareness.

Using the Oral Torah to recreate a God-centered understanding of the world from the midst of this spiritual desert was a staggering feat. Within a human context, this is the equivalent of creating existence from scratch. Since our purpose is to emulate God the Creator by using free will to create,[65] this approached ultimate accomplishment.[66] But it also brought us dangerously close to the snake's prideful temptation: "Eat this fruit and you will be like God," i.e., becoming a maker of worlds.[67] All it took to poison our achievement was the arrogance of attributing our understanding to ourselves. Our challenge was intensified by the Greek context in which it was faced.[68] Greek culture was consciously centered on formulating a vision of reality that was man's creation and possession. The ideals of the larger culture bolstered the snake's incitement.

---

64. Greece was a complex, sophisticated society with many different intellectual strains. We speak now of the aspect of Greek worldview that was spread by Alexander, which was primarily Aristotelian (Aristotle was Alexander's personal tutor).

65. See Chapter 6.

66. We will see momentarily that there is an even higher level on which we can achieve this emulation — when we create ourselves, thus emulating God's necessity of being. This was accomplished under Rome.

67. *Bereishit* 3:5 and *Rashi*.

68. See *Berachot* 17a.

Under Greek rule we were, therefore, faced with a single temptation that had both a revealed and hidden form: (1) to accept the Greek vision of man controlling reality by defining it — which was open capitulation — and (2) to corrupt our own vision so that, though presenting itself as Torah, it was actually a veiled form of the Greek philosophy of human control of understanding — a concealed surrender.

We might think that someone who had the strength to resist the Greek worldview and remain focused in Torah would also have the strength to keep his Torah pure. But this was not necessarily so. Because the infiltration of the forbidden fruit of control into the Oral Torah was subtle, it was not easy to see the corruption stealing in. Greek philosophy, on the other hand, presented a clear enemy to fight against.

Furthermore, the inclination to twist Torah into an egotistical expression was necessarily stronger than the pull of Greek thought itself. As much as the Greek vision was from man, it was formulated through observation of the world and acceptance of what reality presented to the eye. Torah was formulated totally from within the self, in opposition to the interpretation suggested by the world. Because it was more from us, the potential satisfaction of claiming it as our own was that much greater, and, so too, the allure.

Many Jews openly succumbed to the enticement of Greek thought. Greek culture spread to many Jews and the Greek armies against which the Maccabees fought were aided by Jewish Hellenists. The battle against the Greeks was in many respects a civil war amongst Jews.[69] But the compromise of our own tradition was also evident at this time. The cohesion of the Oral Torah began to break up: the Torah leadership was divided between the Prince and the Head of the Court,[70] and in this generation the first dispute in halachah arose.[71]

---

69. See *History of the Jewish People: The Second Temple Era*, ch. 8.
70. Yosi ben Yoezer who, together with Yosi ben Yochanan, formed the first leadership pair (*Pirkei Avot* 1:4), was killed by the Greeks. *Bereishit Rabbah* 65:22.
71. About *semichah* on *Yom Tov*. See *Tosefot Yom Tov, Pirkei Avot* 1:4.

The purity of the Torah was also violated. This was the generation of Tzadduk and Baitus, who rejected the authority of the Oral Torah. They began by perverting their teacher Antigonos' admonition not to be like servants who serve their master for the sake of reward as meaning that there was no reward in the Next World.[72] As well as a breakdown in the continuity of the oral tradition, this specific corruption was clear evidence of Greek ideas seeping into the Oral Torah. The rejection of the concept of reward brought Tzadduk and Baitus in line with Aristotle's understanding that good deeds are for their own sake.[73]

The compromising of the Oral Torah by Greek influence was symbolized in the Greeks profaning the Menorah. Every vessel in the Temple represented a specific aspect of our relationship with God. The Menorah that gave forth a light that we lit represented the Oral Torah.[74] Though the Greeks debased the Temple in general, the special significance of the Menorah to the conflict is seen in the miracle that it uniquely merited in the restoration after the Greeks.

REACHING FOR THE ROOT SELF

We could escape the Greek prison only by full recognition of our dependence upon the transcendent realm. The war with the Greeks presented a perfect opportunity to push us to this recognition. The Jews faced a situation where they were impossibly outnumbered; if they were the ones determining the result there was no hope. Yet if they did not fight, the Jewish people would be lost so they had to act. Yehudah HaMaccabee, who led the actual combat, also guided his troops in the more important struggle for clarity. Before each battle he reminded his followers that God could bring victory to the few as easily as to the many — He could save them just as He saved the Jews from Pharaoh at the sea;[75] they were

---

72. *Avot D'Rebbi Natan* 5:1–2.
73. See *Akeidat Yitzchak, Ha'arot* 24:4.
74. *Shemot Rabbah* 36:2. See Rav Tzaddok HaKohen, *Pri Tzaddik*, Chanukah 10.
75. *History of the Jewish People: The Second Temple Era*, ch. 9.

not responsible for the outcome, only the effort. The Jews fought with this understanding and were delivered. Our awareness of God's involvement was then reinforced by the miracle of the Menorah.

The Jews had been centered in their intellect but then corrupted that faculty as a base for connecting to God. Their repentance in the Chanukah rebellion was not a return to this prior form of connection. We are changed by the experience of transgression and must move on to a relationship that is appropriate to whom we have become. The achievement of clarity about our dependence upon God that extracted us from Greek domination had to come from a new source.

If the intellect was no longer subservient to our larger project of relating to God — if it was not a place from which we could reach to our *tzelem Elokim* — then we had to move our center from the intellect and directly occupy our root connection to God. Through *mesirut nefesh* (self-sacrifice),[76] by discounting our own lives in battle, we shifted the anchor of our personality to an aspect of self that lay beyond all the physical aspects that are contained in the finite, natural world where our individuality is located.[77] By doing this, we recovered our transcendent connection through the inner self. This had already become the basis of our connection to God after the loss of our natural sense for worship but had been accessed through the intellect. Having corrupted that channel, we now integrated with our directly. Once established, this inner bridge was enough to bring about the unnatural military success.[78]

But what of the Torah? It is the medium of our connection with God. With the loss of prophecy there remained only the Oral Torah, which requires the active participation of our intellect. The intellect was corrupted under Greece!

We can no longer center ourselves in the intellect, trusting that it will convey the undistorted perspective of *tzelem Elokim*. But having

---

76. *Peirush HaBach, Tur Orach Chayim* 670:4.
77. See Chapter 9 where we discuss in detail the different facets of human personality: physical energy, individuality, intellect, and our root connection to the Creator.
78. *Berachot* 20a and Rav Chayim Freidlander, *Siftei Chayim* II, pp. 31–39.

located ourselves in our *tzelem Elokim* (our root self) we can still utilize intellect as our tool to develop Torah.

Our enduring anchor in *tzelem Elokim* is not, however, a direct consequence of the *mesirut nefesh* of the Maccabees. Their sacrifice 2,200 years ago did not create a permanent entitlement to this level. Rather, it *made possible* our national identification with our root self. So spiritual a level can only be actualized through our own self sacrifice. The medium for this ongoing self sacrifice is not combat as it was for the Maccabees — at least generally. Rather it is self sacrifice for reaching truth through dedication to the Oral Torah. Every day, through the relentless, uncompromising pursuit of truth and the meticulous removal of selfishness which characterizes true engagement in the Oral Torah, we reach beyond all aspects of physical nature to our root self.[79] At such a depth we leave our ego behind, and with it any veiled philosophical musings masquerading as a connection to God, and we instead achieve true Torah.

THE CHALLENGE OF ROME

As in each of the preceding exiles, the very growth which allowed us to escape Greek dominion also opened the possibility for a new corruption and its resultant exile, in this case our last exile — to Rome. After Greece, however, we are not just susceptible to failure; we are prone to it. Since our physical being, identity, and intellect are no longer viable centers from which to form relationship with God, the only remaining possibility is to anchor ourselves in *tzelem Elokim*; but that can be done only through ongoing *mesirut nefesh*. Whereas we departed all previous exiles by entering a deeper part of our personality which was a safe haven until we actively perverted it, after Greece there is no place to base

---

79. About the Oral Torah it is written… "You will not find it in the land of the living." [Then] will you find it in the land of the dead? [Rather,] this is to tell us that the Oral Torah will not be found with one who seeks the pleasures of this world — desire, honor, and greatness — rather, only with one who "kills himself" for its attainment (*Midrash Tanchuma, Noach* 3, quoted in Chapter 4, pp. 60-61).

ourselves that we can take for granted — we have to strive constantly to achieve our starting point. Self-sacrifice is our responsibility and way of life — our only way of life. Laxity inevitably leads to disaster, for it leaves us in a limbo devoid of any connection to significant being and brings to a breakdown in faith.[80]

This danger of passivity is in addition to the hazard of achievement which is typical of all exiles; that is, just as our escape from each exile centered us in a new facet of self which was vulnerable to a new inclination, so too the new ground we occupy after Greece leaves us vulnerable to a new corruption. In this case, success means sacrificing in an ongoing fashion. The medium for our self sacrifice after Greece is the Oral Torah — the new foundation of our relationship with God. It is different from the prophetic relationship that preceded it. Prophecy was experienced as something received from beyond the self. With the Oral Torah our inspiration is more subtle, coming in the form of a synthesis of man's thoughts with Divine influence.[81]

We experience ourselves as generating the thoughts; Torah is our creative act. Since it is a reconstruction of reality from the perspective of Torah, our act emulates the creation of God. Because after Greece it comes through self-sacrifice, we give up the self we were given and become the self we create; through this we achieve our equivalent of necessity of being and resemble God on the most profound level. This produces the resonance we spoke of earlier as the highest achievement of free will where our being — and therefore also our thoughts — are an

---

80. See Chapter 2, pp 23–24 that *emunah* arises from our connection to significant being. For sources which discuss the risk inherent in being defined by a level which requires active achievement, see *Bemidbar Rabbah* 1:11; *Ketuvot* 66b; Maharal, *Gevurot HaShem*, ch. 60 (on the *maror*). *Bemidbar Rabbah* is particularly relevant to our discussion as it speaks about who we were forced to become after the sin of the golden calf; centering ourselves in the root self is a necessity only after transgressions which recapitulated the golden calf.

81. Ramban, who is cited in note 52 in this chapter, describes it as an intuition for which of the possible interpretations is correct. Our thinking is always built on insight and intuition that arise from an invisible place within our minds. Through the Oral Torah we reach a purer source for those intuitions and insights.

echo of God.[82] While we generate the insights of the Oral Torah, the Creator remains their ultimate Source.[83] We are like the violin whose vibrating string brings forth its rich sound, all the time invisibly energized by a distant instrument.

This very accomplishment, however, presents us with a new and singular challenge: to maintain clarity that *the Divinity* underlying our selves and our inspiration is not our own.[84] To escape Greece we had identified ourselves with our root connection to God. This level of closeness made us profoundly aware of our dependence upon God for the existence of both our self and our inspiration for Torah. But it also narrowed the divide between God and us. With direct awareness of transcendence absent and having lost an appreciation for the unfathomable greatness of God's being, it became possible to confuse identifying our self with our connection to God — which brings utter humility — and identifying that connection to God with our self — which is absolute pridefulness.[85] The extraordinary achievement of emulating God's necessity that we achieve after Greece further blurs the distinction.[86] He is necessary being and

---

82. See Chapter 6, pp. 96–100.

83. This level is related to *shem tov*, a good name, meaning good in essence. This refers to integrating goodness into the essential self, as opposed to merely possessing a good characteristic. The connection of *shem tov* to the Menorah can be seen in *Bemidbar Rabbah* 14:10.

84. This is a subtle but enormously significant shift from the challenge we faced under Greece. The Greek intellectual reconstruction of reality was their own, focused in a sphere where — according to them — God lacked genuine involvement. They denied the relevance of God and therefore assumed His role of defining reality. Greece's rise to empire reflected our attributing our Torah to our selves. Rome, by actually attributing Divinity to man or effectively doing so (by identifying primary being with man), retains God as a concept but He becomes a front for the self. Rather than taking God's role, man becomes God. Rome's rise to empire reflected our attribution of our Divine root to ourselves.

85. See the discussion on Hillel at the end of Chapter 16, pp. 307–308.

86. We strive to resemble God's necessity by earning our existence. The more we earn self, the more deeply we resemble God. Since we earn self by creating relationship with God, the more hidden He is the more we earn it. The extreme hiddenness of God that accompanied the arrival of Greece forces us to take full responsibility for creating our relationship with God and maximizes our resemblance. This very resemblance, however, creates confusion between ourselves and God.

we come to experience ourselves as necessary through the self-creation that comes through self-sacrifice.[87] This all combines to create a powerful temptation to attribute Divinity to ourselves.

This is the most essential expression of evil's seduction, "Eat from the fruit so that you can be like God."[88] All that is required to step over the line is to compromise the purity of our self-sacrifice by mixing in an element of pridefulness.[89] Self-sacrifice brings a sense of spiritual connection. But pridefulness cuts off from God, as it did to our intellect when it colored our Torah under Greece. We end up with a seeming transcendent experience that is really only a thinly veiled connection to ourselves and we come to think that we are God. When we succumbed to this temptation we brought upon us the last of the kingdoms, the one that confused man with God — Rome. In mirroring our difficulty separating ourselves from God, Rome presents us with the ultimate challenge to attaining true self.

The exile of Rome is as deep as the self, yet as empty as man masquerading as God. Rome misses true connection to transcendence so extremely that its cultural expression can come either in a totally religious guise or in a totally secular one, because under the influence of Rome they are fundamentally related. There is no significant difference between "I am God" and "there is no God." If I am God, then God is so diminished that there is no God. Furthermore, if we can experience our self to be self-supported, necessary existence, which is the basis of attributing Divinity to ourselves, then we can project that onto external reality and see it as self-contained and self-supported — that is, without a Source. These denials of God arising from corrupt self-sacrifice

---

87. Rav Moshe Shapiro spoke about our assumption under Rome that our own being is necessary. This insight and my efforts over the years to understand what he meant have been central to the development of important parts of this book. It is worth noting that Rome makes self-sacrifice an explicit, integral part of confusing the self with Divinity.

88. Based on *Bereishit* 3:5. See Chapter 6, pp. 100–101 and Chapter 17, pp. 317–321.

89. Rav Moshe Shapiro at one point identified pridefulness as the corrupting influence. It makes sense based on all that we have said — especially our discussion of the centrality of Rome to the process of exile at the beginning of this chapter.

supplement the danger of denial that comes from a lack of self-sacrifice that we mentioned earlier.

The singular alienation from self and God we suffer under Rome matches the unprecedented difficulty we face trying to escape Rome. In all other exiles we had a higher facet of self to which we ascended in order to skirt the inclination that was ravaging us; even after Greece, though we needed constant effort to reach that higher place within us, there was a place to go. This capability is central to the flax-whacking process. However, we bring Rome upon us by corrupting our attachment to the highest aspect of self, our root connection to God. So under Rome there is ostensibly no untainted access to a place from which we can recover pure relationship with God!

*   *   *

There is an underlying similarity between Greece and Rome. Both substitute man for God — in Greece man takes God's role, in Rome man takes God's place. They express different facets of the transgression of the spies, where we accepted a godless world, just as Babylon and Persia expressed different facets of the idolatry of the golden calf. We can now see how the four modern exiles grow out from the two root transgressions of the generation of the desert that we discussed earlier.[90]

For all their similarities, however, Greece and Rome are still very different. Our focus must now turn to Rome. For though studying exiles of the past gives important context and perspective to our present situation, it is Rome that is of immediate and practical concern, specifically its expression in our present society. We need to understand more deeply what it is to be a part of this exile and how we meet the challenges it poses.

---

90. See Chapter 13.

THE CHALLENGE:

Living
through
Rome

CHAPTER 15

Limited Truth and Limited Self

"'And [Yitzchak] called to [Esav] his greater (meaning elder) son...'[1] Said the Holy One: If in your eyes he is great, in Mine he is small: 'Behold I have accounted you [Edom, a descendant of Esav and a precursor to Rome] small amongst the nations. You are very despicable...'[2]"[3] Esav and his seed [Edom and Rome] have great pride and no humility. The Holy One therefore said, "If in your eyes he is great..." meaning because of the power and extent of his kingship, "in My eyes he is despicable," because he has no true existence.[4]

THOUGH THE SAGES RECOGNIZE today's culture as a consequence and extension of the worldview of Rome, modernity expresses Rome in its own unique way. Our awareness of the Roman roots of our society can give us insight into our present situation. But we are not in ancient Rome. Rather, we live the twenty-first century's variation on a Roman theme. If we want clarity on our task today, it is today that we must understand. We now turn our attention to modern experience to understand its form and the unique challenges it poses as we strive to touch our transcendent root and achieve relationship with the Creator.

---

1. *Bereishit* 27:1.
2. *Ovadyah* 1:2.
3. The whole quote is from *Bereishit Rabbah* 65:11.
4. Maharal, *Ohr Chadash*, p. 130.

What defines our modern experience? What distinguishes it from previous generations? When did it begin? Since works of philosophy accurately reflect the nature of awareness in their day, we can expect both the dawning of modern consciousness and its unique nature to be revealed in works of philosophy.[5]

Many consider truly modern philosophy to begin with the seventeenth-century French philosopher Descartes. It was his resolution to determine reality entirely from his own rational understanding that set him apart from what came before.[6] What was significant in Descartes' project was the assumption that man could reach truth on his own, wielding the tool of logic while firmly planted in his own egoistic experience.

Prior to Descartes it was generally accepted that some form of received wisdom was the basis of understanding. Even the mystic, though starting from the self, did not remain in that self as he searched reality. Rather, he traveled through the self to a deeper level of consciousness that transcended his autonomous individuality. Descartes, however, preferred to view reality from the isolated confines of his individual perspective, rejecting any ideas originating outside of himself.[7] A number of things contributed to the attractiveness of this method of acquiring understanding. In addition to Descartes' faith in the ability of reason to distinguish truth, the benefit that is touted to justify this approach is that it provides a structured methodology to develop understanding and a way to judge the veracity of that development.[8]

---

5. See *The Jewish Self*, "Philosophy and Awareness."

6. The Sages, inheritors of a scholarly tradition that stretches back several thousand years, would view Descartes within a much broader historical context. They would not see him as a beginning, but rather as a mature expression of currents that flowed out from a more distant past, first surfacing during the Golden Age of Greece. We will explore this later in Chapter 17, pp. 314–315.

7. *Discourse on Method*, Discourse 2 and 4.

8. Descartes mentions this in his First Discourse. The modern scientific method, which develops directly from Descartes' methodology, is frequently justified using this argument. We will see later that other less conscious factors also pull man in the context of modern culture toward Descartes' view.

The attitude and approach championed by Descartes unleashed the full power of rationality. As well as a philosophical milestone, Descartes' work was also a major advance toward the modern scientific method and outlook.[9] We are all aware of the enormous benefits this mode of thought has given us — the wealth and power it has produced. We are less aware of the profound loss that has also come in its wake. The control over the development of understanding that Descartes' approach allows comes at the cost of restricting the pursuit of understanding and, ultimately, the designation of truth to a narrow layer of existence — that which can be observed by a subject.

There are alternate relationships with reality — such as the experience of being as opposed to the observation of its appearance. These open us to other ways of knowing and acknowledge other dimensions of truth. Descartes, however, focused us exclusively on working out the implications of the subject-object relationship, which is the basis of his vision. Our single-minded preoccupation with this mode of knowing has progressed to the point where we forget that alternatives even exist and presume that viewing the world as objects reveals all there is to know. The scope of reality has been severely diminished.

But it is not just our view of reality that has been truncated by this approach. We, too, are reduced. Pursuit of understanding is central to our humanity. To an extent, we are what we know. More accurately, we are a reflection of the way we know. There are many facets and levels to our humanity, just as there are many facets and levels to our awareness; different ways of knowing existence and the world emanate from and actualize distinct aspects of the self.

For example, an artist looking at a flower will primarily notice shapes, colors, and textures. Looking at the flower this way is both a

---

9. In his philosophical *Discourse on Method*, Descartes relied on logic. But his rejection of tradition and emphasis on personal determination, when related to understanding the physical world, implied the importance of individual observation in place of received wisdom. Descartes himself engaged in a number of scientific studies but is best known for his fundamental work in geometry.

consequence and cause of the person being an artist. The artistry of the artist directs his concentration to these aspects of the flower, and his focus on them keeps the artist centered in his artistic, aesthetic awareness. A scientist, looking at the same flower, will see something very different. Rather than bold curves and vibrant colors, the scientist will be most vividly aware of functional units within the structure of the flower, and he will wonder about its biochemistry. His eye notices different details; the analytical part of his mind is energized by breaking the flower down, centering him in an aspect of personality very different from that of the artist. The artist knows the world aesthetically and the scientist analytically. Since we are aware of ourselves through the act of being aware of the world, these two people know themselves very differently — certainly if they are the kind of artist and scientist who are always in character, consistently connecting to their surroundings through their defining manner.

The modes of understanding that shut down after Descartes — principally, awareness of being — actualize an aspect of our humanity that is much deeper than the rational faculty. Their omission from the legitimate pursuit of truth, and effectively from our consciousness, brings with it the loss of awareness of that deeper self. Today we actualize only our logical faculty in truth-seeking. Since we are aware of ourselves in the act of knowing, distilling the experience of reality to a purely rational awareness turns us into our intellect. The intellect is our primary tool for interpreting our world. But it is just a *tool* of the self; it is not the actual self.[10] Through the intellect, man becomes an observer, for, as subjects viewing objects, only disinterested observation accesses truth. Any personal response is deemed illegitimate and intentionally screened out, turning our "I" into an "eye." We come to know the world only through looking as opposed to through being, and in the process we forget our own existence.[11]

---

10. See Chapter 9, pp. 146–148 and 150–151.
11. The parallel form that this challenge takes within the Torah world is our distraction from *yirah*, *ahavah*, and *dveikut*. Ramchal speaks about this in his introduction to *Mesillat*

LOGIC'S LIMITED SCOPE

In Descartes' approach, what we can know from the perspective of the observing subject is exclusively accounted as truth. Descartes' subjective perspective is powerful, but it is not all-inclusive. Science provides an example of how specific modes of understanding leave out dimensions of reality. Science is the detailed analysis of physical phenomena and is very powerful in its chosen arena—but it cannot go beyond it, because science's mandate, methodology, and tools only reach to physical phenomena.[12] The contrast between science's deep insight into physical reality and its oblivion to spiritual reality tells us nothing about spirituality's existence or lack of existence. Concluding from this incognizance that spirituality does not exist would be like a deaf person comparing a painter's studio to a jazz concert and determining that music adds nothing of richness and sophistication to life.[13] The creativity of the music resides in sound and is only accessible through the sense of hearing, which the deaf person lacks. Even though he can make insightful comments about paintings, thus establishing his credentials to judge art, the deaf person is utterly unqualified to comment on music. His oblivion to the beauty of jazz is a consequence of *his* limitations, not the limitations of music.

We are confident in our Cartesian understanding because we presume that logic invests it with truth. This confidence is exaggerated, however. Logic is a limited and specific tool. It gives truth only in the sense that it explicates the underlying structure of what we know or the way we know. It can reveal the potential inherent in our perspective, but it remains forever party to this perspective. Science, for example, is very logical. But its logical rigor does not broaden the scope of its access.

Yesharim, but is much stronger about it in the original version of *Mesillat Yesharim* that was only recently published (Machon Ofek, 2004).

12. Scientists would hold this point to be definitional. They aggressively oppose any resort to spiritual explanations in a scientific context as violations of the scientific process.

13. An even more accurate metaphor would be someone who puts in earplugs before going to the concert, because scientists consciously ignore spiritual explanations as outside the defined purview of science.

Science remains a circumscribed investigation of physical phenomena, albeit a logical investigation.

Mathematics, the most logical of all pursuits, provides a pure example of this limitation. In mathematics we begin by establishing axioms that define the space we are analyzing. After we have the axioms, we use logic to deduce theorems, unpacking the structure inherent in the space we have defined. Logic does not give us the axioms that form the space, nor does it change the space, which would require changing the axioms. Logical deduction is wholly confined to the specific context in which it operates.

For example, an axiom of Euclidean geometry is that parallel lines — defined as two lines that are perpendicular to a third line — never meet. When we apply logic to this and the other axioms of Euclidean geometry, we determine what there is to know about Euclidean space. But Euclidean geometry only holds true where the axioms apply — on a flat surface where parallel lines defined this way indeed do not meet. On a sphere, parallel lines do meet, as you can see from looking at longitude lines on a globe.[14] For spherical spaces, Euclidean theorems are false. The same mathematical logic which deduces truths about Euclidean space cannot deduce non-Euclidean space from Euclidean space. If we want non-Euclidean geometry, we need to establish a new set of axioms and then reapply the logical method.

So, too, logic tells us nothing of the larger context within which our subject-object perspective operates. It is blind to other ways of perceiving reality, or how deep our perspective penetrates relative to the other possible views — whether it reaches to the essential depths of reality or not.

Even as a tool for unpacking structure, logic is particular and not universal. Our comparison to mathematics suggested that were we to change the nature of our connection to reality — the equivalent to changing the axioms — we would be able to apply logic to reveal the structure of our new approach. But in the example of mathematics,

---

14. Lines of latitude, which do not meet, are not true parallels in the sense of being perpendicular to a common third line. Rather, latitude lines are composed of those points that lie at a common angle to the equator.

though we are moving from space to space, we remain within the same way of knowing. Just as logic accesses the structure in one space, so does it in the other — both are known in the same way. But the fact that logic successfully unlocks the structure of Descartes' subject-observing-object form of knowledge does not guarantee that it has the same capability in the context of another form of knowing. Dreams, for example, are a way of knowing ourselves and the world that are not a product of observation. Dreams can be understood. But the structure of dreams and the knowledge they can contain do not yield to traditional logic at all.

We cannot rely on logic to elevate Descartes' vision to ontological truth. The way of perceiving reality that we have inherited from Descartes is what it is — a particular view that includes what it includes but has its limitations. What exactly is it missing and how significant are its blind spots?

WHAT DESCARTES LEFT OUT

The vision of a subject observing his world yields the truth of how something appears, but leaves out the truth of what something is. This is because our project of knowing the world operates independently of our awareness of being. But how much is really lost by excluding the experience of being from legitimate understanding? At first glance, being would seem to be the ultimate subjective experience, since the only being that we have access to is our own. Though we observe who we are just as we observe everything else in existence — i.e., we have access to the appearance of our self — our self is exceptional because we also know it in a different way. We not only observe who we are, we also *are* who we are — we experience our being. But it is only our own being that we can experience. We are other to everything except ourselves. Everything else we know from the outside and, therefore, can only know its appearance.

The fact that our experience of being is focused on the self, however, is not necessarily a limitation on what it can access. In an earlier age we could, through the experience of self, reach deeper levels of existence that transcend our individuality and thus touched being beyond our own. In other words, the self mediated rather than delimited the experience. Our source — the Creator — is the source of everything. Therefore, theoretically, we could access God through the self, and through God access the rest of creation.[15] Today, we consider this mystical. But once it characterized everyone's intuitive experience of self.[16] Even today, when this depth is for the most part obscured, we can still, through our own personal experience of being and extrapolating that beyond our individuality, gain some sense of being beyond ourselves.

Acknowledging the experience of being as a legitimate venue for knowing truth exposes a linguistic contradiction deeply embedded in the post-Cartesian worldview which we have been skirting but must be addressed. We can only know being through the experience of our subjectivity, and that experience of subjectivity is inaccessible to outside confirmation and, for the most part, to logical analysis. For that reason, modern vision labels this "subjective" knowledge. The word "subjective" would be appropriate — it is truly the knowledge of the subject — were it not for the fact that in the Cartesian worldview, subjective means "perceived" as opposed to "real" — because it does not allow confirmation. Yet the subjective experience of being is our only access to what something is as opposed to how it appears! Furthermore, when we talk about what something is, as opposed to how it appears, we call it "objective" understanding. The whole concept of "object" presupposes the subject-object split that requires us to relate to things as other, and, therefore, through appearances as opposed to the actuality of their being![17] Employing the

---

15. The prophetic potential of dreams is also a consequence of our self's connection to the Creator. (See Rav Yosef Yehudah Leib Bloch, *Shiurei Daat* I, *Nissim v'Teva* 1, his discussion of dreams.) Dreams can be distracting as an example of an alternative to modern awareness because we are really interested in a different mode of conscious awareness. But dreams do present us with an experience that we still have today that is not mediated through the relation of subject to object. In an earlier era, when our conscious awareness was also not so severely subject-object oriented, we had the possibility of conscious prophecy.
16. See Chapter 14 and *The Jewish Self*, "A Moment of Favor." See also the description of Adam's experience of self at the beginning of Chapter 17.
17. Ontological being would be a more accurate term than "actuality of being" but is too technical for a work of this kind.

accepted usage of these problematic terms, it emerges that our only access to objective reality is considered "subjective knowledge" in Descartes' world, while subjective knowledge — knowledge of appearance from the perspective of the subject — is considered "objective". Appearance becomes essence, and being becomes appearance. This confusion brings into sharp relief the relativity and narrowness of the Cartesian worldview.

In a sense, by objective reality what is meant in the Cartesian view is "testable." But is it legitimate to make testability the prerequisite of truth? Testability does not determine genuine significance, relevance, or priority. For example, if we are interested in the relative intelligence of a group, but we only have a tape measure, we do not organize our sample according to height and claim to have the information we want. We also do not claim, in this example, that because we cannot measure intelligence, it does not exist or is not important. Similarly, only valuing understanding that can be tested *because* it can be tested does not necessarily lead to the deepest truths.[18]

OUR DYING SELF

If the experience of being were just attributed inferior status, it would be a terrible inversion of priority. But in our obsession with observing the world, we forget to experience our being at all! Obviously, if we think about it we are aware that we exist. In fact, the pain of our emptiness can make us acutely conscious of our existence. But even when we are aware, what passes for our self today is little more than a shallow, featureless storehouse for our observations. There is more to us — there is an "I" with content and depth who is experiencing being! But the fact that there is an observer who is more than the sum total of his observations is lost. This loss of true self is the principal victim of Descartes' rational shift.

---

18. Anyone who has had the frustrating experience of dealing with a government program understands this. Generally, governmental bureaucracies work to maximize what is testable, regardless of the testable factor's relevance to the genuine need that created the bureaucracy in the first place, because bureaucracies must demonstrate their usefulness.

It is remarkable that Descartes launches modern philosophy with the insight "I think therefore I am," because there is not much more discussion of the "I" after this initial insight. Descartes' "I" merely provides the basis for a rational approach to knowing the world. But there is more to our "I." Though it is true that we awaken to our existence in the act of perception, ending our experience of being at that is like seeing a sandwich and equating seeing it with eating it. We only know the sandwich is there by seeing it; sight gives us our first encounter with the sandwich. But if we don't then actually eat it we are missing out on what the sandwich is really all about: eating and receiving nourishment. So, too, our total focus on observing the world—which, it is true, has produced the acuity of vision that gives us modern science—has come at the exclusion of being. In our unceasing observation of the world, we know ourselves only in the act of perception. Instead of a first awakening, this becomes the totality of our experience of self. The self who is doing the observing loses content and falls into the background of consciousness—the "I" is lost.

This is not abstruse philosophical spray, of interest only to members of the academies; it has very real consequences for our day-to-day living. Returning to the sandwich metaphor for a moment, if we continue to restrict our connection to the sandwich to our visual senses, we receive compelling evidence that we have missed something important in the sandwich's relevance to us, for we are hungry. And even though we can ignore the hunger, and if we do so for long enough we may forget our hunger, we have compelling evidence that we are still missing something about the sandwich essential to our existence, for we eventually die.

So, too, we have ample evidence that our lack of any experience of being misses something important; while much of our life is dedicated to acquiring, we are eternally unsatisfied—we are hungry. And though with the passage of time we forget that there is such a thing as experiencing being, and we accept our chronic dissatisfaction as part of the experience of life, we have ample evidence that something essential has been lost. While our power continually waxes, our self-confidence only wanes—our self is dying.

For some time now, most of us have had all our subsistence needs met, and beyond that our material substance has continually grown. We have achieved undreamed-of wealth — yet we constantly sense that we are lacking. The line between want and need is hopelessly blurred and life seems to be an unending succession of discoveries of new things we cannot live without. No sooner is one lack filled than we discern another.

We were created in the melding of a boundless, Divine spirit with a finite physical vessel.[19] This means that our humanity and our true experience of our humanity are intrinsically infinite, or at least tied to infinity.[20] When we define, anchor, and develop ourselves around our confined, physical dimension — that part of us we see reflected in our observation and experience of the physical world — we make ourselves into wholly physical, limited beings. This is a profound diminution in the depth of our humanity. We may become oblivious to the crowding caused by the shrinking boundaries of our increasingly finite self, yet it wreaks havoc with our sense of being. Subliminally we experience profound lack in ourselves.

We instinctively react to fill the growing void. But our efforts are directed to the realm where all our attention has become focused, the only reality we know — the external, physical realm that we are continually observing.[21] We attempt to solve our problem by expanding our physical reach, acquiring more and more things. We feel the lack and assume it must be a consequence of our missing some possession, because the alternative, that something is lacking in our self, is not even considered; that the self should have any content is an expectation long ago forgotten. We look around for that which we are missing — or a polite advertiser graciously advises us on this matter. We come to long for that which we think we need, obsessing until we are possessing. Then, moments after we achieve our goal and it becomes ours, we are suddenly looking for the next thing to buy. We find ourselves just as wanting after the acquisition as we were before — even a bit more.

The reason for this is that we never needed the object we sought.

---

19. *Bereishit* 2:7. See also *Rashi* there from *Bereishit Rabbah*.
20. See Chapter 9, p. 148.
21. Ibid., pp. 144–145.

Our lack lay in the shallowness of our self; coming to possess some object cannot fill the real gap. Rather, it is like quenching our thirst with saltwater. Every new acquisition we make merely anchors us more in our physical expression, further distancing us from our infinite root and thereby increasing our neediness. Even the illusion that specific objects will complete us is possible only as long as they do not share in our deficiency. Once in our possession, they, too, become party to our lack and, therefore, cannot satisfy us. In short: we want things only because we are wanting. The things we want, we want only because they are not already ours. Once ours, they cannot satisfy us because they are ours.

It has reached the point where as soon as we acquire something we felt we desperately needed, we immediately begin *searching* for the next thing to need. The experience of needing something, and pursuing it, has become so much a part of us that we are not comfortable without it. The instinct to grow and complete ourselves as people, which we discussed as defining humanity and human purpose, has been corrupted into the need to pursue physical objects we lack. To feel like a growing person, we must be constantly striving to acquire a *something* that we are missing in our physical domain.

We do not experience our emptiness directly because we have forgotten what it is to be full. We have lost our sense of the necessity of connectedness to a deeper, infinite core. We no longer define or experience ourselves as the expression of Being — *Tzelem Elokim* (the image of God). But we *are* that connection, and subconsciously we are aware of the distance between the profound significance of our true being and our actual experience of self. It is this that leaves us wanting, with the depth of the want measuring the extent of the distance. The insatiable consumerism that is the cornerstone of modern economics and society is, therefore, a chilling indicator of our vacuousness — a clear sign of just how hungry we are.[22]

---

22. See *Peirush al Kamah Aggadot* by the Gra, ch. 21 on *histapkut*, satisfaction. There the Gra hints to the converse of this: that only through focusing on our connection to our infinite, spiritual Source can we achieve abiding satisfaction. As long as we search for satisfaction

But if consumerism is the sign that we suffer emptiness, the seriousness of the damage is manifest in our sense of profound inadequacy. We have become something that lacks basis. Our "I" is dissolving — our hunger is advancing toward death.[23]

Though we don't generally walk around conscious of a sense of inadequacy, our inner poverty is evident. Our self is so weak that we despair of achieving true greatness. Instead of building toward significant being, we invest in the appearance of greatness, honoring empty achievements of relative superiority over others, like running faster, being smarter, or having more.[24] True greatness is not relative; it is a reality — you either have it or you don't. It only comes from the significance of being that derives from connection to genuine existence — the necessary, infinite Creator.[25] There is no competition for such a thing. One person having it does not detract from someone else gaining it. Rather, the opposite is true — one person's attainment can only catalyze the achievement of others. But this greatness is very far away from us at

---

from physical things, we will never be satisfied. Our approach should be to look for sufficiency in our physical involvements and seek satisfaction from our connection to the infinite, spiritual realm (sufficiency is not an objective level of subsistence but, rather, is relative to the standards and expectations of each individual — see Rav Yosef Yehudah Leib Bloch, *Shiurei Daat* II, pp. 104–116). When the Jews were in the desert after their departure from *Mitzrayim* they ate *manna*. Everyone ate exactly the same amount, an *omer*, the measure of an individual's basic subsistence. They were content with this amount of food because their source of satisfaction came not from food, but from their connection to God. In fact, it was the *manna* that maintained that connection by falling in such a way that all facets of *emunah* were reinforced. When the Jews became dissatisfied with the *manna* in *Bemidbar*, it was in the context of a series of events that indicated a general weakening of this spiritual connection. In fact, it was soon after they complained about the *manna* that they sinned with sending the spies into Israel — a sin that was motivated by a lack of *emunah* (*Devarim* 9:23) — and brought upon us our history of exile. In the context of equating satisfaction with *emunah* the Gra cites a statement of the Sages that the prohibition against coveting contains the entire Torah. This works well with our conclusion in the first section of this book that the entire Torah is to foster *emunah*.

23. See our discussion of Haman's despising of Mordechai in Chapter 3, pp. 33–36 for another facet of this idea.
24. Regarding the Roman focus on externalities see *Vayikra Rabbah* 13:5.
25. See Chapter 6.

this time. That distance is the smallness of man under Roman dominion to which the *midrash* at the beginning of our chapter refers.

But perhaps this culture's lack of true achievement is not a sign that we have lost all connection to greatness. Maybe we strive for these superficialities only because we have forgotten that real greatness exists. While this would be a troubling sign in its own right, it would not indicate the advanced stage of disease associated with extreme inadequacy.

That would be a possible explanation if we were satisfied with our petty accomplishments. But our focus on shallow goals is matched by the consistent presence of slander in public and private discourse, something that the commentaries single out as a defining characteristic of the last exile. Slander is a way of compensating for failure; by slanderously tearing down any instance of greatness in others we console ourselves over our own failings by convincing ourselves that greatness either doesn't exist or is impossible to achieve. But where is the wholesale failure in modern society that motivates our recurrent chorus of slander? We are not even trying for true greatness! On some level we must know that our accomplishments are meaningless; only because we lack the strength or confidence needed to reach for something higher do we still pursue them. But even when we achieve these empty goals we are aware that we have essentially failed. The pervasiveness of slander in modern culture is indicative of an underlying, if unconscious, sense of inadequacy. Slander is not just one transgression among many. Rather, it is emblematic of humanity's dying core.[26]

---

26. Because modern culture is characterized by hatred between individuals (see Chapter 3) Jewish involvement in slander cuts to the essence of our subjugation to that culture. For this reason, Rav Yisrael Meir Kagan (unfortunately, no direct relation), the leading light of pre-World War II Jewry, devoted endless attention and energy to eradicating slander and wrote his famous work, the *Chafetz Chaim,* on the laws of slander.

CHAPTER 16

Understanding the Sin of Understanding

Rebbi Yehudah said, "[The tree from which Adam ate] was wheat, for an infant does not know how to call out to his father and mother until he has tasted wheat."[1]

W E DISCUSSED, IN THE previous chapter, that we presently understand the world as a subject viewing objects. This new stance toward reality leaves out that which, in prior times, was the basis of our awareness — our experience of being. But what does it mean to understand the world through our experience of being?

It was easier for us to describe the nature of our modern understanding than it will be to gain a sense for what it was before it took its present form. Yet if we do not make the effort to picture this earlier way, we will not know what it is that we have lost or appreciate the significance of the changes that have occurred in consciousness. And though intellectually we may recognize the parochial nature of our experience, with no specific alternative against which to measure our present understanding we will naturally relate to our form of understanding as defining human experience universally across all generations and cultures. This limits our appreciation of human potential, skews our concept of what it is to

---

1. *Sanhedrin* 70b.

be human, and blocks our ability to make meaningful changes.

Let us begin by recognizing the extent of the revolution inherent in Descartes' subject-object format.[2] Our understanding of our world is necessarily a reflection of the way we search — if we look with our eyes we find what is bright, if we look with our ears we find what is loud. By revamping how knowledge is sought, we necessarily change what we know of the world. Through Descartes' approach, we do not simply know more or finer details about our world than we did before; we know different things about it because our focus has changed. Since we know the world differently, the world is different for us. And since, as we mentioned in the previous chapter, we awaken to our existence through the act of knowing, a change in what and how we know necessarily also changes who we are that seeks to know.[3]

The modern way of understanding, then, is a central element in a complex web; it remakes our selves and our world on every level. All these elements — how we know, what we know, who we are that knows — together form a distinct *da'at*. The precise meaning of the Hebrew term *da'at*, which we usually translate as "wisdom" or "judgment," is best understood in contrast to the other classic terms for understanding: *chochmah* and *binah*. The Hebrew term *chochmah* refers to knowledge that we cannot determine on our own but, rather, must receive from outside ourselves.[4] Though an oversimplification, it is most easily understood as the axioms or premises that define our world and our understanding. *Binah* refers to the system of understanding that results from working out the implications of the premises given by *chochmah*.[5] Through *binah* we build a comprehensive, overall vision of our world. *Da'at* refers to this

---

2. We will discuss later when this revolution really took place. We have already recognized Descartes as marking the first mature expression of modern understanding, at least in philosophy. So, for now, we will continue to use him as modernity's representative.
3. This is because we become aware of ourselves in the act of knowing, and the aspect of self actualized and thus discovered depends upon which facet of self is involved in knowing.
4. *Rashi, Shemot* 31:3.
5. Ibid.

system of understanding after it is integrated into us. Whereas *binah* is a systematic intellectual construct that we have the option of utilizing to interpret our world, *da'at* is the system of understanding that is identified with and inseperable from our awareness of self. It is not a way we *can* interpret our world; it *is* our interpretation of our world. It is not something we know so much as something we are. *Da'at* is one with us on a level that outstrips our conscious understanding. It is part of our instinct and intuition[6] and we come to understand it not only through our intellect but also through knowing ourselves.

Da'at is our understanding that, were it taken away, we would no longer recognize ourselves as ourselves.[7] It establishes the structure of our ongoing awareness and, so, also determines who we are that awakens to our own existence through awareness.

Since *da'at* establishes the way we know what is outside ourselves, what we know, and who we are that knows, *da'at*, is our total, integrated, self-contained world. Two people, each with a different *da'at* might physically stand next to one another, but they exist in completely different worlds. They can speak to one another, but only with great difficulty and conscious effort can they communicate. They will appear similar to one another, yet they are completely different sorts of people, having actualized different parts of themselves. They will point to the same objects and use the same words to describe them, but every term will have different meanings and contexts for each of them.

Once we determine that modernity is characterized by a changed *da'at*, if we want to understand better what that *da'at* is and how it differs from our previous *da'at*, we can turn to the Torah. The topic of distinct and competing *da'at*s is well-developed there and, as we will see, the two *da'at*s that the Torah deals with are equivalent to our modern *da'at* and the *da'at* we had before the arrival of modernity.

---

6. Ibid.
7. As heard from Rav Moshe Shapiro.

WHAT IS WRONG WITH KNOWLEDGE?

When Adam was placed in Gan Eden he was prohibited from one thing: eating from the Tree of the Knowledge of Good and Evil. Since the consequence of eating from this tree was the acquisition of knowledge, we understand that it was actually the knowledge of good and evil that was forbidden.[8]

However, when we talk of the prohibition against obtaining the "knowledge of good and evil," we are working with a translation of complex Hebrew terminology. Translating the Torah is an impossibly challenging task — every word needs extensive explanation. This is particularly true of the word we have rendered as "knowledge." The actual Hebrew is *"da'at,"* the word we discussed in the previous paragraphs. Judge for yourself if "knowledge" adequately conveys the depth of meaning implied by the term *da'at*. At the very least, alerting ourselves to the fact that the prohibition in the Garden was against the *da'at* of good and evil reveals the story's relevance to our present discussion. We will soon see that the choice of this specific term has profound implications for understanding the story of the Garden.

The prohibition against acquiring the knowledge of good and evil is particularly significant because it is the first prohibition placed on man. Creation is an economical process. The Creator does not create every individual thing from nothing; rather, He creates specific forms, which are then expressed into physical existence, recurring in various manifestations. The first expression of any form is its archetype, from which all future variations are derived.[9] As the first prohibition, then,

8. The significance of this knowledge coming through eating was discussed earlier in Chapter 2, pp. 15–19. For Adam, eating achieved and represented the definitive human act of actualizing potential. Improper eating, then, realized possibilities in man that distanced him from attaining his true goal in creation. The significance of the food being specifically from a fruit tree can be derived from a discussion we will have momentarily about fruit trees.

9. Since creation descends from its spiritual root to physical expression, the first time something appears in creation it emerges directly from its spiritual root and is, therefore, its most essential expression. The mitzvah to dedicate *bikkurim* (first fruits of a crop) is an outgrowth of this.

refraining from the knowledge of good and evil is the root prohibition, the essence and basis of all proscriptions of the Torah.

It is surprising that the root prohibition should be directed at knowledge. The restrictions that the Creator placed on us hold us back from doing things that block or interfere with the attainment of the goal for which we were created. In the most general terms our purpose is to develop our relationship with the Creator, which we do by actualizing that part of ourselves that is intrinsically tied to the Creator.[10] The pursuit of understanding is central to that effort — Torah study is the foundation of our relationship with God.[11] Knowledge is a good thing! If so, why is the root prohibition on man directed against acquiring the knowledge of good and evil?

In order to answer this question, we must first ask what the situation was in the Garden prior to Adam's transgression — what is our picture of the Garden? Our intuitive first interpretation of the story is that Adam and Chavah were Rousseauian rustics living in blissful, naïve ignorance, at one with their surroundings until they wrecked everything by acquiring understanding. A more thoughtful reading of the story does not support this, however. We are told that Adam was created *b'tzelem Elokim*, in the "image of God," which some commentaries identify with intellect.[12] At the very least, a Neanderthal does not fit the description. And Adam was commanded; the idea of command makes no sense unless the reaction of the one commanded is significant. Adam, then, must have had operational free will, which requires, among other things, that he understand on some level the consequences of his actions. If Adam responded only out of instinct, then the Creator would be controlling everything directly; Adam would be nothing more than a cog. The whole Gan Eden story would be reduced to empty theater and a confounding waste of precious words; God might as well have created existence with the consequences of Adam's actions already built into reality!

---

10. See Chapters 1 and 2.
11. See Chapter 8, p. 120 and Chapter 13, pp. 231–232.
12. Rambam, *Moreh Nevuchim* 1:1; *Seforno, Bereishit* 1:27.

Adam clearly had knowledge and understanding before the sin. If so, the prohibition against eating the fruit was not denying him knowledge per se, but rather it was holding Adam back from a certain type of knowledge — the knowledge of good and evil. What type of knowledge is the knowledge of good and evil? What other type of knowledge is there? The fact that the knowledge of good and evil was prohibited means that it prevents or retards the development of relationship with the Creator. Why and how does specifically the knowledge of good and evil hinder that relationship?

A DEFICIENCY IN THE GROUND

We mentioned that essential significance lies in the command not to eat from the Tree of the Knowledge of Good and Evil because it was the first prohibition placed upon man. It must therefore express the core of what we are not supposed to do — what it is to turn away from the Creator. But as well as recognizing significance in the first prohibition, there is also significance in the first sin. Though Adam's decision to eat from the tree was *man's* first violation of a command of the Creator, it was not the first violation to occur in creation. There was another that was prior to his and, therefore, an even more fundamental turning away. If Adam's sin is the essence of all sins, then this prior transgression is the essence of Adam's sin.

On day three of Creation, the Creator commanded:

> Let the earth bring forth grass, herb yielding seed, and fruit tree bearing fruit after its kind, whose seed is in it upon the earth...[13]

The next verse describes the earth's implementation of this directive. A careful reading reveals subtle departures:

> And the earth brought forth grass, and herb yielding seed after its kind, and tree bearing fruit, whose seed was in it after its kind...[14]

---

13. *Bereishit* 1:11.
14. Ibid., 1:12.

The Sages identify several discrepancies between what the Creator commanded and what the earth did. The one that concerns us is that the earth was directed to bring forth a "fruit tree" bearing fruit, whereas the earth actually brought forth a "tree" bearing edible fruit. The Midrash explains that in the command, the trees, as well as bearing fruit, were supposed to themselves be edible — they were supposed to be "fruit trees."[15] Instead of climbing a tree to pick an apple, one would have just taken a bite out of a branch or the trunk. But the earth instead brought forth trees of the kind we are familiar with, where only the fruit is edible, not the tree. We will discuss in a moment the significance of this particular deviation; but for now we must focus on the fact that there was a deviation.

When God commanded the ground, He was not a parent ordering around a rebellious teenager. Rather, the Source and Basis of all existence was doing the commanding. Any divergence from the command of the Creator under any circumstances is difficult to fathom. We generally only find it with man and explain it by the concept of free will, which was introduced into creation for reasons we have discussed. But here it is the earth that is deviating! How are we to understand the possibility of the inanimate earth acting counter to a command from the Basis of its existence?

If we cannot comprehend the possibility that the earth would "willingly" veer from the command of the Creator, we must understand that it was "unwilling," i.e., that it was incapable of fulfilling the Creator's order. But this answer introduces more questions than it answers. Did the Creator not know that the earth was incapable of fulfilling His command? Could He not create earth that was capable of fulfilling His desires?

We must answer that the Creator intended that the earth be unable to fulfill this command to bring forth a "fruit tree." But then why did the Creator demand it in the first place? We must explain that the Creator

---

15. *Bereishit Rabbah* 5:9. "Fruit trees" could not mean that the trees were supposed to bear fruit, for that is explicitly stated in the verse, "fruit tree bearing fruit." We are using the interpretation of Rebbi Yehudah bar Rebbi Shalom. Rebbi Pinchus reads the verse differently.

was commanding creation to reach its ideal state, but made creation in such a way that it initially fell short, leaving space for man to complete creation.[16] The space between actual and ideal existence — that which man must bridge — is then the distance between a creation filled with "trees" and a creation filled with "fruit trees."

Not only does the ground's shortfall leave over work for man to do in creation, it also makes that task meaningful. Man's responsibility to complete creation is only significant when he does it through his own free choice.[17] The actualization of free will requires a force that pulls away from the Creator.[18] We established earlier that incompleteness gives rise to inclinations;[19] the shortfall of creation from its ideal, its incompleteness, is its separation from the Creator — what we call *ra* or "evil."[20] This produces a force that pulls to exacerbate the separation from the Creator rather than repair it, the *yetzer ha-ra*, or "evil inclination." This force is materialized in the ground.

This same ground contributes to the creation of man. Man came into being when a Divine spirit was invested into a body taken from the earth.[21] The soul, which was pinched off from the Creator, seeks only to return to its source — the Creator,[22] thus providing the necessary pull toward God without which free will would not have the strength to choose correctly. The ground in man pulls him away from God and toward the incompleteness of creation. Since man's efforts to complete the world now operate against a countervailing force they have the quality of choice and are meaningful.[23]

Since the pull away from the Creator that man must overcome

---

16. *Chagigah* 12a; *Bereishit Rabbah* 5:8. See Ramchal, *Da'at Tevunot* 26.
17. Ramchal, *Derech HaShem*, 1:3:1. See Chapter 5.
18. See Chapter 5, p. 75 and Chapter 9, p. 143.
19. See Chapter 9, pp. 143–144.
20. *Ra* literally means "broken off," as we see in *Tehillim* 2:9, "*Tero'eim b'shevet barzel* — Break them with an iron rod."
21. *Bereishit* 2:7.
22. Ramchal, *Da'at Tevunot* 24.
23. See Chapter 9, p. 143.

derives from his component of ground, we can understand the nature of this force in man by investigating the specific inadequacy revealed in the ground through its "transgression" or shortfall. We have already mentioned that the ground was commanded to bring forth a "fruit tree" bearing fruit and instead brought forth a "tree" lacking the succulent, edible qualities of its fruit. What is the implication of this shortfall?

To answer this question we will need to understand the significance of trees and fruit. But first let us examine the basis of meaning and the significance of objects generally.

THE MEANING OF MEANING

Shlomo HaMelech, King Solomon, achieved the deepest human understanding possible.[24] When Shlomo HaMelech put the essence of his wisdom into a book, he called it *Mishlei*. This is rendered in English as Proverbs. The term "proverb" has several meanings. It is specifically in the sense of a parable — an allegorical expression of wisdom — that Proverbs accurately translates the Hebrew term *Mishlei*. An allegory is a story or statement whose primary meaning and intent lies outside the actual story or statement. The story is merely an intermediary to reach a level of understanding that would otherwise be inaccessible. If we do not understand the story, we have no allegory. But if we only understand the story, we have missed the whole point of the allegory.[25]

When Shlomo HaMelech called his book *Mishlei*, he was disclosing the essential truth of his book. To communicate we must speak, but true wisdom is concerned with an arena beyond what can be conveyed directly in words. What we want to communicate can at best be indicated metaphorically, leaving it to the reader to understand wisdom from within himself. Wisdom lies beyond the direct reach of language because

---

24. See *Melachim* I 5:9–14. See *Rashi* on verse 11 from the *Pesikta*.
25. Rav Moshe Shapiro emphasized this point in regard to understanding *Mishlei*.

300 @ THE CHOICE TO BE

the essence of reality is its spiritual root rather than its physical expression. But we live in the physical realm, and our language reflects that. We can still access the spiritual root because our world is the shadow cast by spiritual reality into physical existence — the structure of physical existence therefore mirrors spiritual reality. By titling his book *Mishlei*, Shlomo HaMelech was teaching us to relate to physical experience as allegory. He was showing us how to live through physical experience rather than in it so that we can reach the deeper spiritual root.

More specifically, existence was created to give man an opportunity to form a relationship with the Creator. We have no immediate access to the Creator, for He is not physical and our only door to reality is through physical creation. But physical creation is a medium for encountering the infinite Being of God indirectly. Everything in creation has a role to play in our achieving relationship with God. Therefore, though everything in creation has a function within the context of physical existence, that is only its *story*. Its *message* is connected to our relationship with the Creator. We encounter and understand things in their physical context, but we must also see beyond their immediate purpose in this world in order to perceive their essential significance and meaning.

The language of the Torah makes this clear. We see ourselves as occupying a world full of objects — things devoid of intrinsic meaning and open to the whims of our interpretation. This is because we live very much in the immediate story of physical reality, rather than being aware of its larger context. *Lashon ha-kodesh* — Hebrew with the meanings used in the Torah — pushes us beyond the immediate story to consciousness of the metaphorical implications of physical reality. The Hebrew term *davar,* which we translate with the neutral term "object," is derived from the term *dibur,* which means "speech." *Lashon ha-kodesh* challenges us to live in a world full of words spoken with intention in a conversation with the Creator — with *devarim,* not with something as amoral as "objects."

To apply this to our topic, if we wish to understand trees we must ask ourselves what they signify in the context of our relationship with the Creator — what word they are in the conversation. How does the existence of trees catalyze, facilitate, or inform our relationship with the Creator?

TREE AND FRUIT AS METAPHOR

Trees and their fruit provide an image of the general relationship between Creator and creation; the tree is the source, or creator, while the fruit is its product, or creation. They supply this image throughout Torah and Rabbinic literature.[26] The usage also carries over into English, where we speak, for example, of the fruit of our labor. When the Creator commanded the creation of this metaphor, He specifically instructed the earth to bring forth a "fruit tree" bearing fruit, meaning that the tree should itself be a fruit as well as produce fruit. Why was this important? How would this have affected the meaning communicated by the metaphor?

Were a tree itself to be edible, the tree would have absolute primacy over its fruit, for it would have everything the fruit has in addition to being the source of the fruit.[27] In fact, if a tree were itself fruity, we could question why it needed fruit at all! The verse in *Bereishit* that describes the creation of trees supplies the answer — fruits contain seeds, giving the tree an opportunity to reproduce. In the case of an edible tree, then, the fruit would add nothing to the picture other than giving the tree the ability to exist in a new location. Fruit would utterly serve its tree.

Had the earth brought forth a fruit tree bearing fruit, the defining image of the Creator's relationship to creation would have conveyed the deeper truth that the Creator contains in Himself everything found in creation. Creation would stand revealed to be what it really is: like a fruit of the fruit tree, existing only to allow the Creator expression into physical reality (*tzelem Elokim*, the image of God), utterly and only serving Him.[28]

---

26. *Yeshayah* 3:10; *Tehillim* 1:3; *Ta'anit* 5b.

27. *Bereishit* 1:11. It is important to remember that the first tree did not grow from a fruit seed. It was created as a mature tree bearing fruit. Otherwise, we could reverse the whole image and see the fruit as the source of the tree.

28. See *Yeshayah* 43:7, "For My glory I have created it…" In the beginning of Chapter 4 we discussed the necessity of recognizing that everything in creation is contained in the Creator. We deduced from this that the purpose of creation must be for God to give. Here we derive from the same recognition that God created in order to express His glory into creation. These two ideas — that creation is for God to give and for God to express Himself into physical

But the earth deviated from the command to create a "fruit tree" bearing fruit and, instead, created a "tree" bearing fruit, meaning the tree itself had none of the qualities of the fruit — the situation that we are familiar with in our world. With our kind of trees, when a person plants a seed, his interest is the eventual fruit and not the tree itself. The priority of the fruit and the tree has been reversed, with the fruit becoming the goal and the tree relegated to the role of the means. With the tree-fruit relationship symbolizing the relationship between the Creator and creation, this signifies that the ground's perspective on the enterprise of creation is that creation is the basis of reality and the Creator a means to its existence.

The earth's perversion is the equivalent of our turning to the Creator once we wake up to our existence and thanking Him for His service in bringing us into being but requesting that He please not get in the way because, after all, we are now here, i.e., the goal has been achieved. As a show of our appreciation for His fine efforts, we are willing to worship on Saturdays as long as it does not distract us too much from our own concerns.

Creation sees itself as center rather than as servant. This is the root ra, "evil," incompletion of physical existence — its shortcoming and distance from the Creator and truth. And when man's body was formed from the earth this false view of creation as "the fruit of a tree" became a part of us. It provided a distorting pull away from our true purpose of completing creation by making it over in the image of "a fruit of the fruit tree."

The evil force of the ground was only created to provide an alternative to truth against which we could do battle. It was there to be overcome — to challenge us to achieve our goals through active free will. But that is not what happened. Adam ended up giving in to this darkness and followed the ground into a world of inedible trees. The perspective of the ground, which until that point had been only a voice nagging at Adam, was

being — are actually two sides of the same coin. The good we receive is through our connection to God, which we achieve through recognizing His expression into creation. See Rav Freidlander's introduction to Da'at Tevunot.

transformed into Adam's own perspective. This expressed itself in man eating from the Tree of the Knowledge of Good and Evil. How do we see the influence of the earth expressed in this root transgression?

THE AWAKENING OF EGO

The Torah teaches us that the Tree of the Knowledge of Good and Evil enticed man on a number of different levels:

> And when the woman saw that the tree was good for food, and that it was pleasant to the eyes, and a tree to be desired to make one wise, she took of its fruit, and ate...[29]

The Sages associate each of the attractions of the tree — good for food, pleasant to the eyes, and desirous for wisdom — with a primary inclination in man — desire, jealousy, and honor.[30] They argue over which of them took priority in leading man to sin. This argument takes the form of a dispute over which specific kind of fruit was on the tree, each fruit representing one of the inclinations.[31] Because of our particular interest in understanding and *da'at* we will focus on the opinion of Rebbi Yehudah, quoted at the outset of this chapter, that the fruit was wheat; we will see later that wheat represents the attraction of man's intellect to honor.

> Rebbi Yehudah said, "[The tree from which Adam ate] was wheat, for an infant does not know how to call out to his father and mother until he has tasted wheat."[32]

---

29. *Bereishit* 3:6.

30. Maharal, *Derech Chayim* 4:22.

31. *Sanhedrin* 70b: Rebbi Meir said: That tree from which Adam ate was a vine, for nothing brings woe to man like wine. Rebbi Yehudah said: It was wheat, for an infant does not know how to call out to his father and mother until he has tasted wheat. Rebbi Nechemiah said: It was a fig tree, for with the thing by which they were corrupted they made amends, as it is written, "And they sewed fig leaves together." *Bereishit Rabbah* adds in the name of Rebbi Abba from Acco an *etrog* (citroen). See Maharal, *Derech Chayim* 4:22, for a discussion of these different opinions and their relationship to the inclinations.

32. Ibid.

Rebbi Yehudah's assumption that wheat grew on trees in Gan Eden is a point discussed by the Sages and the commentaries and need not concern us at this time.[33] Even ignoring this issue, Rebbi Yehudah's statement is cryptic. What does an infant's calling to his parents have to do with tasting wheat? And what does it have to do with Adam's sin?

An observation of Jean Piaget, the famous Swiss philosopher and psychologist, will help us. Piaget studied, among other things, the psychological development of infants. He noticed the fact that in early infancy when a child is shown an interesting object, like a bright red ball, the child will be happy and continues to be happy even after the object is taken away. At a certain point in the child's development, however (Piaget said around eight months, but the exact age remains a matter of dispute), when the ball is shown and then taken away, the child reacts in a forceful, negative manner (he screams his head off). Piaget theorized that the older infant has developed a concept of "object constancy" — he recognizes that the ball continues to exist, is not present, and he wants it. What is the situation of the younger infant? Piaget reasoned that the younger child does not scream because "Out of sight, out of mind" — no permanence to the object. Once the object is no longer in front of the infant, it effectively ceases to exist for him.

An alternative interpretation of Piaget's observation, however, is also possible and is implicit in Rebbi Yehudah's statement. This interpretation is dependent upon another issue that is hotly debated among

---

33. The fact that a bread offering inaugurates the bringing of the First Fruit offerings (see *Rosh Hashanah* 16a) indicates that the Torah recognizes wheat as being at essence a fruit of a tree. See also *Berachot* 40a. Wheat originally grew as loaves of bread on trees (*Bereishit Rabbah* 15:7, *Yafeh Einayim*; *Berachot* 38a; *Megaleh Amukot Vayeitzei*; *Pri Tzaddik, Chag Ha-Sukkot* 25) but, as a consequence of the sin of Adam, was diminished to the wheat kernels growing out of the ground that we are familiar with. On the simplest level, bread is symbolic of man (*Bereishit* 39:6, *Rashi*), and the making of bread, the staff of life, is symbolic of man's essential activity and creativity. The sin of Adam broadened man's responsibility in creating himself and his relationship with God; therefore, after the sin, instead of picking finished loaves off of trees, we have to harvest kernels that need a lot of processing to create bread (*Pri Tzaddik, Chag HaSukkot* 25).

developmental psychologists: When does a child become aware of himself as an individual distinct from his surroundings? If we suppose that the child develops his first inklings of self at the time he begins to reveal what Piaget understood to be an awareness of object constancy, we could explain the changing relationship of the child to objects as a consequence of a growing awareness of his permanence of self rather than of the permanence of objects.

We could then understand the effect that Piaget observed as follows: before displaying object constancy, the child cannot distinguish himself as a distinct entity. Once the child is shown the ball he knows that the ball exists and continues to know that it exists even when it is taken away. Since he cannot distinguish himself from the rest of reality, he cannot distinguish himself from the ball. As long as the child has awareness, then, the ball continues to be present for the child even when it is taken away because there is no distinction between the ball and the child — all is one. But this changes with the dawning of a rudimentary ego awareness that allows the child to experience himself as distinct from his world and so of the ball. Instead of awareness merely flowing through him, there is a *he* that is aware. With the arrival of this awareness of a distinct self exclusive of the ball, the child will need the actual presence of the ball to be satisfied. Therefore, when it is taken away he screams.

What Piaget identified as the development of an awareness of object constancy would, according to this understanding, instead be the development of a need for object presence caused by the coalescing of the self. If we substitute the child's parents for the ball in this example we begin to understand Rebbi Yehudah's statement and its relevance to Adam's sin. A child can only call out to his mother and father once he is capable of recognizing their absence. According to Piaget this comes when he recognizes object constancy. According to Rebbi Yehudah it comes when the child is first aware of himself as a distinct entity. Prior to this awakening of self the child would never miss his parents — his awareness of being would be the same as the presence of his parents. A young infant never cries out from loneliness, only from pain. Once he matures enough to experience himself as separate, however, the possibility of abandonment arises. When his mother is not there, he will wonder where she is and call to her. By implication, Rebbi Yehudah is telling us that the effect of eating from the Tree of the Knowledge of Good and Evil was the birth in Adam of ego awareness distinct from God.

What does all this have to do with wheat? When does this rudimentary awareness of self begin in a child? The Sages understood that internal, psychological developments in people take place in parallel to physical changes. Thus, for example, a child reaches the age of majority — when he is held responsible for his actions — at the time he shows signs of puberty.[34] We become responsible for our actions only when we achieve a level of understanding and sense of self sufficient to generate actions from ourselves — to truly choose — rather than merely responding automatically to our environment. Based on our discussion of free will this ability to choose is the equivalent of gaining the ability to create or give birth to our own self.[35] This development parallels gaining the ability to physically reproduce.

Similarly, a child's ability to distinguish himself from his surroundings is paralleled by a corresponding physical change. Before birth, a child has no sense of himself as independent from the rest of existence — specifically from his mother, who is everything for him. This is reflected on a physical level by his total dependence upon his mother for all aspects of sustenance. After birth, the child's lack of individual awareness continues, while his nursing carries on the physical dependence originally channeled through the umbilical cord. The child remains merely an extension of the mother, having come from her and still utterly sustained by her. As the child moves through infancy, however, his experience of himself as distinct from his mother develops. This is paralleled by the equivalent physical change — the child begins to hunger for food that is not derived from his mother. The child's desire

---

34. See *Yevamot* 105b.
35. See Chapter 6, pp. 85–87. See also Chapter 2, pp. 21–22 for our discussion of the double meaning of the term "generations."

to be sustained from the world rather than from his mother reflects and reinforces his growing sense of identity independent of Mom. The first food which can fully sustain a child without his mother is wheat. Thus, the tasting of wheat is an external physical event marking the internal transition to a primal awareness of distinct self. It is then that he becomes aware of his parents' absence and wants their return. Thus, a child does not know how to call out to his father and mother until he tastes wheat.

SELF AND GOD

What do we mean that Adam, like a developing infant, gained ego awareness through the sin? We can transpose the situation of an infant before he knows himself as an individual to that of Adam before the sin through a curious statement made by one of the great Sages of Jewish history, Hillel the Elder. The Talmud relates that when Hillel reached supreme joy, he would say, "If I am here, everything is here."[36] Hillel was famous for, among other things, his great humility.[37] If so, how are we to understand what he was saying?

The answer lies in knowing that "I" can refer to a person's awareness of himself as an individual, but it can also be a name for the *Shechinah*, the Holy Presence.[38] The reason "I" is a name for the *Shechinah* is that individuality, when it is not false, is a level of reality that can only emanate from the Creator Himself, as we explained when we discussed free will.[39] Hillel's joy led him to achieve a connection to the Creator that blurred the line between his distinct being and the Creator.[40] If Hillel maintained his distinct identity while confusing it with the Creator, he would be revealing himself to be psychotically prideful. In this

---

36. At a *Simchat Beit HaShoëivah. Sukkah* 53a.

37. See *Kad HaKemach, Erech Atzeret.*

38. Rav Tzaddok HaKohen, *Komeitz HaMinchah*, 71.

39. See Chapter 6, pp. 96–97.

40. *Toldot Yaakov Yosef, Korach*, paragraph 3.

case, however, Hillel was losing his distinct identity to the Creator, an experience of ultimate humility. His sense of self no longer blocked his awareness of the Creator. Rather, that sense of self was his medium for reaching the Creator. Hillel still had a sense of identity — he used the word "I." But that "I" was located in the Creator, not in himself. He had become transparent to the Creator at the root of his being so that he was more aware of the Creator than he was of his own egotistic experience. He transcended individual self to become a conduit for the Creator's expression into the world.

The greatness Hillel achieved sounds remarkably similar to the experience of early infancy.[41] Just as an infant has not yet gained a self distinct from his mother, Hillel brought himself to the point where he submerged his independent identity in the Creator. This resemblance helps us understand Adam's situation before the sin and provides the key to understanding Rebbi Yehudah's view that the Tree of the Knowledge of Good and Evil was wheat. Rebbi Yehudah is telling us that just as an infant loses his integration of identity with his mother when he tastes wheat, so the result of Adam's transgression was a fall from a state of almost egoless consciousness in which selfhood was located in the Creator.

Adam before the sin was more aware of the existence of the Creator than of his own existence, similar to Hillel. He experienced himself as a limb of the Creator, a conduit for God's expression into the world. Through the sin, Adam broke himself off from the Creator. That much is obvious, for through the act of disobeying God's command, regardless of what the act was, Adam had to become other to God. Some commentaries identify the moment of sin with the plucking of the fruit from the

---

41. The Sages state that a child before birth is in an exalted spiritual state of direct connection to Source and boundless insight. But once the *neshamah* is joined with the body, thereby subjecting the spiritual root of the individual to limitation, this is lost (*Niddah* 30b). Though on some level this occurs at birth, since the integration of the *neshamah* with the body is seen in the capacity of speech and at birth this has not yet been actualized, we can understand this integration to develop over time. Therefore, it makes sense to look at an early infant's awareness as a paradigm for spiritual connection.

tree — the first action that ran counter to the will of the Creator.[42] By identifying the fruit as wheat, Rebbi Yehudah highlights this separation as the essential change accomplished by eating from the tree.

We are now in a position to understand the relationship between Adam's sin and the sin of the ground. The inclination of the ground was revealed when it brought forth a tree bearing fruit rather than a fruit tree bearing fruit. We explained that this represented an inverted perception of the true relationship between Creator and created. Whereas the Creator contains within Himself all reality, with creation nothing more than a means to His expression into physical reality, the ground attributed priority to creation, relegating the Creator to the status of a means to creation's existence. Similarly, Adam began with his identity located in the Creator, experiencing himself as effectively a limb of the Creator, a conduit to His expression into the world — a fruit of the fruit tree. As a result of eating from the Tree of the Knowledge of Good and Evil, Adam perceived himself as an independent entity distinct from God.

Why is this called the knowledge of good and evil? Once Adam experienced himself as an independent center of reality, his primary awareness and the center of his experience of being was his self and he could then only perceive reality from the vantage of that self. Subjective reality, reality viewed from the perspective of the self, is the knowledge of "good and evil" — good to me or bad to me — as opposed to true or false in an objective, externally anchored sense.[43]

---

42. Maharal, *Gur Aryeh, Bereishit* 1:11.

43. Having established that the consequence of Adam's sin was to break his selfhood off from the Creator, we now take the next step of recognizing that this necessarily results in coming to know the world from the perspective of the self. This is what the Torah calls the Knowledge of Good and Evil (Rav Yitzchak Izak Chaver, *Siach Yitzchak*, sec. 1, *Drush l'Shabbat Teshuvah*). Though there is an intrinsic structure to this form of knowing that is accessible through logic, there are also severe limitations to this mode of awareness as we discussed in Chapter 15. A limitation that we did not yet discuss is the absence of any real values from a purely logical system — values (externally anchored morality) are not accessible by logic. As we recognized in Chapter 13, pp. 227–228, when God is hidden

Adam's view of reality from the self necessarily established him as judge of his reality. Moreover, it limited Adam to perceiving the Creator as no more than an element in his world. Just as the ground had inverted the priority of Creator and creation, so had Adam — in place of a fruit of the fruit tree he became the fruit of a tree. This fantasy of status was the subconscious motivation for the sin according to Rebbi Yehudah. For, as we said earlier, Rebbi Yehudah identified wheat as the culprit because he concluded that the primary inclination motivating Adam to sin was intellect's desire for inappropriate honor. We will examine these effects in more detail in the next chapter.

We can now understand why the Torah spoke of the *"da'at"* of Good and Evil. Adam did not gain a specific piece of information through eating from the tree; he transformed his entire perspective on himself and reality. And the perspective he gained precisely matches in form the mode of awareness we have identified with Descartes and modernity — Adam became a subject viewing objects.

---

we must be the ones to determine values — see Maharal, who states (*Derech Chayim* 3:15) that knowing good and evil is a consequence of having free will together with detachment from God; we determine our world and God no longer sets the boundaries of that world. But as opposed to God, who defines objectively true value, we have no basis upon which to assess values other than what is subjectively good to us or evil to us. The 18th-century philosopher Kant accused most moral philosophers of confusing morality with pleasure (good to me). And though Kant attempted to construct a rational morality, most modern moral philosophers either openly embraced the pleasure definition (Bentham, Mills) or rejected any idea of an externally anchored morality (Nietzsche, Sartre), which again returns us to the subjective "good to me." As the secular basis of our society becomes expressed in an increasingly unadulterated form, the subjectivity of its morality becomes increasingly revealed and accepted.

CHAPTER 17

Structures of Perception

The wise expand their understanding to meet reality. Fools reduce reality to meet their understanding.[1]

W E HAVE CONCLUDED THAT knowing the world through good and evil means understanding reality from the perspective of the self.[2] This precisely matches our description of the form of understanding that characterizes our modern, post-Descartes era.

Adam's mode of understanding before the sin, however, was very different. We have explained that Adam experienced his being as centered in the Creator, with himself an instrument or limb for the expression of the Creator into physical reality. We have also established that Adam had conscious intelligence. How, then, did Adam perceive his world? What did his "ego-less" understanding look like?

---

1. Quoted by Rav Yosef Yehudah Leib Bloch, *Shiurei Daat* I, p. 32.
2. In the previous chapter we derived this by interpreting primary sources. For a secondary source that states this almost explicitly, see *Siach Yitzchak* of Rav Yitzchak Izak Chaver, sec. 1. He says there: "The Tree of the Knowledge of Good and Evil, *which is investigation by the human intellect*, is to establish all of reality on his intellect through non-Torah wisdom. This is the source of all error and through this man comes to the denial of God and His oversight... the entire world's evil emanates from this source." The original Hebrew is:

עץ הדעת טוב ורע, שהוא ענין מחקר שכל האנושי, לעמוד הכל על שכלו בחכמה חיצונית, שמזה יוצא מכשול ח"ו, עד שבא האדם לידי כפירה גמורה באלוקותו ית' ובהשגחתו... וכל רשעי עולם משרש זה יצאו.

311

This is impossible for us to fully grasp intuitively because the basis of our outlook is the self, as Descartes affirmed when he identified "I am" as the clearest awareness we have. Our understanding begins with distinguishing our individuality from the world, and our process of acquiring knowledge is entirely filtered through the subject-object relationship.

Our first attempt to envision Adam's perspective might picture him understanding with the Creator's understanding. This suggests a comparison to a child comprehending his world through the outlook supplied by his parents at a time when he still sees them as all-knowing. But though this formulation gives understanding an absolute quality and roots it outside the child, it is still experienced through the medium of the autonomous self. This profoundly affects the understanding and contradicts Adam's experience of himself as an extension of the Creator.

To gain some sense for Adam's understanding, we must begin with the insight that he was aware of himself as a limb of the Creator. Imagine your hand invested with consciousness — how it would experience itself, perceive reality, and understanding. Adam located his center at the point where his root emerged into being from the Creator so that any sense of "I" blurred into his awareness of the Creator.[3] Centering himself in such a deep place not only precluded a clearly articulated individual self, but identified selfhood as an exclusive possession of the Creator, a selfhood in which Adam participated. We have already likened this to Hillel's statement, "If I am here, everything is here."[4] Not

---

3. Rav Chayim Volozhin, *Nefesh HaChayim* 2:17.

4. See the end of the previous chapter. Hillel's statement represents some identification with the deepest facet of the self, what is called the *yechidah*, that is both unified with the Creator and recognizes His unity. This recognition contradicts our individual being, thus when Ben Azzai approached this aspect of self with its attendant level of understanding, he died (*Chagigah* 14b; that three others did not is beyond our discussion). Rambam states, in his introduction to *Moreh Nevuchim*, that even Moshe was not established on this level of clarity but, rather, returned to it continuously. The metaphor of the flashing frames of a movie reel comes to mind. Maharal states that this level of recognition was attained by Moshe by keeping it separate from his actual existence in this world, implying he was established on this level. Maharal and Rambam are not necessarily arguing, however, as Maharal may be speaking specifically about Moshe's experience on Har Sinai or in the Tent of Meeting.

only was the *source* of Adam's understanding located in the Creator and outside Adam's awareness of his individuality, the *understanding itself* was centered there also. Adam understood through participating in God's understanding.

The Creator does not know His world as a subject observing an object external to Himself. He is the basis of the existence of that which He knows. Therefore, He knows it through His experience of His own Being.[5] It was on this understanding that Adam "eavesdropped" in perceiving his world. Today, it is impossible to understand this in any integrated, experiential sense; it may not be possible to understand it even intellectually. In any case, before his sin Adam's understanding of the world came through his experience of being. His *da'at* was focused in precisely that area lacking in our present *da'at*.

ALTERNATE FOUNDATIONS FOR DA'AT

When we look at modern *da'at* and contrast it to any possible alternative designed to correct its shortcomings we come up with essentially the two *da'at*s that opposed one another in the Garden. This suggests that there are only two *da'at*s. Each one may come in a number of variations, but, in essence, there are only two. Either we are isolated individuals observing existence from our personal vantage point, or we are each a part of a larger, all-encompassing reality through which we experience existence.

This reflects the fact that man comes into being through the joining together of two dimensions. He is composed of a boundless *neshamah*, or soul, and a finite, physical body. The *neshamah* emanates directly from the Creator. The body, on the other hand, is composed of material — the

---

Adam before the sin was on this level but it was never again attained by man in this world (Rav Chayim Volozhin, *Nefesh HaChayim*, 2:17).

5. Adam, then, more experienced knowledge than knew it — along the lines of how we experience our own existence. It was not, however, anchored in himself but, rather, in ultimate Being. This would have lent understanding an unimaginable clarity and accuracy beyond even Descartes' experiential first fact, "I think therefore I am."

divisible substance through which man is broken off from his Creator to gain separate existence. Though this is also from the Creator, it is connected only indirectly. The dimension in which we anchor ourselves defines us and our vision. Adam's understanding was the vision or perspective on reality from the vantage point of the *neshamah*, or from man as primarily *neshamah*, with his body providing the medium for individuation and expression (a fruit of the fruit tree). Descartes' understanding, on the other hand, is the vision or perspective on reality from the vantage point of the body, or from a man who is primarily physical, his spirituality providing him with consciousness through which to be aware of and pursue his individual interests (the fruit of a tree).[6]

Once we realize the profound separation between Descartes' view and the alternative, we must wonder at the load we are placing on Descartes and the period in which he wrote. We seem to be asserting that there was a complete revolution of self that came around this time, as evidenced by Descartes' humble work. This impression, however, is mistaken. We began this section with the goal of understanding the specifics of our present experience of reality. Descartes conveniently demarcated the point at which we entered the uniquely modern period. But we never viewed modernity as a new and isolated phenomenon. We have always viewed it as an incremental advance on Roman consciousness that itself developed directly from Greece.

The shift in man's experience of self, from being centered in a connection beyond his individuality to the egoism that characterizes our awareness (along with the corresponding outlook on reality), has evolved over several thousand years. This showed itself in the continual diminution of the depth of prophetic experience, culminating in its disappearance altogether. The passing of prophecy accompanied man's loss of compulsion to worship and the corresponding rise of Greece with its

---

6. In the previous chapter, we intimated that a change in our understanding was the motive force behind the altered *daat* of modernity. From this discussion we see that the engine of change was a modification in the nature of our experience of the self. A change in our awareness of self changed the nature of our understanding and the nature of our world.

philosophical and scientific culture.[7] Under Rome all internal sense of transcendent connection faded, to be replaced by a façade of worship. The primary shift in center that led eventually to modern consciousness, then, occurred nearly 2,500 years ago. Descartes merely articulated a mature, uncluttered *vision* of this shift and thereby gave evidence that we had arrived at a mature, uncluttered *experience* of this *da'at*.

COMPARING PERSPECTIVES

We begin to understand what these two different *da'at*s are. But how do they compare to one another? Which is true? When we pose a question within the context of each of them and arrive at conflicting answers, which answer is correct? Is it even possible to meaningfully ask such a question when each *da'at* sees itself as true, and any answer we give comes from within the context of one of them?

We already mentioned that the modern subject-object *da'at* is the perspective of man defined by his physical being, whereas Adam's *da'at* is the perspective of man defined by his *neshamah*. We recognize that the source of existence, the Creator, is purely spiritual, and reality descends from its spiritual source through levels until taking on physical actualization.[8] Spirituality is primary being, physicality its vessel of expression. Man's *neshamah* is a much deeper reality than his body, emerging directly from the wellsprings of existence. Without a body, man is not man, but it is not his basis or defining essence.[9] Man defined by his *neshamah* is a truer, deeper man than man defined by his physical being. And the perspective of man defined by his *neshamah*, then, is a deeper, truer view of reality.

Someone who is entrenched in the subject-object perspective and lacks *emunah* (faith), however, would deny the primacy of the *neshamah*

---

7. *Yoma* 69b; *Daniel* 11:2–4; *Seder Olam Rabbah*, ch. 30, with *Biur HaGra*. See Chapter 14, pp. 257–258 and pp. 262–263.
8. Ramchal, *Derech HaShem* 1:5:3–4.
9. See Chapter 9, p. 148.

and, therefore, the primacy of its perspective. In fact, as a result of the dominance of his physical experience, this person would question the very existence of a truly spiritual dimension and would regard it, at best, as a phenomenon arising from physical being. For him, the perspective of the body gives the only hope of truth. This book is less directed at him than to someone at least open to the possible reality of the *neshamah*. For that person, just as the existence of the *neshamah* is an open question, so, too, the priority of its perspective.

But even for many who fully accept the reality of the *neshamah*, the question remains. Those lonely men of faith who are torn between their spiritual and physical perspectives are also unsure. They recognize the sanctity of the *neshamah*. But because they find themselves in physical reality, they are not comfortable ignoring or discounting its native subject-object approach. They must ask whether the perspective of the *neshamah* or of the body takes precedence. Can we find some neutral ground from which to compare and evaluate the two views?

There are certain truths that stand independent of our understanding. We can compare our two *da'ats* by examining their perception of these truths. In the section on free will (Chapter 8) we discussed how God's unity is the only Divine attribute to which we have access, and that man's full recognition of specifically this attribute is the purpose of creation. This includes God's singular control over everything that happens in creation. Man was granted free will to choose how he wants the world to be and can act to change the world, but the effects of his actions are mediated through the Creator. There is no entity that acts directly upon existence but God—this is the deeper meaning of the *Shema*, "HaShem is One," and lies at the heart of our recognition of the Creator's omnipotence.[10]

Think of the Creator as a puppeteer and all of creation as his puppets. Man is an exception because his free will allows him to initiate action.[11] Man's movements pull the strings attached to the "fingers" of

10. *Devarim* 6:4. See Ramchal, *Da'at Tevunot* 36.
11. Ramchal, *Derech HaShem* 1:5:4.

God the puppeteer. These "fingers" then cause the other elements in creation to dance.[12] Man *does* affect the world, but only through the puppeteer. There is an important condition, however. The movements of the Creator's "fingers" by man's actions are not automatic. The Creator determines if and to what degree His fingers are moved, depending on the condition of the relationship between man and God. Rather than the strings being stiff, picture them as elastic, allowing the "fingers" flexibility in their response to the movements of the human puppet.

The subject-object perspective cuts all this out and views man as interacting directly with the other elements of creation. Within the framework of this *da'at*, man understands himself to be an independent force affecting the world — in complete violation of the deeper intent of the *Shema* and the understanding of God we were created to achieve.[13] The Creator is diminished and man's sense of his own significance is inflated because man is equated with God. Both act directly on the world and, necessarily, man competes with God to determine the direction of creation.

It is a corollary of man's grant of free will that reality reflects man's interpretation — that is, when we understand the world to be exclusively physical it appears to function in a natural manner and reacts to our seemingly direct interventions. Otherwise we would be confronted with an immediate and compelling reality check that would, in effect, restrict our choice. But the vision is false on any level of reality beyond appearance. God is the only One who affects directly; God is the only One who controls.

TO BE LIKE GOD: FOUNDING REALITY ON THE SELF

But there is a far more basic level on which God's unity is violated by the subject-object perspective. Recognizing the Creator as the Source and Basis of all existence is the foundation of Torah. Even a cursory

---

12. Rav Chayim Volozhin, *Nefesh HaChayim* 1:5.
13. See Chapter 8.

investigation of this belief and its implications leads us to appreciate just how profound the divide is between the Creator and His creation in terms of significance of being.[14] We mentioned earlier that one of the names for the Creator is *Makom*, or "Place,"[15] to tell us: "You might think the world is the place of the Creator. In fact, the Creator is the place of the world."[16] A first attempt to picture the act of creation often views the Creator entering the equivalent of a giant, empty parking lot and beginning to fill it. This completely misunderstands the totality of His omnipotence. Without God there is no parking lot — there is not even space. Absolutely everything comes from the Creator, including the possibility of being that empty space represents.

If we wish to contemplate the enormity of the act of creation, we must begin by attempting to contemplate the absolute nothingness of any existence in any way other to God. The Creator begins by creating "somethingness" where there was nothingness — or, rather, where there was not even nothing — there was not even "there was not." For assuming "there was not" presupposes the possibility that there could or will be, and even this possibility did not exist before creation. Out of this nothing, God created something that was then developed into the reality we are familiar with. Without the Creator's act of creation, there is nothing to an extent that outstrips the imagination of any created being to conceive.[17]

Yet this totality of dependence upon the Creator is subtly yet hopelessly distorted by the introduction of the subject-object perspective. Remembering that the subject-object perspective is synonymous with the knowledge of good and evil, we can uncover this distortion by analyzing the temptation of the snake that led Chavah to eat from the Tree of Knowledge in the first place. The snake told Chavah that it was out of jealousy that the Creator forbade eating from the tree. The snake

---

14. See Chapter 6, pp. 80, 82–83.
15. *Bereishit* 28:11.
16. *Bereishit Rabbah* 68:9.
17. Our awareness contradicts what we are trying to be aware of.

said the Creator Himself ate from the tree to gain the ability to create the world and He wanted to deny it to others.[18] Therefore, continued the snake, "If you eat from the tree you will be like God, knowing good and evil."[19] By "like God" he meant a creator of worlds.[20]

Every lie needs its grain of truth to be believed. The truth in the snake's statement was that eating the fruit would remove man's access to objective truth centered in God, thereby forcing man to create his own subjective understanding of existence — effectively to create his world around himself. The snake neglected to add that this was replacing the reality of the Creator's world with man's fantasy — what we called the subjective world of good and evil in place of the objective world of truth and falsehood, existence and non-existence.

To follow after the seduction of the snake and eat from the tree, man had to, at least on some level, accept the snake's lie that God had eaten from the tree. The implications of this particular slander of the snake are therefore revealing of the world man entered by transgressing. Saying, "God ate from the Tree of Knowledge to create the world," implies that something existed outside of the Creator and His creation. God was reduced by the snake to an operator in a context that existed outside Himself. He was no longer the Creator in the fundamental sense of being the absolute Source and Basis of existence. He was at best a creator in the mundane sense of taking from an environment that pre-existed Him and manipulating it — an intermediary. The perception of God that the snake introduced was idolatrous.

By accepting the snake's vision, we relate to *the* Creator in the Divine sense as *a* creator in the mundane sense. In the snake's vision, we must ask what contains and defines God? Who created Him? Yet, since we are relating to *the* Creator in this manner, this question reveals the effective denial of the existence of a true Creator in the world of the snake. In the post-sin, subject-object world, we instinctively relate to the concept of God

---

18. *Bereishit Rabbah* 19:4.
19. *Bereishit* 3:5.
20. *Rashi, Bereishit* 3:5.

in the snake's diminished, heretical way. This is nothing new. The snake merely repackages the position we ascribed earlier to the earth — that God is a tree to our fruit in place of recognizing Him as *the* fruit tree.[21] God is made into a means to our end. To be more precise, as we concluded at the end of the previous chapter, because we build our understanding of our world from our perspective, the world is necessarily centered around us and God cannot be more than an element in that world. As opposed to the *daat* of the *neshamah* through which we experience self emerging from God, existing in Him and, so, unable to grasp Him, with modern *daat* we stand outside of God. Because we contain Him we perceive Him, try to understand Him and, necessarily, limit Him. We do not articulate this point, but it is the ugly lie behind our subjective vision, a vision that yields to us the authority to judge and define.

With God in the subject-object world reduced to an element, who or what is the basis of existence? On the deepest levels of this perspective — nothing. Regardless of what we may proclaim as our belief, on the deepest levels of our psyche we must actually take existence for granted, for there is nothing to bring it into being. The Greeks, with their vestigial attachment to worship, latched on to the structure of physical reality, imputing semi-divine status to intellect and aesthetics. But since man contains these anyway, it was a short step to the pure expression of the emptiness inherent in the knowledge of good and evil, that denies any larger context to physical existence. Into this vacuum enters the only thing that still holds any strong sense of reality for us: "I am" — our self. That is to say, either I am not in any need of God or I am God.

Had Adam eaten first from the Tree of Life, everything subsequently would have tasted of the Tree of Life. Since life comes through our connection to the Creator, this taste-of-life would have flavored the entirety of our experience with the sense that we exist in the Creator's world.[22]

---

21. See Chapter 16.

22. Rav Tzaddok HaKohen, *Pri Tzaddik, Tazria* 3. The commentaries state that man in the Garden would eventually have been able to eat even from the Tree of Knowledge along with all the other fruits — that the self-centering it fostered could add to man's relationship

But instead Adam ate first from the Tree of Knowledge. This caused everything to taste of the Tree of Knowledge,[23] meaning it was experienced as existing in man's world with man at the center. As children of Adam this is our experience of reality — our subject-object experience of reality — and it constantly reinforces our impression of the primacy of our own being, making us the measure and basis of being.

Through the subject-object relationship that is the foundation of modern *da'at*, man has become "like God" not merely because he determines the nature of his subjective world, but also because man experiences everything as existing in *his* world with himself as primary being. Obviously we do not claim to have physically created existence. But on a metaphysical level, because our sense of self is the only thing that carries any force of reality for us, the self becomes the basis and measure of existence. Thus we experience the world as based in us and coming from us, rather than being experienced by us.

Man can choose how to understand or imagine the world and his place in it. But he has no power to genuinely uphold the existence of reality. We are living a lie. The subject-object perspective thus perverts our understanding of the nature of reality and our place in it on the most profound of levels.

REALITY CHECK

So there we have it. Modern philosophical and scientific *da'at* perverts truth and is therefore discounted. But before we utterly reject its viability, we need to ask some difficult questions about truth and our connection to it. On the deepest level of reality, nothing exists but the Creator; this is implicit in the unity of God.[24] In creation, this level of reality must be hidden to allow us to experience existence and function.

---

with God, but only after eating from the Tree of Life first and experiencing Shabbat (*Be'er Mayim Chayim, Bereishit* 2).

23. Ibid.

24. Rav Yosef Yehudah Leib Bloch, *Shiurei Da'at* II, pp. 109–116, *Plas B'Ma'agal Raglecha*.

The only moment when it was revealed, when God spoke directly to the Jews on Har Sinai, everything stood in silent stillness and everyone died — for if the Creator is the only existence, we do not exist in any way separate from Him.[25] We strive to experience a shadow of this reality when we verbalize the *Shema*, our declaration of the unity of God. The commentaries teach that we should imagine ourselves dying as we finish reciting its last word: *Echad*, One.[26] Rebbi Akiva actually did die through his declaration of the *Shema*.[27]

Remarkably, it is possible for a human being to connect on some level to Unity and still continue to exist — though Moshe died along with the rest of the Jewish people on Har Sinai,[28] he remained alive when God spoke to him individually.[29] These prophetic moments, however,

---

25. *Shabbat* 88b. See Maharal, *Tiferet Yisrael*, ch. 31. We are not talking about biological death, because the very experience that brought death brought new life — the direct connection to the Creator. But at the moment of revelation, the Jews ceased to exist as entities separate from the Creator, and they were different people after the experience. The Midrash also tells us that the nations of the world died at this moment (*Shemot Rabbah* 5:9). Again, this must be meant figuratively: With the revelation of Torah a new level of connection of the Creator to His world was introduced. The nations were not party to that connection, and since life is connection to the Creator, they were, relatively speaking, dead (also discussed by Maharal there in *Tiferet Yisrael*. See also *Rashi, Bereishit* 11:32). For the connection of this discussion to *Shema*, see *Devarim Rabbah* 2:31.

26. Shelah HaKadosh. *B'Eser Maamarot, Maamar* 1.

27. *Berachot* 61b. See Rav Tzaddok HaKohen, *Pri Tzaddik, Vayechi* 10 and *Ohr Zarua L'Tzaddik, Alef Rabati v'Alef Zaira* that Rebbi Akiva did not die from the torture inflicted upon him by the Romans but, rather, through the level he was able to achieve through the *Shema* as a result of the experience.

28. Implied in Maharal, *Tiferet Yisrael*, ch. 31. *Vayikra Rabbah* 1:1, that states explicitly that Moshe lived when the rest of the Jewish people feared death, is speaking about the last eight of the Ten Commandments. That is when the Jews feared death as opposed to the first two when they actually, on some level, died. During the first two, God's Unity was more fully revealed.

29. *Bemidbar* 12:8; *Ramban, Shemot* 25:1. A close reading of the Ramban reveals that he understands Moshe's continuous revelation as not the full revelation of God's unity that occurred during the first two of the Ten Commandments that had required the death of the Jewish people. Rather, it was on a par with the lesser revelation of the last eight commandments. Maharal in *Tiferet Yisrael*, ch. 31 could be understood to say that the same level that was revealed in the giving of the first two commandments was being revealed to Moshe, but

were private to Moshe; no one else could hear God's words.[30] Because of Moshe's remarkable spiritual height, revelation that was only to him did not descend into physical reality to an extent that would contradict God's unity. Rather, it remained with Moshe, who was centered in his *neshamah* where individual autonomy dissolved into its Source.[31]

Even Moshe, however, could not live in continuous recognition of this level of God's Unity. He could only grasp it as it slipped away, like a lightning flash that disappeared as he saw it.[32] With Moshe, these flashes came as consistent bursts, like the frames of a movie. So he had effective connection to this level of Unity. But how many others have come even this close? There are parallels between Moshe and our forefather Yaakov.[33] But we are talking about a handful at most in the entire history of creation.

None of the other prophets approached Moshe's level.[34] They only occasionally achieved flashes of insight.[35] The rest of the time they may have been intellectually aware of the Creator's Unity, but it was not their living reality. The rest of us never genuinely touch this recognition. We live with an awareness of our independent, individual existence. Because on the deepest layers of reality only God exists, this is not merely wrong, it is heretical. We spoke about the *da'at* of Adam — that is aware of God's unity — and modern *da'at* — that is oblivious to it — as two completely

---

because it was not fully revealed into the world Moshe could co-exist with this Unity. However, Rav Zevulun Shwartzman understands from the Gra that the revelations to Moshe were not on the same level as that experienced during the giving of the first two commandments.

30. *Rashi, Vayikra* 1:1; *Bemidbar Rabbah* 1:3; *Tanchuma Ki Tisa* 31.

31. Maharal, *Tiferet Yisrael*, ch. 31. See also note 4 in this chapter. When we discussed free will in Chapter (pp. 95–97), we spoke about achieving selfhood that did not contradict God's unity.

32. See Rambam, *Petichah* to *Chelek* 1 of *Moreh Nevuchim*.

33. See the beginning of Chapter 8. See also Rabbeinu Bechaya, *Bereishit* 32:29. Adam before his sin was on an even higher level than Moshe, but that was in Gan Eden which was a different level of reality (Rav Chayim Volozhin, *Nefesh HaChayim* 2:17. He also mentions there from the *Zohar* that Chanoch was taken from the world when he approached Adam's level).

34. *Devarim* 34:10; *Yevamot* 49b; Rambam, *Petichah* to *Chelek* 1 of *Moreh Nevuchim*.

35. Ibid.

distinct and detached worldviews, and they are. But the way any of us actually put our world together does not fit neatly into either of these two separate visions. Rather, we each create our own personal aggregate.[36]

If so, as we consider the *da'ats* from which man actually reaches toward God, it would be more accurate to speak about deeper *da'ats*, ones that more purely adhere to the *da'at* of Adam and are closer to absolute truth, and *da'ats* that are more in line with modernity, encountering reality superficially. Consequently, we cannot disqualify modern *da'at* as a medium from which to reach toward God even though it corrupts our perception. Human awareness invariably contains falsity, so modern *da'at* is just the extreme of a continuum upon which we all fall.

THE WORLD AS WE EXPERIENCE IT

There is another consideration that is relevant when we examine the viability of modern *da'at*. The fact that Adam's *da'at*, the perspective of the *neshamah*, is deeper and truer does not require that it more accurately represents the world *as we actually experience it*. Just as there are many levels to understanding, each a distinct distance from absolute truth, reality itself can be experienced in many ways. The Torah uses the language of speech to describe the Creator's act of creation.[37] This means that creation, at least as we experience it, is formed through the communication between God and man and is not a fixed, objective thing. Though the Creator speaks with a specific intention establishing objective reality, experience is determined through man's interpretation of that reality, allowing for many possible expressions.

In its highest form, this participation of man in creation shows itself in man's responsibility to apply Torah to the world.[38] Man partnered

---

36. See *Rosh Hashanah* 16b that God inscribes man in three books on Rosh Hashanah: that of the Righteous, that of the Evil, and that of the "Inbetweeners."
37. *Bereishit* 1:3.
38. *Shabbat* 10a. Any judge who judges truly, even for a moment, is considered a partner with the Creator in creation.

with God in setting the structure of time when the Sanhedrin decided which day was the first of each new lunar month and when to add a leap month. This partnership, which continues today through the fixed calendar created by the Sages, establishes the dates of holidays, determining the timing of obligations, prohibitions, and the unique spiritual potential God invests in each holiday.[39] Whatever day the Sages say it is, it is; if someone intentionally violates Yom Kippur he is spiritually cut off by God, though his crime is necessarily based on the Sages' determination of the date.[40] When deciding halachah, the Sages are required to ignore even explicit revelation of heavenly perspective and rule according to their own understanding.[41] In addition to the spiritual structure of reality, halachic decisions also alter physical reality.[42]

But man can also "interpret the world" in ways that distance reality from its source. And these interpretations also carry weight in determining the nature of reality as we experience it. We discussed this in slightly different language when we spoke of the effect of our conduct and self-definition upon the rise and fall of empires.[43] Today's reality, that we experience as governed by natural law, is a consequence of our understanding the world in a Roman fashion as filled with neutral physical objects functioning in a purely natural order.

That, at least, is the face of reality that we see. Though man interprets creation, it is the Creator's speech that is being interpreted, and that speech establishes the foundations upon which reality is built. The *neshamah*'s accurate perception of God's direct and absolute control of reality remains true. Though we see a world driven inexorably by fixed natural laws, in actuality we are observing the shallow interface where

---

39. See *Shemot Rabbah* 15:2, The *malachim* said before the Holy One, "Master of the Universe, when will You make the holidays?"... He answered them, "I and you will accept whatever date the Jews decide."
40. *Shulchan Aruch, Orach Chaim* 611:2.
41. *Bava Metzia* 59b, "*nitzchuni banai.*" See also Maharal, *Be'er HaGolah, Be'er* 4.
42. *Yerushalmi, Sanhedrin* 6a.
43. See Chapter 14.

reality meets our illusion. Like Newton living in Einstein's universe, we see what we see only because we restrict our observations to a particular field of vision. Underneath it lies the vast depth of God's oversight and complete control. The Creator created with a purpose, and that purpose will be achieved. Whatever needs to happen in order for that purpose to be achieved will happen.[44] But God's control is largely hidden from sight, at least at this point in history. Though it governs, other than in extraordinary situations, its workings are nested within and masked by the system of the world determined by man. This is now a natural system.[45]

Reality is a layered affair, and we choose in which layer we anchor ourselves. The "natural layer" created by our subject-object perception is very distant from core reality. But since collectively the overwhelming majority of us today are focused in this superficial layer, we establish nature as the governing paradigm of our world. In other words, modern *da'at* that sees only natural causality is accurate to our experience because, though it is far from truth, it truly is our *da'at*.

POSSIBLE RELATIONSHIPS TO NATURE AND SPIRITUALITY

Just as on a national level we are able to affect God's general conduct of the world, on a personal level we can affect God's conduct toward us as individuals by determining the level of reality to which we are subject. Those rare individuals who can pierce through the veils of nature and genuinely live their lives focused around the Creator's direct control of existence function outside the purely natural system.[46]

The commentaries identify four levels of relationship with physical reality.[47] On the first level is the individual who sees himself living in a

---

44. *Yeshayah* 55:10–11.

45. Ramchal, *Da'at Tevnuot* 48.

46. *Ramban* and Rabbeinu Bechaya, *Bereishit* 18:19. See also Rav Yosef Yehudah Leib Bloch, *Shiurei Da'at* I, *Hashgachah*.

47. The following section is based largely on Rav Yosef Yehudah Leib Bloch, *Shiurei Da'at* I, *Hashgachah*.

natural world and, measure for measure, he does. On the second level is a person who views his world through the lens of the Torah and experiences his life as a relationship with God. For such a person, though there is natural law that can be observed in the world, there is also a deeper spiritual law revealed in the Torah that expresses itself through the medium of natural law. For example, the Torah tells us that blessing comes to a person through giving charity.[48] So even though basic natural law would say that the more one gives the less he has, the Torah informs us that there is a deeper structure to reality that will, all else being equal, bring blessing to a person for giving. No natural law need be violated for this to happen. The person on this second level will detect a pattern arising from within the natural context where blessing and wealth come to those who give. This is both because the world responds differently to him as a consequence of the way he relates to the world and also because he is more sensitive to the nuances of spirituality in his environment.

This second level person is like someone looking at a Magic Eye picture. Magic Eye pictures have one pattern that is completely obscured within another. The hidden pattern is coded in at a different depth than the surface picture and can only be resolved by consciously focusing behind the obvious picture. When one does so, the original picture — though it is still present — disappears before the vividness of the now revealed, deeper pattern.[49] So, too, the person living in the world while defining himself around and interpreting his experience through Torah is connecting to a deeper level of reality embedded within natural reality.

This second level is the domain of individuals on a broad continuum

---

48. *Devarim* 15:7–10.

49. It should not surprise us that two people can observe the same physical phenomena and identify completely different patterns — it depends on what one is looking for and to what he is sensitive. This is even true of physically based patterns. A line widely attributed to Thomas Kuhn is apropos: "You don't see something until you have the right metaphor to let you perceive it."

of spiritual attainment. The applicability of Torah's spiritual laws to a person and his awareness of them are dependent on the intensity and consistency of his spiritual focus. In fact, seeing and experiencing the world as purely natural — what we have labeled the first level — is really just the lowest extreme of what we are now calling the second level.

On the third level is one who has transformed himself into a *neshamah* that is expressed through his body. He is identified and defined by his spiritual dimension and therefore is governed exclusively by the spiritual law of the Torah. He has a body yet he is not subject to its physical laws, just as a person does not get dry cleaned because he is wearing a suit. Examples of individuals who reached this level are Chananiah, Mishael, and Azaria who, we are told in *Sefer Daniel*, were thrown into a furnace because of their beliefs and emerged unscathed.[50] According to the Midrash, this also happened to our forefather Avraham.[51] Someone who is not on this third level and finds himself in a fire, barring specific Divine intervention, dies; the same *midrash* that tells us that Avraham was unaffected by the furnace tells us that his brother Haran, who was thrown in for supporting Avraham but whose commitment was unsure, was consumed by the fire.[52]

On the fourth level, nature ceases to exist. Everything is directly governed by the will of the Creator. This is the deepest level of existence and truth, but is only apparent on those rare occasions when the Creator reveals His unity. These moments are characterized by a wholesale compromise of natural structure, such as in the Exodus from

---

50. *Daniel* 3:15–28. See *Be'er Mayim Chayim, Tetzaveh* 27.

51. *Bereishit Rabbah* 38:13. The Sages do not consider the salvation of Avraham to have been miraculous in the sense of an intervention that ran counter to the consistent functioning of reality. Fire's inability to harm him was a direct and necessary consequence of Avraham's spiritual level. Placing Avraham in the fire was roughly equivalent to placing a piece of metal in a fire. A regular fire does not burn metal; it only burns wood. See *Shemot* 6:3 and Rabbeinu Bechaya there; Maharal, *Gevurot HaShem*, ch. 36; *Be'er Mayim Chayim, Tetzaveh* 27.

52. *Bereishit Rabbah* 38:13.

Mitzrayim.[53] Moshe is our paradigm of the exceptional individual whose awareness is focused on the Creator to the degree necessary to facilitate the expression of this level of the unity of God.[54]

WHERE WE STAND TODAY

Of the four levels we have outlined, the last two are presumably only relevant to singular individuals in history.[55] As we contemplate where we stand in the spectrum of the first two levels — using our earlier language as we determine the specific mixture of the *da'at* of Adam and the *da'at* of modernity that characterizes us — it is important to realize that we are interested in what we are, rather than what we say. The spiritual focus that defines us is not determined by our pronouncements of the primacy of the *neshamah* and the spiritual realm or even our belief that these are important to us. Rather, a person's actual spiritual level is determined by the true integration of spiritual ideals and their implications into his self and life, which is much harder to achieve.

We might claim that the Creator runs the world. We might admit that our doings cannot actually determine outcomes. We might be careful to pray before acting in the world. But in spite of this, our reactions to situations reveal that the overwhelming majority of us live in a reality much more heavily weighted toward a subject looking at objects than to one mediated through and controlled by the Creator. We conduct ourselves as if our acts move the world around us through causal manipulations, where results are determined by us. For example, when we

---

53. This is distinct from level three because the violation of nature occurs where the people involved are not defined around their *neshamah* and should be subject to natural law. We are not, therefore, seeing the necessary expression of a deeper layer of spiritual law. Rather, it is a miracle in which God's will overrides the laws that structure creation, revealing that they are not hard and fast laws at all. Rather, they are merely an expression of an aspect of the Creator's will.
54. See notes 4 and 31 in this chapter.
55. See, however, *Bava Metzia* 85a that Rebbi Zera entered an oven every thirty days and emerged unscathed. This was to check that the fires of *Gehinnom* could not burn him.

are sick our thoughts turn first to the doctor or the medicine cabinet, only later do we remember *teshuvah* (repentance) and prayer.

This is not an incidental or isolated response. Rather, it is representative of our whole connection to reality. Let us examine ourselves. When a clock stops working we first assume that the battery is dead. If we change the battery and it still does not work we check to see if the arms have become loose on the central pin. If that is not it and we are so inclined, we may open the clock to see if one of the gears has slipped from its place.

This series of steps is a consequence of a mode of thinking by which we dissect and analyze our environment based on a complex web of assumtions. The world is, for us, a structure of parts each of which is individually responsible for a specific function that, when taken together, produce a predictable, collective result. It is absolutely intuitive for us to think this way and most of us cannot imagine any other way of approaching a situation. This approach is the foundation of our modern subject-object worldview. It detaches events from any larger relationship or context of meaning, assuming a purely mechanistic, natural world. This removes singular control of existence from God and sets up man as His competitor through man's direct manipulations of the physical structure of reality.

Science is the discipline that builds most directly on this form of thinking and consciously aims to give man the direct control of reality that is definitive of modern *da'at*. This makes science both central and representative of modernity. The depth of our compromise to modern *da'at* is evident in the fact that the scientific process is nothing more than a focused and consistent extension of our native thought process — the one that today structures our experience.

With the exception of those very few individuals who have labored to rise above this form of connection to reality, though we may think of ourselves as spiritual people with consciousness of the omnipotent and unitary God, we actually experience the world through the *da'at* of modernity. We may achieve a façade of spiritual focus, but on a very deep level we are party to modern *da'at* and, therefore, subject to all the distortions inherent in it.

OUR NATIONAL LEVEL

Experience seems to corroborate the reality of modern *da'at* and the science that anchors it; in areas where we have expertise, scientific predictions are increasingly accurate. Based on what we concluded earlier — that the world functions according to our collective interpretation of it — this only further confirms the generality of our integration with modern, mechanistic *da'at*. Because as individuals we almost all interpret the world naturally, it functions in a natural way. But though this is how things are today, it is not the only way things can be and was not always so. There was a time in the past when nationally we lived face-to-face with the Creator.

The Jews in the desert, after departing from *Mitzrayim*, were defined collectively by their *neshamot*, and the spiritual law outlined in the Torah ordered their environment. Natural law played little if any part in their lives. They were in a desert that could not naturally support them, fed by *manna* that fell from the sky, and drank water from a well that traveled with them. They were led by a pillar of fire and protected by an accompanying cloud. The context of their lives was structured by revealed miracle — patterns of functioning inconsistent with the rest of the world. The Jews experienced reality as mediated directly through their relationship with the Creator and, therefore, it was.[56] The Jews themselves would not have been able to bring themselves to play the role of scientist searching for physical causes to explain events — looking at physical reality would have seemed to them like studying the structure of paper to understand what is written in a book.

Even as the level of the people declined after they left the desert, they descended into a natural relationship with reality only slowly. The presence of *tzara'at*, a skin condition discussed extensively in the Torah, indicated this.[57] We understand all illness to be a physical imbalance that ultimately has a spiritual root. But this was particularly true of

---

56. See Maharal, *Gevurot HaShem*, ch. 40.
57. *Vayikra* 13:1–14:57.

tzara'at. While having clearly identifiable physical symptoms, it brought spiritual impurity to its sufferers and could only be cured by a *kohen* and *teshuvah*, a priest and repentance, not a doctor. The character flaws and transgressions that caused *tzara'at* are discussed extensively in Rabbinic literature,[58] and *tzara'at* was understood to be an integral part of the direct and revealed relationship between God and the Jewish people.[59] Instances of *tzara'at* are mentioned in the Written Torah late into the First Temple period.[60] It disappeared from the world only when, as a nation, we lost the ability to relate to it as an aspect of Divine oversight.[61]

STUCK OUTSIDE OURSELVES

Torah basically conveys reality from the same perspective as that of the Jews in the desert — through the prism of Adam's *da'at*, aware of the immediacy of the Creator. Though Torah's vision may not conform to the layer of reality most of us occupy today, we still recognize that it describes the reality of a deeper part of us — we are just alienated from that deeper part. And since the functioning of the world mirrors where we anchor our personality, the world seems alien to Torah. But the present form of reality no more reveals the totality of reality than our present consciousness encompasses our total being.

We could compare our situation to that of a scout evaluating a player for his basketball team. The scout will be more interested in a list of playing statistics of the potential team member than a book of poetry he wrote. We all would admit that the poetry tells us more about the player's humanity — his internal being. But right now we want to form a basketball team, so the statistics are more relevant to us. We may admit that basketball is not all that significant — certainly when compared to our essential humanity. However, though no one is comfortable with a

---

58. *Arachin* 15b–16a.
59. *Seforno, Vayikra* 13:47.
60. *Divrei HaYamim* II 26:19, when King Uziyahu was struck with *tzara'at*.
61. *Seforno, Vayikra* 13:47.

great athlete who is an obvious louse of a human being, we are addicted to the game and so we will still hire him if he is not completely out of control. We might ask how we can cure our infatuation with basketball and return to the more important work of reading and writing poetry, where we focus on things that are more essentially human. But the present situation is that we love the game. It is also true that if we wish to evaluate the player as a potential suitor for our daughter, we *will* grab his book of poetry, though we may struggle to read it because our literary sensitivities have atrophied over the years.

CHAPTER 18

Torah and Science

Rebbi Tzaddok fasted during the forty years leading up to the destruction of Yerushalayim to hold off the disaster. He became so thin that when he would eat you could see the food going down his throat... [Before the actual destruction Rabban Yochanan ben Zakkai asked the conquering general Vespasian for three things:] give me Yavneh and its Sages, the family of Rabban Gamliel, and [Roman] physicians to heal Rebbi Tzaddok.[1]

THERE WAS A TIME when, as a nation, we lived with the immediate awareness of our relationship with God. We experienced His direct intervention in our lives, Torah defined our world, and physical causality had little relevance to us. That time is long past. Most of us now travel in a world that we perceive as running along natural lines and because we perceive it that way it, for the most part, does. We are aware that we have a deeper self, one that we see reflected in the Torah. But we cannot tear ourselves away from our physical focus — we are basically addicted. As a result we are trapped in a natural world.

But though this describes the large majority of the Jewish people at this time, there remain the rare individuals that have managed, through the Torah, to pull themselves out of the mud. They have built themselves around their spiritual core, living their deeper self and defining their

---

1. *Gittin* 56a–b.

world around God and the Torah. Because they do not live in the world as a natural place, the world does not function toward them in a wholly natural manner. Rather, spiritual causality and the direct *hashgachah* or oversight of the Creator govern their world. For them, the Torah perspective is not merely the deeper truth; it also accurately reflects the world in which they operate. What does that actually look like?

We would turn to Adam and Moshe if we wanted to explore the full extent to which a human being can make a reality of the Torah vision. They are, however, so distant from us that their deeds seem fantastic and we cannot recognize even our greatest self reflected in them. Moreover, since the spiritual state of the nation sets the backdrop against which all must act, and context affects what can be achieved, of more interest to us is what level exceptional individuals can reach today when, as a nation, we are so entrenched in the natural world. To what extent can Torah become our reality in place of the natural causality of the subject-object perspective?

Rebbi Chanina ben Dosa, who lived at the end of the Second Temple period, provides us with one example. The Talmud tells us several stories about him. One of them is about a certain Shabbat when his daughter came to him distraught because she had accidentally filled the Shabbat candles with vinegar instead of oil. Rebbi Chanina ben Dosa calmly responded, "He who spoke to the oil and it burned will speak to the vinegar and it will burn."[2] The Talmud tells us that the candles burned until after Shabbat, when the *havdalah* candle was lit from them.[3]

It was common for the scholars of the Talmud to be able to perform miracles. What was special about this incident that the Talmud

---

2. *Ta'anit* 28a.

3. A clear reference to the *ner ma'aravi*. This was the candle of the Menorah in the *Beit Ha-Mikdash* that was given enough oil to burn through the night like each of the other candles, and yet burned through to the next evening so that its flame was used to light the Menorah for the next night. This was a testimony to the world that the Presence of God dwelt with the Jewish people (*Menachot* 86b). By implication, Rebbi Chanina ben Dosa's experience was the testimony that the Presence of God continued to dwell with the Jewish people even after the destruction of the *Beit HaMikdash* and the loss of the testimony of the Menorah.

specifically recalls it? Moreover, they studiously refrained from benefiting from miracles unless absolutely necessary.[4] Why would Rebbi Chanina ben Dosa have asked for a miracle here?

Rebbi Chanina ben Dosa's specific words reveal something unusual about him. Rebbi Chanina ben Dosa did not ask for a miraculous violation of nature when he said, "He who spoke to the oil and it burned will speak to the vinegar and it will burn." Rather, he was stating that there is no such thing as natural causality — that he experienced every event as an expression of the unmediated Will of the Creator. And for Rebbi Chanina ben Dosa, the world responded that way — the vinegar burned. Rebbi Chanina ben Dosa was able to discount nature and live in the physical world with the awareness of his direct relationship with God giving form to his experience of reality.

But this is one incident in the life of one individual. What of the general relationship of the righteous to physical existence? To determine this, we need to examine an area of activity with tangible consequences that requires realism and honesty; otherwise the idealism of the righteous may lead them to act in a manner representative of who they want to become as opposed to who they actually are. We find just such an area in approaches to health and healing.

The Torah recognizes the physical world in all of its aspects as a manifestation of a deeper, spiritual level of reality. Sickness is no exception to this rule, especially when we remember the special Divine oversight that people have as a result of their free will.[5] We have already mentioned *tzara'at*, a disease with revealed spiritual overtones that could only be cured by *teshuvah* and a *kohen*. Even though this disease no longer exists, illness generally has a spiritual cause.[6] The physical imbalance revealed by an illness must be expressing some spiritual imbalance between God and the sick person. It should, theoretically, be curable through personal development, certainly through

---

4. *Ta'anit* 23a-24b.
5. *Bava Kama* 2b.
6. *Ketuvot* 30a.

prayer, unless a person's time has truly come.

On the other hand, modern medicine views the body as a complex, natural machine. Many illnesses can be treated through physical means with a high rate of success. How a person chooses to respond to sickness will tell us a lot about what world he understands himself to be standing in. Moreover, the righteous are under pressure to be realistic in their responses because of a halachic obligation on each individual to guard his life[7] and not to spill blood — including his own.[8]

Returning for a moment to Rebbi Chanina ben Dosa, we are told:

> In a certain place there was once a lizard that used to injure people. They came and told R. Chanina ben Dosa. He said to them, "Show me its hole." They showed him its hole and he put his heel over it. The lizard came out and bit him, and it died. He put it on his shoulder and brought it to the *beit ha-midrash* (the study hall) and said to the students, "See, my sons. It is not the lizard that kills, it is sin that kills!" About this they said, "Woe to the man whom a lizard meets, but woe to the lizard whom R. Chanina ben Dosa meets!"[9]

This seems to imply that it is possible for a person on a sufficiently high level to ignore nature even when it comes to his health.

However, the example of a contemporary of Rebbi Chanina ben Dosa, Rebbi Tzaddok, is instructive of the broader context. Rebbi Tzaddok fasted during the forty years preceding the Second Temple's destruction to try to stave off the disaster. When the time for the destruction arrived, the Jewish leader Rabban Yochanan ben Zakkai asked for three things from the Roman general Vespasian who was to lead the conquest of Yerushalayim: protection for the Sages of Yavneh, protection for the descendants of Rabban Gamliel, and Roman doctors for Rebbi Tzaddok, who was weak from his fasting.[10] Rabban Yochanan

---

7. *Devarim* 4:9.
8. *Bereishit* 9:5 and *Mishnah Berurah* 618:5.
9. *Berachot* 33a.
10. *Gittin* 56a, b.

ben Zakkai's request for these things at that time indicated that he understood them to be essential to the survival and continuity of the Jewish people after the impending destruction. The descendants of Rabban Gamliel preserved the seed of David HaMelech and, therefore, the potential for *Mashiach*. Yavneh preserved Torah for the future. Rebbi Tzaddok, after all his fasting, personified the direct connection to God of service and prayer; Rabban Yochanan ben Zakkai's desire to save him reflected the extent to which Rebbi Tzaddok was identified with this aspect of the Jewish people's relationship with God in that generation.

Rebbi Tzaddok, then, was centered in the most spiritual aspect of Torah — direct relationship between man and God. Yet Rabban Yochanan ben Zakkai requested scientific medical care for him — through Roman doctors, no less! To understand Rabban Yochanan ben Zakkai's request, we must contrast it to the absence of any indication that medical efforts were made to treat Rebbi Tzaddok during the forty years leading up to the destruction. What suddenly changed with the loss of the *Beit HaMikdash* (the Temple)?

The *Beit HaMikdash* was the home that physically contained our relationship with God.[11] We might think then that its destruction would mark the end of that relationship. This, however, was not the case; the relationship between God and the Jewish people is eternal.[12] But it did mark the end of any expression of that relationship into physical reality. The time had come for our connection to God to go internal, where we could nurture it in a place protected from the storms of the material world.[13] But since it is through God's relationship with the Jews that He is connected directly to physical reality,[14] the destruction of the *Beit*

---

11. Though *Beit HaMikdash* refers to the Temple, it literally translates as House (or Home) of Sanctity or Holiness. A home is a vessel to contain a relationship.

12. *Ta'anit* 3b.

13. *Yoma* 69b.

14. The Creator is connected to the world through man's synthesis of the Divine spark with a physical body (*Rashi, Bereishit* 2:7). After the flood, this role of humanity became focused in the Jews. See the beginning of Chapter 10.

HaMikdash also brought with it the end of outward expression of God's connection to physical reality generally.

With the loss of the *Beit HaMikdash* therefore came a profound thickening of the veil that obscures God's direct control of existence. We became subject to nature on a new level and it became immeasurably more difficult to look at the vinegar and genuinely expect it to burn.[15] The ramifications of this change for the righteous were enormous. Prior to the destruction, an individual on Rebbi Tzaddok's level would have been able to operate wholly above nature and would not have needed medical treatment. In fact, for someone on that level, seeking a doctor would have been a conscious departure from a spiritual reality governed by direct Divine oversight to enter the realm of apparent causality, nature, and human control. Such a move would have bordered on heresy.[16]

But Rebbi Tzaddok's ability to live beyond nature — and by implica-

---

15. For a precedent for this transition to a more natural state, see *Rashi, Shemot* 10:10. Only after the sin of the golden calf did the Jews become subject to the natural implications of the stars that they were headed toward destruction in the desert. See Rav Eliyahu Dessler, *Michtav Me'Eliyahu* I, p. 185.

16. *Ramban, Vayikra* 26:11 states this explicitly. This statement of Ramban is controversial, but Rav Dessler takes it as absolutely obvious and attributes any apparent argument on Ramban to a focus on individuals who have not reached the level where Torah is their genuine reality. Rav Dessler says this in a number of places, for example, *Michtav Me'Eliyahu* I, p. 181. Rav Dessler states that Rambam would agree with Ramban on this point; see *Michtav Me'Eliyahu* III, 170–172. Rav Dessler's position on Rambam would seem to be a straightforward extension of Rambam's views on Divine oversight brought in the *Moreh Nevuchim*. They echo the idea of Ramban in *Bereishit* 18:19, that the more focused a person is on HaShem the more direct the oversight he receives. According to Rav Yisrael Salanter in *Ohr Yisrael*, however, *Chovot HaLevavot* argues fundamentally on Ramban, saying that everyone must make an effort within the framework of the natural world because of a Divine decree that man must act. See *Sha'ar HaBitachon, perek* 4. Rav Yisrael Salanter was known to follow his physician's instructions with painstaking exactitude. The commentators explain that his intent was not to give any impression that he was attempting to accomplish anything through the medicine other than to fulfill his obligation to put in effort. The Alter from Kelm would only go to medical technicians rather than to doctors for the same reason — to fulfill his obligation to act but, at the same time, to keep clear that he didn't expect his caregiver to be the one who was healing him — that was up to HaShem. He was only going to the technician to fulfill his obligation to act.

tion everyone else's — was undercut by the destruction of the Temple. Since we are always obligated to guard our health, once Rebbi Tzaddok could no longer do it supernaturally, it became necessary to do it naturally.[17] It would have been irresponsible and, therefore, prohibited to refrain from seeking treatment for Rebbi Tzaddok.[18] According to this understanding, the stories of Rebbi Chanina ben Dosa completely disregarding nature either took place before the destruction of the *Beit HaMikdash*, or he was the exception who remained on the level of earlier generations to connect his deeper relationship with God to the newly orphaned Jewish people.[19]

In a sense, the destruction of the *Beit HaMikdash* brought not only the exile of the Jews from the Land of Israel, but also their exile from physical reality; their defining closeness to God was no longer evident in the material realm. When God withdrew, hiding Himself behind a natural screen, He took His Torah with Him so that it now has only limited connection to physical existence on a revealed level. We are stuck in a

---

17. Rav Eliyahu Dessler, *Michtav Me'Eliyahu* III, p. 172.

18. See *Teshuvot HaRashba* I, *teshuvah* 413, that getting appropriate medical care is a mitzvah, though he himself cites Rebbi Chanina ben Dosa as someone for whom this halachah did not apply.

19. Just as Shimon HaTzaddik carried the relationship of revealed miracle into the era when miracles disappeared. See note 3 in this chapter. In fact, it remains a point of vigorous controversy whether or not it is possible for an individual to reach the level where it would be considered abandoning the oversight of the Creator to turn to doctors. The statement of Ramban cited in note 16 in this chapter is somewhat ambiguous. His comment comes in the context of a discussion of the Jewish people in a time of salvation and revealed relationship with God. Yet Ramban sounds like he is also talking about the present. He cites as one of his proofs Rav Yosef, who was an Amora living hundreds of years after Rebbi Chanina ben Dosa and the destruction of the *Beit HaMikdash*. Rashba, a student of Ramban who tells us we are obligated to use medicine, cites only Rebbi Chanina ben Dosa as the exception and implies anyone of lesser stature is out of the running. From Rav Dessler it sounds like this level of relationship is a thing of the past. Yet the Vilna Gaon, considered the greatest Talmudist of the last 500 years, refused medical treatment at the end of his life until he gave in to the insistence of his family. Practically speaking, this dispute need not concern us because even if it is possible today to rise above the obligation to use medicine, it can only apply to a minute, chosen few.

world that appears to us to function in a purely mechanical fashion.[20]
And although individuals of profound spiritual attainment can come
to understand the workings of the world differently, for the most part it
is beyond their and anyone else's reach to integrate that level of reality
into experience to the point where they can justifiably disregard nature.
We find ourselves in the acutely embarrassing situation where our own
Torah requires all of us — even the great leaders of our generation — to
utilize scientific medicine, even though it *seemingly* repudiates direct
personal oversight by the Creator!

But when a Torah leader today seeks medical assistance he is not
turning away from God. Rather, he is responding to a distance that already exists. In this he is not yielding *reality* to physical causality but,
rather, is recognizing that our outward *experience* in exile is structured
according to causality, and therefore he cannot honestly respond in a
manner that ignores natural causality. Directly manipulating physical
laws to produce a cure is not a denial of relationship with God. The Torah
personality views nature as no more than a medium through which the
Creator presently effects His *hashgachah* — prayer remains our instrument
to influence outcomes, with the doctor and his medicines mere agents.

But a change in our relationship has occurred, and that is painful.
We are like a diplomat who in former times bypassed all the bureaucracy and dealt directly with the president. Now when we enter, though
we are not thrown out of the building, we are politely referred to the un-
der-secretary. As well as the inconvenience of needing to follow proper
protocol, it is demeaning. God seems to have downgraded the level of
our ties. Our direct service is denied; it is raining on our sukkah.[21]

Or so it appears. We understand why our connection with God has

---

20. In a related matter see *Ramban, Vayikra* 18:25 that we are obligated to keep the mitzvot in our exile from the Land of Israel only so that upon our return we will not need to be
commanded anew. In other words, though the obligation remains, the genuine integration
of the mitzvot with reality went missing with the exile.
21. In *Sukkah* 28b the Talmud compares rain on Sukkot to a master who receives a cup of
wine from his servant and throws it back in the servant's face. We come to serve HaShem
by sitting in our sukkah but the rain forces us to return to our houses.

become distant. We have entered exile to the fourth kingdom. Apropos to that, we are experiencing some subtle combination of preparation to further reveal the Oneness of God,[22] pressure to develop another level of character,[23] and a precisely focused *onesh* (punishment) to cure our specific distraction from spirituality.[24] The purpose of achieving complete relationship with the Creator remains the same. All that has changed are the circumstances needed to accomplish the next stage. Rather than a downgrade, God's hiddenness represents a deepened commitment to the relationship.[25] His oversight now must occur nested within natural phenomena, which requires a far greater level of miracle than a mere violation of nature.[26]

From our side, we retain our written record of the times we lived as a nation on a level where it was nature that yielded before the Torah, as well as our memory of individuals who transcended the strictures of physical existence. The loss of our ability to ignore nature does not stop the righteous from rising to the point where they perceive the patterns of *hashgachah* operating underneath the natural patterns obvious to science and work with them. They recognize that the degree to which nature orders the life of an individual is a measure-for-measure response to that person's distortion of reality, not fundamental law. Our ability to fully integrate this knowledge with our physical experience is reduced, affecting our practice, but our understanding remains straight. In fact, our understanding becomes clearer. Because we are no longer integrated with our knowledge, it is less intuitive, and we are forced to articulate ideas much more sharply to understand them.[27] We still have Torah.

But the fact that we have Torah and we have been lowered does not

---

22. See Chapter 8, pp. 121–122, 128–129, 131–135.
23. See Chapter 10.
24. See Chapter 14.
25. *Peirush HaGra al Megillat Esther* 1:2.
26. See Chapter 8, pp. 121–122.
27. *Midrash Tanchuma, Noach* 3; Rav Tzaddok HaKohen, *Pri Tzaddik, Ma'amar Kedushat Shabbat* 4.

permit us to bring the Torah down to our present level and interpret it as an expression of or fitting into natural causation. The Torah does not change with our descent into natural existence. More physical aspects of the Torah are actualized as a result of our coming to it from our new place. But it remains in its own realm, offering us perspective from a higher vantage and a hand with which to pull ourselves up from the lowly place we have come to occupy.

For this reason, it should not surprise us that the Torah looks at reality differently from science. And it should surprise us even less that we are more comfortable with the vision of science — for it is describing a reality with which we are immediately familiar. Torah, on the other hand, is operating from a plane of existence different from that which is actualized in us today. The Torah's vision is much closer to that of our essential self and true identity — but we have become distant from that self. Torah is no longer intuitive to our conscious minds, but it remains dear to our hearts, the organ through which we connect to our spiritual core. If we open ourselves to this deeper self, we can still find internal awareness of the priority of Torah independent of our memories of a miraculous past, for we sense that it is essential and definitive just as it speaks to a part of us that is essential and definitive.

LIVING IN TWO WORLDS

When the *Beit HaMikdash* was destroyed, we became anchored on a national level in physical reality. The Torah greats remain with a defining focus in the spiritual dimension, with Torah as their primary guide. The rest of us are more deeply enmeshed in our physical dimension and are, therefore, more reliant on science to give shape and structure to our surroundings. But though the specific balance between these two facets of our reality will vary from person to person, we all live in two worlds. How do we create one reality out of these two worlds and modes of thought? Are there conflicts between Torah and science which complicate achieving a coherent understanding of and response to the world?

Torah's recognition of the existence and priority of the spiritual dimension implies a very different understanding of action and effect than that of science. We explained in the last chapter that a full recognition of God's omnipotence understands that we have no direct control over what happens in the world. All change is mediated by the Creator, with our efforts no more than requests for results. This contrasts starkly with science's adherence to its vision of physical causality and direct human control.

Though this represents a profound conceptual difference, it does not create any practical conflict for the Torah personality. Recognizing God's singular control of reality still leaves us with the obligation of *hishtadlut*, personal effort. The Torah person will be careful to pray before he acts, understanding that outcomes are not in his hands. But this addition creates no contradiction about what effort is required of us but merely raises questions about how much exertion on our part is too much — at what point we should just leave it to God. In terms of specific actions, however, there are no serious obstacles to meshing our scientific and Torah outlooks.

But Torah's view of action does not only require adding prayer to *hishtadlut*. The physical world is real; we interact with it, but we understand it to be an expression of a more significant, spiritual realm of reality. We therefore act in the physical world with the intent of affecting the more fundamental, spiritual realm. Torah teaches us to live through physical reality rather than in it — this is the overall idea of the Torah.[28] This implies a completely different pathway to success with a different set of actions to accomplish a given goal.

Mitzvot provide an illustration of how we act upon the material world to manipulate its spiritual counterpart in our quest to affect our surroundings. When the Torah commands the mitzvot it does not intend that we change the world through direct physical causality. For example, we are required to wave a *lulav* and *etrog* on Sukkot. The Sages suggest appropriate intentions to have when we do this mitzvah — that we are demonstrating proper use of wealth and improving our character.

---

28. This is related to what we said in the beginning of Chapter 10 about the Jewish people being anchored in the most spiritual aspect of Adam's personality. The Torah guides us to relate to reality in a manner that is appropriate to the locus of our true personality. See also Maharal's discussion of the place of the Jewish people among the nations in *Gevurot HaShem*, ch. 60.

They also reveal expected results — material blessing.[29] We cannot detect any physical effect from the mitzvah of *lulav* that would, in any direct sense, generate wealth or affect character. Torah wants its influence on our internal being and the spiritual plane.[30] This is accomplished through physical action, but the effect is not traveling through physical causality. The effects will eventually reach the physical world, such as bringing blessing.[31] But, these effects only come through changes accomplished on a spiritual plane.[32]

Even this concept of action, however, creates no direct conflict with science. Mitzvot are not an area where our Torah and scientific identities clash because when doing a mitzvah we act solely in our capacity as Torah-observant people. When we are not doing a mitzvah but, rather, acting practically in our era of distance from the Creator, the actual effort, with the exception of our prayers before action, is the same as that which the scientist would advise for success — natural effort. We have already discussed this in terms of health and healing.

As far as results are concerned, we find no conflict with science. We do not expect anything to occur that will openly violate natural causality. We mentioned in the previous chapter that there are numerous levels of interaction between the spiritual and physical realm. Open miracles are possible, which would violate science's purely natural vision of reality. But open miracles ceased by the time science became the dominant paradigm through which we encounter reality. Today, we only experience ongoing spiritual causality nested within natural causality. Though the Torah personality experiences and perceives spiritual influences, they do not directly violate the natural framework.

---

29. See *Vayikra Rabbah* 30:1; *Sukkah* 62a with Rav Tzaddok HaKohen, *Pri Tzaddik, Chag HaSukkot* 46.

30. See Rav Yosef Yehudah Leib Bloch, *Shiurei Daat* I, *Nishmat HaTorah* pp. 50–61 for his discussion of the arena targeted by the mitzvot.

31. See for example *Vayikra Rabbah* 30:1.

32. See *Raiya Mehemna Devarim* 281b, "*Rachmana liba boi*."

DIFFERENT UNDERSTANDINGS

Our distance from the Creator allows for a neat convergence between Torah's and science's expectations for our efforts in the realm of action and their anticipated results. No serious conflicts over what to do need arise for a Torah person living in the scientific age. But what of our understanding of reality? For example, modern science understands our world to be approximately four billion years old and the universe in which it resides to be approximately sixteen billion years old. We will soon discuss the limitations of the approach that leads to this estimate. But the fact remains that anyone looking at the world through scientific eyes at this time in history will see a sixteen-billion-year-old universe. Torah, on the other hand, describes physical reality as unfolding over a six day period. Can the Torah personality, living in a time when he must take science seriously, put these visions together?

There are those who reject out of hand the idea that there can be any inconsistency between the Torah's vision of reality and the natural science of subject-object causality. Science is accurate and Torah is true; therefore they must agree. We are arguing in this book against this assumption, at least in any superficial sense. Our present distance from our deepest self connects us to a very shallow layer of functioning. It is science's very fidelity to our present experience that causes it to see a reality very different from that described by Torah, which emerges from a deeper place. Though the person who has truly integrated himself with Torah and the scientist occupy the same physical space, they live in different worlds. Therefore, attempts to combine a simple understanding of the Torah's account of the first days of creation with modern cosmology on a detailed level are likely to be stretched. But do they, in fact, conflict?

The world encountered by the scientist and the developed Torah personality can be compared to a jazz concert attended by a deaf person and a music connoisseur. These two individuals have widely disparate experiences. The deaf man will be captivated by the bold colors of the crimson, sequined costumes of the musicians shimmering in the lights. During the performance he will savor every visual detail he finds appealing.

The music connoisseur, on the other hand, though he can see the costumes, does not focus on them. He is not going to the concert for an entertainment spectacular; his interest is the artistry of the jazzmen, the brilliance with which they invest the music with their souls. He will be vaguely aware of their attire but its effect will blend imperceptibly into his overall experience; the musicians dress the way they do only to enhance the music, not to distract the audience.[33]

Were we to hear reports of the concert from each of these individuals we would have difficulty recognizing that they attended the same event. The deaf man will recount in great detail the dazzle of the musicians' clothes, focusing on it as the sole significance of the evening. The music connoisseur, after a lengthy discussion of rich sounds and complex harmonies will, at best, give only passing mention to the outfits. The only visual component that might warrant genuine attention in his account is the subtle, swaying dance the artists performed while reveling in their musical ecstasy — for this intensified the connoisseur's appreciation for the artists' immersion in their music. The deaf man, however, without the music to cue him in to the significance of their motions would likely have perceived them as little more than interference complicating his clear view of the far more interesting shirts on the players. He will congratulate himself on the expertise he exercised in correcting for the musicians' movements while resolving the fine pattern of the material of their clothes.

The deaf man will likely consider the connoisseur's account of the event a fantasy of specious connections that misses the real story. "What is all this talk of melody and dancing? Didn't you see the amazing outfits the band was wearing?" Perhaps he can be brought to grudgingly recognize

---

33. I originally intended to compare a deaf person with a blind person to accentuate the difference in the perspectives and to avoid favoring the Torah perspective beyond the strict needs of the metaphor. I changed it because while science as a matter of principle excludes spiritual considerations from its investigation, Torah is cognizant of the physical dimension as well as the spiritual, it is just aware of it differently than science. For this reason, the connoisseur seemed more appropriate — someone conscious of both sight and sound, but giving priority to sound so that the visual component is integrated into the overall experience only as it compliments the music.

that there may have been another dimension to the experience. But he will not be inclined to accept that the faculty he lacks would have accessed a more essential part of the experience — that he basically missed the show.[34] The music connoisseur will view the deaf man as hopelessly distracted by a trivial facet of the performance — akin to a grandmother kvelling over her grandson's shoes rather than over her grandson. Technically speaking, however, their disparate reports do not conflict.

Just as the deaf man is cut off from the essential experience of the concert, the scientist is oblivious to the more essential layers of reality. His focus on the material world allows heightened insight into the details of its makeup. But he has lost the significance of life that founds and frames all understanding for the Torah personality. One who encounters the world through Torah is aware of physical reality, but only

---

34. A scientist might protest that in this particular metaphor since there are sensual components keyed directly to the music that the deaf person can access — the swaying of the musicians to the beat, the vibrations in the floor matching the patterns formed by the moving fingers of the musicians — the deaf person representing the scientist would have recognized that he was missing something. He might further claim that no metaphor can be constructed that will not suffer this same lack because science is not oblivious to something that truly exists. To this we can answer with a line widely attributed to Thomas Kuhn and quoted in an earlier note (Chapter 17 note 49): "You don't see something until you have the right metaphor to let you perceive it." The history of science, of which Kuhn was a great student, is replete with examples where evidence for new scientific discoveries was apparent for years before someone recognized the need for a new paradigm that put all the evidence together. In terms of our topic, science consciously avoids any consideration of spiritual causality, which science dismisses as either beyond its scope or non-existent, depending on the scientist. This is especially true in our time when we no longer experience revealed miracles in physical reality — spiritual matters are only directly felt in our internal, private awareness. Any expressions into physical reality come in subtle and ambiguous forms (see Chapter 21, p. 398). Science and Torah effectively provide their adherents with very different metaphors, and, therefore, they see different things. The scientist and the Torah personality are not merely focusing on different details; they are connecting to physical reality differently. They search for different thing, with different expectations of what they will find because they are anchored in different worlds. For the scientist, physical reality is his entire reality and all that he wishes to know he finds there. For the Torah personality, physical reality is the expression of reality; he searches elsewhere for what is most important to him, scanning physical existence only for indications of and opportunities to actualize what he finds in another realm.

relates to it within its spiritual context. The details of interest are very different, as is the way he puts them together. But as with the accounts of the concert, though there is no similarity in their descriptions, they are not necessarily at odds with one another.

When we encounter a difference between scientific observation and Torah description, our first response should not be to strive to integrate them, which would be like trying to color a pirouette. Nor should we feel compelled to determine which is wrong and which is right. We expect their descriptions to diverge; but that does not necessarily mean they contradict one another. Before we can determine if they conflict or identify the areas where it is likely to occur we need to understand how to read the Torah's descriptions of physical reality — what it means to view reality within its spiritual context.

TORAH PERSPECTIVE ON PHYSICAL REALITY

Creation is physical and spiritual. Spiritual existence is less removed from God and, therefore, is the dimension through which we join ourselves to the Creator. Our experience, however, is anchored in the physical realm, so we grow and gain understanding primarily through our interaction with physical reality. Because physical and spiritual reality are connected both in us and in the world around us, we can affect changes in the spiritual plane through physical actions and gain understanding of the spiritual plane through describing and understanding its physical shadow. Torah, therefore, guides us in how to connect with God through commands to act and descriptions of physical reality. But Torah's intent in relating to physical reality is always as part of a larger context.[35] That is why Torah's descriptions of physical reality are so incomplete from a purely physical point of view. Torah provides only the details that are pertinent to what Torah is conveying — a physical reality

---

35. *Ramban, Bereishit* 1:1 states, "Torah speaks about physical reality, all the time hinting to spiritual reality." But Rama M'Pano in *Eser Maamarot, Chikur HaDin* 3:22 states, "Torah essentially speaks about spiritual existence, hinting only secondarily to physical existence."

that derives meaning and purpose from its spiritual context. In general, the Torah is teaching us that the physical world we inhabit is only one layer of a much deeper reality and that we live in the physical world only as a medium through which to encounter that deeper reality.

We have already given examples of how Torah descriptions of physical phenomena simultaneously reference other dimensions. We explained that when the Torah hints at the evolving association of the sun with the moon in the first days of creation it is teaching us about the relationship between a primary receiver and its source. We learn as much about man's relationship to God from this passage as we learn about the sun and moon.[36]

We also explained that Shlomo HaMelech, in his book *Mishlei*, generalized beyond the Torah this idea of understanding spiritual reality through the experience of physical reality. There he taught that the essence of all human wisdom is to relate to our world as a proverb or allegory — a story whose full significance lies beyond the story.[37] The way the wisdom of *Mishlei* is expressed is affected by its intent to foster the allegorical link. So too Torah describes physical reality differently from what we would expect if it were merely painting a physical picture because of its intent to convey meaning on multiple levels.

TORAH'S DESCRIPTION OF CREATION

Once we are cognizant that Torah sees physical reality in a larger, spiritual context, how do we interpret Torah's imagery? Returning to our earlier question of whether it is possible to integrate Torah's description of creation with science's understanding of the age of the universe, what does the word "day" mean as it is used in the story of creation? What is it communicating to us?

"Day" as it is used in the Torah's account of the first six days means a complete unit of creation beginning with withdrawal, creation of

36. See Chapter 7.
37. See Chapter 16, pp. 299–300.

potential, and actualization. The Torah teaches us in the Ten Commandments that the world "was created six days."[38] The Sages point out that we would have expected the verse to tell us that the world was created "*in* six days" — which would convey a duration of time. Instead we are told "six days" which communicates structure.[39] Six days of creation are six distinct units, the creation of six distinct facets of existence. The fact that there were days, complete units of creation, and that there were six of them is important. The "sixish" character of creation teaches us that creation came through six aspects and layers. These correspond to the disparate character traits of God's revelation that were actualized each day — giving, containment etc.[40] We need to know these because they remain the foundation of existence and the path by which we reach God through emulating Him as a creator.[41] That there are exactly six that represent the complete set from the start of creation until its finish reflects on the specific nature of the traits that compose the set.[42]

We quoted a *midrash* at the beginning of Chapter 12 that breaks

---

38. *Shemot* 20:11.

39. Rebbi Nechuniah ben Hakaneh, *Sefer HaBahir*. See Rav Eliyahu Dessler, *Michtav Me'Eliyahu* II, pp. 151–153 from Ramban and the Gra.

40. See Ramban, *Bereishit* 1:3.

41. For example, see Rav Yitzchak Hutner, *Pachad Yitzchak Rosh Hashanah* 1:4.

42. *Vayikra Rabbah* 30:1 proves the priority of Torah over physical reality because Torah was given in forty days whereas the physical world was created in only six. The comparison is not of the length of time but of the complexity of structure, where the number forty reflects on the nature of Torah in as specific a manner as the six days reflect on the nature of physical reality. This can be roughly compared to a dog and a child, both of whom need to be trained. The dog is good for three things: getting the paper, licking his master, and growling at strangers. The child needs to learn fine motor skills, language, empathy, sharing, consideration, all facets of Torah, mathematics, history, engineering, philosophy, etc. All beings are defined by their purpose. The dog's purpose is threefold. Three distinct units of training and development correspond to its purpose. The child's purpose is unlimited, reflected in the multiplicity of things that must be developed in him. If the dog is slow and needs a year to learn his three duties while the child is talented and learns all he needs in that same year this does not equate them. The dog's purpose remains threefold while the child's remains, in the metaphor, infinite. The *midrash* is explaining that physical reality arises through six significant facets; Torah is associated with forty.

the sixth day of creation down into twelve one-hour units, telling us what happened during each hour: in the first hour God conceived the idea of man, in the second He consulted with the *malachim* (the angels), in the third he gathered the dust...[43] No one can think that the Sages meant to say that the Creator was watching a sundial while doing His Divine work! This *midrash* is a clear indication that the function of time as described in Torah, at the very least during Creation, was not focused on duration as much as on structure. The Sages were communicating that there were distinct facets and layers to the creation of man, each leaving its impression on the finished product.[44]

Creation has a physical component and it is the unfolding of that physical component that is being directly described in the account of the first days.[45] It, therefore, takes place in time. The first word of the Torah, *Bereishit*, "in the beginning," implies chronology and, therefore, time.[46] But what exactly the duration of Creation was is difficult to deduce from the Torah because the Torah is not focused on that kind of detail. It describes physical creation in order to convey some meaning that arises from understanding it in the context of its deeper dimensions. What that meaning is beyond conveying God's character traits is a matter of dispute among the commentaries.[47] But the Torah's purpose is not to give us a precise picture of the development of physical reality in a scientific sense — that is, as a purely physical event devoid of

---

43. *Vayikra Rabbah* 29:1.
44. Hour units are a breakdown of the more fundamental time unit of a day. On distinct days different dimensions were created; in distinct hours different aspects of a dimension were created. We are told what these different dimensions and aspects were, but it is also important for us to know that they were each associated with a distinct day or hour because this reveals structure, relationship, and priority.
45. *Ramban, Bereishit* 1:1 states, "Torah speaks about physical reality, all the time hinting to spiritual reality." See, however, note 35 in this chapter with its reference to Rama M'Pano.
46. The commentaries understand that this first word actually references the physical creation of time. See *Rosh Hashanah* 32a.
47. *Rashi, Bereishit* 1:1 brings a *midrash* to answer the question, but there are different understandings of the meaning of the *midrash*. See *Gur Aryeh, Bereishit* 1:1. See also *Sefat Emet, Sukkot* 632.

meaning. This does not imply that we cannot deduce the duration. But we should not expect it to be an obvious detail of the story.

Torah's account of Creation is like the music connoisseur's description of a jazz concert; though Torah is cognizant of the "clothing" of creation — its physical process — details of these garments do not figure prominently in its description of the event. Were we to carefully analyze the text perhaps we could extract those details; but they are not obvious. In fact, the physical details of Creation are so obscure that the commentaries question why the story was included in the Torah at all.[48]

There was physical creation and that is very important to us. And what that physical creation was is told to us. But what Torah's description of creation communicates about what physically happened — what we would have seen if who we are today with our present interests and categories of understanding had been present to observe the process — is closed to us.[49]

If a scientist could somehow travel back in time to the period before the destruction of the *Beit HaMikdash* he would be able to find individuals immersed in Torah and living in the world exclusively through the vision of the Torah. If he would ask them in how many twenty-four hour intervals the world was created, measuring in hours as we know them today, they would not have an answer in the sense in which the question was intended, because the Torah does not directly address it. They would certainly refuse to enter the analytical frame from which the questioner gets his answer — for someone truly immersed in Torah such a shift would be a conscious movement away from God's *hashgachah*. Besides the *emunah* issues this raises, the whole approach would seem absurd because it is oriented toward achieving a result that is utterly irrelevant — a physical description devoid of spiritual implications and meaning.

It would be like trying to make sense of someone writing a song to

---

48. *Ramban, Bereishit* 1:1. Though it is essential that we know that God created the world, that is told to us in the Ten Commandments. Why do we need the few details that are supplied about the first six days when we cannot make any precise sense of what it means anyway?
49. Ibid.

his beloved by analyzing the act as a purely chemical reaction, focusing simultaneously on all his biochemical processes and their interactions without reference to the fact that the writer is a person acting with emotion and intention. It can be done to some degree, but it would be impossibly complicated and largely inexplicable — reading like a Ptolemaic description of the movements of the solar system. It would also neglect a fundamental layer of causality by leaving out the influence of free will. Most important of all, it would completely miss what is most essential, meaningful, and interesting in the event — the emotion and connection expressed in the act. Besides the fact that looking at it as pure chemistry gives a skewed understanding, a Torah personality from this earlier age might refuse on moral grounds to try viewing the event this way even as an exercise because it dehumanizes both the one being analyzed and the one doing the analysis.

But we live after the destruction of the *Beit HaMikash* in a time when we are much more fully mired in physical reality. Even the Torah-based individual must relate to the immediate causal framework that is the focus of science and submit to its findings, such as in matters of health. This scientific understanding that accurately models our immediate experience and demands our attention also makes claims beyond our experience. As a system of understanding, it offers a vision that encompasses reality from the beginning of time onwards. This includes the period covered in the Torah by the creation story — so the question of how many twenty-four hour intervals were required for Creation is meaningful even to the Torah personality. Yet, he looks to the Torah as his reference for understanding reality on its deepest levels — Torah describes creation as happening in days, but, as we said, not defining specific duration. How will he relate to this question of how long it took to develop physical reality as we see it today? How do these two worlds come together as one reality?

TORAH AND SCIENCE TODAY

Torah speaks to us through descriptions of the physical world, which means that science and Torah do overlap. But because Torah's intent in giving its description is totally different from that of science, what we can glean from those descriptions about that physical reality in terms of the conceptual categories of science, at the very least when we talk about something as distant as creation, is poorly understood.[50] It is, therefore, unclear to what degree theories of astrophysics, geology, and evolution directly contact or cross with Torah. Just clarifying what we do and do not know from the Torah on this issue would be a complex study.

For those genuinely defined by Torah, however, this topic holds surprisingly little interest. There is a reason why Torah does not discuss the concrete details of creation — they have no effect on our present responsibilities, whether in action or thought, and Torah does not teach without purpose.[51] The information Torah supplies on creation is needed, for it reveals the foundations of God's relationship with man, but the specifics of its physical expression are, effectively, theoretical knowledge. And though the Torah personality, like everyone else, must now be cognizant of scientific understanding, he is not pressured because of this to check if this raises contradictions with Torah. The perspective of science does not come to compete with or displace Torah, but as an added layer, existing fully within the Torah vision. If it turns out science conflicts with the Torah, he knows he will resolve the dispute based on Torah.

But how is this so simple if this same person must rely on modern medicine or use the scientist's understanding of electricity to determine what can and cannot be done on Shabbat? There are two aspects to the scientific method: observation and interpretation. There are two categories of interpretation: that which strives to understand the present workings of physical reality and that which strives to enlarge findings to encompass a picture of all of reality, extrapolating beyond human experience. These two endeavors are separable because extending

---

50. *Ramban, Bereishit* 1:1.
51. See the beginning of Chapter 1 that Torah is a practical guide.

science requires an addition to the general premises upon which science rests — the supposition that all physical laws that we see in effect today have always functioned exactly the way we observe them to function now. This assumption is not a logical derivation of scientific thinking, nor is it critical to the immediate scientific project.

The supposition that scientific experiments can be reenacted with identical results in other times and places is essential to scientific progress. But this does not require us to extend deductions beyond the boundaries of possible human experience. Whether it is even legitimate to do so is open to question since the extension is absolutely untestable. Any actual scientific support for this added assumption is built on the assumption itself. In effect, science says if we assume that no forces or processes influence reality other than the physical laws as we know them today, and interpret data with this in mind, then we can explain the origin of much of our reality, and therefore, the laws must always have functioned as they do today.

This is a logical argument rather than a scientific proof in the classical sense, and is refuted — at least as a proof — by the existence of any alternate path to today's reality. It is true that our intellectual instinct for simplicity (Ockham's razor) favors the expanded application of scientific theory — why assume some additional system for organizing reality when one that we see clearly functioning is enough to explain so much of what we see? But this simplicity breaks down before the existence of other layers of reality that do not function along purely natural lines. Individuals who are genuinely defined by Torah see patterns in the world that defy physical causality. And people who are sensitive to their internal experience are aware of a dimension of reality that has nothing to do with natural law.

But more importantly, we are speaking now about the Torah personality who fully accepts Torah and for whom its vision is deeply integrated into his experience of reality. He seeks to assimilate science into Torah, not vice versa. Torah understands reality to function in a manner that flies in the face of this added assumption of consistency. And though the idea of consistency seems straightforward enough to us, its intuitive character is a result of our present *da'at* that has removed our focus from our internal experience and sees reality as based in material substance and fixed. Torah, however, understands our reality to be a consequence of the relationship between man and God, changing with the vicissitudes of that relationship.[52] This is a basic characteristic of man's grant of free will and is, therefore, central to the God-man relationship.[53] And between *Chumash*, the works of the prophets, and the record of the Oral Torah, we have testimony spanning thousands of years to a reality whose functioning is continually shifting.

Accordingly, trying to extrapolate scientific theories into earlier periods of human history is problematic enough because of differences in the functioning of reality, like the former occurrence of open miracles. But extending science to the period before the relationship between God and man even came into being, when the structure of material reality was a result of an unmediated revelation of the Will of the Creator, could be no more than speculation. This is not to say that the present scientific model of the origins of the universe cannot play a role in the Torah defined individual's understanding of reality. But it can only hold the status of a perspective. To accept it with even the kind of conviction that we attach to the immediate functioning of nature — our confidence that fire will result from striking a match or an explosion will occur when hydrogen meets oxygen — runs counter to basic premises of Torah understanding.[54] The Torah personality certainly is not concerned about any conflicts that might arise with Torah from extending scientific theory into any distant past. Science describes the way things look now; it cannot legitimately claim access to timeless truth.[55] The extended scientific vision merely describes the picture that

---

52. See Chapter 17, pp. 326–329.

53. While theoretically we could be confronted with individual choices without the context of those choices changing, we discussed in Chapters 10, 12, and 14 that this fluidity is necessary to utilize free choice to develop the whole self and to correct for bad decisions.

54. Even immediate natural occurrences are hidden miracles utterly dependent upon the will of the Creator (*Ramban, Shemot* 13:16). But in exile, we experience them more like laws.

55. Rav Moshe Shapiro, Rav Zevulun Shwartzman, and Rav Moshe Meiselman.

emerges if we extrapolate present functioning into the past. It does not tell us what was; it tells us how the past appears from the perspective of how things appear now.

UNDERSTANDING OUR DIFFICULTY

But what about the rest of us, those not so immersed in Torah who experience and understand reality in a manner much more bound up with science? It is hard for us to break from the material vision of reality and the assumption of consistency over time that naturally accompanies it. This allows for the perception of conflict between science and Torah and makes that possibility debilitating.

We feel compelled to search out contradictions because we firmly believe that science is true and we are dedicated to the fact that Torah is true. We cannot sacrifice science without losing our minds; we cannot sacrifice Torah without losing our hearts. There is only one truth, so if they are at odds we are faced with an intolerable contradiction. Our anxiety is heightened by a cultural context that has imprinted us with esteem for the truth of the intellect — we feel we know that science is true while only believing that Torah is true — that creates a certain foreboding about how we must resolve the matter if an insoluble conflict really arises. Perversely, at any hint of a problem we feel our innate sense of righteousness awakening to support the truth of science when it seems opposed by Torah.

This is the real source of our difficulty: we are susceptible to science's claim to an all-encompassing vision of reality that implies a truth that stands outside of Torah and binds it. Any concern we have for conflicts between Torah and science is merely a symptom of this much deeper problem. Our sense that Torah is limited by the exigencies of nature, and that if a conflict were to genuinely arise truth would lie with science rather than Torah, is a direct consequence of modernity imposing its form upon our experience. Our struggle with this distortion is one of the primary battle lines in our effort to recognize God's Oneness in the present exile.

Earlier in the book we concluded that the purpose of creation is to reveal God's complete and singular omnipotence — that He is One.[56] This is achieved by passing through various false understandings of independent power that then dissolve before the strength of the Creator. We described how the succession of Jewish exiles are the process by which this occurs, identifying the five ways we can mistakenly attribute power to an alternate source and associating each with an exile. The paradigm for the mistake that is embedded in the Roman worldview was the Christian position that God *could not* forgive the Jews — presuming that He is bound by laws. Torah conveys God's direct will and oversight; He created the natural world with its laws as a medium and means through which it is experienced. Subordinating Torah to science's conclusions about nature is just another variation on the characteristically Roman perversion of subjecting God to law.[57]

We also explained that in tandem with the revelation of God's unity, the purpose of creation is for man to develop himself as an individual in relationship with God. This is achieved through overcoming corruption in the four primary facets of our personality and turning each into an instrument of connection to God. The process unfolds through the Jewish people's passage through exiles to cultures that embody these various perversions of personality and overcoming those perversions.[58] Personal development is linked to recognition of God's unity because our perception of God is dependent upon how we experience our own being.[59]

Perceiving God as limited by law is a natural outgrowth of modern

---

56. See Chapter 8 from Ramchal, *Daat Tevunot*.

57. This parallel is especially precise according to Rav Friedlander's understanding of Ramchal, quoted in Chapter 8, note 52, that the moral laws Christianity subjects God to are of His own making — in this case we merely substitute the natural law of God's creation for His moral code. If scientists understand natural law to be in any way *inevitable*, binding God, then the parallel exists even according to Rav Shwartzman's understanding of Ramchal, quoted in the same note, that the moral laws to which Christianity subjects God exist independent of God, a holdover from Greek *kadmut*.

58. See Chapter 10.

59. See Chapter 8, p. 138; Chapter 10, pp. 172–184; and Chapter 14.

experience. We explained that the nature of modern *da'at* is to determine and judge the world from our individual perspective.[60] We mentioned that this led to a number of distortions, one being that we necessarily construct reality as centered on ourselves. Since this is the form of our perception, regardless of how we claim to understand God, He cannot be more than an element in our world. This echoes and is reinforced by our skewed experience of ourselves as the locus of primary being.[61] Subjecting God to law is a direct consequence of this structure of understanding. It is because we perceive God as contained in our world that we assume He is subject to its laws.

AN INCLINATION TO UNIVERSALITY

After the destruction of the *Beit HaMikdash* we all utilize scientific perspective. But once it is allowed into consciousness, rather than merely providing a structure for indirect relationship with the Creator, science seeks to displace Torah entirely and provide a replacement vision of existence. Though science claims to be independent and indifferent to issues of morality and spirituality, when science becomes all-encompassing its independence of these matters is no longer indifferent. Rather, it in effect denies the existence of transcendence and transcendent morals.[62] Whether or not science's universal claim is articulated, it is implicit so that when it is not articulated it is only more pernicious — it still eats away at our commitment to the truth of Torah, merely doing so without our notice.

What drives science to this universal claim or, rather, us to declare its universality? As we mentioned, there is a certain intellectual satisfaction

---

60. See Chapters 15, 16, and 17.

61. Our sense of self as primary being and the center of our reality is ultimately the basis of our perception of God as only an element in that reality. This illusion is opposed to the deeper truth that God is named *Makom* (Place)because He is the place of the world — the world is not His place. See Chapters 16 and 17.

62. For the importance of our overall understanding of reality to our potential relationship with God, see *Shabbat* 31a–b.

that comes from extending science to include everything — the simplicity it creates is deeply appealing. But there are other internal forces pushing us to recognize the complete hegemony of science. Scientific thinking perfectly reflects man's connection to reality in the context of modernity where man evaluates and judges the world from his perspective.[63] Furthermore, if all of reality is brought within the purview of science, then we understand, define, and control reality. Apart from the appeal this has for our basic power instincts, we need a sense of control over existence because in the context of modernity we experience ourselves as replacing God; science supplies that control. We see how science subconsciously supports modernity's self-concept by the way it is sometimes deployed consciously — to eviscerate any competing spiritual claims. By demonstrating power it is used to confirm the validity of the modern worldview. The intellectual satisfaction we receive from extending our scientific vision is, therefore, vigorously reinforced by science's centrality to modernity and the psychological need it fills. Reality becomes science and science becomes an ideology, philosophy, and theology.

So, it is not the conflicts that may or may not arise from specific conclusions of science that are the root of our difficulties achieving a viable integration of science and Torah. It is as a conceptual framework that science's clash with Torah is problematic. Science threatens to eclipse rather than buffer our relationship with God, undermining the foundation of any reasonable equilibrium we might achieve between our internal spiritual consciousness and our outward natural experience. But it is important to be clear that whatever conflicts there might be lie not with scientific thinking per se and our submission to immediate, natural causality, but with science's projection beyond experience to an all-encompassing vision that displaces Torah.

Science is not an explanation of reality in any fundamental sense. Rather, science describes the functioning of the specific slice of reality

---

63. See note 61 in this chapter.

in which we find ourselves focused today. We legitimately assimilate scientific thinking and practice into our relationship with God. It is a painful step down from direct relationship, but necessary after we distanced ourselves from Him. Science, however, must enter our world not as a substitute, but as an added layer, finding its place in the context of Torah. This is an uneasy coexistence. But just as we are obligated to work with science, we are obligated to recognize the limits of its applicability: nature orders experience as a medium through which God effects His *hashgachah* in exile as a measure for measure response to our own distance from God, nothing more. It is not objective truth.

A person steeped in Torah can achieve this uneasy balance. Most of us, however, stand between the Torah personality and the scientist. We live every day with the conceptual categories of science; it is the laws of nature that define our world. On the other hand we recognize that the Torah holds a deeper truth. We accept the legitimacy of the biochemical view of man and yet have a gnawing sense that something fundamental is missing from the picture. We are committed to the primacy of spiritual reality; in those quiet moments when we are with our selves we are clear that our internal being is our true identity and that, therefore, our spiritual root is our essential being. But that focus is lost rapidly under the onslaught of a return to the noisiness of life.

*   *   *

We experience the confrontation between science and Torah within the confines of the Roman exile. This is the modern version of the test of the spies. At the time of the spies, we were challenged to discern the underlying control of God that we had seen exposed in the desert but that became hidden behind the façade of nature once we entered the Land of Israel. Similarly today, though we have the memory of our historical experience of direct relationship with God, He is now hidden. It is our responsibility to find him and create a relationship in the context of a seemingly natural world. Discussions between the scientist and the Torah personality today directly parallel the debate the ten spies had with Kalev and Yehoshua: "The cities are fortified," cried the spies, who were frightened by the physical strength of the Canaanites. "But

Job is dead," responded Kalev and Yehoshua — there are no righteous individuals with merit to compete with us for God's protection.[64] It is not really a discussion because they are not talking to one another; they look at the same reality and see completely different things because they are basing themselves upon completely different assumptions.

One who denigrates the Torah perspective because it speaks in a different language from the scientific view is like a devoted Newtonian physicist laughing at someone trying to explain Einstein's Theory of Relativity — "Bending space, slowing time, increasing mass! Why must you cling to your fantasies! Throw away your crutch, be courageous and liberate yourself. Live in reality!" The intensity of the Newtonian's disparagement only demonstrates the totality of his limitations. He has never escaped his parochial world of mundane velocities, so he does not even see his shortcomings. He is the deaf person at the jazz concert gazing intently at the sequined shirts and impatient with mindless dribble about harmony. To the knowledgeable observer the scene is comic, ironic, or tragic, depending on the circumstances.

Most of us today are in the position of the Newtonian with regard to science and Torah. We are lost in our mechanical understanding of reality where science speaks clearly. We cannot hear the voice of our inner self and the categories of understanding that are its language. The Torah's descriptions fly past us; we cannot catch their meaning because of our insular narrowness.

If we wish to right this imbalance we cannot simply disparage science or try to drown out its message. The honest person will still sense its clarity and wonder what it is that we are afraid of. But the Newtonian can only hold on to his view as long as he remains in his isolated reality. Were he to venture beyond it, he himself would quickly realize that he needs an entirely different analytical frame to understand that which opens before him. If the deaf man at the concert suddenly gained his hearing he would immediately be struck with wonder. So too with

---

64. *Rashi, Bemidbar* 14:9.

regard to us and our relationship to Torah. The truest method for reset-ting our connection to Torah would be to raise our spiritual level above the layer of reality to which science is directed, centering ourselves in our *neshamah* where we encounter the world through the mediation of the Creator. This would bring the message of the Torah into sharp focus and make science irrelevant.

At this point, however, such an accomplishment is beyond us. The *Beit HaMikdash* still lies in ruins, and only the rarest of individuals achieves even a cursory understanding of how Torah wants us to be in the world, let alone actually experiencing the world that way. For the vast majority — those of us who intellectually recognize the primacy of Torah but, if we are honest with ourselves, must admit that we live in a world of causality, science, and the subject-object split — what is our path forward? We cannot shake the claim that the scientific interpreta-tion makes on our view of reality because it speaks so comfortably to the part of us in which we are normally centered. This is the reality of where we are at, so how do we move forward? How are we to grow?

CHAPTER 19

The Allure of Control

Guard yourself lest you forget HaShem your God and not keep His mitzvot, His judgments, and His statutes... Lest you eat and be satisfied, and build good houses and live in them, and your herds and flocks multiply, and your silver and gold increase, and all that you have grows. And [because of this] your heart becomes prideful, and you forget HaShem your God, who brought you out of the land of Mitzrayim from the house of slavery... And you say in your heart, "My power and the might of my own hand have created this wealth for me."[1]

W E CONCLUDED IN THE previous chapters that our modern experience profoundly compromises our ability to achieve an authentic, integrated relationship with the Creator through Torah. Nevertheless, we continue to work toward it because we exist only for this relationship. But at least part of our effort must be aimed at changing this form of experience that so complicates our efforts. Repair, however, is difficult because the corruption reaches deep within the unified reality that we call our *da'at*. We cannot just decide to cease perceiving existence from the perspective of our autonomous selfhood and, instead, experience ourselves as an expression of our Source. Anyone who is honest with himself realizes that attempting to do so directly would be an exercise

---

1. *Devarim* 8:11–17.

in fantasy rather than spiritual growth. The change in perspective we require can only genuinely come by moving the center of our personality to a deeper level in the self. That movement is not accomplished by pushing a button in an elevator. We are talking about a personal revolution.

Our difficulty in changing perspective is compounded by lack of an accurate sense of what the new outlook we are striving for would be. If we try picturing it, as a matter of course we imagine ourselves pretty much as we are now with an added awareness of connection to God that enhances our sense of self. But this is no more than a beefed-up version of our present experience; it is basically "me, plus."

The reality of the new perspective, as opposed to its fantasy, would require a profound alteration in the weight we attribute to our own existence relative to that of the Source of our being. The new experience would be something like: "I sense my self emanating from a Being whose significance and greatness I cannot fathom. I exist only to give Him expression and my existence is utterly dependent upon His ongoing Will. This obligates me to Him unconditionally. I am aware that this world that contains me physically is from and sustained by the Creator in the same manner as I am, reinforcing my awareness of dependence and indebtedness I and all my actions occur in a context of absolute truth, which makes me both aware of my real motives and that those motives are transparent and judged in the context of that truth."

As we describe it, this change of *da'at* doesn't sound so inviting — loss of self, all obligation, and naked before the truth. But this awareness would rest upon a foundation of deeply felt wholeness, belonging, security, personal integrity, purpose, and love for which we have no precedent in our experience. In any case, we are very far away from a visceral appreciation of the worldview we are striving toward. Even if we could imagine it, it is out of our reach to suddenly shift into this awareness. So how do we move forward?

THE ORAL TORAH

Genuinely changing the self is so daunting because the self is an integrated whole. Therefore, direct change would seem to require that we instantaneously transform our entire being, which seems impossible — at least impossible for us to initiate.[2] But man lives through his consciousness of his surroundings and sees himself reflected there.[3] So we can get to the self indirectly by changing our awareness of the world. Though that awareness is influenced by our experience of self and our self is now spiritually barren, we can consciously override that effect and alter our perception of the world to a more spiritual interpretation. We can slowly and painstakingly reconstruct our vision of reality, coming to see it as it would appear in the context of true relationship with God. Element by element, we can ask, "What is the significance of this object? How does it obligate me or help me fulfill my responsibilities? What role does it play in my relationship with the Creator?" If we do this honestly, we will slowly come to experience ourselves as living in God's world. We will then find our truer self mirrored there.

This requires the monumental undertaking of reunderstanding every detail of existence to fit in the framework of a world created by God. Apart from the difficulty resulting from the magnitude of the undertaking, how are we to know this deeper truth when we are so spiritually cut off? Our guide for this is the *Torah SheBe'al Peh*, the Oral Torah, that applies the principals of the prophetic Written Torah to the details of experience.

Understanding our project this way places the Torah Sages at the head of our efforts to achieve relationship with the Creator, for they are the masters of *Torah SheBe'al Peh*.[4] But, though through them we can all have a relationship with the level of Torah necessary to recover spirituality in our times, obviously we cannot all be them. Does that mean that most of us are sidelined from moving ourselves, the nation, and mankind toward spirituality and purpose?

---

2. We will speak in the next chapter about the kinds of situations that can catalyze such a change.

3. We spoke about this idea in Chapter 15, pp. 279–280, in a slightly different language.

4. See Chapter 4 (pp. 57–61) and Chapter 14 (pp. 269–270) for another facet of the Sages' role in maintaining our spiritual connection when our direct relationship is hidden.

No. We explained earlier that the project of creation requires everyone's involvement. Each of us must play his role by confronting a challenge unique to him and achieve his part in man's overall relationship with God.[5] Though we do not all have the dedication, concentration, and capability to remake our world, we know from our previous discussion of the Greek exile that the intellectual project of the Oral Torah can become misguided.[6] Its success is dependent upon basic character issues that are the purview of all of us. In this we are no different from any previous era. In every generation our national struggle is focused in a particular facet of character, while as individuals we are each responsible for developing our own specific expression of that trait.[7]

What facet of character are we wrestling with today? What is the challenge that defines our era? We have already discussed this point.[8] The final installment in history is not characterized by a specific trait that has been corrupted as much as by the energy of corruption itself.

We exist to connect to God and serve Him. We have a number of facets to our character that can play particular roles in this project. Through history we struggle with the energy to be separate, which perverts each of these facets into opportunities for self-aggrandizement. In the final historical period we face this energy in its unadulterated form. We experience ourselves as other to God and compete with Him both for priority of being and for control of our world.[9]

A CULTURE OF CONTROL

When we think about what characterizes our society we presume that our present culture is uniquely knowledgeable about our world. But this assumption is a consequence of our narrowness, which gives singular priority to our mode of rational thought. Though rational

5. See Chapter 10, pp. 156–158..
6. See Chapter 14, pp. 264–265.
7. See Chapter 10, pp. 156–158.
8. See Chapter 10, pp. 171–172 and Chapter14, pp. 244–247.
9. See Chapter 17, pp. 315–321.

science provides a framework within which to extend our knowledge of a purely physical reality, it comes only with the loss of another form of knowledge, one that is more humane, deep, and satisfying.[10]

We also presume that our present culture is characterized by un-precedented power — giving us the ability to protect ourselves, cure our ills, and create material wealth. But though we are more powerful than the generations that immediately preceded the scientific revolution, the power we have today does not generally characterize this culture and exile. The transition to our present mode of thought began much earlier with the rise of Greece 2,500 years ago. Most of the time since then, science's practical benefit has been limited. Even looking at the power we have today it does not compare to the abilities we had before the changes in awareness that accompanied the rise of Greece. Prior to Greece we experienced existence through relationship with God. This allowed for effective prayer, which brought blessing upon our efforts,[11] and prophecy, which predicted the future better than any computer can today.[12] We have lost power by adopting our present worldview — at the very least we have lost a kind of power.

---

10. See Chapter 15.

11. Since change was effected through the mediation of the Creator, the world also could be impacted in ways that today would be considered impossible. For example, both the prophet Eliyahu and his student Elisha brought dead individuals back to life. It is important to understand that this was not simply a different strategy for achieving selfish goals. Such a relationship to action could only exist in the context of a developed relationship with the Creator. In a developed relationship, we define ourselves as His servant and, therefore, exist to further His goals. We would only want what either effected the accomplishment of those goals or strengthened us as instruments for achieving those goals. That didn't mean that a person never sought his selfish needs, but the determination of what to request was not based on maximizing personal pleasure, but rather on what we realistically needed within the context of our long-term project of developing ourselves as true servants of God. Sometimes one really does need a chocolate bar, or the equivalent. See *Shiurei Daat* II, p. 109–116, *Plas B'Maagal Raglecha*.

12. See *Vayikra* 26:3–13; *Devarim* 28:1–14. See also *Eichah Rabbah* 2:5. If we compare prophecy to computers, computers extrapolate the present into the future. They can only predict a future that results from the play of purely natural factors. Prophecy sees the future that will be, regardless of what path it takes to get there.

372 ⑨ THE CHOICE TO BE

What does genuinely characterize our era? Our sense of control — or at least the illusion of control. Though we could successfully affect our surroundings in the ancient world, as we explained earlier, it was not direct. We experienced reality in a manner comparable to Adam, for whom change was accomplished through the intervention of the Creator. Obviously, after Adam ate from the Tree of Knowledge, man did not experience his dependence upon the Creator with Adam's original clarity. But as long as our awareness remained centered in God more than in our individual ego — before we lost miracle, prophecy, and our intuitive awareness of transcendence — our experience, interpretation, and interaction with reality continued to travel through the Creator. With our involvement in the world filtered through Him, we could choose our efforts, but results were recognized as entirely the domain and decision of God. We did not control.

In the context of our present subject-object approach to reality we interpret our interaction with our environment as direct. By skirting the mediation of God in our connection to reality, we take control of the consequences of our actions and challenge the singular control of God.[13]

Critiques on religion from a modern, scientific perspective almost invariably assume that man turned to religion for solace in his helplessness — which, they imply, is no longer needed because science has given us power. This formulation conveniently views the turn to science as an objective advance in human civilization, and neatly distracts from the self-interest and egotism that accompanied its arrival. In fact, when the worldview that brought us science began, it did not bring us power. We have understood that we do not "turn" toward religion or "turn" toward science. Rather, each is an interpretation of the world that is a direct consequence of a specific way of experiencing self and reality. Rather than power, the mode of experience that brings science, what we have called the subject-object relationship, breeds a sense of control that

---

13. See Chapter 17, pp. 316–317.

turns us into impatient teenagers eagerly seeking independence from the Creator.

A CONSISTENT CHALLENGE

Earlier, we said that the purpose of creation is our recognition of the unity of God — that He alone controls everything which happens in creation.[14] That implies, and the quote that opens our chapter confirms, that acknowledging that the Creator is the basis of being and accepting our dependence upon Him is our ultimate challenge. We have faced it from the beginning of creation, varying only in form and intensity. At the start of man's history the snake tempted Chavah to eat from the Tree of Knowledge and take center stage in creation in place of God.[15] Similarly, at the commencement of Jewish history, we worshipped the golden calf in an effort to obscure God's presence and appropriate to ourselves His role of defining reality.[16] We said earlier that all the transgressions that led to our previous exiles were consequences of this desire for control, albeit experienced indirectly through desires for pleasure, power, and jealousy.[17] In the final exile, however, we confront the desire for control head on.

Our frequent failure to meet this challenge of acknowledging God's control is the consequence of an inherent tension in the structure and purpose of man. We were given the perilous gift of free will to enable

---

14. See Chapter 8.

15. See Chapter 16, p. 309 and Chapter 17, pp. 318–320. Though we mentioned there that the Sages argue over which inclination was primary in leading to the sin, all must acknowledge the significance of man's challenge to God's singular omnipotence, for implicit in the decision to disobey was the assumption that "I am right" regardless of what God commanded. Thus in the time of the Temple the sin offering was a goat, symbolic of stubbornness, for this is the foundation of all transgression.

16. See Chapter 13, pp. 227–228. Even if the ultimate intention of the calf was to justify promiscuity (*Sanhedrin* 63b), taking control of understanding was the prerequisite for achieving that justification.

17. See Chapter 14, p. 247.

us to emulate God by being a creator in our own right. If we rephrase the obligation to emulate God as a command to "be like God," we see that the snake's temptation of Chavah, the most essential expression of evil, was merely a subtle corruption of our central purpose in life. We were commanded to "be like God" in the sense of achieving selfhood, but this put us in danger of being "like God" in an illusion of independence; we were invited to "be like God" in creating the nature of our individual personality, but this put us in danger of being "like God" in creating a fantasy world centered on ourselves.[18] Ironically, this resemblance of the evil inclination to the purpose of life that makes it so seductive also allows it to act as the driving force behind our development — as we saw in the section on the kingdoms. But the reality remains that we have a predisposition to fall into an evil that is difficult to escape.

The end of history finds us exiled to Roman culture, deeply entangled in a worldview that places us in the center of our world. Instead of subjugating ourselves to God, we strive for control of our surroundings, both conceptually and physically, usurping the place of God and blocking the recognition of His unitary Omnipotence. Though in past exiles there was "someplace to go," a facet of self which remained unsullied in its attachment to God and offered a refuge from the conquests of the inclinations, when we face Rome the corruption has reached the deepest recesses of our individuality, leaving us no solid ground on which to stand.[19] How can we turn this distance into the closeness for which we yearn and achieve the relationship with God for which we were created?

Just as we turn to beginnings to discover our root challenges, we can turn to an ending in history for a model of how our difficulty can be resolved. There was a time when we stopped the creeping deterioration in our relationship with God and inverted it to achieve full connection

---

18. See Chapter 6, pp. 100–101; Chapter 14, pp. 272–273; and Chapter 17, pp. 318–320.
19. See Chapter 14, pp. 270–271.

with the Creator and recognition of His singular control. The Purim story, though it comes in the middle of Jewish history, comes at the end of the era characterized by revelation, prophecy, and revealed miracle. That period began with the birth of the Jewish people in their departure from *Mitzrayim* by means of the complete abrogation of nature. It continued through their supernatural experience in the desert and miraculous entry into the Land of Israel. It reached its fullness in the building of the First *Beit HaMikdash* — a place of constant miracle and revelation.[20] The period appeared to end with the destruction of that *Beit HaMikdash*, the departure of God's presence — the *Shechinah*, and the exile of the Jewish people to Babylon.

But this could not have been the true end of the era. Creation was made for a purpose — the complete attachment of man to the Creator. And in a world created by the omnipotent God, that purpose will be accomplished.[21] Just as the cycle of the week ends with Shabbat, which echoes the final reward of the World to Come, so any complete period in history must finish with an experience that at least echoes the achievement of history's goal.

The experience that capped the first full era of Jewish history was not the destruction of the First *Beit HaMikdash* and exile but rather our deliverance from the most threatening point in that exile — our salvation in Persia commemorated at the end of each calendar year on Purim.[22] That event snatched the Jewish people from annihilation, gave them political domination of the Persian Empire, and set up the building of the Second *Beit HaMikdash*; that Second Temple provided

---

20. *Pirkei Avot* 5:5.
21. *Yeshayah* 55:10–11.
22. Though Rosh Hashanah is the new year for certain *halachot*, Pesach, which commemorates our birth as a nation, is considered the first holiday of the year. See *Mishnah Rosh Hashanah* 1:1 and *Shemot* 12:2. This makes Purim, which commemorates the event which completed the historical cycle that began with the departure from *Mitzrayim*, the last holiday of the year. Thus, as we progress through the calendar each year, we recapitulate the process of Jewish history.

the foundation for the next round of Jewish history, of which we are still a part.[23] We turn now to the Persian experience that concluded the first cycle of Jewish history for a precedent of how we can overcome the challenges of our times at the end of this second and final cycle of Jewish history.

23. In contrast to the first cycle, which occurred in the context of revelation, the second cycle differs in that it projects our relationship with the Creator against the backdrop of God's hiddenness.

CHAPTER 20

Purim's Precedent

When Mordechai saw Haman coming toward him leading a horse, he said, "It appears this evil man comes to kill me." His disciples were sitting and learning in his presence. He said to them, "Rise, flee, lest you be burnt by my coal!" They answered him, "Whether to death or to life we are with you and will not desert you!" Mordechai wrapped himself in his prayer shawl and stood in prayer before the Holy One, blessed be He, while his disciples sat and learned. Haman came in and said to them, "What are you studying?" They answered him, "The commandment of the Omer offering that Israel used to bring in the Temple on this day." He asked them, "What was this offering made of, gold or silver?" They replied, "Of barley." He asked them, "And how much was this barley worth? Perhaps ten silver coins?" They replied, "No. Ten pennies worth was sufficient." He said to them, "Arise, for your ten pennies have overcome my ten thousand coins of silver!"[1]

W E HAVE IDENTIFIED THE events of the Purim story as our guide to salvation from our present alienation from self and God. Purim brings to a conclusion the cycle of Jewish history characterized by revelation. Ends echo ends, therefore we expect it to provide a precedent for our own times as we approach the end of the cycle of Jewish history

---

1. *Vayikra Rabbah* 28:6.

characterized by God's hiddenness. Still, it is difficult to imagine how our experience then could be relevant to our experience today. In Persia we were challenged by a worshipping society, albeit idolatrous, while today we are confronted with the extreme secularism of a scientific and technologically based culture. Our times are perfectly captured by the verses that open the previous chapter: "My power and the might of my own hand have created for me this wealth."[2] Persia seemed very different from this.

It is true that the Purim story took place in the context of Persian dominion and the Persian king Achashverosh had no love for his Jewish subjects. Still, the prime threat and mover of events against the Jews was not the king but his minister Haman, who attempted to exterminate the Jews. Haman was an Amalekite[3] and, therefore, a direct descendant of Esav,[4] the personality animating the culture that we find so oppressive today.[5] Purim really commemorates a victory over Esav and everything that he represents, in line with what we are trying to achieve today. The particularly Persian contribution to the Purim story will be discussed later.

The catalyst for Haman's threat against the Jews was the refusal by the leader of the Jewish people, Mordechai, to bow down to Haman after Haman declared himself a god.[6] Declaring oneself a god was not so unusual in the ancient world — we know, for example, that Pharaoh did so.[7] This tendency stemmed from the sensitivity people had then to their spiritual root. Individuals deified themselves because they experienced their connection to their Source so much so that they felt themselves the personification of a particular spiritual energy and its center of expression in the world.

2. *Devarim* 8:17.
3. *Targum Yonatan, Megillat Esther* 1:3.
4. *Bereishit* 36:12; *Esther Rabbah* 7:10.
5. *Yalkut Shemoni, Bereishit* 27:115.
6. *Megillat Esther* 3:5–6.
7. *Shemot Rabbah* 5:14.

It is, however, paradoxical to find this in a descendant of Amalek. We have already identified the essential characteristic of Amalek as isolation from spiritual reality.[8] We saw that this reveals itself in, among other things, an inability to access the *tzelem Elokim*, the image of God, in themselves and in others. Amalekites have an artificial pride — they think their greatness stems from themselves rather than from God. Because of this they deprecate others to an extreme degree — they think their greatness is personal to them and therefore lacking in others.[9] If Amalekites have an unusually weak sense of spiritual connection, what is the basis for an Amalekite declaring himself a god?

An Amalekite declares himself a god precisely from this poverty of transcendent experience. Cut off from any Being beyond his own, the Amalekite presumes that there is no significance of being greater than his own and that, therefore, he personifies God.[10] In other words, it may not have been unusual for people in antiquity to declare themselves *a* god, but when Amalek does it he is declaring himself *the* God.[11] This is a logical but extreme extension of the replacement of God by the self that we have said results from the modern *da'at* of Good and Evil.[12]

Since this inflated sense of self results from a lack of internal connection to transcendent reality, it is actually built upon a fundamental lack of genuine significance — it is man without his *tzelem Elokim*. As we discussed before, man is subconsciously aware of his potential for true greatness and sensitive to his distance from that greatness. Amalek is the extreme of distance from that potential.[13] Therefore, hidden beneath

---

8. See Chapter 3, pp. 29–30.

9. Ibid., pp. 33–36.

10. This parallels our description in Chapter 14 (pp. 272–273) and Chapter 17 (pp. 318–320) of the confusion between self and God which arises within the culture of Rome.

11. In *Shemot Rabbah* 5:14 Pharaoh declares himself "Master of the world." But from Maharal, *Gur Aryeh, Shemot* 8:15 it is clear that this could only mean that Pharaoh was the greatest power on earth. not that he was the only power. Amalek, on the other hand, confuses himself with God that is One.

12. See note 10 in this chapter.

13. See Maharal, *Chiddushei Aggadot* IV, p. 139 and Maharal, *Ohr Chadash*, pp. 130–131.

his pridefulness is a profound sense of inadequacy.[14] Defiance of such a person is very dangerous. Because he himself is so shallow, all he has is other people's impression of him. So when a person challenges him, he does not feel his status threatened, he feels his very existence threatened. When the leader of the Jewish people, Mordechai, refused to bow to the self-proclaimed deity Haman, the reaction was swift and cataclysmic.

Mordechai refused to bow because, as a Jew, his existence was defined around service to the Creator, who is Being itself — something that is expressed through but cannot be contained in an individual.[15] Mordechai's refusal affirmed the existence of a level of reality to which Haman had no genuine connection, directly challenging the legitimacy of Haman's deification. Since Haman's deification was based on his distance from any Higher reality, Mordechai's refusal stirred Haman's sense of inadequacy and vulnerability to its highest level.[16] He harnessed all the machinery of the Persian Empire to annihilate Mordechai and everything that represented Mordechai's values — that is, the Jewish people.[17]

King Achashverosh, because of his idolatry, was also distant from the true Creator. But since he at least worshipped, he had some connection to

---

14. This parallels our description on page 289 in Chapter 15 of the sense of inadequacy that lies at the root of Roman culture.

15. It cannot be contained in the sense of elevating an individual to a deity. All of us share *tzelem Elokim*, the image of God, which is Divinity flowing through us into the world. But we are in no way an independent source.

16. For a comparable situation, see Maharal, *Netzach Yisrael*, ch. 5 that Rome destroyed the *Beit HaMikdash* because through it the Jews connected to God on a higher level than Rome did.

17. The real point here is that any sense of greatness that Amalek has leads inexorably to a sense of deification. Amalek personifies the confusion of the snake — that man becomes like God to the point of substitution for God. Challenging his deification is felt by Amalek as a challenge to any and all of his sense of greatness. It is for this reason that Amalek attacks the Jews with such venom and feels the need to utterly annihilate them. Every Jew, even a single one, personifies an attachment to a level of reality that reminds Amalek of the vacuousness of his existence and must be eliminated, as we have seen in our recent history. See also the previous footnote.

transcendence and, so, was not removed from the Jews to the degree that Haman was. Achashverosh's idol worship, however, prevented him from receiving the full loyalty from the Jews that he could have from his other subjects. So, though he would not himself have initiated Haman's action, he was not opposed to it.[18] The decree to kill the Jews was issued.

The First Temple was destroyed because of idol worship. The Jews found themselves in Persia because of this transgression. We have already shown that idol worship is built on self-worship.[19] Granted, it is not a full-blown expression, as it retains some connection to transcendence. But self-worship is its basis and what it is moving toward. We have also already connected the exile of the First *Beit HaMikdash* to the idol worship of the golden calf, and we explained that transgression as an effort by man to take control of interpreting reality.[20] It was not the complete rejection of worship implicit in the sin of the spies and the transgressions of the Second *Beit HaMikdash*, but the essential energy was already at work.

The attack of Haman therefore mirrored the root problem that had brought the Jews to Persia, and was an anticipation of what the Jews would eventually face in a more developed and less ambiguous form in their confrontation with Rome. Since the Jews made a grab for controlling reality and displacing God in the First *Beit HaMikdash*, here was a very ugly mirror of that transgression in a more developed form. Not

---

18. That the Jews' destruction was convenient for Achashverosh is seen in *Megillah* 14a: "To what can we compare Achashverosh and Haman at this point? To two men one of whom had a mound in the middle of his field and the other a ditch in the middle of his field. The owner of the ditch said, 'I wish I could buy that mound,' and the owner of the mound said, 'I wish I could buy that ditch.' One day they met, and the owner of the ditch said, 'Sell me your mound,' whereupon the other replied, "Take it for nothing, and I shall be only too glad.'" See Maharal's explanation of this *gemara* in *Ohr Chadash*, p. 140. Another reason Achashverosh would not himself initiate the Jews' destruction is found in *Megillah* 11a and *Ohr Chadash*, pp. 67–68. Achashverosh was a king and thus, on some level, represented God in a time of exile. God would not destroy His people so, therefore, neither could his representative. Haman, however, was a man, representing no one but himself.

19. See Chapter 13, pp. 228–229.

20. Ibid., pp. 227–228.

only were we forced to see what man controlling reality really looked like, we were also shown the place of the Jewish people in such a world. Born as a nation through dedication to the service of the Creator in our departure from *Mitzrayim*,[21] a world run by man could only spell one thing for the Jews — eradication.

LOSING CONTROL

How did we repair the assertion of control implicit in our idol worship? How did we escape the clutches of the man we thus empowered, who was so confident of his righteousness and loathing? We have already discussed how God created the world in such a way that our transgressions give rise to the very situation that allows us to grow beyond our shortcomings.[22] In a world controlled by man, we found ourselves utterly helpless and hated. We were helpless because we represented God, and man had been put in control.[23] We were hated because we proclaimed God's authority in the face of man's appropriation of reality. We were forced to recognize that independent of God we had no power. After fasting and repenting for three days and internalizing that messages Haman was dead and all vestiges of his efforts washed away.

The Talmud states that the salvation in Persia and, for that matter, all salvations from Esav's descendants, come through prayer[24]; we do not physically act. In order to avoid any confusion about who is bringing deliverance, we do not manipulate the world directly on any level but, rather, leave it entirely up to the Creator.[25]

This reflects what we described earlier as the national, or "Yehudah," response to the tensions inherent in free will — we fall, but achieve ultimate relationship with God through repentance.[26] At some point we

---

21. See Maharal, *Gevurot HaShem*, ch. 60.
22. See the beginning of Chapter 14.
23. *Megillat Esther* 3:10; Rav Tzaddok HaKohen, *Takanat HaShavim* 58a.
24. *Megillah* 11a. See Maharal, *Ohr Chadash*, p. 68.
25. *Eichah Rabbah, Hakdamah* 30.
26. See the end of Chapter 6 and all of Chapter 7.

just have to recognize our limitations and give up completely to God. Maharal uses this idea to explain the mitzvah on Purim of *ad d'lo yada*, getting drunk.[27] We mirror our situation in Persia of complete help-lessness, for it was that helplessness that actually brought the help. It is through our intellect that we have the capability of standing independent of God, and it is the fact that we have an intellect that gives us the pride to accord ourselves a status separate from God. Through wine we remove the intellect, eliminating the means and reason for separation. With all barriers down, we recover the full intimacy of our natural connection with the Creator and we cannot be harmed for we are part of Him.[28]

This ability to completely merge with God allows us to reach the heights of humanity, the greatness that distinguishes us from the rest of creation, elevating us above even the angels. An angel's greatness is its weakness. Because it is a lofty spiritual being and has no lowly, physical component, it can stand alone as a creation of significance. Man, however, is composed of both a *neshamah*, that connects him to God, and a finite physical vessel. Our physical being is limited and therefore lacking any significance of being. The fact that this lowly existence is part of us drives us to cleave through our *neshamah* to the Creator with incomparable strength. Because of our desperation to escape the meaninglessness of our physical component, we define our-selves by our attachment to the Creator, giving us a deeper existence than any other creation.[29] The endpoint of history brings this despera-tion to its ultimate intensity, as our survival is literally threatened by our distance from God.[30] The sense of utter dependence inverts this to the tightest possible attachment to the Creator, elevating man to his greatest height. And since the attachment is motivated by our complete powerlessness, it leads to our appreciation of God's total control that

---

27. *Shulchan Aruch, Orach Chayim* 695:3.
28. See, among many examples, the end of Maharal's *Ohr Chadash* and Maharal's discus-sion of *Terumat HaDeshen* in *Drosh al Shabbat HaGadol*. See *Devarim* 32:9.
29. Maharal, *Tiferet Yisrael*, ch. 24.
30. Maharal, *Ohr Chadash*, p. 221.

we said was the purpose of creation in the first place.[31]

We learn from our experience in Persia that our final national redemption will come through complete national repentance. In Persia,
a situation arose that forced the entire Jewish people to despair and,
through that, to achieve complete return. A comparable event may be
in our future to bring our era of Jewish history to its conclusion. But
our job is not to wait for such a situation. Rather, we must each strive
to achieve what we can as individuals to preclude the need for such an
occasion. In other words, we must try to follow Yosef's example of righteous achievement even though we know that our relationship with the
Creator may eventually come as part of a national repentance in the
style of Yehudah. The Purim story also reveals how achievement in the
style of Yosef looks at the end of history. To see this we will first have to
delve a bit deeper into the story.

THE MERIT OF THE OMER OFFERING

Haman was hung on the afternoon of the 16th of Nissan.[32] Haman's
fall from favor began that morning when Achashverosh asked him to
parade Mordechai through the city, publicly declaring Mordechai's
value to the king.[33] The opening quote of this chapter records that when
Haman went to fetch Mordechai, Haman found Mordechai's students
learning Torah. Haman asked the students what they were learning.
They replied that on that day — the 16th of Nissan — when the *Beit
HaMikdash* stood, a special sacrifice was brought: the Omer offering.
They were learning its laws to make up for the fact that since the *Beit
HaMikdash* was in ruins it could not be brought that year.[34] Haman
declared to them that the merit of the Omer offering had saved the Jews
from his decree. The Midrash itself cautions us to be careful with the

---

31. See Chapter 8.
32. *Vayikra Rabbah* 28:6. The date can be derived directly from *Megillat Esther* 3:12, 4:16,
5:1–8. See Maharal, *Ohr Chadash*, pp. 182–184.
33. *Megillat Esther* 6:10–11.
34. *Megillah* 31b.

Omer offering because in its merit we were saved from Haman.[35]

What was the Omer offering and what about it protected the Jews from Haman and all that he represented? The Omer offering was composed of the first ripened grain of the new year — the first fruit of the barley crop.[36] The word "*omer*" refers to a small volume measurement of approximately two and a half liters.[37] Every year, one *omer* of barley was brought on the Altar for the entire Jewish people,[38] and until it was offered no grain of the new crop could be eaten by anyone.[39]

Generally, when we want to understand something in the Torah, we look at its name. This is also true of sacrifices, where their names tell us their significance. A sin-offering is to atone for a sin, a peace-offering brings peace. The fact that this barley offering was called "Omer" indicates that its significance lay in the specific quantity of barley that was brought.

The other place where we see this measurement used is in relation to the manna, or *man*.[40] This was the miracle bread that fell for the Jews in the desert, with each individual receiving exactly one *omer* of *man*

---

35. *Vayikra Rabbah* 28:6.
36. See *Sefer HaChinuch*, mitzvah 302.
37. *Shemot* 16:36 using the measurements of R. Aryeh Carmell, *Aiding Talmud Study* (Feldheim, 1998).
38. *Vayikra Rabbah* 28:3; Rambam, *Hilchot Tamidim u'Musafim* 7:12. Rambam states that the measure of the Omer was an *isaron*, a tenth of an *eifah*. An *eifah* is three *se'ah*. The Omer offering was made from three *se'ah* of barley, from which an *isaron*, one tenth, was removed. This gave one *omer* of barley flour.
39. *Sefer HaChinuch* 302.
40. *Shemot* 16:16. The measurement is also used for *challah* and for the *menachot* (Rashi, *Shemot* 16:36), but there it is called an *isaron*. The term *omer* is only used in conjunction with the Omer offering and with the *man*. It is also used for *shichechah*, the measure of wheat stalks forgotten in the field during harvesting that must be left for the poor (*Devarim* 24:19). The term *omer* in that context means "sheaf" — its usage in the Writings — but is interpreted to also relate to the measurement (see Rashi there). *Shichechah*, however, is kabbalistically connected to the Omer offering. See Rav Moshe Cordavero, *Tomer Devorah*, Perek 5, *Biur Middat Sefirat HaChessed*. On the simplest level, *shichechah* is like *man* to the poor person for it comes to him without the intention of its donor; it is, in effect, from God just like the *man*.

every day.[41] The fact that the quantity of barley in the Omer offering was exactly the same as the amount of *man* that each person received in the desert, and that the offering was named for this measurement, clearly links this offering to the *man*.[42]

The uniqueness of *man* as a food was that it made our dependence upon the Creator absolutely clear. It was our sole sustenance and fell directly from the heavens. Each day we could only collect what we needed for that day and could not save it overnight — every day we were reminded of our total dependence upon the Creator as we picked up our ration.[43] *Man* even fell in a manner that reflected the state of our personal relationship with the Creator — if we were not fulfilling our responsibilities it fell far away, the distance correlated to our individual distance from God.[44] The *man* was faith food.

The Midrash combines the Omer offering's reference to the *man* with the halachah that we could not eat from our new crop before bringing the offering to derive the intent of the sacrifice. The Omer was brought to remind us that despite our extensive efforts to grow our crops, when we eat our produce, we are still effectively eating *man*. For without the Creator's support of nature in general, and all the specific things we need to grow our crops in particular, we would have nothing.[45] Produce is slightly veiled *man*. The Omer teaches us that we control nothing, even when we are manipulating the forces of nature; our actions are frosting on the Creator's cake, a request for His blessing and no more. This is the awareness we identified earlier as the basis of our recognition of God's unity — His singular existence and omnipotence.[46]

It is this recognition that brings us salvation from Amalek, who represents the extreme of directionless nature and human control of

41. Ibid.
42. *Vayikra Rabbah* 28:3.
43. *Shemot* 16:16–21, and see *Rashi*.
44. *Yoma* 75a.
45. *Vayikra Rabbah* 28:1–3.
46. See Chapter 8.

events. This is reflected in our first encounter with Amalek just after we left *Mitzrayim*. Through the Exodus from *Mitzrayim* we saw the Creator's unassailable strength to abrogate nature. This was enough to establish the relationship of the Jewish people with God, but was not the full revelation of God's singular control of reality for which the world was created. To recognize God's Oneness we needed to see God as more than just stronger than nature. We had to understand that nature has no reality independent of God whatsoever — that nature is His instrument to work through as easily as to nullify.[47] This required that we recognize God's complete control even in a purely natural context. To develop that recognition, after departing *Mitzrayim* the intensity of the miracles by which God led us through the desert gradually diminished. As our experience of reality became increasingly natural, we were challenged to retain our awareness of God's oversight despite the thickening of nature. But to fully achieve this recognition will require a level of personal development that only the experience of history can produce.[48] Fresh out of *Mitzrayim*, we came to a point where we were unable to perceive God's guiding hand behind events and we reverted to a natural outlook. This empowered Amalek, the people who personified the natural, mechanistic worldview, to attack.[49]

Amalek's assault forced us to fight. During the battle Moshe ascended to the top of a hill where the Jews could see him.[50] As long as he held his hands toward heaven, the Jews were victorious; when he lost strength and his hands drooped down toward the ground, the Amalekites began to overcome the Jews.[51] Moshe's hands held heavenward symbolized that the power of our hands comes from God. As long as the Jews kept this idea clear in their minds, their leader and representative Moshe was able to keep his hands up. When their clarity waned and

---

47. See *Ramban, Shemot* 13:16. See Chapter 8, pp. 121–122.
48. Ramchal, *Da'at Tevunot* 40.
49. *Rashi, Shemot* 17:8; *Rashi, Devarim* 25:18. See Chapter 3.
50. *Shemot* 14:10.
51. Ibid., verse 11.

388 ⑨ THE CHOICE TO BE

they began to think that their own strength and skill was carrying the day, Moshe lost the ability to hold his hands high and the Jews began to lose.[52] This pressed the Jews to clarify to themselves that everything that happens in the world — even the effects of human actions — are only an expression of the Will of the Creator; our efforts are nothing but a vessel to receive blessing.[53] To be successful we need to at least pray before we act. The next higher level, that which was demanded of the Jews as they fought Amalek after the Exodus, was to achieve a state of prayer while they were acting. This is an expression of what we described as the Yosef approach to free will — acting within a context of clear recognition of the Creator's total control over results.

ESTHER'S RIGHTEOUS ACT

Where do we see the Omer's lesson reflected in the Purim story? Though on a national level we were Yehudah, utterly helpless with nothing to do but return in complete, subservient repentance, on an individual level we do see one direct action taken to bring about our salvation. This was when Esther went to Achashverosh to beg him to intervene on behalf of the Jews. She carefully prepared the ground beforehand to bolster her chances of getting the king to act. She threw two parties for him and invited Haman so that the king's jealousy would be awakened against Haman.[54]

When the moment finally arrived, Esther broke down and cried out, "If I have found favor in your sight, the king, and if it please the king, let my life be given me at my asking, and my people at my request — for

---

52. *Mishnah Rosh Hashanah* 3:8.

53. See Chapter 17, pp. 316–317. In Chapter 8 we explain that perceiving the unity of God requires that we recognize that He is the only One who controls what happens. We spoke there about realizing this in relation to the enemies of God — the kingdoms. But recognizing our own lack of control is just as important to the revelation of God's unity.

54. This could have resulted in both Esther and Haman being killed, but Esther would have considered that an acceptable outcome also, as long as the threat to the Jews was removed (*Megillah* 15b).

we are sold, I and my people, to be destroyed, to be slain, and to be annihilated."

In shock, the king asked, "Who is it that wants to do this?" Esther replied, "A man who is a foe and an enemy, this evil Haman."[55] From the fact that Esther first spoke about a man who was an enemy and only afterwards identified him as Haman, the Talmud learns that Esther originally pointed at Achashverosh as the villain. A *malach* (angel) came and pushed her hand toward Haman.[56] The commentaries explain that Esther despised Achashverosh — he hated the Jews and was responsible for their situation like Haman. That being the case, how could Esther turn to Achashverosh for help?

The answer lies in a *midrash* that states that anywhere in *Megillat Esther* where the term "king" is used without naming Achashverosh it is actually referring to the Creator.[57] When we reexamine Esther's request of the king in this light, we realize that she was not talking *to* Achashverosh as much as *through* him — she was praying to the Creator through the face of the king.[58] Esther took action — her words were also directed at Achashverosh and had meaning to him; in fact they were a cunning, carefully orchestrated manipulation of Achashverosh. But her words had another level of meaning to them, for her true target was not Achashverosh at all. Rather, she directed herself toward the Creator. For what would happen when Achashverosh's hatred of the Jews and respect for Haman was weighed against his love for Esther and the gnawing doubts she had awakened about Haman's loyalty? No one could predict, regardless of how clever her preparation or precise her implementation. This was a situation that Esther could have no illusion of controlling.

---

55. *Megillat Esther* 7:3–6.
56. *Megillah* 16a.
57. *Midrash Abba ben Gurion*, ch. 1.
58. Prayer relates to the Creator's trait of kingship. In a time of exile, the expression of the Creator's kingship is corrupted and comes into the world through the only expression of kingship available in the world, the king of the ruling empire. Thus the appropriate conduit to reach the Creator through prayer is through the face of the king. This was heard from Rav Moshe Shapiro.

She turned to the only One who could determine the outcome, transforming her action into prayer.

Here Esther went a step beyond what the Jews were pushed to achieve in the desert against Amalek in their first encounter. Then the Jews acted and were pressed to recognize that their success was not caused by their actions. They were effectively praying *while* they were acting. Esther transformed action *itself* into prayer. For the Jews in the desert, action and prayer were simultaneous; for Esther, action and prayer were synonymous, bringing perfect synthesis to man's initiative and dependence on the Creator.[59] This represented full internalization of the lesson of the Omer offering. By yielding control to the Creator, this act fully recognized His Oneness, providing a paradigm for righteous action at the end of history.

YAAKOV'S PRECEDENT

From where did Esther derive the strength for this singular accomplishment? As with all our spiritual talents, we look to our forefathers whose experiences, actions, and achievements created the human capabilities from which we, their children, draw strength to meet our challenges.[60] Since the significance of Esther's act lay in its recognition of the Oneness of God, we know to search the life of Yaakov for Esther's source; he is the forefather we most identify with this awareness.[61] In fact, Esther's achievement of saving the Jews from annihilation by turning action into prayer echoes an event at the dawn of Jewish exile when Yaakov saved his family from Esav by turning action into prayer.

The Sages identify Esav as the archetypal exiler.[62] This is due to his

---

59. See Chapter 6, pp. 91–97, that this is an example of fully actualizing free will: we assert our individuality through a creative choice to act, but our action is one of utter subservience to God. See the beginning of Chapter 8 that a true act of choice brings us to recognize the unity of God.

60. "The acts of the fathers are a sign for their children." *Midrash Tanchuma, Lech Lecha* 9.

61. See Chapter 8, pp. 118–127.

62. *Bereishit Rabbah* 75:1.

character of living in the world cut off from spirituality,[63] which is the essence of the experience of exile.[64] In practice also, Esav caused Yaakov to flee from the Land of Israel to the house of Lavan — effectively our first exile. And his cultural progeny, Rome, expelled the Jewish people from the Land of Israel for the final and longest time. Even though other nations preceded Rome in exiling the Jews, they were all infected to varying degrees with the essential quality that made Rome our exiler, that of being separate from God and so separating us from God.[65]

Yaakov's return to Israel after twenty years in the house of Lavan precipitated a direct confrontation with Esav. Because Esav personified the force of exile, we learn from Yaakov's handling of that encounter how we, his descendants, should approach exile for the remainder of history.[66]

---

63. See Chapter 3, pp. 29–30, 35–36.

64. See Chapter 11, pp. 187–188.

65. See Chapter 14, pp. 244–247. Esav and Rome personify the actual separation from God, as opposed to the other exilers, who corrupted a facet of connection to God thereby introducing a level of separation.

66. This is true of all exiles (see *Bereishit Rabbah* 75:5), but there was also significance in this meeting specific to our confrontation with Haman under Persian rule. See *Bereishit Rabbah* 86:3 and compare to *Yalkut Shemoni, Iyov*, ch. 3, *remez* 897. There the Sages associate the particular pains Yaakov suffered with the exiles of the Jewish people. This second *midrash* also appears in *Shemot Rabbah* 26:1, but in the *Yalkut* the order of associations connects Yaakov's face-to-face meeting with Esav to the Persian exile. This creates an exact parallel between the chronology of Yaakov's troubles and the chronology of the exiles. When Yaakov met Esav, Yaakov's loss of Yosef, which presaged the long exile to Rome, was yet to come. The house of Lavan was preparation for the exile to Bavel, while the capture of Dina that came after Yaakov's meeting with Esav and before the loss of Yosef echoed the Greek exile. The exile to Lavan, where Yaakov was out of the Land, is associated with Bavel, since Bavel actually exiled the Jews from the Land — that was an essential part of their exile. Dina is associated with Greece because the essential core of that exile was the profaning of the sanctity of the Jews — both intellectually and through the profaning of women. See chapter 8, note 23. Yosef's disappearance mirrored the Roman exile for many reasons, not least its seemingly endless quality (see *Ohr Gedaliyahu, Likutei Vayishlach* 4 and *Likutei Vayigash* 1). In addition to the chronology there is another reason why it makes sense to associate Yaakov's experiences with the exiles in this way. Yaakov's face-to-face meeting with Esav mirrors our experience in Persia where we directly confronted Haman, a biological descendant of Esav. When Yosef was lost to Yaakov, however, he was actually held by *Mitzrayim*, not Esav. What made it Esav-like was the separation from Yosef, not who captured

As with all confrontations with Esav and his representatives, the immediate threat was annihilation; Esav rode toward Yaakov, his wives, and his sons, with four hundred troops intending to kill everyone. To preempt the slaughter, Yaakov prayed and sent massive tribute. When the two finally met face to face, as Yaakov approached Esav Yaakov bowed seven times. Instead of fighting, Esav suddenly embraced Yaakov and kissed him, even going so far as to confirm Yaakov's status as the rightful heir of Yitzchak.[67] What happened?

The event is understood in light of an incident that is recorded in the Talmud. Abayei, a prominent 4th century Talmudist, had a yeshivah that was occupied by a demon who was constantly injuring the students. Abayei heard that another Sage, Rav Yaakov brei d'Rav Acha bar Yaakov, was coming to visit the town. Abayei arranged that the townspeople deny the traveler lodging so that Rav Yaakov would have to sleep in the yeshivah. That night, while in the yeshivah, a seven-headed demon appeared to Rav Yaakov. He bowed seven times and each time he did, one of the heads of the demon fell off. In the morning, Rav Yaakov exclaimed, "Had there not been a miracle, I would have been in danger."[68]

A demon is a semi-spiritual force of destruction that works against the Creator's intention to give us good. We empower demons through our confusion about the existence of centers of power separate from the Creator. The seven-headed demon represents the most powerful demonic force that exists. A head represents an independent source of being — in

---

him. This resembles the long Roman exile that has been suffered under peoples who were poisoned by the influence of Esav's culture rather than being direct biological descendants of Esav. The language of the *midrash* is that Rome "rules over every nation" or "levies troops from every nation" (*Bereishit Rabbah* 70:8, quoted in a number of *midrashim*). The exact translation is in doubt, but it is clear that the intention is that Rome rules through all other nations. This also fits well with our premise that Rome essentially represents our modern *daat* that influences us regardless of where we live and who rules over us. There are other meanings to this *midrash*, but they are beyond the scope of this work.

67. *Bereishit* 32:6–33:9, and *Rashi, Bereishit* 33:9.

68. *Kiddushin* 29b.

the Torah "appointing a head" is a language of idol worship.[69] The demon of seven heads is the most powerful because there are seven distinct facets to physical existence, the arena in which we can suffer the delusion that there is existence separate from the Creator. The seven heads represent all seven facets of potential separation from the Creator united into one entity.

Bowing is an act of subservience. Someone as righteous as Rav Yaakov was not likely to be bowing to the demon. And if he did, we would not expect the demon to lose a head as a result. Remember that a demon's strength is a function of our own misunderstanding of reality, our illusion of a force independent of the Creator. Rav Yaakov was bowing to the Creator, each time focusing on a facet in himself associated with one of the seven dimensions of reality represented by one of the heads of the demon. By nullifying that facet's independence through subjugating it to the Creator, he reconnected that facet of reality back to its source. The head of the demon signifying the independent existence of that facet then fell off. After bowing seven times to the Creator, all of reality was reunited with its source. That God is One was expressed in the world and the demon was no more.[70]

Yaakov's bowing in front of Esav needs to be understood in the same manner as Rav Yaakov's bowing before the demon. Though Yaakov's act of bowing had meaning to Esav — it spoke to Esav's deepest need for external recognition — Yaakov was primarily directing his action toward God, before whom he bowed in submission.[71] Esav personified the separation of this world from its source — reality as governed by natural forces and for the sake of temporal existence. Effectively, he is the eight headed demon. Esav and those who represent him only have strength in the world as long as we to some degree relate to the world as they do.[72] Because of the distortions inherent in a post-sin physical

---

69. *Rashi, Bemidbar* 14:4.
70. This interpretation is based on Maharal, *Chiddushei Aggadot* II, pp. 131–132.
71. See note 58 in this chapter.
72. *Bereishit* 25:23, 27:40. See Chapter 14.

394 ⑤ The Choice to Be

world, concerted effort is required to avoid Esav's view of reality, so Esav is naturally strong. When Yaakov bowed, however, he brought himself to an unprecedented closeness to God. He submitted all facets of his personality, and with them, of reality to God, undercutting Esav's base and rendering him powerless. In Chapter 8 we discuss Yaakov's achievement of full recognition of God's Oneness. The source which proves Yaakov reached this height refers to the night before this meeting with Esav when Yaakov was preparing himself for the confrontation.

Though Esav's hatred of Yaakov emanated from the deepest recesses of his character, Yaakov had removed the basis of that hating character so that what was left was overcome with love and goodwill for Yaakov — at least at that moment. This confrontation between Esav, the root of exile, and Yaakov, the root of the Jewish people, was brought to a satisfactory conclusion by Yaakov acting in a manner that was meaningful to Esav but was actually a prayer directed through Esav to God. Against Esav's vision of extreme secularism and personal control, Yaakov transformed action into prayer, denying even himself any power separate from the Unitary Creator. Yaakov returned the world to its source, depriving Esav of any independent standing and leaving him a limp puppet in the hands of his Maker, and the seed of the Jewish people was saved.

When Esther prayed through the face of Achashverosh, she was drawing on strength developed by Yaakov. Esther, as a true child of Yaakov, achieved the same level of integration between action and prayer as Yaakov had and brought the first round of Jewish history to a successful conclusion.

WHAT REMAINS TO DO?

When we originally turned to our salvation from the Persian exile for guidance on how to gain deliverance from our Roman exile, we were concerned that the two situations were too different for us to learn anything that would be applicable from one to the other. When we recognized that the primary agent of our danger in Persia was Haman, an Amalekite and, therefore, a descendant of Rome's progenitor Esav, we realized that the two exiles were fundamentally similar.

We have concluded that in Persia the attack of Haman drove us as a people to a state of national repentance and self-nullification. Concomitantly our leaders were pressed to perfect their awareness of their dependence on the Creator and transform themselves and their actions into prayer.[73] The parallel between the Persian event and our present experience implies that repentance and prayer are also the direction in which our deliverance lies. This is consistent with the statement in the Talmud cited earlier that in any situation involving Esav or his descendants, salvation comes through prayer.[74]

We learned in the section on the kingdoms that no generation strives to create total relationship with the Creator, only to complete the part that is theirs.[75] Our accomplishments over history are never left behind. Rather, they remain as we build, generation after generation, toward a complete relationship with the Creator. History never repeats itself. Similar situations may occur, but the precise facet of self that each period in history allows to be actualized always differs in some way from what has been accomplished in the past — either because of changes in context, the strengths we bring to the situation, or the specific nature of the challenge. Otherwise, there is no point in repeating. If we turn to the Persian experience to learn what our focus should be today because ends echo ends, we must also ask what differentiates the present from Persia. We already humbled ourselves in the face of Rome's representative, Haman; what does our present situation, where we also face Rome, press us to achieve that goes beyond that?

---

73. *Tehillim* 109:4.
74. *Megillah* 11a; Maharal, *Ohr Chadash*, p. 68.
75. See Chapter 12, p. 214 and Chapter 14.

CHAPTER 21

A Deeper Darkness

THE SIGNIFICANCE OF ESTHER'S achievement in Persia was immeasurable. Against a backdrop of national repentance, she saved the Jewish people from destruction and tied off the era of revelation in history. Haman, who had sought with his unprecedented wealth and power to eradicate the nation, was killed and replaced by Mordechai who took over his position and assets. The Jews, instead of being destroyed by their enemies, were allowed to destroy those very enemies.[1] The salvation was complete... almost.

The Jews remained in exile. The end of Jewish history had not yet arrived. There was more to do. We mentioned earlier that choices are affected not only by the challenges we face and the strengths with which we face them but also by the context in which the choices are made.[2] Though in the Purim story we faced Esav's representative in Persia, it was Esav's representative *in Persia*. That is to say we struggled against the spiritual emptiness of Haman in the context of a society that at least supported the concept of worship, even if their worship was a corrupt one. There remained the need to create ourselves in opposition to Esav's representative but against the backdrop of a whole new level of God's hiddenness, one in which worship was absent and seemingly irrelevant. We needed to face Rome *in Rome*. The significance of the events in Persia, therefore, lay not only in the salvation of the Jews from

---

1. *Megillat Esther* 8:1–2, 11.
2. See the beginning of Chapter 10.

destruction at that time, but also in the manner in which the Jewish people were readied to face the thickening darkness that lay ahead.

The approaching darkness was already evident in the events of Purim. *Megillat Esther* does not mention God's name — an unprecedented omission in the books of the Written Torah. A name labels a relationship. The absence of God's name means that no specific incident in the story revealed God's involvement sufficiently to attach His name to it. There were no clear miracles — God was hidden.[3] The events in Persia inaugurated our modern era in which we have to make our way in the world in the absence of any obvious signs of God's presence.

Megillat Esther was written to prepare us for the spiritless future that awaited us. Though God was invisible in Persia as a participant in specific acts, the Sages showed in the *Megillah* that He was clearly present as a director. Nine years worth of history was condensed into an eighteen-minute story to highlight those details that, when lined up, revealed God's hand firmly steering events toward His intended outcome. The missing names of God in the book were filled by the story as a whole, revealing God's involvement. The book itself became, in effect, a name of God.

For a hidden miracle, the Purim salvation was unusually transparent — filled with uncanny coincidences, remarkable timing, and a seamless integration of all the different parts. The Sages used this relatively clear case to write *Megillat Esther* as a kind of Magic Eye manual to train us in the art of picking out those details that testify to the presence of God's hidden hand.[4] This was a skill we would need for the darkening future.

As the natural world of causality was taking root in our consciousness, it was not just the ability to recognize God's oversight of specific events that was required. In the context of God's seeming absence, we experienced existence as neutral — to be interpreted and engaged as we

---

3. Maharal, *Ohr Chadash*, p. 125 and p. 184.
4. Magic Eye pictures are explained in Chapter 17, p. 327. They are pictures that reveal a surface image but have another image coded in at a different depth. If one consciously focuses on this deeper level while looking at the picture a completely different image appears.

desired. We needed guidance to to recover our understanding of reality as a communication with God, defined by meaning and purpose. We needed Torah. But, as we discussed earlier, at this time prophecy was passing.[5] The form in which the *Megillah* was written came to answer this need.

Though it was composed at the end of the prophetic period with the assistance of the last prophets, *Megillat Esther* itself was not prophetic. The Divinity of its inspiration was sufficiently weak that the Talmud records a debate over including it in Scripture.[6] Its lack of prophetic insight was filled in by the extraordinary wisdom invested in it by the one hundred and twenty Sages who contributed to its formulation. The document provided a transition from the prophetic Written Torah to the wisdom of the Oral Torah that was replacing it as the central vehicle of connection to God in post-prophetic times.[7]

The flip side of the shift to Torah that was filtered through wisdom and human intellect was the danger it introduced. With God's role in Torah hidden and ours enlarged we were tempted to pridefully attribute Torah to our own personal genius.[8] *Megillat Esther* strengthened us against this threat to the extent that was possible. Teaching us to distinguish the hidden miracles of the Creator operating behind the façade of a natural world it also gave us the ability to recognize the hidden inspiration of the Creator in our own insight.[9]

The Oral Torah became the foundation of our relationship with God when the Jews accepted the Rabbinic command to read *Megillat Esther* on Purim, implicitly accepting the general authority of the Oral Torah.[10]

---

5. See Chapters 14, p. 260.

6. *Megillah* 7a.

7. See Chapter 10, pp. 179–180; Chapter 14, pp. 259–261; and Chapter 19.

8. See Chapter 14, p. 265.

9. Rav Tzaddok HaKohen, *Likutei Maʾamarim, Sefer Yehoshua.* See Chapter 14.

10. The Jews explicitly accepted the authority of the prophetic Written Torah at Har Sinai in the negotiations that preceded the revelation at Sinai. The Oral Torah was only accepted under the compulsion of overpowering revelation at the actual giving of the Torah (*Midrash Tanchuma, Noach* 3). That acceptance only held weight as long as the

As queen of Persia, Esther went on to bear a child who, when he became king, financed the building of the Second Temple. The Second Temple provided the necessary environment for the Oral Torah to be developed, concretized, and take root to the point where it could withstand the long exile to come and provide an ark for the Jews in an increasingly empty world.[11]

YISHMAEL'S ADDITION

The qualitatively deeper darkness that Purim heralded is our unique challenge. The salvation of Purim both anticipated the coming reduction in the level of spiritual experience and created the framework for us to continue developing a relationship with the Creator under our new circumstances. But beyond the profound increase in the hiddenness of the Creator, there is another element that distinguishes our current exile from that in Persia.

We have spoken much about the four kingdoms that exiled the Jewish people, culminating in Rome. But we have been silent about the Arabs, who both oppressed a large segment of our people for over a thousand years and are the primary agents of physical pressure on the Jews today. Culturally our oppressor remains Rome, so the Arabs must be understood as an added element that comes to color the end of the Roman exile.[12] But what is the color that they add?

---

circumstances under which it had been accepted continued — a context of revelation (Rav Tzaddok HaKohen, *Likutei Ma'amarim*, 4). With the final masking of the face of the Creator behind a natural world, the Oral Torah needed to be accepted voluntarily. This happened through the acceptance of the mitzvah to read *Megillat Esther* (*Shabbat* 88a).

11. *Pirkei HaHeichalot*, ch. 27.

12. As much as the Arab element constitutes a difference between our present circumstances and those under which the Purim salvation occurred, it also highlights an aspect of similarity, for Yishmael and Persia are deeply entwined with one another. Iran's adoption of Islam and alignment with Arab politics is only a recent development but is at least indicative of a deep connection. (Islam only emerged in the 7th century of the Common Era. Our exile to Persia was hundreds of years before the Common Era, at a time when Persia was Zoroastrian rather than Islamic.) But there are commentaries who equate the ancient

The Arabs have yet to exile the Jewish people, so they are in a different category than the four kingdoms.[13] The Arabs also differ from the four kingdoms because of the level of their connection to the Creator. Babylon, Persia, Greece, and Rome were all societies whose religious attachment was fundamentally compromised — either by idol worship, in Babylon and Persia, or with a man-centered *da'at*, in Greece and Rome. Both of these perversions precluded a full connection to God. With the Arabs, for the first time we face a people with a relationship to monotheism uncompromised by either idolatry or deep-rooted secularism.

The Arabs are descendants of Yishmael, a son of Avraham. Yishmael literally translates as "God will hear." He is born and named for God hearing and answering the cries of his mother, Hagar.[14] God also answered a prayer of Yishmael in the Torah.[15] Since Yishmael's name derives from his ability to pray, we understand that this is his and his descendants' principal strength. If we apply the concept we established earlier, that nations that have the opportunity to attack us have been given that opportunity as a mirror of our lacks, we conclude that our present vulnerability to the Arabs must derive from a lack in our prayers.[16]

In Persia our direct adversary was a descendant of Esav and, therefore, essentially not religious. All we had to do to remove his base of

---

Persian Empire with Yishmael (See Maharal, *Netzach Yisrael*, ch. 21). This has to do with an underlying cultural commonality, which is beyond our present scope. Both in the Persian exile and today we are dealing with a combination of Esav and Yishmael, the difference being that at Purim, Haman representing Esav operated in the context of the Persian Empire representing Yishmael, whereas today Yishmael is operating within the context of Esav (Rome).

13. The Arabs never exiled us from the Land of Israel; they only oppressed us after we were already out of the Land. Even then, it was only to a portion of the Jewish people. Though Greece also never forced the Jews out of the Land of Israel, they did culturally dominate us in the Land at a time when the bulk of the Jewish people were living in the Land — which is the equivalent of exile.

14. *Bereishit* 16:11.

15. Ibid., 21:17.

16. As heard from Rav Moshe Shapiro.

power was to achieve genuine devotion, and we strove to achieve this from within a larger social context that was religious — compromised by idol worship, but still with a concept of service of a transcendent source. Today we are faced with the Arabs, who are themselves genuinely religious. To overcome them it is not enough merely to become God's servants — which they also are. Rather, we are forced to perfect our service, especially in the area of prayer.[17] This must be accomplished under the influence of Roman culture, which is essentially not religious.

THE END GAME

In the final exile, then, we are stretched in both directions. The standard of achievement is raised and the challenge of our circumstances is intensified. We are pushed to actualize our free will on the highest possible level. How are we to succeed in our weakened state?

As was the case in Persia, there is the path for the group — recognizing our complete helplessness and utter dependence upon the Creator — and the path of the individual — striving to integrate the necessity of human action with an awareness that the Creator runs the world. We begin with the path of the group.

We discussed in the previous chapter that the unique greatness of man among all other creations is his combination of a *neshamah* connecting to the most sublime spiritual heights and a body that is finite and opaque to our deeper levels of being. We would think that our bodies lower our overall spiritual level. But because our *neshamah* is aware of what is possible, the existence of our physical component only

---

17. Our vulnerability to the prayers of Yishmael is mentioned by the Sages. There are those who expand this to other areas where we are religiously weak, seeing them mirrored in vulnerability to the Arabs. For example, the Oral Torah can only be truly learned in a context of *mesirut nefesh*, giving up one's life for Torah (see Chapter 14, p. 270). Our weakness in this area is reflected in our vulnerability to suicide bombers (as heard from Rav Moshe Shapiro). It is worth noting that we find weakness specifically in the areas that are most important in countering the influence of Rome and its corrupt worldview — prayer and the Oral Torah.

drives us to cleave more tightly to the Creator as we strive to escape its limitations and mortality. A corollary of this is that the greater our sense of limitation at any given time, the greater the desperation and intensity with which we long, consciously or not, for connection to God. Paradoxically, then, the further we are from God, the closer we are to recovering closeness to Him. Our increasing distance creates a pull to return that increases in step with the distance.[18] Eventually, that energy must reach the point where the barriers constraining it crumble.

Today we are distant from God to an unprecedented degree. We already discussed how our present cultural setting creates a gnawing sense of inner emptiness.[19] Our inner vacuum is mirrored in our outer understanding of our inconsequentiality. When we experienced God as the basis of existence in general, and our existence in particular, we understood ourselves to occupy the center of reality in a metaphysical sense. This was reflected in our understanding of ourselves as occupying the center of reality in a physical sense. As our integration with our present perspective strengthens, we come to see ourselves less and less central to existence metaphysically. In parallel, we have come to see ourselves physically standing further and further from the center. Though a critical aspect of the subject-object view is the disassociation of physical reality from meaning, our increasingly peripheral location cannot but affect and reflect on our sense of self.

Today, we view ourselves as a speck on an insignificant planet revolving around a smallish and insignificant star, one of hundreds of billions of stars in an insignificant galaxy, one of hundreds of billions of galaxies in what may be one of countless universes! The triviality we attribute to our existence is incomprehensible.[20] This is just in the spatial dimension of cosmology, a science that is neutral to humanity's significance. There are other branches of science where the effort to undermine human significance is more conscious and no less successful.

---

18. See Appendix 2, A Modern Gathering of Straw.
19. See the end of Chapter 15.
20. This was a point that Rav Feldman emphasized a number of times.

I recently read a book on the history of science that opened with the following line, "The most important thing that science has taught us about our place in the Universe is that we are not special."[21] "*The most important…*" This attitude is not universally held among scientists but neither is it, from my experience, unusual.

This sense of insignificance and distance from God has created an enormous need to return that boils below the surface of our consciousness. Any spiritual awakening propels a person to search for meaning and can lead to a genuine embrace of the Creator. We see evidence for the imminence, or at least the proximity of return to God, in the unprecedented number of people coming back to Torah in our time. At this moment, a full return to God on a national level remains blocked by our extreme secular perspective. But that situation could change in an instant because of the powerful subconscious hunger for change. National repentance is as close as it is far.

In Persia we required a threat to bring to consciousness the realization of how far we were from connection to God and how desperately we needed that connection both spiritually and physically. The Creator has demonstrated in the recent past that He is not averse to using extreme methods to make this idea clear. It is frightening to consider the possibilities available today to make this point. Will rounding off our era of history require this kind of intervention again?

There still remains the individual path, which is built on acting in the context of clarity about our utter dependence upon God. This achievement is also sandwiched between extremes of challenge and opportunity as a result of our deepening exile. On the one hand, we have gained the ability to manipulate nature to an extraordinary degree of precision, bolstering our conviction of our control over the world. On the other hand, we have achieved this by focusing our personality in an aspect of our humanity that leaves us utterly out of control of ourselves.

---

21. John Gribbin, *The Scientists: A History of Science Told Through the Lives of Its Greatest Inventors* (Penguin Books, 2002), p. xviii.

The explosion of psychology and pop psychology bears witness to how much we as individuals are casting around for help. On a societal level, the industries we require to bring us comfort threaten our wellbeing through pollution and oppression born of raging greed. The weapons we design to protect us threaten our continued existence because of wild anger and jealousy. Technology that should connect us as people puts an electronic interface between us that blocks true human sharing. Our addiction to media and entertainment distracts us from human interaction. Our appetite for information prevents thought and wisdom. Wealth becomes poverty through unrestrained desires. To a developed person, the idea that we control anything seems utterly farcical. The frightening deterioration in our humanity pushes us to break out of our mold and center ourselves in a deeper part of our personality, with its wholly different understanding of our dependence on God and our relationship with action.

There is no question that history will conclude with a national return to recognition of and dependence upon God. Though Persia offers a precedent for that awakening being catalyzed from without, that does not preclude the possibility of an awakening from within. The internal awaking is an individual and personal affair. But, ultimately, our nation is composed of individuals. We have discussed Yosef's individual path of righteousness and Yehudah's public path of repentance as if they belong exclusively to two distinct categories of people. In truth, they are both facets of everyone's life project. Even the spiritually weak strive for righteousness. Even Moshe, for all of his achievements, in the end could only ask from God because of God's grace.[22]

As much as we are all part of the larger community, we still retain our individuality and are responsible and able to strive toward clarity. We have a well-developed Oral Torah to guide us in this project and ample motivation provided by the barrenness of the larger culture that presses upon us. We can as individuals, each on our own level, accept

---

22. *Devarim Rabbah* 2:1.

upon ourselves the responsibility to turn inward and touch a deeper self connected to our true Source of Being.

*   *   *

The poverty of our spiritual experience compared to previous generations can lead to despair over our ever being able to bring history to its completion. This debilitating thought can bring to a rejection of purpose, and a lack of purpose leads to a denial of creation — if history has no end then it has no beginning. In this book we have argued that such a reaction is based on a fundamental misunderstanding of the functioning of history. If we can learn to relate to history as a process, our present shallowness defines our challenge rather than proving our failure.

Our job today is not the impossible task of reaching the awesome heights of previous generations, for we already stand upon their shoulders. This does not make us any greater in our own right. It simply means we stand closer to our goal, for all the work they did belongs to us also. What remains for us today is merely to complete the little they left unfinished.

We must achieve, from within a spiritually barren world, a basic but integrated *emunah* in God and His complete dominion. This will express itself in earnest prayer. Through prayer we affirm that what we want can come only from God, for He is the sole master of existence.[23]

This achievement is only one small facet of mankind's overall task of creating relationship with God. But our lives are made no less meaningful by the narrowness of our focus, for this facet is the most essential of them all. It is also incredibly difficult to achieve because we must dig deeply within ourselves at a time when all the doors to our internal world are closed. But even though we approach the end of the historical process, the statement of Rebbi Tarfon in *Pirkei Avot* remains true:

---

23. See Maharal, *Netivot Olam* I, *Netiv HaAvodah*, ch. 1, and Maharal, *Be'er HaGolah*, *Be'er* 4 regarding *Berachot* 7a.

It is not upon you — meaning as an individual — to complete the task, but neither do you have the right to refrain from trying.[24] God does not demand that we do what we *cannot* do. But he does demand that we do what we *can* do. This requires that we each concentrate on our individual obligation of making ourselves better tomorrow than we are today, all the while laboring to appreciate the presence of God in our world and ourselves.

If we all face up to this responsibility, perhaps we can prevent being confronted with the kind of peril that would be required to externally force our return as a nation. The choice to be is ours — let us seize it. "HaShem! Return us to You, and we will return. Renew our days as they once were."[25]

---

24. *Pirkei Avot* 2:16.
25. *Eichah* 5:21.

Appendices

Synopsis

BARE ESSENTIALS

Section I: Our longing and purpose is to actualize our deepest self. Since this is the part of us that emerges directly from the Creator into individual being, its actualization is synonymous with attaching ourselves to God. Our guide to accomplish this goal is the Torah; through its mitzvot we develop all facets of our personality as expressions of our root self. This development brings recognition of our connection to God in all spheres of experience: in our outward awareness we are conscious of the utter dependence of existence on God, in our inner awareness we experience the depth of our own being, which echoes God — our Source, and in our relationships with others we engage their underlying Divinity. Complete recognition of God is an alternate understanding of our defining purpose.

   Section II: Our connection to God is initially hidden, allowing us to utilize free will to create ourselves as individuals connected to Him. Through creating ourselves, we emulate God the Creator, and the resulting creative self resembles Him on the highest level possible. This process of creation is, therefore, our deepest connection to God and our deepest actualization of self. Who we are determines how we perceive God so this process of resembling God fully is also the process of recognizing God's complete omnipotence, that He is One. So the ultimate goal of self development is identical with the ultimate goal of recognition of God, and they are achieved through the same process.

412 ❾ The Choice to Be

Section III: We begin as unfinished beings, lacking true connection with God. As we develop, the focus of our identity ascends through our various facets of personality and we are challenged to shape each one into a vehicle for relationship with God. To be a creative self, which is synonymous with saying to be creative of self, this process cannot be automatic but, rather, must come from us through choices made in the face of countervailing pulls. These pulls are provided by our inclinations, each a unique form of self-centeredness arising from the incompleteness of one of our aspects. Each facet, when we master its associated inclination and bring it to completion, plays a unique part in our overall relationship with God. We go through a parallel process on a national level over historical time. The various kingdoms who have exiled us serve the role of the inclinations against which we achieve self, and each generation contributes its unique part in building our overall relationship with God.

Section IV: As we move through this process, both personally and nationally, we are centered in increasingly sophisticated aspects of our personality. Though less physical, these give us a deeper sense of independent worth and, therefore, increasingly undermine our awareness of dependence on God, making us less spiritual. Thus, for example, we move from exiles amongst idol worshiping nations to exiles amongst nations that deny the legitimacy of worship altogether. We are presently late in the final exile. All of experience is processed through our rational intellect, blocking any sense of infinite, spiritual reality and all of its accoutrements: miracle, prophecy, and an intuitive need for worship. We are profoundly cut off from God. This does not prove national failure at connecting with Him; it merely defines our specific challenge and task in the historical process. It is left to us to take the initiative to create the most basic foundation of our relationship with God, our faith in His existence and His involvement in our lives. Our job is complicated by the remarkable mastery over physical reality modern rationality seems to have achieved; man appears to compete with God for control, contradicting God's singular omnipotence. In the past, such circumstances have set the stage for remarkable events that produced the inversion of our understanding needed to appreciate the the true unity of God.

GENERAL OVERVIEW

In the first section we recognize in man an innate hunger in every dimension of his experience to touch reality on a level that transcends the boundaries of his individual ego. This longing is a reaction of the soul to the constriction it suffered when it was pinched off from the Creator to enter individual, physical being and is a thinly veiled desire to return to the infinite God. Since this need arises with and as a consequence of our coming to individual existence, it is the essential motive force of the self.

Our purpose in creation is defined by the obligations placed upon us by the Creator — His mitzvot. The first of these, and therefore the root and essence of all of them, was to eat from all the fruit of Gan Eden. Since, conceptually, eating is an act by which we fill lack, the mitzvot — which are all extensions of the original root mitzvah — are acts through which we fill our lack. But what is it that we lack?

Names articulate essence. Man, *adam*, was named for the *adamah*, the earth, from which he was drawn because of the characteristic he uniquely shares with it of actualizing potential. Adam's name reveals that his essence is to actualize potential. His defining lack, then, is his unfulfilled potential — his need to develop himself.

Since we emerge into individual being from the Creator, the foundation of our humanity and deepest part of ourselves is our root connection to Him. Since the nature of individuality is to obscure this, we are all, to varying degrees, unaware of this connection and it is our deepest unrealized potential. Through the mitzvot, we develop ourselves by actively transforming every facet of our humanity into an expression of our connection to the Creator thus actualizing our identity as a being emanating from God. This fulfills our innate longing for attachment to God. Thus our deepest desire leads us to achieve our purpose.

This achievement manifests itself in our consciousness as *emunah*, or faith. In the context of our direct awareness of God, this *emunah* is experienced as a sense of complete dependence on Him. In the context of our individual awareness, this *emunah* shows itself in our sense of significance and connectedness to infinite Being, experiencing the self as a echo, conduit, and servant of God. In the context of our relationships with others, this *emunah* shows itself as sensitivity to the Divinity that lies at the root of each person's individuality and the significance and honor that radiates through it from his *tzelem Elokim.*

In the second section we ask the obvious question: if our purpose is to connect to God in these various ways, why is He so hidden? Why do we need to go through such a challenging process of development to uncover our internal root and find the Creator in a dark world? The sharpness of the question is intensified when we recognize that fundamental to our understanding of the Creator and His relationship with existence is that He created in order to give good. *Emunah* is our purpose because connection to the Creator is the greatest true joy we can experience. The opacity of reality and self to their Divine Source blocks this good. But not only does it hinder this positive experience, it also allows the negative experience of evil. Mankind's suffering seems to contradict the Creator's goodness or omnipotence. What can warrant the darkness which allows this?

The Creator hides Himself in creation to allow for the actualization of free will. God created in order to give. But giving to one's self is not an act of giving so there must be someone other to the Creator to whom He can give — someone with self. Yet anything that is created is an extension of its creator, and is therefore not other — otherness cannot be created. The opportunity for its emergence, however, can be. Free will and the circumstances under which it can act — God's hiddenness — give man the capacity and opportunity to earn his being and determine his nature, thus achieving selfhood. The development of self, which we identified in the first section as man's purpose, is really the development of *a* self and occurs through the free choices that man makes. The darkness which allows free will to operate is, then, a prerequisite to the accomplishment of the goal of creation.

However, the self thus achieved is not merely a means to God's giving. The opportunity to create self is *the* gift of the Creator; for the achievement of self is the achievement of being and without this we have nothing, for we are nothing. Our task, therefore, is to gain self. There is a serious difficulty in identifying this as our goal, however, because if we are other to God we do not exist — for He is the only thing that truly exists. To exist, then, we seemingly must cease to exist?!

This apparent contradiction is resolved when we look more deeply at how free choice operates. The only choices through which we achieve selfhood are those involving values that define us. There are many examples and permutations of these choices but, on the most essential level, in all of them we choose whether to serve the Higher cause and attach ourselves to God or to act selfishly. Since our true self emanates from and is therefore subservient to God, such a choice is not between equivalent options. Rather, it is a choice between seizing an opportunity to actualize true self by serving or to decline it by acting egocentrically; being selfish is the equivalent of allowing the true self to be washed away by inclinations that, though part of us, are foreign to our essential being. Since we only achieve self through subjugation to the Creator, the only self we can create is transparent to the Creator as its source. Thus, when we defined man's purpose in the first section, we did not state generally that he must develop himself. Rather, we were specific: man's purpose is to develop himself as a person connected to God.

We still have a difficulty, however, because even if we are a self "connected to God" it does not change the fact that selfhood is synonymous with independence. A "self" that is attached would seem to be a contradiction in terms.

Self is achieved through our own creative act: that we are and who we are comes from us—this defines selfhood. To the degree possible within the context of creation, when we do this we emulate the Creator's quality of necessity, whereby He exists from Himself.[1] Rather than

---

1. The Creator is necessary. This reflects the unique significance of His being and is expressed both in *that* He is—His existence is necessary—and *Who* He is—the necessity of His being requires that He is fully actualized. No other being can match this by definition, since we exist only by virtue of God's act of creation. When we develop ourselves through freely chosen, righteous acts, however, within the context of the system of justice God established, we earn and receive our existence by necessary right rather than as a gift. This emulates God's necessity of existence. We also govern our particular development, rather than it being externally imposed by another; this emulates the necessity of His actualization. These emulations are obviously not total but, rather, are to the extent possible within the limits of creation. God's being is necessary without reliance on anything external to Him-

breaking us off from God, this ties us to Him on the deepest possible level. Through emulating God, we recognize God as the Source and Basis of whichever quality we are emulating, and we become attached to Him like a branch arising from its root. Attachment through emulation reaches its highest level in emulating the quality of necessity because we recognize God's quality of necessity from His role as Creator of existence.[2] Therefore, through this quality He is most profoundly our root. Furthermore, when we emulate through ourselves becoming creators, the emulation is closest because the branch after His root that we become is itself a root — just as He is a creator, we are a creator.

All that truly exists is God and we derive our being from Him. This occurs most directly and fully when we remove from our self those qualities that hide Him, effectively becoming a revelation of God. This comes in our emulation of His necessity through free choice. Since God is revealed through His quality of necessity, when we display that necessity through self-creation in emulation of Him, it is His necessity that is displayed. God is then manifest in the world through us. We are who we are and exist from ourselves, yet that existence originates in God, traveling through us like one instrument resonating with another.

The distinction is subtle, however, between emulating God through creation of self to gain connection to Him, and following the exhortation of the snake to "be like God" — gaining existence to compete with God and displace Him. This subtlety leads many to error, who then only regain connection through repentance. The act of repentance is itself a profound exercise of free will, albeit a less complete expression of it than when someone consistently maintains his righteousness.[3] The Jewish

---

self whereas our necessity is only within the framework of a system of justice that God has established. Our actualization is not necessary, but at least emanates from within ourselves rather than being imposed by another. But by at least tasting creation's equivalent of God's necessity we achieve a degree of being that echoes that of the Creator.

2. Existence testifies to a source that has the significance of being to uphold it. This is the quality of necessity.

3. Those who relate through repentance emulate the necessity of God's actualization since, through the act of repentance, the determination of who they are comes from within them-

people are composed of the exceptional, consistently righteous few and the national majority whose connection is based on repentance after falling. Each plays its role in achieving a full relationship of the nation with God. There are aspects of the bond that the repentant's dependence on God's mercy creates that the completely righteous person lacks.

*　　　*　　　*

Up until now we have spoken about the need for operative free will to achieve a *self* connected to the Creator. But it is just as essential to our understanding of *God* to whom we are connecting. We said that through free will we come from ourselves, emulating and connecting to God's quality of necessity. In the language of our Sages this is called "being alone," meaning we come from ourselves undetermined by any other being; we emulate God's quality of "being alone." In reference to God, "being alone" refers to the fact that God is One — the only one who truly exists, a consequence of His necessity. Through using our capacity for free will to fully develop ourselves, then, we connect to God's unique unity or Oneness. This connection primes us to, on some level, perceive and understand this quality of God.

Unity is the only characteristic of God about which we can gain any understanding. Intellect is a fundamental element of our being and therefore a necessary component in any relationship that would be considered whole or complete. Since God created existence for the purpose of man developing full relationship with Him, and only in recognizing the unity of God can that be achieved, its revelation is the purpose of creation. Thus, as we achieve our personal purpose through free will of becoming "alone," we prepare to perceive that which the world was created to reveal — that God is One.

---

selves. In fact, the act of repentance accomplishes this to the highest degree possible — in repentance we directly choose who we are. But since the repentant are dependent upon God's mercy to accept their repentance rather than on His character of strict justice, they have not earned their relationship with God and therefore it is not their own by necessary right. They do not emulate the necessity of God's existence, which the consistently righteous do.

God's unity is accessible to understanding because it is perceived through the negation of its opposite rather than through attempting to directly grasp God's incomprehensible, infinite qualities. God's unity implies that nothing has any control in existence except Him. When we err and perceive some power as operating independently, and then watch it eventually falter and resolve into an instrument of God's will, we are left with the clarity that "God is the only One." As this occurs over and over, we achieve an ever deepening sense of God's singular control of events.

Nationally, this happens through the succession of empires that conquer us. Our sins, also the product of our free will, leave us vulnerable to the conquest of kingdoms that come to destroy or profane God's Temple. Each kingdom's power is built upon a unique illusion of power independent of God: that God's servants have independent power (Babylonian idolatry), that there are multiple sources to reality (Persian idolatry), that nature functions independent of God's oversight (Greece), that God is limited by laws (Rome), and that we can manipulate God's system of oversight to our selfish advantage (misdirected Jews). Each kingdom in its hour of glory appears omnipotent, or at the very least in possession of power to oppose God, which seems to corroborate their claim to an independent base of power. After each kingdom fulfills its purpose of pushing us to repentance, it disappears from history, revealing that it had no independence and was nothing more than God's tool. Since it is specifically in the movement from error to truth that the conviction of God's unity is achieved, free will and the hiddenness of God that allows it to function — our ability to make mistakes and recover from them by recognizing truth — powers the process through which God's unity becomes clarified.

Our purpose of developing ourselves as individuals in relationship with God and our purpose of recognizing God's unity complement one another. Personal development primes us to recognize God's unity. In fact, in general, our perception of God and reality is a consequence of who we have become. Similarly, our recognition of God is the basis of any relationship we have with Him; the end point of relationship will come with our recognition of God's unity.

But if the historical process is structured to reveal God's unity, how can we face the challenges necessary for individual development? Like the revelation of God's unity, the proper context within which we develop self is the succession of kingdoms that have conquered us. These two processes are really one and the same.

In the third section we trace the process of self-creation. We are charged with the responsibility to create true selfhood, which is the self attached to God. We cannot create that which already exists. Therefore, God's attachment to us must be hidden, which, for all its darkness, is nothing more than the opportunity to create self.

An individual through the course of his life faces a characteristic pattern of oblivion to the centrality of his attachment to the Creator against which he must labor to give birth to himself as a whole person. This is experienced as a succession of four primary inclinations each arising through the perversion of a facet of personality that exists to serve as a means to connect with God.

We have physical energy to do mitzvot. But when that energy becomes an end unto itself we are consumed by lust. We have a sense of self, allowing us to emulate God's kingship by ruling over our environment as His representative. Untamed, however, it deteriorates into the desire for power. We have an intellect to receive Torah and understand reality as an expression of spiritual existence. But unchecked it jealously usurps the role of defining reality for the sake of man. And we have a root self connecting us to God that, if allowed to atrophy, leaves us empty, inadequate, and prone to violence, whether physical or verbal. By sequentially overcoming each of the inclinations as they arise and confining each corrupted facet of personality to its proper role, we, in effect, create our entire self.

We strive to create a self attached to God because God created in order to have relationship with us. The common inclinations we all meet provide a general structure for the challenges that must be faced to achieve this relationship. But the Creator's desire for total relationship with man requires an additional level of detail that precludes any single individual giving form to all the necessary facets of personality. This is because developing certain elements of the overall relationship require contradictory circumstances. For example, to achieve full dedication to God we must battle satisfaction with the pleasures of this world, which requires that we have wealth; on the other hand, to achieve satisfaction we must battle discontent, which requires that we experience want. The Creator, therefore, relates to a generation as a whole as well as to the individual in order to separate out and distribute the responsibilities that must be filled to achieve relationship with man in all of its facets.

But a single generation is also insufficient to achieve all that is needed. The precise challenge faced in making any choice is also affected by the cultural background against which the choice is made — for example choosing true faith from a context of idolatry is different from choosing it from a context of severe secularism — each choice builds us in a different way. To develop the totality of our humanity, then, we must be faced with various cultural settings. Since each generation operates only within the context of its specific culture, just as no individual can face all challenges to actualize all of human potential, so too no single generation can face all the challenges. Rather, God's relationship with man unfolds across history.

After the sin of the Tower of Bavel, the development of God's relationship with man was narrowed to the Jewish people, to be channeled through them to the rest of humanity. The vehicle for providing the varying cultural challenges needed to bring out the totality of human potential became the Jewish people's subjugation to a succession of conquering societies, each with a culture animated by one of the inclinations we face as individuals. These are the exiles to the kingdoms of Babylon, Persia, Greece, and Rome — the very nations we said conquered us to reveal God's unity. Together with the common trials of personal development and the difficulties uniquely faced by each individual in a given generation, this historical dimension provides the full gamut of challenges against which we must use our free will to choose relationship with God and create humanity.

Since each inclination arises from a corruption of a different aspect of personality, each of these societies, by being focused on a different inclination, anchors personality in a different aspect of self. Thus, as we move from kingdom to kingdom, not only does the inclination we face and the cultural context in which we face it change, the "we" who is facing it also changes — our experience of self is very different in each of these exiles. As we travel through history the locus of our personality shifts toward facets that are increasingly delineated and seemingly complete unto themselves.

In the midst of all of these various cultural contexts, we strive for relationship with God, which ultimately means recognizing His unity. This Oneness, however, contradicts the independent self. So the more strongly we perceive our self, the more compromised is our recognition of God's omnipotence. As we move through the historical process, shifting our focus of personality to increasingly sophisticated and independent facets of self, the challenge to recognize God's unity shifts and intensifies in tandem.

We are initially focused in our more physical aspects. When corrupt, these aspects are experienced as desires that, though very powerful, do not define us; when centered in them we still crave dedication to an external Authority. Babylon and Persia, cultures centered on power and lust, were thus idol worshipping societies, each founded on a form of idolatry appropriate to its inclination. While in exile to these countries, we needed to develop ourselves in the larger context of choosing worship of the One God over idols. Greece and Rome, on the other hand, were cultures arising from man centering himself in the intellectual and spiritual facets of personality. Corruptions in these spheres lead man to define the world for himself and deny any larger context, or at least the relevance of any larger context. When under the rule of these cultures, the struggle to develop relationship with the unitary God was and is against inclinations to deny the legitimacy of worship or to substitute ourselves as the object of our worship.

The challenges against which we must struggle to develop self determine the challenges against which we must struggle to recognize God's unity. A single, integrated historical process presents us with the medium through which to attain both selfhood and full recognition of God.

*   *   *

The way we have presented God's selective hidings both in an individual's life and in the life of the nation understands them to be an intrinsic part of the process of creation — the necessary context for the full expression of man's free will to develop himself and recognize God. Our own responsibility for the hiding of God's face must also be recognized. When we sin, either as an individual or nationally, there are consequences. These consequences are called in Hebrew *onesh*, from the root *nash*, meaning "fall away." Through sin we internally distance ourselves from God and change the starting point from which relationship must be achieved. The *onesh* for this is the process by which God hides Himself to actualize the distance we have created. This awakens our innate desire for relationship and creates the circumstances that allow us to repent and recover closeness. Distance is experienced as pain, thus we associate it with punishment; but the pain is directly purposeful, which is why the association can be misleading. The term "*onesh*" more precisely captures the meaning, for the painful distance is not punitive. Rather, the distance causes the effects of sin to "fall away" allowing us to continue our project of building connection with God. *Onesh* is forward looking.

For example, when we as a nation were overwhelmed by our inclination for power and began running our lives as if power was our defining value, we created an internal distance between ourselves and God. Our *onesh*, the actualization of that distance, was to elevate the inclination for power to dominance in man globally, which resulted in the ascendance of Babylon, the nation whose culture was intrinsically based on that inclination. They then conquered us, allowing us to experience the full implications of our distance while we still had enough spiritual strength to react and return to our true focus on creating relationship with God. The concept of *onesh* provides us with another lens through which to analyze our history of exile — how the principal inclinations of pleasure, power, jealousy, and contempt sequentially came to dominate us leading to exiles to the corresponding kingdoms.

These two modes of God's hiding — that intrinsically built into creation to advance relationship and that consequent to our transgressions to recover relationship — actually complement one another and form one integrated system. This is because when we return to God from the distance created by sin, our *teshuvah* (repentance) does not merely recover the ground that was lost. A relationship that is broken cannot be restored in its original form; once the aspect of self that served as the foundation of the connection suffers corruption its defenses are weakened and it is forever susceptible to renewed breakdown. Achieving *teshuvah* requires that we shift the focus of our personality to a higher aspect of self in order to regain relationship with God. Our transgression catalyzes God's hiding, which then pushes us beyond our original starting point, pressing us not only to recover what was lost, but also to move forward in developing our relationship.

History is the process of man achieving complete relationship with God, which is synonymous with man completing himself. It is the ongoing story of progress, failure, recovery, and continued progress toward this goal. The overall project is one for humanity as a whole over time. Each individual in each generation plays his part by facing his unique challenge in order to create his appointed facet of personality, adding his piece to the achievement of his generation. The work of each generation is conserved so that successive generations do not need to accomplish what was already done. They merely need to complete their appointed task, which is then added to the composite accomplishments of mankind until, over the course of time, we create all facets of humanity that connect us to God.

This understanding of the process of human development answers an otherwise deeply troubling question that nags at us as we contemplate history. How can we expect mankind to achieve its purpose and bring history to its conclusion when each successive generation seems further from God than the one preceding it? The Talmud does state that the *Mashiach* will come either in a generation that is totally righteous or totally guilty. We could throw up our hands and say we are going the second route. But the "totally guilty" option means the *Mashiach* comes because there is no longer hope of our creating salvation, so there is no purpose in continuing the process. Relying on this option conveniently absolves us of responsibility but does not conform to our situation. Our free will is still operating; people are growing. We can act. But how can our actions be understood to meaningfully advance the process when earlier generations, who were operating on a much higher level, could not conclude the project? Our understanding of development answers this question. As we come closer and closer to the historical goal of humanity achieving complete self, we as individuals do not need to become more complete, for we are part of a larger process. In fact, just the opposite is true.

If we return for a moment to the development of an individual — which is always our model for understanding the historical development of mankind — we find that the facet of self in which our personality is focused, and therefore the locus of corruption upon which we must work, goes from the most physical to the more spiritual over the course of a lifetime. We might think, therefore, that people become more spiritual as they age but, again, the opposite is the case.

The reason for this is that the spiritual greatness of a person does not reside in his individuality. A human being is a composite of his individuality and his connection to God, and it is that connection to God that gives man his distinct greatness. As we mentioned a moment ago, when we are focused in our more physical aspects, even when they are corrupted, they do not exclude spiritual connection; they merely pervert its nature. But at least there is some form of connection. The intellectual and spiritual corruptions of the later cultures actually exclude spiritual awareness entirely. Thus, for example, we find simultaneous with the rise of Greece the loss from human experience of prophecy and any instinct for worship. Though an extreme diminution in the depth of man's experience of reality, it was still progress in the sense of providing the new challenge of a barren secular context from which to strive toward spiritual awareness and develop new facets of human potential.

The job of each generation is not to create all facets of relationship with God, only the specific one that is uniquely its responsibility. For this reason, though we presently experience spiritual poverty, this does not reflect on our success or failure in leading humanity over time to relationship with God. The spiritual desolation of our generation merely defines our task. As painful as it is to bear, it is our opportunity to create that which no generation before us was able to create. Earlier generations took for granted the foundation of their connection with God — their recognition of His existence and omnipotence; because they had *emunah*, they could not create it. Our generation's complete lack of spiritual intuition allows us to create that very foundation.

In the fourth section we examine the nature of modern experience to understand precisely the challenge we face today as we strive to achieve selfhood through gaining faith in God's existence and singular control of events.

Our present experience is an extension of the secular, man-centered mode of awareness that blossomed when Greece rose to empire and the inclination for idol worship passed. It reached maturity under the dominion of Rome, when all genuine connection to internal depth was lost. Though our present society is a direct cultural descendant of Rome, the unadulterated secular vision that specifically characterizes modernity emerged around the time of Descartes. It was then that all respect for tradition was rejected to clear the way for constructing a purely rational vision of reality based on the observations of man filtered through logic.

We are capable of knowing the world in different ways. Each mode of knowing emanates from and speaks to a different facet of character. For example, scientific vision arises from our analytic self and artistic vision arises from our aesthetic self. How we know the world reflects where we are centered in ourselves. And when we know the world a particular way, we further reinforce the specific part of our personality from which that way of knowing stems. Our modern vision processes observation almost exclusively through the rational intellect, so the aspect of self we awaken to in the act of knowing is centered in rationality.

While intellect is a refined aspect of the self that was created to serve spiritual ends, unto itself it is a product of physical as opposed to spiritual reality — that is, intellect is from the realm broken off from God. Its domination of the self results in an inner experience lacking any genuine connection to spirituality. Unlike the more crude physical aspects that were the self's center in earlier generations, when intellect is in control it rejects external definition even from a spiritual source.

Greece's intellectual focus was the result of the self being centered in the intellect. Since intellect is not material, this center at least attributed reality to nonmaterial, quasi-spiritual existence, yielding a relatively rich inner experience. For example, Greece related to aesthetics not as a quality of material but as a fundamental aspect of reality, with material its vessel of expression.

The root of Roman experience, however, is not the intellect. Rather, intellect is the medium through which we experience awareness. But that awareness originates in a deeper place, from where we should sense our root connection to Transcendence. But that place can only be reached through *mesirut nefesh* (self sacrifice), and when that sacrifice is missing we are left with emptiness. By default, we focus almost exclusively on material existence, resulting in a disastrously shallow experience of being. Spiritual concepts lack any vital internal reference — leaving them without substance. Our sense of God, for example, is so weak under Rome that we can confuse Him with a man, or ourselves with primary being. Our isolation from meaningful levels of being leaves us with a gnawing sense of inadequacy that bubbles below the surface of our consciousness.

The Roman intellect encounters the world as a subject observing objects, which restricts what we can know about reality to the appearance of things, as opposed to their actual existence or being, bolstering our anchor in an external, purely physical reality. Rationality focused on physical existence results in scientific thinking. Through science we probe nature to the point where we can manipulate it with sufficient precision and power to foster a compelling illusion of human control over reality. This further undermines any ability to appreciate God and His singular omnipotence.

Since intellect rejects definitions that come from outside it, we formulate our own vision of the world. By determining reality from our own perspective, we are placed at the center of existence, facing out. We are elevated to the status of God, becoming the judges of reality while the resulting structure of our knowledge necessarily relegates God to the status of an element in our world. Regardless of what we might proclaim about His omnipotence, the power we can authentically attribute to Him is limited. This leaves us subject to the false limitation placed on God's unitary omnipotence that characterizes this exile — the presumption that God is subject to laws. In the early generations of this exile we faced this primarily in the Christian form, where God was understood to be incapable of forgiving the Jews. In the more modern form this same error presents itself as requiring God's oversight of the world to conform to our scientific understanding of the laws of nature.

We are very far from our goal of recognizing God's singular omnipotence. How are we to move forward? Perhaps we can open the Torah and, through its deeper insight into reality, reawaken our deeper self. When we look to the Torah, however, instead of adding depth to our understanding, we find ourselves presented with what seems to be an alien, imaginary world.

It should not surprise us that the Torah's vision is foreign to us. Though Torah speaks about physical reality, it knows physical reality from the perspective of our deepest self, that part of us that emerges into individual being from the Creator. Just as at that level of self we are a spiritual being entering physical reality to take on expression, so, too, at that level of self we perceive the world as a spiritual reality taking on expression through physical existence. Science, however, knows the world from the perspective of the isolated, rational self, cut off from spirituality, and knowing itself — and therefore the world — as a wholly physical reality. Since we, too, in the context of this exile are centered in our rational self, the Torah vision looks foreign.

In the body of the book we compared the relationship between Torah's and science's vision of reality to the contrasting experiences of a music connoisseur and a deaf man at a jazz concert. The two concertgoers have very different experiences. Though both experiences are real, they are not equal. The deaf man has certainly missed the essence of the event because he is focused on an area that is secondary to the event's purpose.

Actually, the relationship is more complex than what this metaphor can convey. At the concert, both the visual and the audio components equally exist; what the eyes see is simply much less important. Modernity's vision of a purely physical world governed by physical causality and resolvable through science is not merely less significant than the Torah vision. Though it accurately corresponds to our experience, the world as we perceive it through modern awareness is real in only an ambiguous sense.

The grant of free will we spoke about in section two not only allows us to choose how we react to situations; through free will we also determine the nature of the situations we encounter. We are in a relationship with God and, as in any relationship, the attention of one party mirrors the attention of the other. God relates to us based on the way that we relate to Him. But since an aspect of God's relationship to us is the reality in which we live, our attitude toward Him establishes the form of our reality. The natural perspective of modern man, which excludes God's relevant involvement in events, results in a world that responds as if it were almost exclusively natural. The modern perspective accurately understands the functioning of the world not because it has access to truth in any ontological sense of the word, but because the way we look at the world determines the general nature of the world's functioning.

There are, however, deeper levels to reality, ones that approach actual existence as opposed to functional fantasies created by our errant free will. These deeper levels correspond to the deeper levels of our humanity and allow genuine connection to the Creator — the only true existence. But they are only accessible by those deeper facets of our personality. Most of us are no longer anchored in the depths of our being. We are located in very physical parts of ourselves that genuinely relate only to a more physical world. Therefore, though the Torah vision reflects reality and the modern vision does not, most of us experience reality in a manner reflected in the modern vision and not in the Torah vision, making the modern vision seem real to us and the Torah vision surreal.

It was not always so. When the Jews wandered through the desert after departing *Mitzrayim*, they were focused in their inner, spiritual essence and connected to reality within the context of an unmediated relationship with God. The laws of nature had minimal impact on their day-to-day functioning. With the passage of time, as our identity shifted to parts of ourselves increasingly distant from our connection to God, our reality became structured more and more by natural law as opposed to direct Divine oversight. The destruction of the Second Temple marked the watershed after which it became nearly impossible for anyone, even Torah greats, to achieve an unadulterated focus on God and retain a relationship of revealed, direct oversight. Effectively, no one can remain above physical reality to the extent that they can honestly ignore the functioning of nature observed by science, such as in matters of health and medicine. Not that this is a replacement for Divine oversight. Rather, it is the reality of relationship with God when we are distant. For the person truly defined by Torah, natural causality is nothing more than the medium through which God indirectly relates to us as a measure-for-measure response to our alienation from the aspect of our self that is truly connected to Him.

But the scientific perspective claims, at least intuitively, an all-encompassing vision that either excludes or at least limits God's relationship with man. The overwhelming majority of us are subject to this claim of science and struggle to develop our relationship with God in the face of its pull. This is the challenge of modernity: to seek genuine relationship with God and recognize His singular omnipotence in the context of an impoverished inner experience that saps any sense of reality from spirituality. This diminishes our concept of God, inflates our own status, and focuses us in physical reality in a manner that gives us seeming control over our world. How are we to proceed?

For us to read the Torah and expect to jump to its perspective is unrealistic. Since we are not anchored in the aspect of humanity naturally associated with Torah, presuming to adopt the Torah vision would be fantasy, for it does not relate to reality as we experience it. If we want to achieve a deeper perspective that is grounded, and thus awaken our truer self, we need to build from where we are toward this deeper vision.

The Oral Torah is the aspect of Torah that allows us to recover a deeper perception of reality even when we are not centered in our depths. In prophetic times, when our perception was based in our spiritual being, the prophetic Written Torah spoke directly to us and the Oral Torah played the role of bridging spiritual concepts to physical reality. Through the Oral Torah we unraveled the particular details of actions by which ideals could be expressed. But eventually we ceased perceiving reality from the vantage of the soul. This was evident in the passing of prophecy from human experience and the loss of any inclination to worship, which both occurred as Greece rose to empire and our modern perspective was born. At that time the basis of our awareness shifted from our spiritual self to our physical being.

After this change the Oral Torah continues its role of bridging physical expression and the spiritual principles of the prophetic Written Torah that are its basis. But the Oral Torah's direction has reversed. Through it we now derive, from the detailed expression of ideals, what those ideals are and how every element of our world is perceived from a spiritual perspective. This gives us the ability to recover our spiritual vision from the midst of the physical world in which we stand, even though spirituality is no longer intuitive.

Man sees himself reflected in his world. When we build meticulously from where we actually stand and genuinely regain the spiritual view, we awaken the deeper part of ourselves to which it speaks. The Oral Torah is our ladder to climb out of the pit of modern consciousness. The Oral Torah is essential to the continued connection of the Jewish people to God. But only a few individuals master it to the point of recovering spirituality. The rest of us have an obligation to be connected to these individuals by connecting ourselves to Torah. But our contribution to the project of relationship with God does not come through immersion in the Oral Torah. What is our part in actively advancing this relationship?

There is a basic corruption of character that led us to adopt the modern perspective that is the root of our problem. Repairing this is everyone's responsibility. This obligation is more fundamental than the mastery of Torah, for Torah can also be tainted if not approached with the proper character. The primary inclination that drove us to adopt the modern perspective — in spite of the profound loss of self that came in its wake — was a desire for control. We must devote our efforts to curb and redirect this craving.

The soul's perspective recognizes that God is the only one who determines what happens in existence. This is God's quality of unique and singular omnipotence. We do not change the world directly. Our actions are no more than requests for blessing from God, with their actual results dependent upon our overall relationship with Him. The modern perspective ignores God's mediation, attributing to man direct influence upon his environment. This brings with it a loss of self and a loss of genuine connection to God. Self is lost because we must be focused superficially to perceive ourselves as in control; genuine connection to God is lost because by attributing to ourselves this control we effectively compete with God, diminishing Him beyond recognition. Since our self is the only thing we have and our connection to God is the only thing we truly desire, this is an unacceptable cost. But to recover this self and connection we must transcend our present perspective. This requires that we deal directly with our confusion over control.

The task is made difficult by the seeming power we have acquired through our insight into the workings of nature. At the same time, the challenge is eased by the obvious loss of self and self-control that has accompanied this physical insight, revealing the inadequacy of our present mode of being in the world. Exceptional individuals can directly recover the clarity that the consequences of our actions come from God. Most of us, the nation as a whole, are unable to voluntarily break away from our addiction to power — at least according to precedent.

The salvation in Persia commemorated on Purim provides a paradigm for recovering full relationship with God. It reflects our present situation, for our opponent was a representative of Rome and its worldview — Haman. Haman assumed personal control of the world and sought to replace God with himself. He appeared all-powerful. We could not challenge Haman; in fact, it appeared that nothing could challenge Haman. We were forced to turn to God for our salvation and, when we did, within three days Haman was dead, with all of his wealth, power, and influence shifted to Mordechai, the leader of the Jews. A force that appeared omnipotent pressed us to *teshuvah* and then was washed away before God. The fact that God is One was revealed along with our true dependence on Him.

In Persia, it took the threat of annihilation to force an awareness of our own powerlessness and catalyze the repentance required to return control to God. Contemplating the likely threat that could bring such a result today is chilling. We retain, however, the individual option of deepening our personal awareness of God, each one of us on his own level. If we can become a nation of such individuals we can circumvent the need for such extreme intervention. We remain with the choice to be. Let us seize it.

APPENDIX 2

The Media:
A Modern Gathering of Straw[1]

A S WE CONSIDER HOW to respond to the intrusion of technology into our lives we easily ignore one of its most important effects. Discussions about the Internet, for example, often focus on the temptation to visit inappropriate sites with content that is spiritually harmful and, potentially, destroys lives. While this danger is real, there is a much more pervasive influence from Internet that, while less extreme on an individual level, is profoundly affecting our community because of its commonality. Even when viewing innocuous material — news, cute videos, occasional shopping — the Internet, perhaps even more than TV, provides easy, inviting, and potentially endless diversion. And while surfing the Internet we are not likely to be probing the depths of our souls. Though pages can be found with genuinely meaningful content, their rarity confirms that the Web does not facilitate encounters with the roots of our being. Similarly, after screening out inappropriate material from TV, the shock lies in the astonishing banality of the programming. As these media shunt our minds into superficial layers of personality, they powerfully support the cell phones, iPods, and pocket video devices that modern society has supplied to distract us from being alone with ourselves. If we think this distractedness is merely an irritating

---

1. This article appeared in a slightly altered form in the first issue of *Dialogue* magazine.

addition to the real challenges of modern life, a study of the origins of exile teaches us otherwise.

Exile is a process of repair. Some lack exists in the Jewish people. Since the Jewish people are complete through their relationship with the Creator, any lack is necessarily a lack in our closeness and connection to Him. Paradoxically, the path to repair lies in exile, where we are drawn even further away from Him. God allows our internal distance from Him to be actualized in the world, resulting in our painful subjugation to foreign powers. This burns out the dross in our personalities that caused the distance in the first place. And because the very basis of Jewish personality lies in our connection to God, this distance also creates a buildup of desire to return to Him, eventually leading to the *teshuvah* (repentance) and *tefillah* (prayer) that bring redemption. With the circumstances separating us from God removed, we rush toward Him with a force that results in a much tighter bond with Him than had existed prior to the cycle of exile and redemption.

Since the goal is the resulting closeness, the success of exile depends upon the distance from God that we reach. Like a rubber band that is stretched, the eventual closeness between the two ends depends upon how far they are pulled apart before being released. So, too, the depth of suffering and longing that eventually bring salvation determine the level of subsequent closeness we attain.[2]

This process can be seen in our experience in *Mitzrayim* (Egypt). The Sages identify four decrees made by Pharaoh that were each a distinct attempt to destroy the strength and will of the Jewish people: the decree of heavy labor, the command that the midwives murder all boys at birth, the killing of all boys born at a certain period, and the requirement that the Jews collect their own straw for making bricks.[3] Each affliction had a specific purpose and each ended up facilitating exactly what it was meant to prevent.

---

2. *Shemot Rabbah* 6:4; *Seforno, Devarim* 16:3.
3. *Shemot Rabbah* 1:12, 1:13, 1:18, 5:18.

The decree of heavy labor was intended to stop the growth of the Jews by forcing the men to sleep in the fields, thus cutting them off from their wives. Instead, the women followed their men and met them in the fields.[4] Moreover, the intense work broke any pridefulness in the men, purifying them spiritually. This allowed them to reach the heights from which *tzelem Elokim* (the image of God) is brought into the world, vastly accelerating the rate at which they multiplied.[5]

Once the first decree failed to curb Jewish growth, Pharaoh commanded the midwives to kill all male children at birth. His intent was to eliminate the carriers of tradition and thus erase any independent identity in the Jews so that the women could be absorbed into *Mitzrayim*. But Pharaoh's command forced these midwives to choose between upholding their defining values and protecting themselves. They chose their values — instead of killing the children, they attended to them even more than usual.[6] The midwives were Yocheved and Miriam, the future mother and sister of Moshe. As a reward for their courage and dedication they were blessed with descendants who brought Torah to the world and founded the houses of priesthood and kingship.[7] These are the three pillars of our relationship with God[8] and, therefore, the defining institutions of our unique national identity.[9]

The third decree came when Pharaoh's astrologers reported the birth of the savior of the Jews. Pharaoh responded by ordering that all boys born at that time, whether Egyptian or Jew, should be thrown into

---

4. *Shemot Rabbah* 1:12.

5. Maharal, *Gevurot HaShem*, ch. 15.

6. *Shemot Rabbah* 1:15.

7. *Shemot Rabbah* 1:17. Moshe received the Torah. Aharon, his brother, founded the line of the priests. King David descended from Miriam. Torah is not mentioned in this *midrash* because the verse tells us the midwives merited "houses," meaning an inherited status. Priesthood and kingship are inherited, but Torah is not. Rather, Torah is earned by each individual who acquires it. That Yocheved also merited Moshe because of this act of courage can be found in *Shemot Rabbah* 40:1.

8. *Pirkei Avot* 4:13.

9. Maharal, *Gevurot HaShem*, ch. 60.

the Nile.[10] To mask from the astrologers that Moshe had eluded death, he was sent floating down the river in a reed basket, only to be picked up by Pharaoh's daughter and brought to Pharaoh's palace. This was the only place Moshe could develop into the leader of the Jews.[11]

The pattern was consistent. Pharaoh's affliction created whatever repair was needed in the nation — *galut* created *geulah*. The pattern broke down, however, with the final decree. Though the Jews had been making bricks since the first decree, the final decree added that the Jews collect the straw needed to make those bricks. This catalyzed the actual redemption. But unlike the other afflictions that pushed the Jews to a deeper spirituality or commitment, thus building them as a people, this one threatened their destruction, requiring God to act. What was this decree all about?

The decree of the straw was promulgated by Pharaoh as he faced an enlarged Jewish population with an intensified national identity and led by an aggressive leader who was demanding their freedom. All of Pharaoh's efforts at weakening the Jews as a nation had failed. There remained only one point of attack — the individual. The decree of the straw was aimed at destroying the Jews as individuals by dissolving their personalities.

At first glance the harshness of collecting straw is hidden. What could it add to the heavy labor of constructing bricks and buildings — straw is light? The Gra points out the insidious logic behind the decree. As opposed to heavy work, from which a laborer has no choice but to rest, light work can be pursued continuously.[12] The addition of the requirement of straw meant that whenever the Jews were not building, they were collecting. There was no longer any such thing as rest.

The Midrash tells us that the Jews had scrolls that spoke of an impending redemption. They read them on Shabbat — which sustained them. The decree of the straw took away Shabbat and, so, took away

---

10. *Shemot Rabbah* 1:18.
11. Maharal, *Gevurot HaShem*, ch. 18.
12. *Peirush HaGra, Shir HaShirim* 2:7.

hope.[13] But breaks in time have a more basic significance to us. We learn in the beginning of *Sefer Vayikra* that the purpose of pauses is to allow for contemplation.[14] When we first learn something we can only understand it on a surface level — we need time to think about it more deeply, compare it to the other things we know, integrate it with the rest of our knowledge, and internalize it. Just as we need time to deepen our understanding of Torah, we need time to understand the events of our lives. When things happen rapidly without a moment to inquire after the meaning of our experiences or link them to our deeper self, our awareness becomes centered in increasingly shallow layers of our self, pulling the anchor of our personality with it.

The significance of this thinning of the self is revealed by Moshe. At a certain point, Moshe killed an Egyptian to stop his beating a Jew. The next day he saw two Jews fighting. When he intervened they taunted him, "Who made you our judge? Will you kill us as you did the Egyptian?"[15] We are then told, "Moshe was afraid and said, 'Then the matter is known.'"[16] Though these words have a straightforward meaning — Moshe's killing of the Egyptian was public knowledge and there was reason to fear he would be caught — the Midrash understands them on another level. "The matter is known" refers to the answer to a question that had troubled Moshe — why the Jewish people were subject to such a painful exile. Seeing Jews who spoke about things that should be kept secret, he understood that they were deserving of exile. Moreover, he was afraid perhaps they did not merit redemption.[17]

This startling interpretation by the *midrash* is explained by Maharal.[18] People are either centered inside themselves or outside themselves. When a person knows something he must bring it to his center for it to

13. *Shemot Rabbah* 5:18.
14. *Rashi, Vayikra* 1:1 from *Torat Kohanim*. See also Ramchal, *Mesillat Yesharim*, ch. 2.
15. *Shemot* 2:14.
16. Ibid.
17. *Rashi, Shemot* 2:14.
18. Maharal, *Gur Aryeh, Shemot* 2:14.

be alive for him. A person who is externally centered must talk about all that he knows. Someone who is internally centered can hold that which he knows within him. The existence of Jews who talked openly about a matter that could cause another's death — that which should be kept secret — indicated that the anchor of Jewish personality had shifted outward.

Why would this spell exile and place in doubt the possibility of redemption? Because the Jews exist as a nation for their relationship with God and that can only be discovered and cultivated internally. The external world is physical. Our only possibility for seeing beyond this physical shell to its Divine source is to be focused in the part of us that is aware of its connection to that Divine source — our *penimiut*, or internal self. Only from that vantage point can we recognize the deeper reality.

The fact that some Jews revealed secrets indicated that, as a people, we were losing our center in that internal place. The only reason for redemption is to recover our connection to God. That recovery is dependent upon our being defined by that connection so that releasing enslavement results in a rush back to our defining closeness. If we were no longer centered in that connection, the process would not work.

The incident with Moshe took place long before Pharaoh had required the Jews to collect straw. But it reveals the destructiveness of losing our inner focus and defines the essence of distance from God. And if this is the essence of distance, it is also the ultimate direction toward which the process of exile pulls us as it builds the energy that, when released, will result in complete closeness and relationship with God.

The instrument for bringing this distance in *Mitzrayim* was the straw — the relentless work that stole from the Jews the pauses in life that allowed for inner focus. That loss of focus defines the core of the experience of exile. The *Chumash* hints to this at the dawn of Jewish exile in *Parashat* (portion) *Vayechi* at the end of *Sefer Bereishit*. Usually, an extra space — indicative of a pause — is left between words that form the transition from one *parashah* to the next. As we move from *Parashat Vayigash* to *Parashat Vayechi*, however, that extra space is missing. The Midrash tells us this was because the enslavement to *Mitzrayim* began from the death of Yaakov recorded in *Parashat Vayechi*.[19] Exile is thus intimated by a lack of space, a lack of pause. The opposite is also true — *geulah* (redemption) brings with it *shirah* (song). The sections of *shirah* are written in the Torah with extra spaces, marking the depth of insight of the *ruach ha-kodesh* (Divine inspiration) that powers *shirah*.[20]

The decree of the straw, as well as causing the externalization of personality in the exile to *Mitzrayim*, also hinted at how the process worked. The straw was needed for building bricks. The role of the straw was to bind each brick together. The strongest materials are made up of a hard but brittle solid to which is added some extended material that binds the solid, preventing it from fracturing. The metal poles in reinforced concrete and the fibers in resin forming fiberglass all work the same way. The straw added this connectedness to the clay in the bricks. When the Jews lacked the straw that connects the brick together and had to work ceaselessly to find it, all connectedness was lost from their life experience. The absence of any breaks in the labor meant they had no time to be aware of themselves as individuals, process their experiences and string them into a continuous, coherent life. It shattered their experience into a succession of disconnected events destroying any sense of a unified self.

The unity of our personality, like all unities, lies in the spiritual realm, ultimately emanating from the Oneness of God. The self that we have any access to is composed of the *nefesh, ruach,* and *neshamah*. The *nefesh* is our physical animation. The *ruach* is our sense of autonomous awareness that connects our distinct physical being to our spiritual consciousness. The *neshamah* is that spiritual consciousness — our awareness of connection to a higher, transcendent Source.[21] After the decree of the straw came into force, the *Chumash* tells us that when Moshe promised the coming of redemption the Jews could no longer accept what he was

---

19. *Rashi, Bereishit* 47:28.

20. Rav Gedaliah Shor, *Ohr Gedaliyahu, Vayechi*.

21. *Nefesh HaChayim* 1:14–15 and Maharal, *Derech HaChayim* 4:22.

saying because of "*kotzer ruach*," a shortness of *ruach*.[22] The *ruach* had become too "short" to reach to the spiritual *neshamah* so they could no longer comprehend the possibility of redemption. With the spiritual source of their unity of personality beyond reach, the Jews, as individuals, began to disassociate and disintegrate as coherent personalities.

At this point Moshe, as leader of the Jews, turned to God and in effect said, "We cannot take this anymore."[23] God responded by saying in so many words, "In that case I will take you out immediately, but you must know that this means the Jews will require exile in the future."[24] *Galut* creates *geulah*, exile creates redemption — distance, when the force causing it is removed, results in closeness. But then if the suffering of *galut* and the distance it represents does not reach its full extent, the consequent closeness and relationship will also be incomplete and future *galut* will be required.[25]

The *midrash* makes clear that Moshe's plea cut short the process of repair of the Jewish people. When the Jews were required to collect the straw they still needed to make as many bricks as before. When they fell short of their quota, Jewish children were placed in the brickwork to replace the missing bricks.[26] Moshe cried out in anguish over this and God said to him in so many words, "If you are not happy with the way I run my world take a child out and see what happens." Moshe removed a child from a building. It turned out to be Michah,[27] who was responsible for the building of the *egel ha-zahav*, the golden calf.[28] That which would have been destroyed by the *galut* had Moshe not intervened caused the sin that brought the decree of future exile.

This is not to say that Moshe was wrong in contending that the

---

22. *Shemot* 6:9.
23. *Shemot* 5:21–23.
24. *Rashi, Shemot* 6:1. This is the effective upshot of prophesying that Moshe would not enter the Land. See Maharal, *Netzach Yisrael*, ch. 33.
25. See Ohr HaChayim, *Shemot* 3:8.
26. *Rashi, Sanhedrin* 101b.
27. Ibid.
28. *Rashi, Shemot* 32:4.

Jews could not have survived the afflictions of *Mitzrayim* any longer.[29] They had reached the forty-ninth level of *tumah* (impurity) and the *geulah* needed to begin immediately. Had they left a moment later than they did, they would have been lost.[30] But it still remains true that the Exodus came before the preparations necessary to achieve complete closeness were finished. The first three decrees of Pharaoh reached their full severity and resulted in their intended repair to the Jewish people in *Mitzrayim*. But the final affliction of the straw was not able to reach the point where it could catalyze total closeness to God. As a result, future exiles were needed to pull us to where the decree of straw was pointing us — far enough from our internal center to trigger the return to God that will complete history.

Every subsequent exile has had its focal inclination upon which to base a false vision of self and distract us from our true center. There was power-hungry Bavel, licentious Persia, and honor-seeking Greece.[31] Now, in the later stages of our final exile to Rome, the process is unmasked, reaching its full, unadulterated expression. Instead of being distracted by an inclination, the inclination we face is the inclination to distraction — with Internet, TV, iPod, cell phone, and video serving as facilitators. This temptation is not a side point of our *galut*. It is the essence of the *galut*,[32] threatening our destruction by undermining our ability to connect to reality in a way that allows for true relationship with God. We are once again lacking straw. Our challenge is to retain a grip on our internal self and genuine connection to God against the pressure of these forces until *teshuvah* brings *geulah*, allowing our unmitigated embrace of God.

In *Mitzrayim*, however, when collecting the straw brought the Jews to a distance from God approaching what was necessary to bring a total

---

29. Implicit in *Ohr HaChayim, Shemot* 3:8.
30. *HaAlshich, Shemot*, ch. 12 from the *Zohar*.
31. Maharal, *Ner Mitzvah* and Chapter 10.
32. The relationship between this distraction and *sinat chinam* will be discussed in a moment.

geulah, they began to break down and had to be taken out. How, then, asks the Ohr HaChayim, can we be brought to this distance in modern exile? How can we remain intact long enough to repair what needs to be repaired and transform it into the ultimate closeness to God? He answers that in *Mitzrayim* the Jews did not have Torah whereas today we have Torah.[33]

The Ohr HaChayim presumably meant that, despite the powerful pulls on our personality toward superficiality and the fracturing that is its consequence, our involvement in Torah allows us to remain centered around our inner spiritual root. At the very least, Torah gives us the spiritual perspective on reality of that spiritual root so that, regardless of where we are naturally drawn in our personality, we remain connected to that inner place. This function of Torah would have served as the necessary counterweight to the burden of the straw had we had Torah in *Mitzrayim*. It certainly served this purpose against the enforced, grinding poverty of Poland and Russia.

But the Ohr HaChayim's comment takes on another meaning in today's world where instead of being faced with relentless hoeing to survive, we are choosing endless movie downloads to entertain. From the perspective of today, the Ohr HaChayim tells us that Torah presents us with the only vision sufficiently compelling and the only endeavor sufficiently engaging to compete with our inclination to easy distraction.

What is so compelling about the Torah? To answer this we must begin by asking what the attraction is of modern media. At first glance it is hard to understand how a *yetzer* (inclination) for something so empty can be so strong. Phrasing the question this way recalls a *midrash*:

In the future all animals will gather around the snake and ask, "A lion crushes and eats, a fox shreds and eats, but you, what pleasure do you have from biting and poisoning?" The snake will answer, "And what pleasure is there to one who speaks *lashon ha-ra* (slander)?"[34]

---

33. *Ohr HaChayim, Shemot* 3:8.
34. *Yalkut Vayikra* 14:559.

There is no pleasure in *lashon ha-ra*. Why do we speak it? Because we are empty. We feel the poverty of our own selfhood and we protect ourselves from guilt and pain by slandering everyone around us to convince ourselves that it is impossible for a human being to be any better. The prevalence of *lashon ha-ra* in our day testifies to a deep and endemic emptiness. The attraction of different forms of media is a consequence of this same emptiness. We are drawn to media not because of what it is but because of what it is not. It is not us. We seek distraction from our selves because of our inner vacuum. This explains the success of media despite its poor quality and blandness. A show does not need to be great to serve its purpose of relieving us of awareness of our own painfully inadequate self. If it is truly entertaining that is better. But if not, we will watch it anyway.

We have been discussing distraction as the defining *yetzer* of our times. Yet, we know that *sinat chinam* (baseless hatred) and *lashon ha-ra* are the basis of our difficulties.[35] We explained earlier, however, that our hatred of others is also based on our inner vacuum.[36] Distraction and *sinah* are two sides of the same coin. Our underlying problem in this, our last *galut*, is that we are empty.

Our humanity, our center, is our connection to God. In previous *galuyot* we experienced our center corruptly — our connection was distorted through idolatry or its equivalent. In this *galut* our true humanity, our connection to God, is too weak to be experienced at all — it is absent.[37] We feel no genuine connection. We either react in rage by slandering those around us who remind us of our emptiness or we strive to forget ourselves through distraction.

The compelling nature of Torah lies in the fact that, rather than distracting us from our emptiness, it reattaches us to our true center. Though the place where our personality has become anchored is detached from God, our spiritual substructure, the *neshamah*, remains intact and

---

35. *Yoma* 9b. See Chapter 3.
36. See Chapter 3 and the end of Chapter 5.
37. See Chapters 10, pp. 181–182 and Chapter 14, p. 270–273.

rooted in Him.[38] By reconnecting with the *neshamah* we reconnect with God. Torah is the Will of God and, therefore, the perspective of the *neshamah*. By studying Torah we both accentuate the *neshamah* within us and realigned our personality with it. As our personality becomes a vessel to give expression to our *neshamah*, we become attached to it, and through it to our source in God. Since learning Torah is effectively returning home, it combines the familiarity of a recovery of self with the power of truth. Torah expresses our true being and makes us at home in our selves and our world. It resonates with us on a level far deeper than the *yetzer*.[39]

The evil inclination has the power of the vacuum and pulls the whole world after it like a horse with a ring through its nose. Alone against such a force, we lose every time.[40] But there is one thing more powerful than non-existence, and that is existence — God. Through Torah we authentically bind ourselves to Him.

The implication of this is that our approach to the challenges of media and technology should not be centered on trying to prevent people from using them to make space for Torah. Rather, our primary focus needs to be on magnifying the attraction of Torah. Rav Shach *ztz"l* said years ago that in our times when the false sweetness of the street is so available and pulls so strongly, we must emphasize the *ahavah* (love) of Torah over the *yirah* (fear) — we must push its sweetness.

We must help our children taste the *geshmack* of learning and the satisfaction of understanding; we must present them with a more powerful and more attractive alternative. Exactly how to do that is its own investigation. Realizing why it is so important to lead with Torah provides the proper context within which to explore and develop our approach. Our battle is with oblivion. Torah is our guide to our true selves, the one portal that is still open to God and meaning.

---

38. *Nefesh HaChayim* 1:18.
39. See *Vayikra Rabbah* 35:5.
40. *Sukkah* 52b.

Birkat Gevurot

G OD CREATES MAN CLOSE to him. Man, urged on by an inclination for independence, forcefully introduces distance into the relationship. Once we experience the distance, we regret our move away from God, realizing that we do want relationship. But the reality is that we have become distant. We must now create relationship under the new circumstances of distance.

The relationship of distance is one where we have to assume more responsibility. We must utilize our free will to choose connection in an environment where revelation no longer determines it. This creates us as individuals, the drive toward which, in a corrupt form, created the distance in the first place. In other words, our inclination toward ego drives us toward a more intense actualization of the goal of creation — the existence of an independent receiver, receiving good from God. This is true only in a specific sense, as explained in Chapter 7. After recovering from sin, we need to make more choices and more profound choices, taking more responsibility for who we are, intensifying our independence. Yet, on another level, the whole process of judgment must occur in a context of mercy, making our existence more dependent.

God creates through *chessed*, revelation without containment, which limits the indepent existence of the receiver. To achieve more sense of self, man distances himself from God. God becomes more hidden from man because of the distance but, also, because man's move away from

God is, by definition, sinful. This requires a relationship through *din* (judgment); a relationship of judgment is more contained because, in judgment, giving is restricted to what is deserved, not the limitless giving that the giver wants to give. Since we can never truly deserve relationship (certainly after sin), we recover it through *rachamim* (mercy), a combination of *chessed* and *din* — giving filtered through earning. Since what we get is affected by what we deserve, we are more of a participant in the relationship, accentuating our selfhood. This is kept within boundaries because it happens in a context of mercy, maintaining our dependence.

This process is reflected in the second blessing of the *Shemoneh Esrei, Atah gibor*:

> You are forever powerful, my Lord, You give life to the dead, You are abundantly able to bring salvation, You bring down the dew. You support the living through *chessed*, You give life to the dead with great *rachamim*. You support those who fall, You heal the sick, You release those who are bound, You maintain faith in those who sleep in the dust... You are reliable to bring life to the dead...

"You are forever powerful... You give life to the dead," meaning even when we kill ourselves by choosing to accentuate our ego over relationship by moving away from You (the equivalent of death), "You give life"; You reconnect to us [which is life] even in our distance. Because of this, You are powerful. Power, *gevurah*, is equivalent to *din*, containment, for it takes power to contain. Here we are saying that God is so powerful he can contain containment and connect to us even within the context of containment, bringing life out of death.

God is *rav lehoshia*, abundantly able to bring salvation, meaning able to save under all circumstances — no matter how far we move away from Him. God can restrict His expression to fit within whatever narrow confines we set for the relationship when we move away. God can hide Himself within whatever world we have created by distancing ourselves from Him. He will still be able to connect to us in a way that allows the eventual accomplishment of the goal of a relationship we choose to create, no matter how far away we set the starting point.

Thus, "You bring down the dew," meaning when we make ourselves so distant that it is inappropriate for You to reveal Your sustenance of the world through rain, You sustain the world in a hidden way through dew. With dew the true source of the water is hidden — you contain your expression even to the point where we cannot see You — a hiddenness we have made necessary through our transgressions; but You are still there.

"You support the living with *chessed*" — those that have not turned away and instead have chosen a living connection over deadening ego, You sustain through *chessed* — open, uncontained relationship.

"You give life to the dead with great *rachamim*" — those who have turned away through choosing individual ego over connection and thus made themselves dead You bring to life through *rachamim*, through *chessed* filtered through *din* which is *rachamim*. You restrict Your expression to a form that can connect to us in our distance. The restricted connection is filtered through *din* — which is an earned relationship. This allows us to create true individuality, for the relationship is unique to each person, depending on what he has earned. The drive toward individuality in a corrupt form initiated the whole process when we distanced ourselves from God in pursuit of ego (evil is the engine of growth) and through this process we repair or sanctify that energy.

"(1) You support those who fall, (2) heal the sick, (3) release those who are bound, and (4) uphold faith in those who sleep in the dust." This line hints to the exiles of the four kingdoms. When we stand up in pridefulness, defining ourselves around greatness originating in ourselves, we "fall" (the opposite of standing tall in pridefulness). This is because we are cut off from our true honor that derives from our *tzelem Elokim*, which we obscure through pridefulness. This fall comes through the conquest of Babylon, who was enamored with the pridefulness of power. After our fall, we require the constant "support" of God. We are more dependent because we rely on the mercy of God for connection when we don't deserve it. Thus, "You support those who fall."

When we become totally subject to our physical lusts, we become focused in our individuality separate from God even more intensely than through pride, we become "sick" (the opposite of experiencing physical pleasure. Our physical aspect brings us suffering). This refers to the conquest of Persia, who dominated us through the strength of their lust. God "heals" us and we recover our awareness of our dependence on God — for it is He that "heals the sick."

The idol worship brought on by pridefulness and lust requires us to nullify worship through hiding God's revelation. Then we must rely on our intellect to reach toward Transcendence. When we create our world through our own intellect, we eventually fall prey to the temptation to see our insights as our own creation. This cuts us off from boundless spirituality and imprisons us — leaves us "bound" — in the limited reality of the human intellect (the opposite of the expansive claims of the intellect). This is the conquest of Greece. God brings inner inspiration and, in response to the self-sacrifice of *mesirut nefesh*, He brings miracles to "release" us from the constricted world that we have come to occupy.

Eventually, we identify that inner inspiration with ourselves and make ourselves a substitute for God. We are completely cut off from spirituality because we confuse ourselves with God — thus we are "in the dust." That very confusion makes us think we are very spiritual, thus we are "asleep in the dust." This brings the conquest of Rome, substituting man for God.

Even when we are asleep to our distance from God, He peeps through the cracks to allow us to "maintain faith" in the utter darkness we have created. "You are reliable to bring life to the dead." No matter how far we stray, You will be able to constrict Yourself to the point where we can connect to You from the distant location where we have placed ourselves.

Glossary

AHAVAH: Love. The numerical value of the letters is the same as in the word *echad*, one. The love relationship is where we retain a semblance of individual existence while unifying with the Creator through emulation.

AKEIDAH: Lit., "binding." This refers to Avraham's binding of Yitzchak when God commanded him to bring Yitzchak as a sacrifice.

BAAL TESHUVAH: One who has done TESHUVAH (repented).

BEIN ADAM L'ATZMO: Between man and himself.

BEIN ADAM L'CHAVERO: Between man and his fellow man.

BEIN ADAM L'MAKOM: Between man and God.

BEIT HAMIKDASH: the Temple. Literally, The House of Sanctity. The foundation of the First Beit HaMikdash was built by David HaMelech and the structure by his son Shlomo HaMelech. It was a place of revealed miracles and direct awareness of the Creator. The Second Beit HaMikdash was built by the Men of the Great Assembly after the return of the Jewish people from the Babylonian and Persian exile. It did not exhibit revealed miracles but was the center from which the Oral Torah was developed.

BEMIDBAR: Lit., "in the desert"; the fourth book of the Bible.

BEREISHIT: Lit., "in the beginning"; the first book of the Bible.

CHESSED: Internally motivated kindness; giving entirely determined by the desire of the giver to give.

CHUMASH: From the word *chameish*, "five." Hebrew term for the five books of the Bible.

DA'AT: Fully developed, integrated, and internalized system of knowledge.

DEVARIM: Lit., "words"; the fifth book of the Bible.

DIN: The trait of judgment. Associated with restricted revelation for it contrasts with CHESSED, the unrestricted giving of kindness.

EMUNAH: Faith.

GAN EDEN: The Garden of Eden.

HASHGACHAH: Divine oversight.

HISHTADLUT: Effort.

KOHEN: Priest.

KORBAN: Translated as sacrifice, or offering. The Hebrew term comes from the root *karov*, meaning "close," or *kireiv*, meaning "approach." Through an offering, the individual recognizes that all belongs to God, giving him a sense of dependence and closeness to his Creator.

MALACH, MALACHIM (PL): Translated as "angel." It refers to a spiritual force through which God effects His will directly. The literal translation is "agent" or "agency."

MALCHUT: Kingship, ruling.

MAKOM: Place; also used as a name of God.

MASHIACH: Messiah.

MEGILLAT ESTHER: The "scroll" of Esther. A book in the Writings of Scripture that describes the events in Persia that we celebrate on Purim.

MIDRASH: Collections of halachic and aggadic statements by Sages of the Tannaic and Amoraic periods, generally ordered according to the verses in Scripture.

MISHNAH: The collection of statements by Sages of the Tannaic period compiled by Rabbi Yehudah HaNasi as an encapsulation of the entire Oral Torah.

MITZVAH, MITZVOT (PL): Command. The root of the word, *tzav*, means connect.

MITZRAYIM: Egypt.

NEFESH: The portion of the soul that animates us physically.

NESHAMAH: The portion of the soul that transcends our individuality, connecting us to God. From the word *neshimah*, meaning breath. God breathes our soul into us, and therefore our soul, by being God's expression into and connection with physical reality, is the "breathing" of God.

NISAYON: Test. A hiding of God's relationship with us to force us to take responsibility for creating relationship with Him. This can either be to recover a level of connection that was lost through sin (flax-whacking) or in order to earn our relationship and receive reward (pot-tapping).

ONESH: Usually translated as punishment. *Onesh*, however, does not refer to a punitive consequence. Rather, it refers to consequences that allow the attainment of the original goal, which has been made more distant as a result of transgression.

RACHAMIM: Mercy. A combination of CHESSED and DIN — giving that is affected but not limited by judgment.

RUACH: The portion of the soul that gives us a sense of independent identity.

SEFER: Book.

SHECHINAH: The Holy presence or manifestation of God's connection to the world.

SHEMA: Lit., "hear." This refers to the first word of, "*Shema Yisrael* (Hear Israel), the Lord (HaShem) is our God, the Lord (HaShem) is One." This is the statement by which we declare our recognition of the unity of God and accept His kingship.

SHEMONEH ESREI: Lit., "eighteen." Refers to the central prayer of the morning, afternoon, and evening weekday service which was originally composed of eighteen blessings.

SHEMOT: Lit., "names"; the second book of the Bible.

TALMUD: The *Mishnah* along with the Gemara — a compilation of the debates of the Sages of the Amoraic period, elaborating the implications of the *Mishnah*.

TEHILLIM: Psalms.

TEFILLAH: Prayer.

TESHUVAH: Lit., "return," meant in the sense of returning to God or, more precisely, the return of the self to its essence. That is the return of the self to being centered and defined by that aspect of our personality that is directly connected to the Creator; repentance.

TORAH SHEBE'AL PEH: The Oral Torah. The portion of the Torah given on Har Sinai that was not intended to be written down. Rather, it was to accompany the Written Torah as an oral tradition. It contained the detailed implementation of the general mitzvot of the Written Torah and the tools of logic for extending them into new situations. The Oral Torah became the primary vehicle of our connection to God with the passing of prophecy.

TZELEM ELOKIM: Image of God. Expression of the Creator into the world through man. This can, among other things, refer to man's intellect or his NESHAMAH.

VAYIKRA: Lit., "and He called out"; the third book of the Bible.

YIRAH: Fear. Refers to our awareness of the utter dependence of existence upon the Creator's ongoing will. In the *Yirah* relationship with God, we unite by disappearing as an independent entity into God.